Workbook to Accompany

Understanding Health Insurance

A Guide to Billing and Reimbursement

8TH EDITION

Susan A. Brisky, BPS, RHTT

Instructor
Department of Physical & Life Sciences, Alfred State College, Alfred, NY

Ruth M. Burke

Medical Billing and Coding Program Specialist
The Community College of Baltimore County, MD
Adjunct Faculty, The Community College of Baltimore County, MD
Adjunct Faculty, Harford Community College, MD
Consultant on Administrative Procedures to Health Care Practices in Maryland and Virginia
President of the Independent Medical Billers Alliance (IMBA)
Member of the Maryland Medical Group Management Association (MGMA)

THOMSON

DELMAR LEARNING ™ Australia Canada Mexico Singapore Spain United Kingdom United States

THOMSON

DELMAR LEARNING

Workbook to Accompany Understanding Health Insurance: A Guide to Billing and Reimbursement, 8th Edition

by Susan A. Brisky and Ruth M. Burke

Vice President, Health Care Business Unit:
William Brottmiller

Editorial Director:
Mathnew Kane

Acquisitions Editor:
Rhonda Dearborn

Developmental Editors:
Marjorie A. Bruce

Editorial Assistant:
Debra Gorgos

Marketing Director:
Jennifer McAvey

Marketing Channel Manager:
Tamara Caruso

Marketing Coordinator:
Kimberly Duffy

Technology Director:
Laurie Davis

Technology Project Manager:
Mary Colleen Liburdi

Technology Project Coordinator:
Carolyn Fox

Production Director:
Carolyn Miller

Art and Design Coordinator:
Alexandros Vasilakos

Senior Production Editor:
James Zayicek

Project Editor:
Natalie Pashoukos

Library of Congress Cataloging-in-Publication Data
ISBN 1-4018-9609-X

NOTICE TO THE READER

Contents

Introduction

INTRODUCTION

The workbook is designed to help learners apply the concepts presented in the text-book. This is accomplished through application-based assignments that are directly related to the content of the textbook. This edition of the workbook is updated and redesigned for maximum effectiveness.

This workbook can be used by college and vocational school programs to train health insurance specialists, medical assistants, medical office administrators, and health information technicians. It can also be used as an in-service training tool for new medical office personnel and independent billing services, or independently by insurance specialists who wish to increase their skills and scope of knowledge.

OBJECTIVES

After completing the assignments in each chapter, the learner will be able to:

1. Contact and interview a health insurance specialist (or similar professional) and explore career opportunities.
2. Create a professional cover letter and résumé.
3. Conduct an effective job search utilizing the Internet and local resources.
4. Access networking sites for professionals, such as Listservs.
5. Interpret health insurance statistics.
6. Explain the effects of managed care on a physician's office.
7. Interpret remittance advice and explanation of benefits documents.
8. Differentiate between fraud and abuse.
9. Accurately assign ICD and CPT/HCPCS codes.
10. Accurately enter required information on CMS-1500 claims according to individual payer requirements.

FEATURES NEW TO THE EIGHTH EDITION

- Chapter 1 contains assignments that assist the learner in conducting a comprehensive, professional job search. The chapter also provides the learner with an opportunity to prepare a journal abstract, as well as become acquainted with professional networking resources, such as Listservs.

- Chapter 2 includes assignments that guide learners in the interpretation of health statistics and the creation of charts using spreadsheet software. Step-by-step instructions for preparing a research paper are also provided.

- Chapter 3 contains assignments that emphasize the history of health insurance legislation, the role of quality assurance programs in health insurance plans, and factors that influence the managed care industry.

- Chapter 4 focuses on the payment of health insurance claims, specifically the encounter form, remittance advice, and explanation of benefits. The chapter includes exercises that teach learners how to interpret the information contained in each of these documents.

- Chapter 5 contains assignments that emphasize confidentiality, address fraud and abuse issues in health care, and examine the importance of privacy and security.

- Chapter 6 is redesigned to provide learners with numerous ICD-9-CM coding practice assignments that increase in level of difficulty, from basic to advanced diagnosis coding. An ICD-9-CM procedure coding assignment is provided.

- Chapter 7 is restructured to provide learners with coding exercises organized in the same order as the CPT manual, beginning with using the index.

- Chapter 8 guides learners through coding assignments based on the organization of the HCPCS Level II manual, beginning with an assignment that teaches how to locate codes in the index.

- Chapter 9 focuses on reimbursement systems. Assignments assist learners in determining payment based on the outpatient prospective payment system (OPPS) and interpreting a DRG-decision tree.

- Chapter 10 is expanded to provide learners with assignments that require them to identify the first-listed diagnosis, link diagnoses with procedures/services, interpret national coverage determinations, and complete additional coding assignments to include case scenarios, SOAP notes, and operative reports.

- Chapter 11 provides an assignment that assists learners in identifying errors in a CMS-1500 claim, explaining optical scanning guidelines, and appropriately entering diagnosis and procedure codes on the CMS-1500.

- Chapters 12 through 17 offer "real-world" assignments to assist learners in accurately completing CMS-1500 claims based on individual payer requirements. The assignments also allow learners to develop skills in completing primary and secondary claims for patients and filing supplemental insurance claims.

  > NOTE: Case studies in Chapters 12 through 17 require learners to assign codes for diagnoses and procedures/services. Following completion of the CMS-1500 claims, the instructor can provide learners with a coding answer key to check the diagnosis and procedure/service codes on their completed CMS-1500 claims. The instructor may prefer to provide the answer key before learners begin the case studies so that they can concentrate on the claim completion process rather than coding.

INSTACLAIM DEMO CD-ROM

The CD-ROM included with the workbook contains InstaClaim software, which automates claims processing. Once learners enter patient registration and insurance information, it is saved and can be used to generate claims for future encounters. The data entry screen is logically organized, and CMS-1500 claims are quickly and easily generated. A tutorial is provided to guide learners through the use of the CD-ROM.

## CHAPTER 1

Health Insurance Specialist Career

INTRODUCTION

This chapter familiarizes students with interviewing a professional, creating a résumé and cover letter, interpreting (and understanding) information from professional journal articles, networking with other professionals via professional discussion forums, and interpreting professional codes of ethics.

ASSIGNMENT 1.1 Interview of a Professional

OBJECTIVES

At the conclusion of this assignment, the student should be able to:

1. State the responsibilities of a professional employed in this field of study.

2. Explain whether this position would be one the student would be interested in obtaining.

OVERVIEW

Health insurance specialists often have similar educational backgrounds; however, their job responsibilities and roles vary greatly depending upon the organization by which they are employed. This assignment will familiarize the student with specific job responsibilities of a professional employed in this field.

INSTRUCTIONS

1. Prepare 10 questions that you would like to ask of a professional employed in your field of study.

   NOTE: Your instructor might devote classroom time to brainstorming such questions (or use a discussion board forum if you are an Internet-based student). This will allow you to share questions with other students in your course and obtain additional questions to ask of the professional.

2. Identify a credentialed professional in your field of study (e.g., CCS, CPC, and so on), and contact the professional to schedule an onsite interview. When you contact the professional, conduct yourself in a professional manner, and explain that you are a student completing a required assignment.

NOTE: If it is not possible to schedule an onsite interview, check with your instructor to determine whether a telephone or e-mail interview would be acceptable.

3. Prepare for the interview by reviewing and organizing the questions you will ask of the professional.

4. Dress appropriately (as if for a job interview), and arrive 10 minutes early for the interview.

5. Adopt a professional and respectful manner when asking interview questions, and be prepared to answer questions asked of you. Be sure to take notes as the professional responds to the interview questions. If you choose to tape-record the interview, be sure to ask the professional for permission to do so.

6. After the interview, thank the professional for his or her time. Be sure to follow up the interview within 10 days by mailing a handwritten thank-you note.

7. Prepare a three-page, double-spaced, word-processed document summarizing the interview, as follows:

   a. Identify the professional's name, position, and facility.

   b. Writing in the third person, summarize the professional's responses to your interview questions. Be sure to organize the interview content in logical paragraphs. (A paragraph consists of at least three sentences.) *Do **not** prepare this paper in a question/answer format.* If you have questions about how to write this paper, ask your instructor for clarification.

   c. In the last paragraph of the paper, summarize your reaction to the interview and state whether you would be interested in having this professional's position (along with why or why not). Also, predict your future by writing about where you will be in 10 years (in terms of employment, family, etc.).

   d. Check and double-check spelling, grammar, and punctuation. Have at least one other person review your document (e.g., college writing lab, English teacher, family member or friend who has excellent writing skills, and so on).

ASSIGNMENT 1.2 Ready, Set, Get a Job!

OBJECTIVES

At the conclusion of this assignment, the student should be able to:

1. Conduct a job search using local resources and the Internet.
2. Create a professional career résumé and cover letter.
3. Research organizations in preparation for a job interview.
4. Determine personal worth to an organization, to facilitate salary negotiation.
5. Anticipate questions that could be asked during a job interview.
6. Describe appropriate follow-up to be performed after a job interview.

OVERVIEW

Begin your successful job search by creating a professional career résumé and cover letter. Prepare for a job interview by practicing for the interview, researching the organization, and determining your worth. Follow up after the interview by mailing a handwritten thank-you note to the interviewer.

NOTE: Some facilities require students to submit a cover letter and résumé for consideration by the clinical supervisor prior to placement for professional practice. This assignment will assist in that process.

Searching for a Job

To conduct a successful job search, you must assess your skills, establish goals, plan your job search, and understand the job market (Figure 1-1). Because it can take six to nine months to complete a successful job search, be sure to contact your school's career services department at least three months before graduation. Be prepared to complete the job search approximately six months after graduation. (Some job searches can take longer!) Consider following these steps to conduct your job search:

1. Perform a self-assessment by identifying your accomplishments, experience, goals, interests, skills, and values. (You have to figure out what you want from a job before you can determine what you have to offer prospective employers.)

2. Research career options and employers. Completing an internship or obtaining part-time or summer employment in your field of study will allow you to network with professionals in that field, leading to job opportunities. Researching prospective employers helps you decide which ones to contact for possible employment.

3. Plan your job search by establishing a target date for obtaining a position, remembering that it can take six to nine months to find a job. Decide how much time you can devote to your job search, get organized, and spend time each week working on your search. Consider using multiple strategies (Figure 1-1) to seek employment; the more contacts you make, the more interviews you will get.

4. Document your job search by keeping a record of résumés mailed, interviews scheduled, and thank-you notes sent. This process allows a job seeker to easily follow up with contacts and increases credibility with prospective employers.

5. Searching for a job is very hard work, and you must be persistent because it can be discouraging. Treating the search like a job will help you produce results. (After your successful job search, establish an action plan for career progression that includes continuing education and professional networking.)

NOTE: It is acceptable to submit your résumé to a prospective employer more than once. Some employers maintain resumes for only 30 days, so if your job search takes months, it is possible that you will need to submit your résumé more than once. Such persistence also demonstrates your enthusiasm and interest in that employer.

INSTRUCTIONS

1. Go to http://www.advisorteam.com, and click on the "Take the Temperament Sorter II Personality Instrument" to complete an online personality assessment that helps individuals discover their "innate tendencies, preferences, and motivations to arrive at an integrated view of their personality."

2. Go to http://www.monstertrak.com, and click on the **Students/Alums** link to begin your research process about available jobs and internships, résumé writing, career contacts (e.g., alumni), salary surveys, employer profiles, and more.

3. Go to the *Occupational Outlook Handbook* at http://www.bls.gov/oco. This "is a nationally recognized source of career information, designed to provide valuable assistance to individuals making decisions about their future work lives.

Classified ads. The "Help Wanted" ads in newspapers list numerous jobs. You should realize, however, that many other job openings are not listed, and that the classified ads sometimes do not give all of the important information. They may offer little or no description of the job, working conditions, or pay. Some ads do not identify the employer. They may simply give a post office box to mail your resume to, making follow-up inquiries very difficult. Some ads offer out-of-town jobs; others advertise employment agencies rather than actual employment opportunities. When using classified ads, keep the following in mind:

- Do not rely solely on the classifieds to find a job; follow other leads as well.
- Answer ads promptly because openings may be filled quickly, even before the ad stops appearing in the paper.
- Read the ads every day, particularly the Sunday edition, which usually includes the most listings.
- Beware of "no experience necessary" ads, which may signal low wages, poor working conditions, or commission work.
- Keep a record of all ads to which you have responded, including the specific skills, educational background, and personal qualifications required for the position.

Community agencies. Many nonprofit organizations, including religious institutions and vocational rehabilitation agencies, offer counseling, career development, and job placement services, generally targeted to a particular group, such as women, youth, minorities, ex-offenders, or older workers.

Employers. Through your library and Internet research, develop a list of potential employers in your desired career field. Employer websites often contain lists of job openings. Websites and business directories can provide you with information on how to apply for a position or whom to contact. Even if no open positions are posted, do not hesitate to contact the employer and the relevant department. Set up an interview with someone working in the same area you wish to work. Ask them how they got started, what they enjoy or dislike about the work, what type of qualifications are necessary for the job, and what type of personality succeeds in that position. Even if they don't have a position available, they may be able to put you in contact with other people who might hire you and they can keep you in mind if a position opens up. Make sure to send them your resume and a cover letter. If you are able to obtain an interview, be sure to send a thank you note. Directly contacting employers is one of the most successful means of job hunting.

Federal government. Information on federal government jobs is available from the Office of Personnel Management through a telephone-based system. Consult your telephone directory under U.S. Government for a local number or call (912) 757-3000; Federal Relay Service (800) 877-8339. The first number is not toll free, and charges may result. Information is available on the Internet at http://www.usajobs.opm.gov.

Internet networks and resources. The Internet provides a variety of information, including job listings and job search resources and techniques. However, no single network or resource will contain all of the information available on employment or career opportunities, so be prepared to search for what you need. Remember that job listings may be posted by field or discipline, so begin your search

(continues)

FIGURE 1-1 *Job search methods (Reprinted according to Bureau of Labor Statistics reuse policy.)*

using keywords. When searching employment databases on the Internet, it is sometimes possible to send your resume to an employer by e-mail or to post it on-line. Some sources allow you to send e-mail free of charge, but be careful that you are not going to incur any additional charges for postings or updates.

Labor unions. Labor unions provide various employment services to members, including apprenticeship programs that teach a specific trade or skill. Contact the appropriate labor union or State apprenticeship council for more information.

Personal contacts. Your family, friends, and acquaintances may offer one of the most effective ways to find a job. They may help you directly or put you in touch with someone else who can. Such networking can lead to information about specific job openings, many of which may not be publicly posted.

Private employment agencies and career consultants. These agencies can be helpful, but they are in business to make money. Most operate on a commission basis, with the fee dependent upon a percentage of the salary paid to a successful applicant. You or the hiring company will pay a fee. Find out the exact cost and who is responsible for paying associated fees before using the service. Although employment agencies can help you save time and contact employers who otherwise might be difficult to locate, the costs may outweigh the benefits if you are responsible for the fee. Contacting employers directly often will generate the same type of leads that a private employment agency will provide. Consider any guarantees the agency offers when determining if the service is worth the cost.

Professional associations. Many professions have associations that offer employment information, including career planning, educational programs, job listings, and job placement. To use these services, associations usually require that you be a member of their association; information can be obtained directly from an association through the Internet, by telephone, or by mail.

School career planning and placement offices. High school and college placement offices help their students and alumni find jobs. They set up appointments and allow recruiters to use their facilities for interviews. Placement offices usually have a list of part-time, temporary, and summer jobs offered on campus. They also may have lists of jobs for regional, nonprofit, and government organizations. Students can receive career counseling and testing and job search advice. At career resource libraries they may attend workshops on such topics as job search strategy, resume writing, letter writing, and effective interviewing; critique drafts of resumes and watch videotapes of mock interviews; explore files of resumes and references; and attend job fairs conducted by the placement office.

State employment service offices. The State employment service, sometimes called Job Service, operates in coordination with the U.S. Department of Labor's Employment and Training Administration. Local offices, found nationwide, help jobseekers find jobs and help employers find qualified workers at no cost to either. To find the office nearest you, look in the State government telephone listings under "Job Service" or "Employment."

- *Job matching and referral.* At the State employment service office, an interviewer will determine if you are "job ready" or if you need help from counseling and testing services to assess your occupational aptitudes and interests and to help you choose and prepare for a career.

(continues)

FIGURE 1-1 *Continued*

After you are "job ready," you may examine available job listings and select openings that interest you. A staff member can then describe the job openings in detail and arrange for interviews with prospective employers.

- *America's Job Bank*, sponsored by the U.S. Department of Labor, is an Internet site that allows you to search through a database of over one million jobs Nationwide, create and post your resume online, and set up an automated job search. The database contains a wide range of mostly full-time private sector jobs that are available all over the country. Job seekers can access America's Job Bank at: http://www.ajb.org. Computers with access to the Internet are available to the public in any local public employment service office, school, library, and military installation. *Tips for Finding the Right Job*, a U.S. Department of Labor pamphlet, offers advice on determining your job skills, organizing your job search, writing a resume, and making the most of an interview.

- *Job Search Guide: Strategies For Professionals*, another U.S. Department of Labor publication, discusses specific steps that jobseekers can follow to identify employment opportunities. This publication includes sections on handling job loss, managing personal resources, assessing personal skills and interests, researching the job market, conducting the job search, and networking. Check with your State employment service office, or order a copy of these and other publications from the U.S. Government Printing Offices Superintendent of Documents by telephone: (202) 512-1800 or via the Internet at: http://www.gpo.gov or at: http://www.doleta.gov/etaindex.asp.

- *Services for special groups*. By law, veterans are entitled to priority for job placement at State employment service centers. If you are a veteran, an employment representative can inform you of available assistance and help you deal with problems. States have One-Stop Service Centers that provide various special groups and the general public with employment, training, and related services available under the Workforce Investment Act of 1998.

FIGURE 1-1 *Continued*

Revised every two years, the *Handbook* describes what workers do on the job, working conditions, the training and education needed, earnings, and expected job prospects in a wide range of occupations."

4. Go to http://www.hoovers.com to access its database of 12 million companies and research information on prospective employers.

5. Select one or more of the following general Web sites to research available positions:

Career Builder	http://www.careerbuilder.com
Federal Jobs	http://www.fedworld.gov/jobs/jobsearch.html
Job Search Engine	http://www.job-search-engine.com
Monster	http://www.monster.com
Nation Job	http://www.nationjob.com
Riley Guide	http://www.rileyguide.com

6. Select one or more of the following health care Web sites to research available positions:

Advance for Health Information Professionals	http://www.advanceforhim.com
American Academy of Professional Coders	http://www.aapc.com
American Association of Medical Assistants	http://www.aama-ntl.org
American Health Information Management Association	http://www.ahima.org
For the Record	http://www.fortherecordmag.com
Health Information Job Search	http://www.hipjobs.net
H.I.M. Recruiters	http://www.himjobs.com
Insights Search	http://www.insights-search.com
MedHunters.com	http://www.medhunters.com
Medical Workers.com	http://www.medicalworkers.com
Professional Association of Health Care Office Management	http://www.pahcom.com

Creating a Résumé and Cover Letter

A résumé won't get you a job; however, it can eliminate you from the pool of candidates if unprofessionally prepared. Employers often identify interview candidates by reviewing résumés to eliminate those unqualified. Résumés or cover letters that contain typographical errors or evidence of poor communication skills are discarded because employers are unwilling to spend valuable time interviewing such candidates.

Carol Woughter, Director (Retired)

Placement & Transfer, Alfred State College

Your cover letter (Figure 1-2) is actually a marketing tool because it focuses on your qualifications as a prospective employee. It should be well written so that the employer will review your résumé. When creating your cover letter, be sure to consider the following:

1. Research the prospective employer's organization to personalize the letter. Your knowledge of the organization demonstrates your interest in the employer.

2. Briefly explain several special abilities or significant accomplishments so the employer will be interested in you. Be sure you do not misrepresent your experience or skills. If you do not meet every job qualification, emphasize your strengths.

3. Group similar information within the same paragraph, and organize paragraphs logically so the cover letter is easy to read. Use action verbs to make the cover letter interesting and display energy.

4. Write in a formal style. Be clear, objective, and persuasive (as opposed to just describing your education and experience background).

5. Do not include any information that might cause the employer to question your ability to do the job. (Everyone has weaknesses, but there is no sense pointing

Street Address
City, State Zip
Current date

> Call the human resources department at the prospective employer to find out to whom the cover letter should be addressed.

Name
Title
Company
Street Address
City, State Zip

Dear Mr./Ms.:

Paragraph 1—Explain why you are writing, and identify the position and your source of information. Summarize your strongest qualifications for the position using a series of phrases. (e.g., I am applying for the Coding & Reimbursement Specialist position as advertised in *The Alfred Sun*, October 9, YYYY. My coding/insurance processing skills and attention to detail are my strongest qualifications for this position.)

Paragraph 2—Detail your strongest qualifications and relate them to the position requirements. Provide evidence of related education and employment experiences. Refer to your enclosed resume. (e.g., I will graduate in May YYYY with a Certificate in Insurance and Reimbursement Specialist from Alfred State College, where I completed extensive coursework in coding and insurance processing. My 240-hour professional practice experience allowed me to perform coding and insurance duties at Alfred State Medical Center. The completed evaluation of this experience documents my attention to detail, excellent work ethic, and superior coding and insurance processing skills. My education also included general education courses, which has provided me with an excellent background in computer applications and human sciences. I plan to take the C.C.A. certification examination in June YYYY, after I graduate. Please refer to the enclosed resume for additional information.)

Paragraph 3—Request an interview and indicate how and when you can be contacted. Suggest that you will place a follow-up call to discuss interview possibilities. Thank the employer for his/her consideration. (e.g., Please contact me at (607) 555-1234 after 4 p.m., Monday through Friday, to schedule an interview at a mutually convenient time. I will contact you next week to ensure that you received my cover letter and resume. Thank you for your consideration.)

Sincerely,

[handwritten signature]

Your typed name

Enclosure

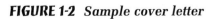

FIGURE 1-2 *Sample cover letter*

them out to a prospective employer in your cover letter! Save this information for the interview, where it will allow you to appear modest about your professional skills.)

6. Check and double-check spelling and grammar. Consider having at least one other person review your cover letter (e.g., school career services professional, English teacher, and so on).

If you are a recent graduate, your career résumé (Figure 1-3) should probably be limited to one page; however, if you have extensive work experience in a health-related field, a two-page résumé is acceptable. Because the purpose of your résumé is to get an interview, the résumé should contain information appropriate to the position you wish to obtain so that it convinces a prospective employer that you have the skills necessary for the available position. In addition, when preparing your résumé, be sure to focus on

---

SALLY S. STUDENT

| 5 Main Street | Alfred, NY 14802 | (607) 555-1111 |

JOB OBJECTIVE	An entry-level insurance and coding specialist position.
EDUCATION	STATE UNIVERSITY OF NEW YORK, COLLEGE OF TECHNOLOGY AT ALFRED, Alfred, N.Y. Candidate for Associate in Applied Science, Coding & Reimbursement Specialist, May YYYY.
	HONORS & AWARDS: Dean's List, Fall YYYY, Spring YYYY, and Fall YYYY. Recipient, Outstanding Coding & Reimbursement Specialist Student Award, May YYYY.
CERTIFICATION	C.C.A. eligible, June YYYY.
PROFESSIONAL AFFILIATIONS	Student Member, American Health Information Management Association. Member, Alfred State College Health Information Management Club.
WORK EXPERIENCE	**Coding and Insurance Professional Practice**, Alfred State Medical Center, Alfred, N.Y. Assigned ICD-9-CM, CPT, and HCPCS Level II codes to inpatient, outpatient, and emergency department records. Abstracted inpatient cases using MediSoft abstracting software. Generated CMS-1500 and UB-92 claims. Processed denials by correcting claims and resubmitted for payment. Summer YYYY.
	Cashier, Burger King, Hornell, N.Y. Assisted customers, operated cash register, and opened/closed store. August YYYY – Present.
AVAILABILITY	May YYYY.
REFERENCES	Available upon request.

FIGURE 1-3 *Sample career résumé*

the prospective employer's needs. This may mean revising your résumé each time you apply for a position (e.g., rewrite the job objective in the résumé).

EXAMPLE: You see an advertisement for a position that seems perfect for you, and along with plenty of others you send the employer a cover letter with your résumé. By the application deadline, human resources personnel are ready to review hundreds of résumés. (A job notice routinely pulls in between 100 to 1,000 résumés.)

The cover letters and résumés are reviewed quickly, with those containing any errors immediately discarded to narrow the applicant pool. Your résumé, however, is not only perfectly written but also well organized and pertinent to the available position. Thus, it is carefully reviewed and placed on the small stack of résumés that will be used to schedule interviews.

The Interview Process

An interview gives you the opportunity to demonstrate your qualifications to an employer, so it pays to be well prepared.

Bureau of Labor Statistics

During a job interview, you are evaluated on how well suited you are for the available position. Therefore, when preparing for a job interview, be sure that you have a good understanding of the organization, job responsibilities and duties, corresponding skills required, and how your experience relates to the position.

Job Interview Tips. (Permission to reprint in accordance with Bureau of Labor Statistics reuse policy.)

Preparation

- Learn about the organization
- Have a specific job or jobs in mind
- Review your qualifications for the job
- Prepare answers to broad questions about yourself
- Review your résumé
- Schedule a mock interview with your school's career services office
- Arrive before the scheduled time of your interview

Personal Appearance

- Be well groomed
- Dress appropriately (e.g., professionally)
- Do not chew gum or smoke

    NOTE: Avoid smoking prior to the interview, because the smell of tobacco can be obvious and offensive to a nonsmoking interviewer.

The Interview

- Relax, and answer each question concisely

    NOTE: It is acceptable to ask that a question be repeated. You can also bring a pen and paper to the interview to record questions and take notes.

- Respond promptly
- Maintain eye contact and good posture

- Use good manners
- Do not interrupt the interviewer
- Highlight ways in which you can be an asset to the organization based on your experience, education, skills, and knowledge

  NOTE: Be absolutely truthful. Do not misrepresent any information about yourself.
- Learn the name of your interviewer and shake hands as you meet
- Use proper English; avoid slang
- Be cooperative and enthusiastic
- Ask questions about the position and the organization (e.g., salary range, working hours, clarification of job functions, working environment, and when the interview results will be available)
- Do not speak negatively about a previous place of employment
- Thank the interviewer verbally when you leave and, as a follow-up, in writing

Testing. Some organization require applicants to complete an exam onsite to demonstrate proficiency (e.g., coding, medical terminology, and so on).

- Listen closely to instructions
- Read each question carefully
- Write legibly and clearly
- Budget your time wisely and do not dwell on one question

Information to Take to an Interview

- Social security card
- Government-issued identification (e.g., driver's license)
- If professional certification is required for the job (e.g., coding credential), bring evidence of certification
- Résumé

  NOTE: Although an employer may not require applicants to bring a résumé to the job interview, you should be able to furnish the interviewer with information about your education, training, and previous employment. Because you may become nervous during the interview, it is helpful to have your résumé available to prompt you for this information.
- References

  NOTE: Employers typically require three professional references. Be sure to obtain permission before using anyone as a reference, and make sure the person will give you a good reference. Avoid using relatives and friends.

@@@@@@@@@@@@@@@
INTERNET LINKS
The following Web sites contain more information about preparing for an interview:

College View	http://www.collegeview.com
Job-Interview	http://www.job-interview.net/
Resume Magic	http://www.resumemagic.com/

Following up After the Interview. Be sure to send the interviewer a handwritten thank-you letter (Figure 1-4) after an interview. The letter indicates that you are considerate and polite, and it also allows you to reemphasize your positive attributes to the interviewer. The thank-you letter should be written the same day of the interview and mailed that night.

Dear [name of interviewer]:

Thank you for interviewing me for the [name of position] position at [name of organization]. After meeting with you, I am convinced that my background and skills will meet your needs.

I appreciate that you took so much time to familiarize me with the organization. I believe I could learn a great deal from you and would certainly enjoy working with you.

In addition to my qualifications and experience, I will bring excellent work habits and judgment to this position. With the countless demands on your time, I am sure that you require people who can be trusted to carry out their responsibilities with minimal supervision.

I look forward to hearing from you concerning your hiring decision. Again, thank you for your time and consideration.
Sincerely,

[your signature]

FIGURE 1-4 *Sample thank-you letter*

Be sure to thank the interviewer for his or her time and mention something that happened or was discussed to remind the interviewer of who you are.

Evaluating a Job Offer. (Permission to reprint in accordance with Bureau of Labor Statistics reuse policy.)

Once you receive a job offer, you are faced with a difficult decision and must evaluate the offer carefully. Fortunately, most organizations will not expect you to accept or reject an offer immediately. There are many issues to consider when assessing a job offer. Will the organization be a good place to work? Will the job be interesting? Are there opportunities for advancement? Is the salary fair? Does the employer offer good benefits? If you have not already figured out exactly what you want, the following discussion may help you develop a set of criteria for judging job offers, whether you are starting a career, reentering the labor force after a long absence, or planning a career change.

The Organization

Background information on an organization can help you decide whether it would be a good place for you to work (Figure 1-5). Factors to consider include the organization's business or activity, financial condition, age, size, and location. You can generally get background information on an organization, particularly a large organization, by telephoning its public relations office. A public company's annual report to the stockholders tells about its corporate philosophy, history, products or services, goals, and financial status. Most government agencies can furnish reports that describe their programs and missions. Press releases, company newsletters or magazines, and recruitment brochures also can be useful. Ask the organization for any other items that might interest a prospective employee. If possible, speak to current or former employees of the organization.

Does the organization's business or activity match your own interests and beliefs? It is easier to apply yourself to the work if you are enthusiastic about what the organization does.

How will the size of the organization affect you? Large firms generally offer a greater variety of training programs and career paths, more managerial levels for advancement, and better employee benefits than small firms. Large employers may also have more advanced technologies. However, jobs in large firms may tend to be highly specialized. Jobs in small firms may offer broader authority and responsibility, a closer working relationship with top management, and a chance to clearly see your contribution to the success of the organization.

Should you work for a relatively new organization or one that is well-established? New businesses have a high failure rate, but for many people, the excitement of helping create a company and the potential for sharing in its success more than offset the risk of job loss. However, it may be just as exciting and rewarding to work for a young firm that already has a foothold on success.

Does it make a difference if the company is private or public? An individual or a family may control a privately owned company, and key jobs may be reserved for relatives and friends. A board of directors responsible to the stockholders controls a publicly owned company and key jobs are usually open to anyone.

Is the organization in an industry with favorable long-term prospects? The most successful firms tend to be in industries that are growing rapidly.

FIGURE 1-5 *Questions to ask before you accept the position (Permission to reprint in accordance with Bureau of Labor Statistics reuse policy.)*

Background information on the organization may be available at your public or school library. If you cannot get an annual report, check the library for reference directories that may provide basic facts about the company, such as earnings, products and services, and number of employees. Some directories widely available in libraries include:

- *Dun & Bradstreet's Million Dollar Directory*
- *Moody's Industrial Manual*
- *Standard and Poor's Register of Corporations*
- *Thomas' Register of American Manufacturers*
- *Ward's Business Directory*

Stories about an organization in magazines and newspapers can tell a great deal about its successes, failures, and plans for the future. You can identify articles on a company by looking under its name in periodical or computerized indexes in libraries. However, it probably will not be useful to look back more than two or three years.

The library also may have government publications that present projections of growth for the industry in which the organization is classified. Long-term projections of employment and output for more than 200 industries, covering the entire economy, are developed by the Bureau of Labor Statistics and revised every two years—see the *Monthly Labor Review* for the most recent projections. The *U.S. Industry and Trade Outlook,*

Where is the job located? If the job is in another section of the country, you need to consider the cost of living, the availability of housing and transportation, and the quality of educational and recreational facilities in that section of the country. Even if the job location is in your area, you should consider the time and expense of commuting.

Does the work match your interests and make good use of your skills? The duties and responsibilities of the job should be explained in enough detail to answer this question.

How important is the job in this company? An explanation of where you fit in the organization and how you are supposed to contribute to its overall objectives should give you an idea of the job's importance.

Are you comfortable with the hours? Most jobs involve regular hours—for example, 40 hours a week, during the day, Monday through Friday. Other jobs require night, weekend, or holiday work. In addition, some jobs routinely require overtime to meet deadlines or sales or production goals, or to better serve customers. Consider the effect the work hours will have on your personal life.

How long do most people who enter this job stay with the company? High turnover can mean dissatisfaction with the nature of the work or something else about the job.

FIGURE 1-6 *Questions to ask before you accept the position (Permission to reprint in accordance with Bureau of Labor Statistics reuse policy.)*

published annually by the U.S. Department of Commerce, presents detailed analyses of U.S. industries. Trade magazines also may include articles on the trends for specific industries.

Career centers at colleges and universities often have information on employers that is not available in libraries. Ask a career center representative how to find out about a particular organization.

Nature of the Job. Even if everything else about the job is attractive, you will be unhappy if you dislike the day-to-day work. Determining in advance whether you will like the work may be difficult (Figure 1-6). However, the more you find out about the job before accepting or rejecting an offer, the more likely you are to make the right choice. Actually working in the industry and, if possible, for the company would provide considerable insight. You can gain work experience through part-time, temporary, or summer jobs, or through internship or work-study programs while in school. All of these can also lead to permanent job offers.

Opportunities Offered by Employers. A good job offers you opportunities to learn new skills, increase your earnings, and rise to positions of greater authority, responsibility, and prestige. A lack of opportunities can dampen your interest in the work and result in frustration and boredom. The company should have a training plan for you. Be sure to ask the following questions:

- What valuable new skills does the company plan to teach you?

- What promotion possibilities are available within the organization?

- What is the next step on the career ladder?

- If you have to wait for a job to become vacant before you can be promoted, how long does this usually take?

- When opportunities for advancement do arise, will you compete with applicants from outside the company?
- Can you apply for jobs for which you qualify elsewhere within the organization, or is mobility within the firm limited?

Salaries and Benefits. Wait for the employer to introduce the subjects of salaries and benefits. Some companies will not talk about pay until they have decided to hire you. To know if an offer is reasonable, you need a rough estimate of what the job should pay. You may have to go to several sources for this information. Try to find family, friends, or acquaintances recently hired in similar jobs. Ask your teachers and the staff in placement offices about starting pay for graduates with your qualifications. Help-wanted ads in newspapers sometimes give salary ranges for similar positions. Check the library or your school's career center for salary surveys, such as those conducted by the National Association of Colleges and Employers or various professional associations.

If you are considering the salary and benefits for a job in another geographic area, make allowances for differences in the cost of living, which may be significantly higher in a large metropolitan area than in a smaller city, town, or rural area.

You also should learn the organization's policy regarding overtime. Depending on the job, you may or may not be exempt from laws requiring the employer to compensate you for overtime. Find out how many hours you will be expected to work each week and whether you receive overtime pay or compensatory time off for working more than the specified number of hours in a week.

Also take into account that a starting salary is just that—the start. Your salary should be reviewed on a regular basis; many organizations do it every year. How much can you expect to earn after one, two, or three or more years? An employer cannot be specific about the amount of pay if it includes commissions and bonuses. Benefits can also add a lot to your base pay, but they vary widely. Find out exactly what the benefit package includes and how much of the cost you must bear (e.g., health insurance).

If You Do Not Get the Job. If you do not get the job, consider contacting the organization to find out why. Ask the following questions:

- What was your general impression of me during the interview?
- In what ways could I improve the way I interview?
- What were my weaknesses, and how can I strengthen them?
- What things did impress you, and why?
- What suggestions do you have for improving my cover letter and/or résumé?
- Is there anything else you would advise me to work on?
- What were the characteristics of the successful candidate?
- Do you have any other positions available for which I might be suitable?
- Finally, is there anything else I should ask you?

Remember that there will be additional opportunities for job interviews. Try not to get so discouraged that you discontinue your job search. Although it is hard to be turned down, it is part of the search process. Keep looking, and you will find the right job with the right employer.

@@@@@@@@@@@@@@@
INTERNET LINKS
The U.S. Industry and Trade Outlook is available at http://www.outlook.gov.
The Monthly Labor Review is available as a link from http://www.bls.gov.

National, state, and metropolitan area data from the National Compensation Survey, which integrates data from three existing Bureau of Labor Statistics programs—the Employment Cost Index, the Occupational Compensation Survey, and the Employee Benefits Survey—are available at http://www.bls.gov/ncs.

Data on earnings by detailed occupation from the Occupational Employment Statistics Survey are available/at/: http://www.bls.gov/oes.

ASSIGNMENT 1.3 Journal Abstract

OBJECTIVES

At the conclusion of this assignment, the student should be able to:

1. Identify the name of the professional association's journal.

2. Write a journal abstract of an article from a professional association's journal.

OVERVIEW

Professional association journals communicate information about health care advances, new technology, changing regulations, and much more. This assignment familiarizes students with the contents of professional journals in their fields and requires students to prepare an abstract (summary) of a selected article.

INSTRUCTIONS

1. Locate the name of your professional association's journal in Table 1-1.

2. Locate a journal by:

   a. going to its Web site (many journals are posted online).

   b. borrowing a journal through interlibrary loan (e.g., college library, local library).

   c. contacting a professional in your field of study or your instructor to borrow a journal.

   NOTE: Borrowing a journal from a professional in your field of study is an excellent way to start the networking process that will lead to employment. If you borrow a journal, be sure to return it promptly, and include a thank-you note. (Student members of professional associations do receive their profession's journal. Because it can take eight weeks to receive your first journal after joining your professional association, your best option is to go to the library or borrow a journal.)

Table 1-1 *Professional Journals*

PROFESSION	PROFESSIONAL JOURNAL	PROFESSIONAL ASSOCIATION	WEB SITE
Coding & Reimbursement Specialist	*CodeWrite*	Society for Clinical Coding (of the American Health Information Management Association)	http://www.ahima.org
	Coding Edge	American Academy of Professional Coders	http://www.aapc.com

3. Select and read an article from a recent edition (e.g., within the past year) of your professional association's journal.

4. Prepare a one-page, double-spaced, word-processed document that summarizes the journal article. Be sure to include the following information:

   a. Name of article

   b. Name of author

   c. Name of journal

   d. Date of journal

   e. Summary of journal article

   NOTE: Do *not* include your opinion about the article's content.

5. Check and double-check spelling, grammar, and punctuation. Have at least one other person review your document (e.g., college writing lab, English teacher, family member or friend who has excellent writing skills, and so on).

ASSIGNMENT 1.4 Professional Discussion Forums (Listservs)

OBJECTIVES

At the conclusion of this assignment, the student should be able to:

1. Explain the value of joining profession discussion forums.

2. Join a professional discussion forum.

3. Review discussion forum contents to identify topics relevant to a particular field of study.

4. Participate in a professional discussion forum.

OVERVIEW

Networking, or sharing information among professionals, is a valuable professional activity. The Internet has made it much easier to network with other professionals by using Web-based professional forums. This assignment familiarizes the student with the value of Internet professional discussion forums.

INSTRUCTIONS

1. Go to http://list.nih.gov, and click on "What is LISTERV?" to learn all about online discussion forums (listservs).

2. Select a professional discussion forum from Table 1-2, and follow its membership instructions.

   NOTE: Joining professional discussion forums is usually free!

3. Access archived forum discussions and observe current discussions for the period designated by your instructor (e.g., one to three weeks), noting topics that are relevant to your field of study.

4. Post a discussion comment or question on the forum and observe responses from subscribers.

5. At the end of the period of observation and participation, determine whether the forum would be helpful to you on the job.

Table 1-2 *Discussion Forums and Internet Sites for Professionals*

PROFESSIONAL	NAME OF FORUM	INTERNET SITE
AHIMA members	Communities of Practice	http://cop.ahima.org
Coders	Bulletin Boards	http://www.advanceforhim.com Scroll to "Resources," click on "Bulletin Board," and scroll down to click on "Coding."
Medicare Part B claims specialists	Part B News® (Medicare PartB-L)	http://www.partbnews.com Click on "Joint PartB-L Listserv."
Reimbursement specialists (Medicare)	Medicare Prospective Payment Communication	http:/list.nih.gov Click "Browse," scroll down and click on the "PPS-L."

ASSIGNMENT 1.5 Multiple Choice Review

1. The concept that every procedure or service reported to a third-party payer must be linked to a condition that justifies that procedure or service is called medical
   a. condition.
   b. necessity.
   c. procedure.
   d. requirement.

2. The administrative agency responsible for establishing rules for Medicare claims processing is called the
   a. Centers for Medicare and Medicaid Services (CMS).
   b. Department of Education and Welfare (DEW).
   c. Department of Health and Human Services (DHHS).
   d. Office of Inspector General (OIG).

3. Many insurance companies allow a time frame during which an insurance specialist may resubmit (rebill) a claim. What is that time frame?
   a. 30 to 45 days
   b. 6 months
   c. 1 year
   d. unlimited

4. Which organization is responsible for administering the Claims Specialist certification exam?
   a. AAPC
   b. NEBA
   c. AHIMA
   d. CMS

5. Which clause is implemented if the requirements associated with preauthorization of a claim prior to payment are not met?
   a. eligibility
   b. hold harmless
   c. no fault
   d. nonparticipation

6. Which type of condition will most likely require special handling for release of medical information requests?
   a. cancer
   b. dysthymia
   c. trauma
   d. tuberculosis

7. The exchange of information between provider and third-party payer, using a standardized machine-readable format, is called
   a. electronic data interchange.
   b. medical coding.
   c. posting payments.
   d. proving medical necessity.

8. The process of reporting diagnoses, procedures, and services as numeric and alphanumeric characters on an insurance claim is
   a. billing.
   b. coding.
   c. electronic data interchange.
   d. preauthorization.

9. Which is another title for the health insurance specialist?
   a. claims examiner
   b. coder
   c. health information technician
   d. medical assistant

10. If a patient is seen by a provider who orders a chest X-ray, which diagnosis should be linked with the procedure to prove medical necessity?
    a. abdominal distress
    b. heartburn
    c. shortness of breath
    d. sinus pain

11. The principles of right or good conduct are known as
    a. bylaws.
    b. ethics.
    c. rights.
    d. standards.

12. The notice sent by the insurance company to the provider, which contains payment information about a claim, is the
    a. claim form.
    b. electronic data interchange.
    c. explanation of benefits.
    d. remittance advice.

13. When an individual chooses to perform services for another under an express or implied agreement and is not subject to the other's control, the individual is defined as a(n)
    a. casual employee.
    b. dependent contractor.
    c. independent contractor.
    d. statutory employee.

14. Employers are generally considered liable for the actions and omissions of employees as performed and committed within the scope of their employment. This is known as
    a. the chain of command.
    b. errors and omissions.
    c. respondent superior.
    d. the scope of practice.

15. To assign codes to the written narratives documented by the health care provider, health insurance specialists must draw upon their knowledge of
    a. billing practices.
    b. insurance regulations.
    c. medical necessity.
    d. medical terminology.

16. Which type of insurance should be purchased by health insurance specialist independent contractors?
    a. bonding
    b. errors and omissions
    c. medical malpractice
    d. workers' compensation

17. A health insurance specialist who is able to demonstrate competency in facilitating the claims reimbursement process from the time a service is rendered by a provider until the balance is paid can qualify for which certification?
    a. Certified Coding Specialist (CCS)
    b. Certified Healthcare Reimbursement Specialist (CHRS)

c. Certified Medical Reimbursement Specialist (CMRS)

d. Registered Health Information Technician (RHIT)

18. Which certification fulfills the need for an entry-level coding credential?

a. Certified Coding Assistant (CCA)

b. Certified Coding Specialist (CCS)

c. Certified Healthcare Reimbursement Specialist (CHRS)

d. Certified Professional Coder—Hospital (CPC-H)

19. *High blood pressure* is an example of a

a. code.

b. diagnosis.

c. procedure.

d. service.

20. According to the *Occupational Outlook Handbook,* which setting offers the fastest employment growth and majority of new jobs for health information technicians (including those who perform insurance specialist functions)?

a. health insurance companies

b. hospitals

c. physician offices

d. schools/colleges

## CHAPTER 2

Introduction to Health Insurance

INTRODUCTION

This chapter familiarizes students with health insurance coverage statistics and major developments in health insurance. Students will interpret health insurance coverage statistics and create an Excel chart to display health insurance data. Students will also perform a literature search to evaluate resources appropriate for preparing a research paper, which explains major developments in health insurance and their impact on health care access, delivery, quality, reimbursement, and technology.

ASSIGNMENT 2.1 Health Insurance Coverage Statistics

OBJECTIVES

At the conclusion of this assignment, the student should be able to:

1. Interpret U.S. health insurance coverage statistics.
2. Compare U.S. health insurance coverage in 2002 and 2003.
3. Create a pie chart to display U.S. health insurance coverage statistics using Microsoft Excel.

OVERVIEW

The ability to properly interpret health insurance statistics and effectively communicate findings is a valuable skill for the health insurance specialist. This assignment requires students to interpret statistical data and display it by creating a pie chart using Microsoft Excel.

INSTRUCTIONS

1. Review the information about U.S. health insurance statistics in Chapter 2 of your textbook.
2. Refer to Figure 2-1 to answer the following questions:
   a. Which type of health insurance coverage decreased for the U.S. population?
   b. What was the percentage change in Medicaid coverage from 2002 to 2003?
   c. Which type of health insurance coverage remained statistically the same?

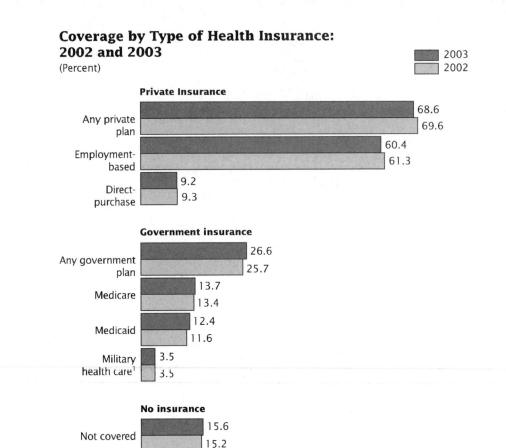

Coverage by Type of Health Insurance: 2002 and 2003
(Percent)

■ 2003
□ 2002

Private Insurance

Any private plan — 68.6 / 69.6

Employment-based — 60.4 / 61.3

Direct-purchase — 9.2 / 9.3

Government insurance

Any government plan — 26.6 / 25.7

Medicare — 13.7 / 13.4

Medicaid — 12.4 / 11.6

Military health care[1] — 3.5 / 3.5

No insurance

Not covered — 15.6 / 15.2

FIGURE 2-1 *Coverage by type of health insurance: 2002 and 2003 (Permission to reuse granted by U.S. Census Bureau.)*

    d. Which two factors explain the decrease in the number of individuals covered by private health insurance?

    e. Which three concerns face individuals who do not have health insurance coverage?

3. Refer to Figure 2-2 to answer the following questions:

    a. What does Figure 2-2 illustrate?

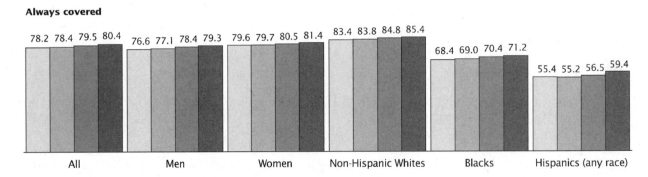

Annual Health Insurance Rates: 1996 - 1999
(In percent)

□ 1996
▨ 1997
▩ 1998
■ 1999

Always covered

All — 78.2 78.4 79.5 80.4

Men — 76.6 77.1 78.4 79.3

Women — 79.6 79.7 80.5 81.4

Non-Hispanic Whites — 83.4 83.8 84.8 85.4

Blacks — 68.4 69.0 70.4 71.2

Hispanics (any race) — 55.4 55.2 56.5 59.4

FIGURE 2-2 *Annual health insurance rates: 1996–1999 (always covered) (Permission to reuse granted by U.S. Census Bureau.)*

b. Compare the percentage of men and women with health care coverage between 1996 and 1999. What conclusion can you draw from comparing these two populations?

c. Which population group had the smallest percentage of individuals with continuous health insurance coverage?

d. What trend applies to every population group identified in Figure 2-2?

4. **Case Study:** Dr. Jason Brook is an orthopedist in a small, rural town in New York state. His practice consists of a high percentage of patients who either have Medicaid or Medicare with Medicaid as a secondary payer. Dr. Brook will meet with colleagues and representatives of the state government to discuss the impact a proposed cut in Medicaid funding will have on providers who practice in rural areas of New York, including the impact on patient access to health care. Dr. Brook has asked you, his health insurance specialist, to assist him by preparing a document that illustrates his patient population. Use the data in Table 2-1 to create a pie chart in Microsoft Excel (Table 2-2), illustrating the breakdown of health insurance coverage in the practice. (Dr. Brook has also instructed you to use vibrant colors and to create a three-dimensional effect.)

Table 2-1 *Dr. Brook's Patient Population According to Health Insurance Coverage*

TYPE OF HEALTH INSURANCE COVERAGE	PERCENTAGE OF PATIENTS COVERED
HMO	45%
Medicaid	18%
Medicare	23%
Military	4%
Self-pay	10%

Table 2-2 *Instructions for Creating a Pie Chart in Microsoft Excel*

1. Open Microsoft Excel.

2. Click File, Open to create a new document.

3. Enter "Type of Health Insurance Coverage" in cell A1.

4. Enter "Percentage of Patients Covered" in cell B1.

5. Enter the types of health insurance coverage plans from column one in Table 2–1 in cells A2 through A6, respectively.

6. Enter the data from column two in Table 2–1 in cells B2 through B6, respectively.

	A	B
1	Type of Health Insurance Coverage	Percentage of Patients Covered
2	HMO	45%
3	Medicaid	18%
4	Medicare	23%
5	Military	4%
6	Self-pay	10%

(continues)

Table 2-2 *Continued*

7. Save your document.

8. Click Insert, Chart, and select Pie from the Standard Types column. Click Next.

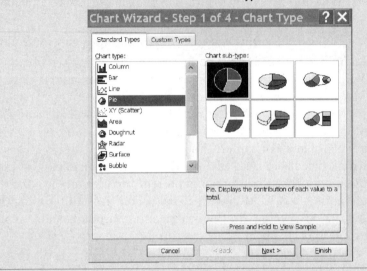

9. Click Next (on the Chart Wizard — Step 2 of 4—Chart Options page).

10. On the Chart Wizard—Step 3 of 4—Chart Options page, edit the Chart title so that it reads "Percentage of Patients Covered by Health Insurance." Click Next.

(continues)

Table 2-2 *Continued*

11. On the Chart Wizard—Step 4 of 4—Chart Location page, click Finish.

Chart Wizard - Step 4 of 4 - Chart Location ? X

Place chart:

○ As new sheet: | Chart1

◉ As object in: | Table 2-1 ▾

Cancel   < Back   Next >   Finish

12. The pie chart is located on Sheet1 of your Excel file. To create a three-dimensional effect, right-click on the pie chart, select Chart Type, click on Custom Types, and scroll down to select Pie Explosion. Click OK.

NOTE: Right-click on the pie chart, select Chart Type, and choose a different type of chart to change the image to a bar graph, line graph, and so on.

	A	B
1	Type of Health Insurance Coverage	Percentage of Patients Covered
2	HMO	45%
3	Medicaid	18%
4	Medicare	23%
5	Military	4%
6	Self-pay	10%
7		
8		
9		

Percentage of Patients Covered by Health Insurance

■ HMO
■ Medicaid
□ Medicare
□ Military
■ Self-pay

ASSIGNMENT 2.2 Major Developments in Health Insurance (Research Paper)

OBJECTIVES

At the end of this assignment, the student should be able to:

1. Use information literacy skills to research topics.

2. Perform a literature search to evaluate resources appropriate for a research paper.

3. Prepare an annotated bibliography.

4. Cite literature sources to avoid plagiarism.

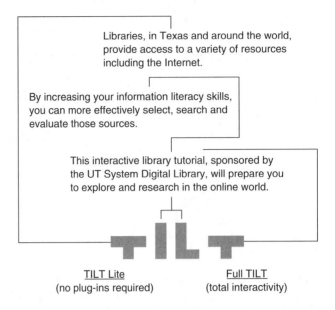

Libraries, in Texas and around the world, provide access to a variety of resources including the Internet.

By increasing your information literacy skills, you can more effectively select, search and evaluate those sources.

This interactive library tutorial, sponsored by the UT System Digital Library, will prepare you to explore and research in the online world.

TILT Lite
(no plug-ins required)

Full TILT
(total interactivity)

FIGURE 2-3 *Texas Information Literacy Tutorial (TILT) (Reprinted according to the TILT Open Publication License at http://tilt.lib.utsystem.edu/yourtilt/agreement.html.)*

5. Write a research paper that explains major developments in health insurance for a specific period of time.

6. Demonstrate relationships between major developments in health insurance and their impact on health care access, delivery, quality, reimbursement, and technology.

OVERVIEW

Performing a literature search to select and evaluate information resources is the first step in writing a research paper. TILT (Figure 2-3) is an interactive literacy tutorial created by the University of Texas to teach students how to perform literature searches. An annotated bibliography (Figure 2-4) contains citations (reference sources, such as books or journal articles) and a brief description of each cited item that summarizes the accuracy, quality, and relevance of the source. Writing a research paper is an excellent way for students to demonstrate their understanding of concepts that require interpretation and critical thinking skills (e.g., impact of health insurance regarding current health care issues).

Plagiarism is the act of stealing someone else's words or phrases and presenting them as your own. This means that when content is cut and pasted from an article into a research paper, the literature source must be cited. Your college may require you to review and sign a plagiarism policy; a sample policy is shown in Figure 2-5.

Texas Information Literacy Tutorial (TILT)

1. Go to http://tilt.lib.utsystem.edu, and select TILT Lite (if you use a dial-up connection to access the Internet) or Full TILT (if you are connected to the Internet via cable, DSL, satellite, or another broadband service).

2. Register to complete TILT's modules, where you will learn about information literacy and how to conduct searches for information.

3. Submit each completed module quiz to your instructor's e-mail address.

This informative, practical article by the project director of the Payment Error Prevention Support Peer Review Organization (PEPSPRO) in Texas discusses the issue of diagnosis related group (DRG) billing as a major contributor to inaccurate Medicare payments and describes the negative consequences of undercoding and upcoding for the hospital. Recommendations are made and tools provided for completing a comprehensive assessment of records, staff qualifications, training, and use of coding resources; coding policies; and safeguards against upcoding. The author also discusses the various aspects of following up on a completed assessment, including implementing new policies, providing appropriate training, and monitoring compliance.

Fletcher, Robin. "The Importance of Addressing Inaccurate Diagnosis Related Group Assignment as a Risk Area." Journal of Health Care Compliance 4.5 (Sept./Oct. 2002): 40–46.

The author reports on the trend of hospitals using Internet-based automated compliance checking in place of more traditional billing methods to fulfill the requirements of the Medicare Correct Coding Initiative (CCI). Using Holy Cross Hospital in Ft. Lauderdale, Florida, as a case example, the author fully details the many benefits of using the automated system, including the reduction of billing errors, ease of use, evaluation of coding risk areas, and preventing noncompliance and the resulting penalty fees.

Moynihan, James J. "Automated Compliance Checker Helps Ensure Billing Accuracy." Healthcare Financial Management 54.7 (July 2000): 78.

FIGURE 2-4 *Sample annotated bibliography with two works cited*

Avoiding Plagiarism

Plagiarism is the act of stealing someone else's words or phrases and presenting them as your own. This is most commonly done when students "cut and paste" from an article directly into their report without citing the literature reference. There are two basic types of plagiarism:

Accidental plagiarism—you did a "cut and paste" of some key points into a working draft copy of your report but failed to remove them from the final version.

Deliberate plagiarism—you knew what you were doing when you did it, and you just hoped that you wouldn't get caught.

So, how do you avoid either type of plagiarism?

Cite the source! If you are using a phrase and think that it is perfect, then you insert it something like this:

According to Edna Huffman, the old adage "in God we trust, all else must document" is as true today as it was in the 1940s when Ms. Huffman first used the phrase (Huffman 1940).

On the reference page, you then list this source:

Huffman, E. 1940. Health Information Management, 10th ed. Physicians' Record Company.

Paraphrase! Even if you don't use the exact words, but rely heavily on another author's work, you should still give credit. It might read like this:

(continues)

FIGURE 2-5 *Sample plagiarism policy to be signed by students (Permission to reuse granted by Patricia Peterson, RHIA.)*

These days, everyone has a grudge about documentation standards, but those standards exist for a reason. The country may trust in God, but the court systems trust only in the record.

Huffman put you on the right track—so, give her credit in the reference page; besides, your paper will be stronger for showing more references.

Take notes, and then take a break! A good strategy is to read several pages and take notes in your own hand. Then go away and come back to write the report just from your notes—don't look at the reference materials. In this way, you are forced to choose your own words and make your own logical conclusions.

Have enough confidence in yourself and what you know. Draw your own conclusions—even when your opinion is different that what you read in the published literature.

I have read the plagiarism policy above, and I understand the policy.

_____   _____

Student's Name   Date

FIGURE 2-5 *Continued*

Annotated Bibliography

1. Select a health care topic that interests you (e.g., health insurance programs for children in poverty).

2. Go to your academic library to locate citations (e.g., journal articles) about your topic. (Refer to Table 1-1 for a list of professional journals.)

3. Review the citations to determine whether they contain useful information and ideas about your topic, and select two to read thoroughly.

4. Prepare the annotated bibliography in the American Psychological Association (APA) style or the Modern Language Association (MLA) style, depending on your instructor's preference (refer to Figure 2-4).

   NOTE: The APA has established a style that is used in all its published books and journals, and many authorities in social and behavioral sciences have adopted this style as their standard. The MLA style is recommended for the preparation of scholarly manuscripts and student research papers. Be sure to ask your instructor which style you should use.

@@@@@@@@@@@@@@@@

INTERNET LINK
Go to http://www.thewritesource.com, and click on the APA link (below Research) or the MLA link to view examples of reference citations.

5. Summarize the article, incorporating at least four of the items below:
   - Description of the content and/or focus of the article
   - Consideration of whether the article content is useful

- Limitations of the article (e.g., outdated)
- Audience for which the article is intended
- Evaluation of any research methods used in the article
- Author's background
- Any conclusions the author(s) made about the topic
- Your reaction to the article

6. Check and double-check spelling, grammar, and punctuation. Have at least one other person review your paper (e.g., college writing lab, English teacher, family member or friend who has excellent writing skills, and so on).

Plagiarism Policy

1. Review the plagiarism policy in Figure 2-5.
2. Sign and date the policy.
3. Remove the policy from the Workbook and submit to your instructor.

Research Paper

INSTRUCTIONS

1. Select a period of time (e.g., 1990–1999) during which to conduct research on the major developments in health insurance, along with their impact on health care quality, access, technology, reimbursement, and so on.

2. Select a minimum of five references (other than the *UHI* textbook) to include in your paper:
   - Two references should be articles (consider using the two sources cited in your annotated bibliography).
   - Two references should be books.
   - One reference can be an Internet Web site.
   - A sixth reference can be the *UHI* textbook.

   NOTE: You will need to conduct a literature search of at least 15 to 20 references before selecting just 5 to use as references in your paper.

3. Write an introductory paragraph that indicates the period of time selected and lists major developments in health insurance for that period. The last sentence of this paragraph should include a list of health care issues affected by those developments.

4. For each subsequent paragraph, explain how major developments in health insurance affected each health care issue (e.g., access, delivery, and so on). Write a separate paragraph for each issue.

5. Write a concluding paragraph that summarizes all of the points made in your paper, and indicate which health care issue was affected most significantly by developments in health insurance and why.

6. Write a bibliography in APA (or MLA) style. (Check with your instructor to see if footnotes are required.)

7. Check and double-check spelling, grammar, and punctuation. Be sure to double-space your paper and follow the format required by your instructor. Have at least one other person review your reference paper (e.g., college writing lab, English teacher, family member or friend who has excellent writing skills, and so on).

ASSIGNMENT 2.3 Multiple Choice Review

1. Which type of insurance is defined as reimbursement for income lost as a result of a temporary or permanent illness or injury?
   a. automobile
   b. disability
   c. health
   d. liability

2. Which type of automobile insurance coverage pays for loss of or damage to a vehicle such as that caused by fire, flood, hail, theft, vandalism, or wind?
   a. collision
   b. comprehensive
   c. liability
   d. medical

3. Which auto insurance employee reviews health care bills, submitted to the insurance company for treatment of injuries sustained as the result of a motor vehicle accident, to determine coverage for the injured person?
   a. analyst
   b. broker
   c. medical adjuster
   d. medical attorney

4. Health insurance benefits are generally _____ to liability insurance.
   a. primary
   b. secondary
   c. supplementary
   d. tertiary

5. What do third-party payers review on claims to determine whether a liability payer should be considered primary?
   a. diagnosis codes
   b. location of treatment
   c. name of treating physician
   d. procedure codes

6. Evidence of the first health insurance policy to provide private health care coverage for injuries that did not result in death appeared in which year
   a. 1842
   b. 1860
   c. 1915
   d. 1920

7. The Hill-Burton Act provided federal grants for modernizing hospitals that had become obsolete because of lack of capital investment during the Great Depression. In return for federal funds, facilities were required to
   a. charge less than facilities that did not receive Hill-Burton funds.
   b. provide services for free or at reduced rates to patients who were unable to pay.
   c. provide temporary shelter for individuals who were without housing.
   d. reimburse the federal government through daily room rate surcharges.

8. An *inpatient* is a person admitted to a hospital for treatment with the expectation of remaining in the hospital for a period of at least
   a. 12 hours.
   b. 18 hours.
   c. 24 hours.
   d. 36 hours.

9. *Current Procedural Terminology* (CPT) was developed by which organization in 1966?
   a. American Hospital Association
   b. American Medical Association
   c. Social Security Administration
   d. World Health Organization

10. A patient with end-stage renal disease is eligible to receive which benefits?
    a. Medicaid
    b. Medicare
    c. Medigap
    d. Workers' Compensation

11. If a veteran is rated as 100% permanently and totally disabled as a result of a service-connected condition, which program will provide benefits to the veteran's dependents?
    a. CHAMPUS
    b. CHAMPVA
    c. COBRA
    d. TRICARE

12. Which coding system was created in 1984?
    a. CPT
    b. DSM
    c. HCPCS
    d. ICD-9-CM

13. Coverage for catastrophic or prolonged illnesses and injuries is known as _____ insurance.
    a. catastrophic
    b. major medical
    c. prolonged care
    d. supplemental

14. Three or more health care providers sharing equipment, supplies, and personnel create a(n)
    a. group practice.
    b. independent practice association.
    c. managed care organization.
    d. sole proprietorship.

15. CMS developed the national Correct Coding Initiative (CCI) to
    a. decrease the amount of money paid out by the Medicare program.
    b. eliminate improper coding and promote national correct coding methodologies.
    c. encourage coders to further their education to qualify for advancement.
    d. reduce the number of codes in the CPT and HCPCS coding systems.

16. The skilled nursing facility prospective payment system (SNF PPS) generates which type of payments for each skilled nursing facility admission?
    a. capitation
    b. cost-based
    c. fee-for-service
    d. per diem

17. In 2000, which type of health plan was introduced as a way to encourage individuals to locate the best health care at the lowest price possible, with the goal of holding down health care costs?
    a. consumer-driven
    b. major medical
    c. private
    d. retrospective

18. By whom is the employer identification number (EIN) assigned?
    a. Centers for Medicare and Medicaid Services
    b. Department of Health and Human Services
    c. Internal Revenue Service
    d. Social Security Administration

19. The identification of disease and the provision of care and treatment by members of a health care team to persons who are sick, injured, or concerned about their health status is the definition of
    a. emergency care.
    b. health care.
    c. medical care.
    d. preventive care.

20. Although the presence of health insurance was increasing in the early 1900s, most Americans continued to pay their own health expenses. This usually meant that
    a. the average household spent more than 50% of household income on health expenses.
    b. the quality of care provided to those without health care insurance was inferior.
    c. their expenses were covered by plans sponsored by the federal government.
    d. those who had no insurance usually received charity care or no care.

## CHAPTER 3

Managed Health Care

INTRODUCTION

This chapter familiarizes students with types of managed care plans, legislation that has affected the managed care industry, and ways in which consumers and professionals can obtain information about the quality of health insurance plans.

ASSIGNMENT 3.1 National Committee for Quality Assurance (NCQA) Health Plan Report Card

OBJECTIVES

At the conclusion of this assignment, the student should be able to:

1. State the purpose of the NCQA health plan report card.
2. Generate and interpret an NCQA health plan report card.

OVERVIEW

The NCQA health plan report card is an interactive tool that helps consumers and professionals evaluate health plans. Report card results are based on an assessment of health plan processes and systems, clinical quality, and member satisfaction.

INSTRUCTIONS

1. Create a customized report card about health plans in your state by going to http://hprc.ncqa.org, clicking on the "create report card" link, and entering the required information.

2. Prepare a one-page, double-spaced, word-processed document that summarizes the results of the report card generated. Be sure to include the following information in the summary:

   a. Comparison of accreditation outcomes for the plans

   b. Number of health plans that earned an "excellent" rating

   c. Significance of an "excellent" rating

3. Check and double-check spelling, grammar, and punctuation. Have at least one other person review your document (e.g., college writing lab, English teacher, family member or friend who has excellent writing skills, and so on).

ASSIGNMENT 3.2 Managed Health Care Federal Legislation

OBJECTIVES

At the conclusion of this assignment, the student should be able to:

1. List managed health care federal legislation and year of implementation.

2. Identify legislation that most significantly influenced the growth of managed care, and state why this legislation was significant.

INSTRUCTIONS

1. Review Table 3-2, "Timeline for managed health care federal legislation," in Chapter 3 of the textbook, and select legislation that most significantly influenced the growth of managed care. (You can select more than one piece of legislation for this purpose.)

   NOTE: Base your selection of significant legislation on classroom discussion as well as the textbook description of each piece of legislation. You are welcome to select more than one piece of legislation.

2. Conduct a literature search to locate at least 10 articles about the legislation you selected. Print (or make a copy of) each article.

   NOTE: If you selected more than one piece of legislation, be sure you conduct literature searches on each. You will probably locate more than 10 articles.

3. Carefully review each article to identify reasons the legislation you selected most significantly influenced the growth of managed care. (Using a highlighter pen to mark pertinent material in the articles may be helpful. Be sure you mark up a *copy* of the article, not the original article.)

4. Prepare a two- to three-page, double-spaced, word-processed document that summarizes your findings. Be sure to organize the document as follows:

   a. First paragraph—legislation you selected as most significantly influencing the growth of managed care

   b. Second and subsequent paragraphs—reasons that support your choice of that legislation as being the most influential regarding the growth of managed care (based on content in articles)

   c. Last paragraph—conclusion about the growth of managed care as the result of the legislation you selected as being most influential

   d. Bibliography (of 10 articles located as the result of performing the literature search)

5. Check and double-check spelling, grammar, and punctuation. Have at least one other person review your paper (e.g., college writing lab, English teacher, family member or friend who has excellent writing skills, and so on).

1. Employees and dependents who join a managed care plan are called
   a. beneficiaries.
   b. enrollees.
   c. sponsors.
   d. subscribers.

2. Which act of legislation permitted large employers to self-insure employee health care benefits?
   a. ERISA
   b. HEDIS
   c. OBRA
   d. TEFRA

3. If a physician provides services that cost less than the managed care capitation amount, the physician will
   a. lose money.
   b. lose his or her managed care contract.
   c. make a profit.
   d. reduce the patient load.

4. The primary care provider is responsible for
   a. ensuring that enrollees pay their premiums.
   b. providing care according to the enrollee's preferences.
   c. supervising and coordinating health care services for enrollees.
   d. the quality of care provided by consultants.

5. Which is a method of controlling health care costs and quality of care by reviewing the appropriateness and necessity of care provided to patients?
   a. administrative oversight
   b. preadmission certification
   c. quality assurance
   d. utilization management

6. Which type of integrated delivery system (IDS) is usually owned by physicians or a hospital and provides practice management services to individual physician practices?
   a. group practice without walls (GPWW)
   b. integrated provider organization (IPO)
   c. management service organization (MSO)
   d. physician-hospital organization (PHO)

7. Which type of health plan funds health care expenses by insurance coverage and allows the individual to select one of each type of provider to create a personalized network?
   a. capitated plan
   b. customized sub-capitation plan
   c. health care reimbursement account
   d. health savings security account

8. Which type of consumer-directed health plan carries the stipulation that any funds unused will be lost?
   a. flexible spending account
   b. health care reimbursement account
   c. health reimbursement arrangement
   d. health savings security account

9. Which is assessed by the National Committee for Quality Assurance?
   a. ambulatory care facilities
   b. hospitals
   c. long-term care facilities
   d. managed care plans

10. A case manager is responsible for
    a. educating enrollees about their health plan benefits.
    b. overseeing the health services provided to enrollees.
    c. providing health care services to enrollees.
    d. submitting claims on behalf of enrollees.

11. The event directly responsible for the dramatic increase in U.S. health care costs was the
    a. conviction of the AMA for violating the Sherman Antitrust Act.
    b. creation of the first Blue Cross plan.
    c. formation of Kaiser Permanente.
    d. implementation of Medicare and Medicaid.

12. What was the cost per month to each enrollee of the first recognized prepaid health plan?
    a. $0.50
    b. $5
    c. $50
    d. $500

13. Which was created to provide standards to assess managed care systems in terms of indicators such as membership, utilization of services, quality, and access?
    a. ERISA
    b. HEDIS
    c. HIPAA
    d. TEFRA

14. Which act of legislation provided states with the flexibility to establish HMOs for Medicare and Medicaid programs?
    a. BBA
    b. COBRA
    c. OBRA
    d. TEFRA

15. Which would likely be subject to a managed care plan quality review?
    a. amount of money spent on construction upgrades
    b. cost of new equipment for a member facility
    c. number of patient payments made by credit card
    d. results of patient satisfaction surveys

16. The Quality Improvement System for Managed Care (QISMC) was established by
    a. the Joint Commission on Accreditation of Healthcare Organizations.
    b. Medicaid.
    c. Medicare.
    d. National Committee for Quality Assurance.

17. Arranging for a patient's transfer to a rehabilitation facility is an example of
    a. concurrent review.
    b. discharge planning.
    c. preadmission review.
    d. preauthorization.

18. Administrative services performed on behalf of a self-insured managed care company can be outsourced to a(n)
    a. accrediting agency.
    b. external quality review organization.
    c. third-party administrator.
    d. utilization management company.

19. Before a patient schedules elective surgery, many managed care plans require a(n):
    a. payment applied to the cost of the surgery.
    b. physician incentive plan disclosure.
    c. quality assurance review.
    d. second surgical opinion.

20. A *health delivery network* is another name for a(n):
    a. exclusive provider organization (EPO).
    b. integrated delivery system (IDS).
    c. preferred provider organization (PPO).
    d. triple option plan (TOP).

CHAPTER 4

Life Cycle of an Insurance Claim

INTRODUCTION

This chapter familiarizes students with the encounter form, remittance advice, and explanation of benefits (EOB) form used in the payment of health insurance claims. Students will learn the contents of an encounter form, as well as how to interpret data contained on a remittance advice and an explanation of benefits.

ASSIGNMENT 4.1 Payment of Claims: Encounter Form

OBJECTIVES

At the conclusion of this assignment, the student should be able to:

1. Explain the purpose of an encounter form.
2. Interpret the information contained on an encounter form.

OVERVIEW

An *encounter form* is the source document used to generate the insurance claim. In addition to patient identification information and the date of service, it contains abbreviated diagnosis and brief procedure/service descriptions and corresponding codes (e.g., ICD, CPT, HCPCS). The provider circles the appropriate codes on the encounter form, and the insurance specialist enters the office charge, amount paid by the patient, and total due.

INSTRUCTIONS

Review the encounter form in Figure 4-1 to familiarize yourself with its organization and contents. Use the encounter form to answer the following questions:

1. The physician entered a check mark in front of "Inj. Tendon 20550" on the encounter form, but did not select a diagnosis code. Which diagnosis code should be selected?

PATIENT INFORMATION

PATIENT'S LAST NAME	FIRST	INITIAL	BIRTHDATE		SEX ☐ MALE ☐ FEMALE	TODAY'S DATE

ADDRESS	CITY	STATE	ZIP	RELATIONSHIP TO SUBSCRIBER	INJURY DATE

SUBSCRIBER OR POLICYHOLDER	INSURANCE CARRIER

ADDRESS	CITY	STATE	ZIP	INS. I.D.	COVERAGE CODE	GROUP

ASSIGNMENT AND RELEASE: I HEREBY AUTHORIZE MY INSURANCE BENEFITS TO BE PAID DIRECTLY TO THE UNDERSIGNED PHYSICIAN. I AM FINANCIALLY RESPONSIBLE FOR NON-COVERED SERVICES. I ALSO AUTHORIZE THE PHYSICIAN TO RELEASE ANY INFORMATION REQUIRED.

IDENTIFY

OTHER HEALTH COVERAGE ☐ YES ☐ NO

DISABILITY RELATED TO:
☐ ACCIDENT ☐ INDUSTRIAL ☐ ILLNESS ☐ OTHER

DATE SYMPTOMS APPEARED, INCEPTION OF PREGNANCY, OR ACCIDENT OCCURRED:

SIGNED _____ (PATIENT, OR PARENT, IF MINOR) _____ Date _____

✓	DESCRIPTION	CPT/MD	FEE	✓	DESCRIPTION	CPT/MD	FEE	✓	DESCRIPTION	CPT/MD	FEE
	OFFICE VISITS	NEW PT			LABORATORY (Cont'd.)				PROCEDURES		
	Moderate Complex	99203			Wet Mount	87210			EKG	93000 93005	
	Moderate/High Comp.	99204			Pap Smear	88150			Resp. Function Test	94010	
	High Complexity	99205			Handling	99000			Ear Lavage	69210	
	OFFICE VISITS	EST. PT			Hemoccult Stool	82270			Injection Inter. Jt.*	20605	
	Minimal	99211			Glucose	82948			Injection Major Jt.*	20610	
	Self Limited Comp.	99212			INJECTIONS				Anoscopy	46600	
	Low/Moderate Comp.	99213			Vitamin B12/B Complex	J3420			Sigmoidoscopy	45355	
	Moderate Complex	99214			ACTH	J0140			I & D*	10060	
	High Complexity	99215			Depo-Estradiol	J1000			Electrocautery*	17200	
	CONSULTATIONS	OFFICE			Depo Testosterone	J1070			Thromb Hemor.*	46320	
	Moderate Complexity	99243			Imferon	J1760			Inj. Tendon*	20550	
	Mod. to High Comp.	99244			Tetanus Toxoid	J3180					
	HOME	EST. PT			Influenza Vaccine - Flu	90724			MISCELLANEOUS		
	Moderate Complexity	99352			Pneumococcal Vaccine	90732			Drugs, Supplies, Materials	99070	
	ER				TB Tine Test	86585			Special Reports	99080	
	Moderate Severity	99283			Aminophyllin	J0280			Services After Hrs.	99050	
	High Severity	99284			Terbutaline Sulf.	J3105			Services 10pm - 8am	99052	
	LABORATORY				Demerol HCL	J0990			Services Sun. & Holidays	99054	
	Urinalysis - Complete	81000			Compazine	J0780			Counseling	99403	
	Hemoglobin	85018			Injection Therapeutic	90782					
	Culture, Strep/Monilia	87081			Estrone Susp.	J1410					

DIAGNOSIS:

☐ Allergic Rhinitis	477.9	☐ Chronic Fatigue Synd.	300.5	☐ Hemorrhoids ... 455.6
☐ Anemia	280.9	☐ COPD	496	☐ Hiatal Hernia ... 553.3
☐ Angina Pectoris	413	☐ Costochondritis	733.99	☐ Hiatal Hernia & Reflux ... 530.1
☐ Anxiety	300.00	☐ CVA	431	☐ HVD ... 402.10
☐ Aortic Stenosis	424.1	☐ Cystitis	595.9	☐ Hyperlipidemia ... 272.4
☐ ASCVD	429.2	☐ Deg. Disc. Disease, CX	722.4	☐ Hypoestrogenism ... 256.3
☐ ASHD	414.9	☐ Deg. Disc. Dis., Lumbar	722.52	☐ Hypothyroidism ... 244.9
☐ Asthma	493.9	☐ Depression, Endogenous	296.2	☐ Impacted Cerumen ... 380.4
☐ Atrial Fibrillation	427.31	☐ Dermatitis	692.9	☐ Influenza, Viral ... 487.1
☐ Bigeminy	427.89	☐ Diabetes Mellitus, Adult	250.0	☐ Irritable Bowel Syndrome ... 564.1
☐ BPH	600	☐ Diarrhea	558.9	☐ Laryngitis ... 464.0
☐ Bronchitis, Acute	466.1	☐ Diverticulitis	562.11	☐ Menopausal Syndrome ... 627.2
☐ Bronchitis, Chronic	491.9	☐ Esophagitis	530.1	☐ Mitral Insufficiency ... 396.2
☐ Bursitis	726	☐ Fibrocystic Breast Disease	610.11	☐ Moniliasis ... 112
☐ Cardiomyopathy	425.4	☐ Fissure in Ano	565.0	☐ Myocardial Infarction ... 410.9
☐ Carotid Artery Disease	433.1	☐ Gastroenteritis	558.9	☐ Neuritis ... 729.2
☐ Cerebral Vascular Disease	437.9	☐ Gout	274.9	☐ Osteoarthritis ... 715.9
☐ CHF	428.0	☐ HCVD	429.2	☐ Osteoporosis ... 733.0
☐ Cholecystitis	575.1	☐ Headache, Vascular	784.0	☐ Otitis Media ... 382.9
		☐ Headache, Migraine	346.9	☐ Parkinsonism ... 332

☐ Peripheral Vascular Dis. ... 443.9
☐ Pharyngitis ... 462.0
☐ Pneumonia, Bacterial ... 482.9
☐ Pneumonia, Viral ... 480.9
☐ Prostatitis, Chronic/Acute ... 601
☐ Rectal Bleeding ... 569.3
☐ Renal Failure, Chronic ... 585
☐ Rheumatoid Arthritis ... 714.0
☐ Sinusitis ... 461.9
☐ Supraventr. Tachycardia ... 427.0
☐ T.I.A. ... 435.9
☐ Tachycardia ... 426.89
☐ Tendinitis ... 726.90
☐ Tonsillitis ... 463
☐ Ulcer Duodenal ... 532.9
☐ Ulcer Gastric ... 531.9
☐ URI ... 465.9
☐ UTI ... 599.0
☐ Vaginitis ... 616.10
☐ Vertigo ... 780.4

DIAGNOSIS: (IF NOT CHECKED ABOVE)	REF. DR. & #

DOCTOR'S SIGNATURE / DATE	NO SERVICES PURCHASED	SERVICE PERFORMED	ACCEPT ASSIGNMENT	TODAY'S FEE	

INSTRUCTIONS TO PATIENT FOR FILING INSURANCE CLAIMS

1. MAIL THIS FORM DIRECTLY TO YOUR INSURANCE COMPANY.
   ATTACH YOUR OWN INSURANCE COMPANY'S FORM.

PLEASE REMEMBER THAT PAYMENT IS YOUR OBLIGATION, REGARDLESS OF INSURANCE OR OTHER THIRD PARTY INVOLVEMENT.

OFFICE ☐   YES ☐   AMT. REC'D TODAY

E.R. ☐   NO ☐

HOME ☐   TOTAL DUE

FIGURE 4-1 *Encounter form (Courtesy of Bibbero Systems, Inc., Petaluma, CA, 800-242-2376.)*

2. The provider will accept as payment in full whatever the payer determines is the allowed fee. Should the provider enter a check mark in the YES box for "ACCEPT ASSIGNMENT" on the encounter form? What is the name of the section of the encounter form that the patient signs to authorize payment to the provider?

3. Which block on the CMS-1500 claim form would contain an entry based on information contained in the encounter form section "DATE SYMPTOMS APPEARED, INCEPTION OF PREGNANCY, OR ACCIDENT OCCURRED?"

4. If the provider placed a check mark before the word "industrial" under the statement "DISABILITY RELATED TO," what type of payer should process the claim?

5. Which CPT codes included on the encounter form are reported for new patient office visits? (Refer to your CPT coding manual to answer this question.)

6. The provider conducted a home visit for a patient. What is the title of the section of the encounter form where the provider would indicate "home visit" as the place of service?

7. The provider rendered services to a patient on a Sunday morning. Identify the CPT code located on the encounter form that would be reported for this service.

8. The patient was referred to this provider by another physician. Identify the section of the encounter form where referring physician information is entered.

9. During processing of the encounter form (to generate the claim), the insurance specialist notices that the provider entered a check mark in front of the procedure, "Hemoccult Stool," and a check mark in front of the diagnosis, "Gout." Because *medical necessity* requires the diagnosis selected to justify the procedure performed, what should the insurance specialist do next?

10. How many CPT codes for an EKG are listed on the encounter form?

ASSIGNMENT 4.2 Payment of Claims: Remittance Advice

OBJECTIVES

At the conclusion of this assignment, the student should be able to:

1. Explain the purpose of a remittance advice.
2. Interpret data contained in a remittance advice.

OVERVIEW

Once the claims adjudication process has been finalized, the claim is either denied or approved for payment. The provider receives a remittance advice, which contains information used to process payments and adjustments to patient accounts. Payers often include multiple patients on the same remittance advice, which means that the insurance specialist must carefully review the document to properly process payments and adjustments. The remittance advice is also reviewed to make sure that there are no processing errors, which would result in the office resubmitting a corrected claim (e.g., coding errors).

INSTRUCTIONS

Review the remittance advice forms in Figures 4-2 through Figure 4-7 to familiarize yourself with the organization and legend (explanation of abbreviated terms).

NOTE: Use the remittance advice in Figure 4-2 to answer questions 1 through 5.

1. What is the check number and amount paid to the provider as recorded on the remittance advice? (HINT: This information is recorded in two different places on the remittance advice.)

2. What was patient John Cofee's coinsurance amount for his visit on 0406YYYY?

3. Patient James Eicher was not charged a coinsurance amount for his 0415YYYY visit. What is the explanation for this?

4. What is patient Jenny Baker's account number?

5. What is the allowed amount for procedure code 99213?

NOTE: Use the remittance advice in Figure 4-3 to answer questions 6 through 10.

6. What is patient John Humphrey's health insurance claim number?

7. How many patients in Figure 4-3 authorized assignment of benefits to Dr. Wilkins?

8. Patient Grayson Kihlberg had a coinsurance amount of $27.00 for CPT code 99204. What does this amount represent?

9. What was Craig Zane's coinsurance amount for code 73600?

10. What was the amount billed for patient Angel Brennan's visit?

NOTE: Use the remittance advice in Figure 4-4 to answer questions 11 through 15.

11. What was the date of service for patient Christopher Hesse?

12. What procedure code is listed for patient Mary Schwartz?

13. How much did the provider bill the insurance company for the care of patient Andrew Gagner?

14. Identify the place-of-service code for each patient.

15. According to the remittance advice, how much was Dr. Kelley paid?

NOTE: Use the remittance advice in Figure 4-5 to answer questions 16 through 20.

16. What does the abbreviation "NET" represent, according to the legend at the bottom of the remittance advice?

17. How much was the allowed amount for code 11442?

18. What was the total coinsurance amount paid on the Figure 4-5 remittance advice?

19. How much is patient Paulette Melfi's coinsurance amount for her visit on 05/01/YY?

20. What is patient Susan Brisbane's account number?

NOTE: Use the remittance advice in Figure 4-6 to answer questions 21 through 25.

21. How much was Dr. Horne paid by the insurance company for patient Jason Brook's visit?

22. What is Dr. Horne's provider number?

ABC INSURANCE COMPANY
100 MAIN STREET
ALFRED, NY 14802
1-800-555-1234

REMITTANCE ADVICE

DAVID MILLER, M.D.
101 NORTH STREET
ALFRED, NY 14802

PAGE #: 1 OF 1

PROVIDER #:   123456
DATE: 05/05/YY
CHECK#:   235698

	SERV DATES	POS	PROC	BILLED	ALLOWED		COINSURANCE		PROVIDER PAID
BAKER, JENNY	HICN 235962541		ACNT BAKE1234567-01			ICN 1235626589651	ASG	Y	MOA MA01
236592ABC	0405 0405YY	11	99213	75.00	60.00		15.00		60.00
PT RESP: 15.00		CLAIM TOTAL: 75.00							
									NET: 60.00
COFEE, JOHN	HICN 569856217		ACNT COFE2326254-01			ICN 23562145898547	ASG	Y	MOA MA01
326526ABC	0406 0406YY	11	99214	100.00	80.00		20.00		80.00
PT RESP: 20.00		CLAIM TOTAL: 100.00							
									NET: 80.00
DAVIS, JEANNE	HICN 562659452		ACNT DAVI2369214-01			ICN 6265975312562	ASG	Y	MOA MA01
123652ABC	0410 0410YY	11	99212	50.00	40.00		10.00		40.00
PT RESP: 10.00		CLAIM TOTAL: 50.00							
									NET: 40.00
EICHER, JAMES	HICN 626594594		ACNT EICH2365214-01			ICN 5695321453259	ASG	Y	MOA MA01
126954ABC	0415 0415YY	11	99385	125.00	0.00		0.00		125.00
PT RESP: 0.00		CLAIM TOTAL: 125.00							
									NET: 125.00
FEINSTEIN, ED	HICN 365956214		ACNT FEIN1236521-01			ICN 9652154125632	ASG	Y	MOA MA01
695214ABC	0420 0420YY	11	17000	750.00	150.00		150.00		600.00
PT RESP: 150.00		CLAIM TOTAL: 750.00							
									NET: 600.00

TOTALS:

# BILLED CLAIMS	ALLOWED AMOUNT	COINSURANCE AMOUNT	TOTAL AMOUNT	PROV PAID AMOUNT	CHECK AMOUNT
5	905.00	195.00	1100.00	905.00	905.00

LEGEND
HICN (health insurance claim number)
SERV DATES (dates of service)
POS (place-of-service code)
PROC (CPT procedure/service code)
BILLED (amount provider billed payer)
ALLOWED (amount authorized by payer)
COINSURANCE (amount patient paid)
PROVIDER PAID (amount provider was reimbursed by payer)
NET: (amount provider billed payer)
PT RESP: (amount patient paid)
ACNT (account number)
ASG Y (patient has authorized provider to accept assignment)
MOA MA01 (indicator that if denied, claim can be appealed)

FIGURE 4-2 *Remittance advice (multiple claims) (Current Procedural Terminology © 2004 American Medical Association. All Rights Reserved.)*

XYZ Insurance Company
500 South Street
Chicago, Illinois 60186
1-800-555-4321

Cynthia Wilkins, M.D.
100 State Street
Denver, Colorado 80200

Remittance Advice

Provider #: 654321
Date: 05/31/YY
Check #:   871267

Aldridge, Morton	HICN 370553029	ACNT ALDR4557516-01			ASG Y		
112233XYZ	05/05 05/05/YY	11	10120	120.00	100.00	20.00	100.00
PT RESP: 20.00		CLAIM TOTAL:	120.00		NET:		100.00

Brennan, Angel	HICN 703459203	ACNT BREN5761282-01			ASG Y		
757557XYZ	05/05 05/05/YY	11	99213	80.00	65.00	15.00	65.00
PT RESP: 15.00		CLAIM TOTAL:	80.00		NET:		65.00

Humphrey, John	HICN 454545544	ACNT HUMP6721357-01			ASG Y		
673112XYZ	05/10 05/10/YY	11	29130	50.00	35.00	15.00	35.00
PT RESP: 15.00		CLAIM TOTAL:	50.00		NET:		35.00

Kihlberg, Grayson	HICN 716372688	ACNT KIHL1242495-02			ASG Y		
876543XYZ	05/12 05/12/YY	11	99204	135.00	125.00	27.00	98.00
PT RESP: 27.00		CLAIM TOTAL:	125.00		NET:		98.00

Zane, Craig	HICN 737682574	ACNT ZANE4963518-01			ASG Y		
302353XYZ	05/17 05/17/YY	11	99213	80.00	65.00	15.00	65.00
			73600	55.00	45.00	0.00	45.00
PT RESP: 15.00		CLAIM TOTAL:	110.00		NET:		110.00

TOTALS:					
# BILLED CLAIMS:	ALLOWED AMOUNT:	COINSURANCE AMOUNT:	TOTAL AMOUNT:	PROVIDER PD. AMT:	CHECK AMOUNT:
5	435.00	92.00	527.00	435.00	435.00

LEGEND
HICN (health insurance claim number)
SERV DATES (dates of service)
POS (place-of-service code)
PROC (CPT procedure/service code)
BILLED (amount provider billed payer)
ALLOWED (amount authorized by payer)
COINSURANCE (amount patient paid)
PROVIDER PAID (amount provider was reimbursed by payer)
NET: (amount provider billed payer)
PT RESP: (amount patient paid)
ACNT (account number)
ASG Y (patient has authorized provider to accept assignment)
MOA MA01 (indicator that if denied, claim can be appealed)

FIGURE 4-3 *Remittance advice (multiple claims) (Current Procedural Terminology © 2004 American Medical Association. All Rights Reserved.)*

Acme Insurance Company
911 Red Light Drive
Dallas, Texas 52222
1-800-555-5555

Remittance Advice

Ross Kelley, M.D.
100 State Street
Buffalo, New York 14202

Provider #:   5872
Date: 05/31/YY
Check #:   37767

		POS		Code(s)	Billed	Allowed	Copay/Ins	
Gagner, Andrew	HICN 621884549		ACNT GAGN032974-01			ASG Y		
745221	05/07	05/07/YY	11	99204	150.00	135.00	15.00	135.00
				74247	320.00	285.00	57.00	228.00
PT RESP: 72.00		CLAIM TOTAL: 420.00					NET:	420.00
Hesse, Christopher	HICN 258369147		ACNT HESS3129657-01			ASG Y		
246810	05/08	05/08/YY	11	99213	80.00	65.00	20.00	45.00
PT RESP: 20.00		CLAIM TOTAL: 65.00					NET:	45.00
Schwartz, Mary	HICN 147953128		ACNT SCHW4963813-01			ASG Y		
999924	05/10	05/10/YY	11	46600	212.00	185.00	37.00	148.00
PT RESP: 37.00		CLAIM TOTAL: 212.00					NET:	148.00
Stave, Gabriella	HICN 752319567		ACNT STAV462978-04			ASG Y		
225932	05/12	05/12/YY	11	99212	90.00	80.00	10.00	70.00
PT RESP: 10.00		CLAIM TOTAL: 80.00					NET:	70.00
Thomas, Michael	HICN 121770222		ACNT THOM699224-02			ASG Y		
930512	05/17	05/17/YY	11	83013	110.00	95.00	30.00	65.00
PT RESP: 30.00		CLAIM TOTAL: 95.00					NET:	65.00

TOTALS:

# BILLED CLAIMS:	ALLOWED AMOUNT:	COINSURANCE AMOUNT:	TOTAL AMOUNT:	PROVIDER PD. AMT:	CHECK AMOUNT:
5	845.00	169.00	1014.00	845.00	845.00

LEGEND

HICN (health insurance claim number)
SERV DATES (dates of service)
POS (place-of-service code)
PROC (CPT procedure/service code)
BILLED (amount provider billed payer)
ALLOWED (amount authorized by payer)
COINSURANCE (amount patient paid)
PROVIDER PAID (amount provider was reimbursed by payer)
NET: (amount provider billed payer)
PT RESP: (amount patient paid)
ACNT (account number)
ASG Y (patient has authorized provider to accept assignment)
MOA MA01 (indicator that if denied, claim can be appealed)

FIGURE 4-4 *Remittance advice (multiple claims) (Current Procedural Terminology © 2004 American Medical Association. All Rights Reserved.)*

UPAY Insurance Company
1000 Main Street
Boston, Massachusetts 02100
1-800-555-5432

Remittance Advice

George Williams, M.D.
25 South Street
Norfolk, Virginia 23500

Provider #: 21137
Date: 05/31/YY
Check #:   665821

		POS		Code(s)	Billed		Allowed		Copay/Ins	
Brisbane, Susan	HICN 125692479		ACNT BRIS396715-01				ASG	Y		
456212UPAY		05/01	05/01/YY	11	11402	105.00	100.00		20.00	80.00
PT RESP:	20.00		CLAIM TOTAL:		100.00			NET:		80.00
Melfi, Paulette 1	HICN 746931251		ACNT MELF551374-02				ASG	Y		
221123UPAY		05/01	05/01/YY	11	99211	40.00	25.00		0.00	25.00
PT RESP:	0.00		CLAIM TOTAL:		25.00			NET:		25.00
Swanson, Lynn	HICN 446285791		ACNT SWAN333333-01				ASG	Y		
821547UPAY		05/06	05/06/YY	11	11442	220.00	190.00		38.00	152.00
PT RESP:	38.00		CLAIM TOTAL:		190.00			NET:		152.00
Wilson, Stacey	HICN 020868543		ACNT WILS211232-01				ASG	Y		
323215UPAY		05/08	05/08/YY	11	99203	140.00	125.00		15.00	110.00
PT RESP:	15.00		CLAIM TOTAL:		125.00			NET:		110.00
Zigler, Peggy	HICN 702515313		ACNT ZIGL945625-03				ASG	Y		
565981UPAY		05/10	05/10/YY	11	11720	75.00	70.00		10.00	60.00
PT RESP:	10.00		CLAIM TOTAL:		70.00			NET:		60.00

TOTALS:

# BILLED CLAIMS:	ALLOWED AMOUNT:	COINSURANCE AMOUNT:	TOTAL AMOUNT:	PROVIDER PD. AMT:	CHECK AMOUNT:
5	510.00	83.00	593.00	510.00	510.00

LEGEND
HICN (health insurance claim number)
SERV DATES (dates of service)
POS (place-of-service code)
PROC (CPT procedure/service code)
BILLED (amount provider billed payer)
ALLOWED (amount authorized by payer)
COINSURANCE (amount patient paid)
PROVIDER PAID (amount provider was reimbursed by payer)
NET: (amount provider billed payer)
PT RESP: (amount patient paid)
ACNT (account number)
ASG Y (patient has authorized provider to accept assignment)
MOA MA01 (indicator that if denied, claim can be appealed)

FIGURE 4-5 *Remittance advice (multiple claims) (Current Procedural Terminology © 2004 American Medical Association. All Rights Reserved.)*

```
White Health Care Systems
500 Seaside Lane
San Francisco, California 94100
1-800-555-2468                                                    Remittance Advice

David Horne, M.D.                                                 Provider #:    31055
1 Eyeball Lane                                                    Date:          05/31/YY
Orlando, Florida 31000                                           Check #:       26854
```

		POS	Code(s)	Billed	Allowed	Copay/Ins	
Brook, Jason	HICN 123456789	ACNT BR00444444-01		ASG Y			
WHCS242678	05/15	05/15/YY	11	99203	112.00	95.00	20.00	75.00
PT RESP: 20.00		CLAIM TOTAL:	95.00			NET:	75.00
Captain, Teresa	HICN 875123466	ACNT CAPT5881125		ASG Y			
WHCS082543	05/16	05/16/YY	11	65205	80.00	72.00	15.00	57.00
PT RESP: 15.00		CLAIM TOTAL:	72.00			NET:	57.00

TOTALS:

# BILLED CLAIMS:	ALLOWED AMOUNT:	COINSURANCE AMOUNT:	TOTAL AMOUNT:	PROVIDER PD. AMT:	CHECK AMOUNT:
2	167.00	35.00	202.00	167.00	167.00

LEGEND
HICN (health insurance claim number)
SERV DATES (dates of service)
POS (place-of-service code)
PROC (CPT procedure/service code)
BILLED (amount provider billed payer)
ALLOWED (amount authorized by payer)
COINSURANCE (amount patient paid)
PROVIDER PAID (amount provider was reimbursed by payer)
NET: (amount provider billed payer)
PT RESP: (amount patient paid)
ACNT (account number)
ASG Y (patient has authorized provider to accept assignment)
MOA MA01 (indicator that if denied, claim can be appealed)

FIGURE 4-6 *Remittance advice (multiple claims) (Current Procedural Terminology © 2004 American Medical Association. All Rights Reserved.)*

23. What is the telephone number for White Health Care Systems?

24. What is the billed amount for code 99203?

25. What does "POS" represent, according to the legend at the bottom of the remittance advice?

    NOTE: Use the remittance advice in Figure 4-7 to answer questions 26 through 30.

26. What is Dr. Brown's title?

Southeast Administrators
24 Hour Street
Miami, Florida 33010
1-800-555-6789

Mark Brown, D.O.
1500 Angler Boulevard
Norfolk, Virginia 23500

Remittance Advice

Provider #: 21137
Date: 05/31/YY
Check #:   665821

		POS	Code(s)	Billed	Allowed	Copay/Ins	
Brister, Suzette	HICN 121113659	ACNT BRIS061667-04			ASG Y	MOA	MA01
SA4452814	05/20	05/20/YY	11	99214	135.00	120.00	0.00	120.00
PT RESP: 0.00		CLAIM TOTAL:		120.00		NET:	120.00
Smith, Kathleen	HICN 112167258	ACNT SMIT081159-05			ASG Y	MOA	MA01
SA216552	05/22	05/22/YY	11	99212	90.00	75.00	5.00	70.00
PT RESP: 5.00		CLAIM TOTAL:		75.00		NET:	70.00
White, Amos	HICN 020347181	ACNT WHIT020347-03	ASG Y	MOA	MA01		
SA12300405	05/22	05/22/YY	11	30300	75.00	65.00	15.00	50.00
PT RESP: 15.00		CLAIM TOTAL:		65.00		NET:	50.00

TOTALS:

# BILLED CLAIMS:	ALLOWED AMOUNT:	COINSURANCE AMOUNT:	TOTAL AMOUNT:	PROVIDER PD. AMT:	CHECK AMOUNT:
3	260.00	20.00	280.00	260.00	260.00

LEGEND
HICN (health insurance claim number)
SERV DATES (dates of service)
POS (place-of-service code)
PROC (CPT procedure/service code)
BILLED (amount provider billed payer)
ALLOWED (amount authorized by payer)
COINSURANCE (amount patient paid)
PROVIDER PAID (amount provider was reimbursed by payer)
NET: (amount provider billed payer)
PT RESP: (amount patient paid)
ACNT (account number)
ASG Y (patient has authorized provider to accept assignment)
MOA MA01 (indicator that if denied, claim can be appealed)

Figure 4-7 *Remittance advice (multiple claims) (Current Procedural Terminology © 2004 American Medical Association. All Rights Reserved.)*

27. What was the date of service for Kathleen Smith's visit?

28. On what date was the remittance advice generated?

29. How many patient visits were listed for 05/22/YY?

30. How much was the allowed amount for code 30300?

OBJECTIVES

At the conclusion of this assignment, the student should be able to:

1. Explain the purpose of an explanation of benefits.

2. Interpret data contained in an explanation of benefits.

OVERVIEW

Once the claims adjudication process has been finalized, the claim is either denied or approved for payment. The patient receives an explanation of benefits (EOB), which contains information about the claim with regard to what was paid by the insurance company and what amount (if any) is the patient's responsibility for payment. The patient should review the explanation of benefits to make sure that there are no errors. If the patient detects an error, the patient may contact the provider's office and speak with a health insurance specialist for assistance and resubmission of a corrected claim as necessary.

NOTE: If the physician is a nonparticipating provider (nonPAR), the office will not receive a remittance advice from Medicare. To assist patients in obtaining Medicare reimbursement so that they can pay the bills mailed to them by the physician's office, the insurance specialist will need to review the EOB that the patient received from Medicare. This exercise provides students with practice in interpreting an EOB.

INSTRUCTIONS

Review the explanation of benefits form in Figure 4-8 to familiarize yourself with the organization and the comments. Use the EOB form in Figure 4-8 to answer the following questions:

1. How much was The Keystone Plan charged for Mary Sue Patient's visit of 04/05/YYYY?

2. How much has Mary Sue Patient paid out of pocket year to date?

3. What is Mary Sue Patient's identification number?

4. What was the allowed amount charged by Dr. Miller for Mary Sue Patient's visit of 04/05/YY?

5. What is Mary Sue Patient's annual medical/surgical deductible, according to the explanation of benefits?

THE KEYSTONE PLAN

P.O. BOX 900
ALFRED NY 14802-0900
(800) 555-9000

DATE: 04/05/YYYY
ID #: BLS123456789
ENROLLEE: MARY SUE PATIENT
CONTRACT: 300500
BENEFIT PLAN: STATE OF NEW YORK

MARY SUE PATIENT
100 MAIN ST
ALFRED NY 14802

EXPLANATION
OF BENEFITS

SERVICE DETAIL

PATIENT/RELAT CLAIM NUMBER	PROVIDER/ SERVICE	DATE OF SERVICE	AMOUNT CHARGED	NOT COVERED	AMOUNT ALLOWED	COPAY/ DEDUCTIBLE	%	PLAN BENEFITS	REMARK CODE
ENROLLEE 5629587	D MILLER OFFICE VISITS	04/05/YY	40.25		40.25	8.00	100	32.25*	D1

PLAN PAYS	32.25

*THIS IS A COPY OF INFORMATION SENT TO THE PROVIDER. THANK YOU FOR USING THE PARTICIPATING PROVIDER PROGRAM.

REMARK CODE(S) LISTED BELOW ARE REFERENCED IN THE *SERVICE DETAIL* SECTION UNDER THE HEADING *REMARK CODE*

(D1)   THANK YOU FOR USING A NETWORK PROVIDER. WE HAVE APPLIED THE NETWORK CONTRACTED FEE. THE MEMBER IS NOT
RESPONSIBLE FOR THE DIFFERENCE BETWEEN THE AMOUNT CHARGED AND THE AMOUNT ALLOWED BY THE CONTRACT.

BENEFIT PLAN PAYMENT SUMMARY INFORMATION	
D MILLER	$32.25

PATIENT NAME	MEDICAL/SURGICAL DEDUCTIBLE		MEDICAL/SURGICAL OUT OF POCKET		PHYSICAL MEDICINE DEDUCTIBLE	
	ANNUAL DEDUCT	YYYY YEAR TO-DATE	ANNUAL MAXIMUM	YYYY YEAR TO-DATE	ANNUAL DEDUCT	YYYY YEAR TO-DATE
ENROLLEE	$249.00	$0.00	$1804.00	$121.64	$250.00	$0.00

THIS CLAIM WAS PROCESSED IN ACCORDANCE WITH THE TERMS OF YOUR EMPLOYEE BENEFITS PLAN. IN THE EVENT THIS CLAIM HAS BEEN DENIED, IN WHOLE OR IN PART, A REQUEST FOR REVIEW MAY BE DIRECTED TO THE KEYSTONE PLAN AT THE ALFRED ADDRESS OR PHONE NUMBER SHOWN ABOVE. THE REQUEST FOR REVIEW MUST BE SUBMITTED WITHIN 60 DAYS AFTER THE CLAIM PAYMENT DATE, OR THE DATE OF THE NOTIFICATION OF DENIAL OF BENEFITS. WHEN REQUESTING A REVIEW, PLEASE STATE WHY YOU BELIEVE THE CLAIM DETERMINATION OR PRE-CERTIFICATION IMPROPERLY REDUCED OR DENIED YOUR BENEFITS. ALSO, SUBMIT ANY DATA OR COMMENTS TO SUPPORT THE APPEAL.

THIS IS NOT A BILL.

Figure 4-8 *Sample explanation of benefits (EOB) form*

ASSIGNMENT 4.4 Multiple Choice Review

1. Which is an example of supporting documentation?
    a. completed CMS-1500 claim form
    b. explanation of benefits
    c. operative report
    d. remittance advice

2. Which term does the CPT coding manual use to refer to supporting documentation?
    a. attachment
    b. detailed report
    c. enclosed note
    d. special report

3. Which claim status is assigned by the payer to allow the provider to correct errors or omissions on the claim and resubmit for payment consideration?
   a. clean
   b. denied
   c. pending
   d. voided

4. A public or private entity that processes or facilitates the processing of nonstandard elements into standard data elements is called a(n)
   a. clearinghouse.
   b. covered entity.
   c. network.
   d. third-party administrator.

5. The intent of mandating HIPAA's national standards for electronic transactions was to
   a. decrease the costs associated with Medicare and Medicaid programs.
   b. improve the continuity and the quality of care provided to patients.
   c. improve the efficiency and effectiveness of the health care system.
   d. increase the number of individuals enrolled in government health plans.

6. Electronic claims are more accurate because they are
   a. always submitted by health insurance professionals who are certified by the AAPC.
   b. checked for accuracy by billing software programs or a health care clearinghouse.
   c. not complicated by such requirements as claims attachments or other documents.
   d. submitted directly to payers for the processing of reimbursement to providers.

7. Which CPT modifier will require supporting documentation for payment?
   a. -22 (unusual procedural services)
   b. -26 (professional component)
   c. -50 (bilateral procedure)
   d. -57 (decision for surgery)

8. Patients can be billed for
   a. extended procedures.
   b. noncovered procedures.
   c. reduced services.
   d. unauthorized services.

9. Medicare calls the remittance advice a
   a. Medicare Explanation of Benefits.
   b. Medicare Summary Notice.
   c. Provider Remittance Advice.
   d. Provider Remittance Notice.

10. The person in whose name the insurance policy is issued is the
    a. beneficiary.
    b. patient.
    c. policyholder.
    d. provider.

11. The life cycle of an insurance claim is initiated when the
    a. health insurance specialist completes the CMS-1500 claim form.
    b. patient contacts the provider's office and schedules an appointment.
    c. patient pays the copay or coinsurance required by the policy contract.
    d. provider completes the encounter form after treating the patient.

12. Which form is considered the financial source document?
    a. history and physical exam
    b. patient registration
    c. statement of charges
    d. superbill or encounter form

13. Another name for the patient account record is the patient
    a. day sheet.
    b. encounter form.
    c. explanation of benefits.
    d. ledger.

14. A chronological summary of all transactions posted to individual patient accounts on a specific day is recorded on a(n)
    a. day sheet.
    b. encounter form.
    c. patient ledger.
    d. remittance advice.

15. What special handling is required if a patient requests a copy of the remittance advice (RA) that contains information about multiple patients?
    a. Patients are not permitted to view or receive copies of the RA.
    b. Remove identifying information about all patients except the requesting patient.
    c. The patient must sign a confidentiality statement prior to receiving a copy of the RA.
    d. The provider must document the request for a copy of the RA in the patient's record.

16. Which federal law protects consumers against harassing or threatening phone calls from collectors?
    a. Fair Credit and Charge Card Disclosure Act
    b. Fair Credit Billing Act
    c. Fair Credit Reporting Act
    d. Fair Debt Collection Practices Act

17. The time period between the point at which a claim is submitted and when the claim is paid is called the _____ period.
    a. aging
    b. collection
    c. delinquent
    d. past-due

18. The provision in group health insurance policies that specifies in what sequence coverage will be provided when more than one policy covers the claim is
    a. accepting assignment.
    b. assignment of benefits.
    c. claims adjudication.
    d. coordination of benefits.

19. A clearinghouse that coordinates with other entities to provide additional services during the processing of claims is a
    a. claims processor.
    b. network commission.
    c. third-party administrator.
    d. value-added network.

20. To determine if a patient is receiving concurrent care for the same condition by more than one provider, the payer will check the claim against the
    a. common data file.
    b. electronic flat file.
    c. insurance claims registry.
    d. patient's billing history.

CHAPTER 5

Legal and Regulatory Issues

INTRODUCTION

This chapter emphasizes the importance of maintaining the confidentiality of protected health information (or patient information). In addition, students will review case studies to determine if health care fraud or abuse was present.

ASSIGNMENT 5.1 HIPAA: Student Confidentiality Statement

OBJECTIVES

At the conclusion of this assignment, the student should be able to:

1. Explain the importance of maintaining the confidentiality of patient information.

2. State the significance of signing a student confidentiality statement prior to beginning a professional practice experience (or internship).

OVERVIEW

Health insurance specialist students who complete professional practice experiences (or internships) as part of their course of study will have access to protected health information (PHI) at the provider's office. It is essential that students maintain the confidentiality of PHI at all times. This assignment allows the student to review and sign a student confidentiality statement.

INSTRUCTIONS

1. Carefully review student confidentiality statement in Figure 5-1.

2. Sign and date the statement, and have a witness sign and date the form.

3. Submit the completed form to your instructor.

PROTECTED HEALTH INFORMATION (PHI) CONFIDENTIALITY STATEMENT

In consideration of my status as a student at _____ and/or association with health care facilities and provider offices that offer internship opportunities, I agree that I will not at any time access or use protected health information, or reveal or disclose to any persons within or outside the health care facility or provider office, any protected health information except as may be required in the course of my duties and responsibilities and in accordance with applicable legislation, and corporate and departmental policies governing proper release of information.

I understand that my obligations outlined above will continue after my association with the School and/or facility ends. I further understand that my obligations concerning the protection of the confidentiality of health information relate to all protected health information whether I acquired the information through my association with the School and/or facility.

I also understand that unauthorized use or disclosure of such information will result in a disciplinary action up to and including involuntary expulsion from the School, the imposition of fines pursuant to relevant state and federal legislation, and a report to my professional regulatory body.

_____   _____
Date Signed   Signature of Student

                                 _____
                                 Student's Printed Name

_____   _____
Date Signed   Signature of Witness

FIGURE 5-1 *Student confidentiality statement (Permission to reuse granted by Alfred State College.)*

ASSIGNMENT 5.2 HIPAA: Preventing Health Care Fraud and Abuse

OBJECTIVES

At the conclusion of this assignment, the student should be able to:

1. Define health care fraud and abuse.
2. Differentiate between forms of health care fraud and abuse.

OVERVIEW

HIPAA defines *fraud* as "an intentional deception or misrepresentation that someone makes, knowing it is false, that could result in an unauthorized payment." *Abuse* "involves actions that are inconsistent with accepted, sound medical, business or fiscal practices."

INSTRUCTIONS

Review Chapter 5 content on page 101 of your textbook to familiarize yourself with examples of fraud and abuse. Then determine whether each situation below is fraud (F) or abuse (A).

_____ 1. An insurance company did not follow applicable rules when setting rates it charged for health care benefits under its Federal Employees Health Benefits Program (FEHBP) contracts, and failed to give the health care program the same discounted rates it gave similarly situated commercial customers. It also failed to coordinate FEHBP benefits with those provided to Medicare eligible annuitants and submitted statements to the Office of Personnel Management (OPM) that failed to fully disclose rate adjustments due to FEHBP.

_____ 2. The state of California and the County of Los Angeles billed Medicaid for services provided to minors when these jurisdictions had no basis for concluding that these individuals financially qualified for Medicaid services. The services at issue in this matter were treatment for drug and alcohol abuse, pregnancy and pregnancy-related services, family planning, sexual assault treatment, sexually transmitted diseases treatment, and mental health services.

_____ 3. A physician documented the medical necessity of a number of medical supplies for a patient's care in the office. Upon review, Medicare denied reimbursement for the claim, stating that the number of medical supplies ordered was excessive.

_____ 4. An insurance company failed to process Medicare claims properly, and then submitted false information to CMS regarding the accuracy of and the timeliness with which it had handled those claims.

_____ 5. The provider ordered a number of the same laboratory tests on several different patients, carefully documenting the medical necessity of each. Upon review, Medicare determined that half of the patients did not need to have those tests performed, and reimbursement was denied.

_____ 6. An insurance company breached its Medicare contract by failing to report errors identified in the quality assurance process. It concealed its true error rate by deleting claims selected for review by CMS and replacing them with claim files that would not significantly affect the error rate (and thus preserve its standing within carrier performance rankings).

_____ 7. A chiropractor performed ultrasonography to follow the progress of a patient treated for back pain. Medicare denied the payment because it determined that this was not a legitimate use for ultrasonography.

_____ 8. An ambulance company submitted false claims for reimbursement to Medicare.

_____ 9. A consulting firm submitted false hospital cost reports to the Medicare and Medicaid programs on behalf of its client hospitals. The consulting firm knowingly made claims that were false, exaggerated, or ineligible for payment, and it concealed errors from government auditors, thereby permitting the client hospitals to retain funds to which they were not entitled.

_____ 10. A spinal videofluoroscopy was performed to demonstrate the extent to which joint motion of a patient was restricted. Medicare determined that physical examination procedures (e.g., asking the patient to bend) provided enough information to guide treatment of the patient and denied reimbursement.

OBJECTIVES

At the conclusion of this assignment, the student should be able to:

1. Explain the HIPAA privacy and security rules.
2. Differentiate between privacy and security provisions of HIPAA.

OVERVIEW

The *privacy rule* establishes standards for how protected health information should be controlled, and it establishes the uses (e.g., continuity of care) and disclosures (e.g., third-party reimbursement) authorized or required, as well as the rights patients have with respect to their health information (e.g., patient access). The *security rule* defines administrative, physical, and technical safeguards to protect the availability, confidentiality, and integrity of electronic PHI. HIPAA provisions require covered entities to implement basic safeguards to protect electronic PHI from unauthorized access, alteration, deletion, and transmission.

INSTRUCTIONS

Determine whether the statements below are associated with the HIPAA privacy rule (P) or the security rule (S).

_____ 1. Defines authorized users of patient information to control access.

_____ 2. Implements a tracking procedure to sign out records to authorized personnel.

_____ 3. Establishes fines and penalties for misuse of protected health information.

_____ 4. Limits record storage access to authorized users.

_____ 5. Gives patients greater access to their own medical records and more control over how their personal health information is used.

_____ 6. Creates national standards to protect individuals' medical records and other personal health information.

_____ 7. Requires that record storage areas be locked at all times.

_____ 8. Addresses obligations that physicians, hospitals, and other health care providers have to obtain a patient's written consent and an authorization before using or disclosing PHI to carry out treatment, payment, or health care operations (TPO).

_____ 9. Exempts psychotherapy notes from a patient's right to access his or her own records.

_____ 10. Requires the original medical record to remain in the facility at all times.

ASSIGNMENT 5.4 Multiple Choice Review

1. A provider was ordered by a judge to bring a patient's medical record to a court hearing. Which document was served on the provider instructing him to comply?
   a. deposition
   b. interrogatory
   c. subpoena duces tecum
   d. subpoena

2. The type of law passed by legislative bodies is known as _____ law.
   a. common
   b. criminal
   c. regulatory
   d. statutory

3. Which civil case document contains a list of questions that must be answered in writing?
   a. deposition
   b. interrogatory
   c. precedent
   d. regulation

4. Which federal law has regulated the conduct of any contractor submitting claims for payment to the federal government since 1863?
   a. False Claims Act
   b. Federal Claims Collection Act
   c. Privacy Act
   d. Social Security Act

5. The Federal Claims Collection Act requires Medicare administrative contractors to
   a. attempt to recover any reimbursement funds sent as overpayment to providers and beneficiaries.
   b. enforce civil monetary penalties upon those who submit false or fraudulent claims to the government.
   c. protect the privacy of individuals identified in information systems maintained by government hospitals.
   d. provide free or reduced-charge medical services to persons unable to pay, in return for federal funds.

6. Since the creation of the Occupational Safety and Health Administration in 1971, workplace fatalities have decreased by
   a. 7%.
   b. 40%.
   c. 50%.
   d. 56%.

7. The Physicians at Teaching Hospitals (PATH) legislation was passed to
   a. increase reimbursement amounts paid to teaching hospitals and other types of health care facilities.
   b. increase the number of physicians and other health care providers available to teach medical students.
   c. limit the types of patients that are seen by medical school residents in PATH health care settings.
   d. monitor Medicare rule compliance for payment of Part B services and proper coding and billing practices.

8. An individual can conduct a comprehensive review of a practitioner's past actions by referring to the
   a. Clinical Data Abstracting Center.
   b. Health Insurance Portability and Accountability Act.
   c. Healthcare Integrity and Protection Data Bank.
   d. Peer Review Improvement Act.

9. One of the provisions of HIPAA designed to improve portability and continuity of health care coverage is
   a. excluding enrollment of employees with a history of poor health.
   b. increasing exclusions for preexisting conditions.
   c. prohibiting a change from group to individual coverage.
   d. providing credit for prior health coverage.

10. Which Department of Health and Human Services agency is responsible for investigating a Medicare provider who is suspected of committing fraud?
    a. Centers for Medicare and Medicaid Services
    b. Office of Inspector General
    c. Social Security Administration
    d. U.S. Attorney General

11. In addition to civil, criminal, and administrative penalties, those who commit health care fraud can also be tried for
    a. breach of contract.
    c. mail and wire fraud.
    b. criminal negligence.
    d. medical malpractice.

12. The first step a physician practice can take to identify areas in the practice that are vulnerable to fraud and abuse is to
    a. conduct appropriate training and education sessions for employees.
    b. designate a compliance officer to monitor and enforce standards.
    c. enforce disciplinary standards through well-publicized guidelines.
    d. perform periodic audits to internally monitor billing processes.

13. An example of an overpayment is
    a. duplicate processing of a claim.
    c. payment based on incorrect charge.
    b. incorrect application of coinsurance.
    d. payment made to wrong payee.

14. Unless the case involves fraud, administrative contractors are prohibited from seeking overpayment recovery when the
    a. amount paid in excess was less than or equal to $100.
    b. office manager sends a letter to request an exception.
    c. overpayment is not reopened within 48 months after payment.
    d. provider did not know the reasonable charge for the service.

15. Code combinations that cannot be reported on the same claim are called
    a. code groups.
    c. edit combinations.
    b. coding conventions.
    d. edit pairs.

16. The most controversial of the proposed unique identifiers in the administrative simplification provision of HIPAA is the
    a. National Health PlanID.
    b. National Individual Identifier.
    c. National Provider Identifier.
    d. National Standard Employer Identification Number.

17. The agency that assigns the National Standard Employer Identification Number (EIN) is the
    a. Centers for Medicare and Medicaid Services.
    b. HHS Office of Inspector General.
    c. Internal Revenue Service.
    d. Social Security Administration.

18. Claims that are considered appropriate for electronic data interchange (EDI) are _____ claims.
    a. computer tape
    c. facsimile
    b. computer-generated paper
    d. photocopy

19. Assigning passwords to users who are authorized to access patient records is a form of
    a. confidentiality.
    b. privacy.
    c. privilege.
    d. security.

20. What special handling is required to release medical information for a patient who is HIV positive?
    a. A special notation should be made on the standard release of information.
    b. The insurance company must speak with the patient directly about the HIV diagnosis.
    c. The patient must sign an additional authorization statement for release of information.
    d. The provider must not release HIV-related information unless subpoenaed.

CHAPTER 6

ICD-9-CM Coding

INTRODUCTION

This chapter familiarizes students with coding diseases and conditions using ICD-9-CM. Students will code diagnostic statements and case studies by applying ICD-9-CM coding conventions, principles, and rules.

ASSIGNMENT 6.1 ICD-9-CM *Index to Diseases*

OBJECTIVES

At the conclusion of this assignment, the student should be able to:

1. Identify the condition in a diagnostic statement that would be considered the main term in the ICD-9-CM *Index to Diseases*.

2. Locate main terms in the ICD-9-CM *Index to Diseases*.

INSTRUCTIONS

In each of the following diagnostic statements, underline the condition that would be considered the main term in the ICD-9-CM *Index to Diseases*.

1. Acute confusion

2. Tension headache

3. Brain stem infarction

4. Allergic bronchitis

5. Bronchial croup

6. Newborn anoxia

7. Acute abdominal cramp

8. Insect bite

9. Radiation sickness

10. Car sickness

ASSIGNMENT 6.2 Basic Coding

OBJECTIVES

At the conclusion of this assignment, the student should be able to:

1. Locate main terms in the ICD-9-CM *Index to Diseases.*
2. Identify codes in the ICD-9-CM *Index to Diseases* and verify them in the *Tabular List of Diseases.*

INSTRUCTIONS

Assign codes to the following conditions using the ICD-9-CM *Index to Diseases.* Be sure to verify the code(s) in the ICD-9-CM *Tabular List of Diseases.*

1. Herpes zoster   _____
2. Parkinson's disease   _____
3. Maxillary sinusitis   _____
4. Pneumonia with influenza   _____
5. Hiatal hernia   _____
6. Skene's gland abscess   _____
7. Skin eruption due to chemical product   _____
8. Infectional erythema   _____
9. Polydactyly of fingers   _____
10. Blindness due to injury   _____

ASSIGNMENT 6.3 Multiple Coding

OBJECTIVES

At the conclusion of this assignment, the student should be able to:

1. Assign ICD-9-CM codes to conditions, using the *Index to Diseases* and *Tabular List of Diseases.*
2. Sequence codes in proper order according to ICD-9-CM coding principles and rules.

INSTRUCTIONS

Assign codes to each condition, and sequence the codes in proper order according to ICD-9-CM coding principles and rules (e.g., manifestation coding rule). Be sure to verify the code(s) in the ICD-9-CM *Tabular List of Diseases.*

1. Parasitic infestation of eyelid due to pediculosis   _____
2. Post-infectious encephalitis due to measles (20 years ago)   _____
3. Peripheral neuropathy in hyperthyroidism   _____
4. Cerebral degeneration due to Fabry's disease   _____
5. Myotonic cataract due to Thomsen's disease   _____
6. Acute and chronic conjunctivitis   _____

7. Xanthelasma of the eyelid due to lipoprotein deficiency _____

8. Cholesteatoma, middle ear and mastoid _____

9. Varicose vein with inflammation and ulcer due to pregnancy _____

10. Psoriatic arthropathy and parapsoriasis _____

ASSIGNMENT 6.4 Combination Coding

OBJECTIVES

At the conclusion of this assignment, the student should be able to:

1. Use the *Index to Diseases* and *Tabular List of Diseases* to locate ICD-9-CM codes.

2. Interpret ICD-9-CM principles and rules to assign an appropriate combination code.

INSTRUCTIONS

Assign a combination code to each diagnostic statement below, using the ICD-9-CM *Index to Diseases*. Be sure to verify the code(s) in the ICD-9-CM *Tabular List of Diseases*.

1. Diabetes with ketoacidosis _____

2. Detached retina with giant tear _____

3. Rheumatic fever with heart involvement _____

4. Acute lung edema with heart disease _____

5. Atherosclerosis of the extremities with intermittent claudication _____

6. Emphysema with acute and chronic bronchitis _____

7. Acute gastric ulcer with perforation and hemorrhage _____

8. Diverticulosis with diverticulitis _____

9. Acute and chronic cholecystitis _____

10. Fractured fibula (closed) with tibia _____

ASSIGNMENT 6.5 Coding Hypertension

OBJECTIVES

At the conclusion of this assignment, the student should be able to:

1. Interpret the ICD-9-CM hypertension table.

2. Assign ICD-9-CM codes to diagnostic statements that document hypertensive disease.

INSTRUCTIONS

Code the following diagnostic statements using the Hypertension table in the ICD-9-CM *Index to Diseases*. Be sure to verify the code(s) using the ICD-9-CM *Tabular List of Diseases*.

1. Hypertension, benign _____
2. Hypertension due to brain tumor, unspecified _____
3. Malignant hypertension with congestive heart failure _____
4. Newborn affected by maternal hypertension _____
5. Hypertensive disease due to pheochromocytoma _____
6. Chronic venous hypertension due to deep vein thrombosis _____
7. Malignant labile hypertension _____
8. Benign renovascular hypertension _____
9. Secondary hypertension due to Cushing's disease _____
10. Necrotizing hypertension _____

ASSIGNMENT 6.6 Coding Neoplasms

OBJECTIVES

At the conclusion of this assignment, the student should be able to:

1. Interpret the ICD-9-CM Neoplasm table.
2. Assign ICD-9-CM codes to diagnostic statements that document neoplastic disease.

INSTRUCTIONS

Code the following diagnostic statements using the Neoplasm table in the ICD-9-CM *Index to Diseases.* Be sure to verify the code(s) in the ICD-9-CM *Tabular List of Diseases.*

1. Carcinoma of the right palatine tonsil _____
2. Metastatic ovarian cancer to the liver _____
3. Stomach cancer _____
4. Lipoma of right forearm _____
5. Osteosarcoma of the left femoral head _____
6. Neurofibromatosis _____
7. Hodgkin's sarcoma _____
8. Chronic lymphocytic leukemia _____
9. Intrathoracic reticulosarcoma _____
10. Adenocarcinoma of the rectum and anus _____

ASSIGNMENT 6.7 Assigning V Codes (Factors Influencing Health Status and Contact with Health Services)

OBJECTIVES

At the conclusion of this assignment, the student should be able to:

1. Interpret content in the V code supplementary classification of ICD-9-CM.
2. Assign ICD-9-CM V codes to diagnostic statements that document factors influencing health status and contact with health services.

Code the following diagnostic statements using the ICD-9-CM *Index to Diseases*. Be sure to verify the code(s) in the ICD-9-CM supplemental classification for V codes (located in the *Tabular List of Diseases*). (Assign just the V code to each statement.)

1. Exercise counseling   _____

2. Personal history of alcoholism   _____

3. Counseling for parent–child conflict   _____

4. Screening, cancer, unspecified   _____

5. Follow-up exam, postsurgery   _____

6. Health check, adult   _____

7. Routine child health check   _____

8. Fitting of artificial eye   _____

9. Flu shot   _____

10. Family history of breast cancer   _____

ASSIGNMENT 6.8 Coding Burns, Fractures, and Late Effects

OBJECTIVES

At the conclusion of this assignment, the student should be able to:

1. Use the *Index to Diseases* and *Tabular List of Diseases* to locate ICD-9-CM codes.

2. Interpret ICD-9-CM principles and rules to assign appropriate codes to burns, fractures, and late effects.

INSTRUCTIONS

Code the following diagnostic statements using the ICD-9-CM *Index to Diseases*. Be sure to verify the code(s) in the ICD-9-CM *Tabular List of Diseases*. As appropriate, also assign the E code.

1. Second-degree burn, right upper arm and shoulder   _____

2. Burns of the mouth, pharynx, and esophagus   _____

3. Third-degree burn, trunk, 35% of body surface   _____

4. Open fracture of coccyx with other spinal cord injury   _____

5. Bennett's fracture, closed   _____

6. Fifth cervical vertebra fracture, closed   _____

7. Scarring due to third-degree burn of left arm   _____

8. Hemiplegia due to old CVA   _____

9. Flail arm due to car accident 10 years ago   _____

10. Brain damage due to old cerebral abscess   _____

ASSIGNMENT 6.9 Assigning E Codes (External Causes of Injury and Poisoning)

OBJECTIVES

At the conclusion of this assignment, the student should be able to:

1. Use the *Index to External Causes of Injury and Poisoning* in ICD-9-CM.
2. Interpret ICD-9-CM principles and rules to assign appropriate codes for external causes of injury and poisonings.

INSTRUCTIONS

Code the following diagnostic statements using the ICD-9-CM *Index to Diseases* and the *Index to External Causes.* Be sure to verify the code(s) in the ICD-9-CM supplemental classification for E codes (located in the *Tabular List of Diseases*). (Assign just the E code to each statement.)

1. Assault by hanging and strangulation   _____
2. Brain damage due to allergic reaction to penicillin   _____
3. Self-inflicted injury by crashing of motor vehicle, highway   _____
4. Exposure to noise at nightclub   _____
5. Struck accidentally by falling rock at quarry   _____
6. Dog bite   _____
7. Accidental poisoning from shellfish at restaurant   _____
8. Foreign object left in body during surgical operation   _____
9. Fall from ladder at home   _____
10. Accident caused by hunting rifle at rifle range   _____

ASSIGNMENT 6.10 Coding Procedures

OBJECTIVES

At the conclusion of this assignment, the student should be able to:

1. Use the *Index to Procedures* and *Tabular List of Procedures* to locate ICD-9-CM codes.
2. Interpret ICD-9-CM principles and rules to assign appropriate codes to procedures.

INSTRUCTIONS

Code the following procedural statements using the ICD-9-CM *Index to Procedures.* Be sure to verify the code(s) in the ICD-9-CM *Tabular List of Procedures.*

1. Incision and drainage of pelvic abscess (female)   _____
2. Cataract extraction with lens implant   _____
3. Insertion of Swan-Ganz catheter   _____

4. Jaboulay operation _____

5. Esophagogastroduodenoscopy (EGD) with closed biopsy _____

6. Replacement of arteriovenous shunt for renal dialysis _____

7. Insertion of bilateral myringotomy tubes _____

8. Extracorporeal shock wave lithotripsy (ESWL) of staghorn calculus, left kidney _____

9. Forceps delivery with partial breech extraction _____

10. Repair of claw toe by tendon lengthening _____

ASSIGNMENT 6.11 Coding Patient Cases

OBJECTIVES

At the conclusion of this assignment, the student should be able to:

1. Identify diagnoses in case studies, and locate codes in the ICD-9-CM *Index to Diseases.*

2. Interpret ICD-9-CM principles and rules to assign appropriate diagnosis codes.

INSTRUCTIONS

Code the following case studies using the ICD-9-CM *Index to Diseases.* Be sure to verify the code(s) in the ICD-9-CM *Tabular List of Diseases.* (Assign just the diagnosis codes for each case study. Do not code procedures or services.)

1. **PATIENT CASE #1**

   HISTORY: The patient is an 87-year-old white male who has coronary artery disease, systolic hypertension, exogenous obesity, peripheral venous insufficiency, and recently had a kidney stone removed. He claims that his only symptom of the stone was persistent back pain. Since the surgery, he has been doing fairly well.

   PHYSICAL EXAMINATION: The exam showed a well-developed, obese male who does not appear to be in any distress, but has considerable problems with mobility and uses a cane to ambulate. VITAL SIGNS: Blood pressure today is 158/86, pulse is 80 per minute, and weight is 204 pounds. He has no pallor. He has rather pronounced shaking of the arms, which he claims is not new. NECK: No jugular venous distention. HEART: Very irregular. LUNGS: Clear. EXTREMITIES: There is edema of both legs.

   ASSESSMENT:

   1. Coronary artery disease

   2. Exogenous obesity

   3. Degenerative joint disease involving multiple joints

   4. History of congestive heart failure

   5. Atrial fibrillation

   6. History of myocardial infarction

   PLAN: The patient will return to the clinic in four months.

2. **PATIENT CASE #2**

S: No change in gait instability. When the patient had to lie quietly with neck extended, gait instability was much worse for 20 to 30 minutes after the test. Medications: Warfarin, digoxin, verapamil.

O: Alert. Ataxic gait with foot slapping and instability in tandem walking. Mild distal weakness and wasting. Barely detectable DTRs. Impaired vibratory sense below the hips. Impaired position sense in toes. Head CT shows diffuse atrophic changes. EMG: Distal demyelinating axonal neuropathy.

A: Gait disorder with central/peripheral components in the context of cervical spondylosis and peripheral neuropathy.

P: Have patient obtain a B12/folate test. Reassess in one month.

3. **PATIENT CASE #3**

CHIEF COMPLAINT: Feels tired all the time and no energy.

HISTORY OF PRESENT ILLNESS: The patient is an 80-year-old man with the following diagnoses: hyperlipidemia, coronary artery disease, cerebrovascular disease, esophageal reflux, and anxiety with depression. The patient was last seen in July of this year for the above problems. The patient is new to our clinic and is requesting follow-up for the fatigue and lack of energy, in addition to the problems noted above.

PHYSICAL EXAMINATION: The patient is 57 inches tall and weighs 184 pounds. Blood pressure is 122/70. Pulse is 60 per minute. Respiratory rate is 18 per minute. HEENT: Basically within normal limits. The patient wears glasses. Hearing aids are present bilaterally. NECK: Supple. Trachea is midline. LUNGS: Clear to auscultation and percussion. HEART: Regular, without murmur or ectopic beats noted. ABDOMEN: Slightly obese and nontender. Bowel sounds were normal. EXTREMITIES: The lower extremity pulses were present. He has good circulation with some very mild edema around the ankles.

ASSESSMENT:

1. Hyperlipidemia
2. Coronary artery disease
3. Cerebrovascular disease
4. Esophageal reflux
5. Anxiety with depression

PLAN: The patient will be referred to Psychiatry. I will see him again in three months.

4. **PATIENT CASE #4**

HISTORY OF PRESENT ILLNESS: The patient is an 88-year-old veteran with chronic constipation, mild dementia, and positive PPD test with negative X-ray. He complains of soreness around the anal region and incontinence of stool and sometimes urine.

PHYSICAL EXAMINATION: The patient is alert and well-oriented today. Vital signs as per the nursing staff. CHEST: Clear. HEART: Normal sinus rhythm.

ABDOMEN: Soft and benign. RECTAL: The anal area and surrounding perianal area is erythematous and there is a tear going from the rectum to the anal region. Slight oozing of blood was noted. Rectal exam was done, and I could not feel any masses in the rectum; however, the exam was painful for the patient.

ASSESSMENT: Anal tear with hemorrhoids.

PLAN: Sitz bath. Protective ointment around the area. Surgical consult. Give donut ring to the patient to keep pressure off the area.

5. *PATIENT CASE #5*

S: The patient is still having pain in the right hip area. She has a new complaint of pain and pressure in the right orbital area.

O: Blood pressure today was 132/82. Pulse was 76 and regular. Temperature was 100.6 degrees. Pain and tenderness in the right frontal sinus region. The eyes appear slightly puffy. Examination of the right hip reveals point tenderness in the region of the head of the femur.

A: Probable sinusitis. Right hip pain; rule out trochanteric bursitis.

P: The patient will be sent for a sinus X-ray and right hip X-ray. I suspect the patient has a sinus infection due to the symptoms and fever. If the X-ray of the hip does not reveal any other pathology, will offer cortisone injection to the patient for relief of the right hip pain.

ASSIGNMENT 6.12 Multiple Choice Review

1. Codes in slanted brackets are
   a. eponyms.
   b. manifestations.
   c. modifiers.
   d. subterms.

2. When coding a late effect, the primary code is the
   a. acute disease.
   b. main symptom.
   c. original cause.
   d. residual condition.

3. Which is an example of an outpatient setting?
   a. emergency department
   b. nursing home
   c. rehabilitation hospital
   d. residential care facility

4. A concurrent condition that exists with the first-listed diagnosis is a
   a. comorbidity.
   b. complication.
   c. manifestation.
   d. symptom.

5. If a patient develops bleeding at the site of operative wound closure, this is a(n):
   a. comorbidity.
   b. complication.
   c. encounter.
   d. manifestation.

6. A 45-year-old patient presents with polyuria and polydipsia. The physician documents "suspected diabetes mellitus." Which would be reported by the physician's office on the CMS-1500 claim?
   a. diabetes mellitus
   b. polydipsia only
   c. polyuria only
   d. polyuria and polydipsia

7. On May 1, a patient presents with a blood pressure of 150/90 and is asked to rest for 10 minutes. Upon reevaluation, the blood pressure is 130/80, and the patient is asked to return to the office on May 15 to rule out hypertension. Which would be reported by the physician's office on the CMS-1500 claim submitted for the May 1 office visit?

    a. benign hypertension

    b. elevated blood pressure

    c. malignant hypertension

    d. rule out hypertension

8. A patient presents with wheezing and a productive cough. The physician recorded "probable bronchitis, pending chest X-ray results." X-ray results confirmed bronchitis. During this visit, the patient's glucose was checked to determine the status of his diabetes. The patient reported that his previous indigestion and diarrhea were currently not a problem. Which would be reported by the physician's office on the CMS-1500 claim?

    a. bronchitis, diabetes mellitus

    b. bronchitis, diabetes mellitus, indigestion, diarrhea

    c. bronchitis, indigestion, diarrhea

    d. productive cough

9. A patient presents complaining of tenderness in the left breast and a family history of breast cancer. Upon examination, the physician discovers a small lump in the left breast. The patient was referred to a breast surgeon and X-ray for mammogram. The physician documented "questionable breast cancer of the left breast." Which would be reported by the physician's office on the CMS-1500 claim?

    a. breast cancer

    b. breast lump; breast pain; family history of breast cancer

    c. breast pain; breast cancer

    d. personal history of breast cancer

10. A 19-year-old patient was brought to the emergency room from a fraternity party because of nausea, vomiting, and lethargy. The diagnosis was alcohol poisoning. Which E code should be reported for "alcohol poisoning"?

    a. accident

    b. assault

    c. therapeutic use

    d. undetermined

11. What effect will reporting E codes have on CMS-1500 claims processing?

    a. The claim processing will be expedited because the circumstances related to an injury are indicated.

    b. The claim will automatically be denied; the claim should be paid by another payer if an E code is present.

    c. The claim will be automatically paid without difficulty because a higher level of detail has been included.

    d. The provider will receive a higher reimbursement amount due to the specificity of the information on the claim.

12. A neoplasm that is considered life-threatening and has spread outside its margins of origin is called

    a. benign.

    b. in situ.

    c. malignant.

    d. precancerous.

13. ICD-9-CM *Index to Diseases* subterms that are indented below the main term, to clarify the main term that must be contained in the diagnostic statement for the code to be assigned, are called

    a. eponyms.   c. nonessential modifiers.
    b. essential modifiers.   d. notes.

14. The condition "Lyme disease" is an example of a(n)

    a. category.   c. manifestation.
    b. eponym.   d. modifier.

15. Four-digit codes in ICD-9-CM are called _____ codes.

    a. category   c. subcategory
    b. classification   d. subclassification

16. A severe form of hypertension with vascular damage and a diastolic reading of 130 mm Hg or greater is called _____ hypertension.

    a. benign   c. malignant
    b. chronic   d. unspecified

17. When assigning an ICD-9-CM code from the Neoplasm table, which is referenced first?

    a. anatomic site   c. category
    b. behavior   d. specificity

18. The appearance of a pathologic condition caused by ingestion or exposure to a chemical substance properly administered is considered a(n)

    a. accident.   c. assault.
    b. adverse effect.   d. poisoning.

19. When multiple injuries are documented during the same episode of care on a patient's record, in what order are ICD-9-CM codes for the injuries reported on the CMS-1500 claim?

    a. The least severe injury is reported first, followed by more severe injuries.
    b. The severest injury is reported first, followed by next severe injury, and so on.
    c. The injury costing the least to treat is reported first, followed by the next costliest.
    d. A head-to-toe order of injury according to body assessment is reported.

20. When coding late effects, the first code reported is the residual condition and the second code is the

    a. etiology.   c. sign.
    b. manifestation.   d. symptom.

CHAPTER 7

CPT Coding

INTRODUCTION

This chapter familiarizes students with coding procedures according to CPT. Students will code procedural statements and case studies by applying CPT coding conventions, principles, and rules.

ASSIGNMENT 7.1 CPT Index

OBJECTIVES

At the conclusion of this assignment, the student should be able to:

1. Identify the word in a procedural statement that would be considered the main term in the CPT Index.

2. Locate main terms in the CPT Index.

INSTRUCTIONS

In each of the following procedural statements, underline the word that would be considered the main term in the CPT Index.

1. Ankle amputation

2. Lower arm biopsy

3. Artery angioplasty

4. Bone marrow aspiration

5. Bladder aspiration

6. Bladder neck resection

7. Rib resection

8. Salivary duct dilation

9. Wrist disarticulation

10. Drinking test for glaucoma

11. Dwyer procedure

12. New patient office visit

13. Well baby care

14. Wound repair of pancreas

15. Inpatient hospital discharge

ASSIGNMENT 7.2 Evaluation and Management (E/M) Coding

OBJECTIVES

At the conclusion of this assignment, the student should be able to:

1. Use the CPT Index to locate E/M codes.

2. Verify codes in the E/M section of CPT.

INSTRUCTIONS

Assign CPT Evaluation and Management codes to the following services. (Refer to Figures 7-10A through 7-10D in the textbook for assistance.)

1. Follow-up inpatient consultation, expanded _____

2. Subsequent nursing facility care, problem focused _____

3. Initial office visit, problem focused _____

4. Initial observation care, detailed _____

5. Subsequent hospital care, expanded _____

6. Initial home visit, detailed _____

7. Follow-up home visit, comprehensive _____

8. Observation care discharge _____

9. Initial inpatient consult, detailed _____

10. Initial confirmatory consult, problem focused _____

ASSIGNMENT 7.3 Anesthesia Coding

OBJECTIVES

At the conclusion of this assignment, the student should be able to:

1. Use the CPT Index to locate Anesthesia codes.

2. Verify codes in the Anesthesia section of CPT.

INSTRUCTIONS

Assign CPT Anesthesia codes to the following procedures. Be sure to include the physical status modifier, which indicates information about the patient's physical status in relation to anesthesia services provided. Where appropriate, assign one or more of the four codes (99100–99140) from the Medicine section that report qualifying circumstances for anesthesia.

1. Coronary angioplasty of two vessels; patient has severe coronary artery disease   _____

2. Amniocentesis; patient has petit mal epilepsy   _____

3. Extracorporeal shock wave lithotripsy; patient has controlled hypertension   _____

4. Percutaneous liver biopsy; patient has chronic alcoholism   _____

5. Debridement of third-degree burns of right arm, 6% body surface area; patient is 2 years old and otherwise healthy   _____

6. Total hip replacement, open procedure; patient has controlled diabetes mellitus   _____

7. Biopsy of clavicle; patient is postoperative mastectomy 2 years ago and is undergoing biopsy procedure for suspected metastatic bone cancer   _____

8. Hand cast application; patient is otherwise healthy   _____

9. Arthroscopic procedure of the ankle joint; patient has generalized arthritis   _____

10. Total cystectomy; patient has bladder cancer, which is localized   _____

ASSIGNMENT 7.4 Surgery Coding

OBJECTIVES

At the conclusion of this assignment, the student should be able to:

1. Use the CPT Index to locate Surgery codes.
2. Verify codes in the Surgery section of CPT.

INSTRUCTIONS

Assign codes to the following procedural statements using the CPT Index. Be sure to verify the code(s) in the CPT Surgery section.

NOTE: Convert inches to centimeters when calculating wound size. The formula is: inches x 2.54. Or, go to http://www.manuelsweb.com/in_cm.htm and use the online conversion calculator.

1. Excision, 1-inch benign lesion, left leg   _____

2. Simple repair of 2-inch laceration on the right foot   _____

3. Layer closure of 3-inch stab wound of the neck   _____

4. Excision, half-inch malignant lesion, left first finger   _____

5. Intermediate repair of 5-inch laceration of the right thigh   _____

6. Open reduction with external fixation of fracture of great toe phalanx fracture   _____

7. Closed reduction of nasal bone fracture with stabilization   _____

8. Surgical elbow arthroscopy with removal of loose body _____

9. Segmental osteotomy of the mandible _____

10. Trigger finger release _____

11. Tracheobronchoscopy through existing tracheostomy incision _____

12. Secondary rhinoplasty with major reconstruction of nasal tip to correct results of an initial rhinoplasty done elsewhere _____

13. Surgical thoracoscopy with excision of pericardial tumor _____

14. Total pulmonary decortication _____

15. Extraplural enucleation of empyema _____

16. Direct repair of cerebral artery aneurysm _____

17. Femoral-popliteal bypass graft _____

18. Coronary artery bypass graft (using two arterial grafts) _____

19. Complete cardiac MRI with contrast _____

20. Insertion of dual-chamber pacemaker with electrodes _____

21. Complete cleft lip repair, primary bilateral, one-stage procedure _____

22. Laparoscopic cholecystectomy with exploration of the common duct _____

23. Umbilectomy _____

24. Pancreatectomy with Whipple procedure _____

25. Percutaneous drainage of subdiaphragmatic abscess _____

26. Inguinal hernia repair without hydrocelectomy; the patient is a 14-month-old male. _____

27. Cystourethroscopy with fulguration of large (6.5 cm) bladder tumor _____

28. Manometric studies through pyelostomy tube _____

29. Nephrorrhaphy of right kidney wound _____

30. Injection of contrast for voiding urethrocystography _____

31. Laser removal of three condylomata from penis _____

32. Incisional biopsy of the prostate _____

33. Marsupialization of Bartholin's gland cyst _____

34. Total bilateral salpingectomy and oophorectomy _____

35. Antepartum care, 10 visits _____

36. Burr holes with evacuation and drainage of subdural hematoma _____

37. Craniotomy for repair of cerebrospinal fluid leak and rhinorrhea _____

38. Thoracic laminectomy with exploration, two vertebrae _____

39. Stereotactic biopsy of spinal cord _____

40. Neuroplasty of the sciatic nerve _____

41. Evisceration of eye with implant _____

42. Laser iridectomy for glaucoma _____

43. Total dacryocystectomy _____

44. Removal of bilateral cerumen impaction _____

45. Successful cochlear implant _____

ASSIGNMENT 7.5 Radiology Coding

OBJECTIVES

At the conclusion of this assignment, the student should be able to:

1. Use the CPT Index to locate Radiology codes.
2. Verify codes in the Radiology section of CPT.

INSTRUCTIONS

Assign codes to the following procedural statements using the CPT Index. Be sure to verify the code(s) in the CPT Radiology section.

1. Complete radiographic examination of the mandible _____
2. Urography, retrograde _____
3. Pelvimetry _____
4. Orthoroentgenogram, scanogram _____
5. Chest X-ray, two views, with fluoroscopy _____
6. X-ray of the facial bones, four views _____
7. CAT scan of the abdomen, with contrast _____
8. Gastroesophageal reflux study _____
9. X-ray of the cervical spine, two views _____
10. Barium enema _____

ASSIGNMENT 7.6 Pathology and Laboratory Coding

OBJECTIVES

At the conclusion of this assignment, the student should be able to:

1. Use the CPT Index to locate Pathology and Laboratory codes.
2. Verify codes in the Pathology and Laboratory section of CPT.

INSTRUCTIONS

Assign codes to the following procedural statements using the CPT Index. Be sure to verify the code(s) in the CPT Radiology and Laboratory section.

1. Red blood cell count _____
2. Blood gases, pH only _____

3. Glucose-6-phosphate dehydrogenase screen _____

4. Glucose tolerance test, three specimens _____

5. KOH prep _____

6. HIV antibody and confirmatory test _____

7. HDL cholesterol _____

8. Rapid test for infection, screen, each antibody _____

9. Herpes simplex virus, quantification _____

10. Urine dip, nonautomated, without microscopy _____

ASSIGNMENT 7.7 Medicine Coding

OBJECTIVES

At the conclusion of this assignment, the student should be able to:

1. Use the CPT Index to locate Medicine codes.

2. Verify codes in the Medicine section of CPT.

INSTRUCTIONS

Assign codes to the following procedural statements using the CPT Index. Be sure to verify the code(s) in the CPT Medicine section.

1. Right heart catheterization, for congenital cardiac anomalies _____

2. Medical testimony _____

3. Services requested between 10:00 p.m. and 8:00 a.m. in addition to basic service _____

4. Acupuncture, one or more needles, with electrical stimulation _____

5. Hypnotherapy _____

6. One hour of psychological testing with interpretation and report _____

7. Wheelchair management/propulsion training, 15 minutes _____

8. Massage therapy, 45 minutes _____

9. Nonpressurized inhalation treatment for acute airway obstruction_____

10. Educational videotapes for the patient _____

ASSIGNMENT 7.8 Assigning CPT Modifiers

OBJECTIVES

At the conclusion of this assignment, the student should be able to:

1. Use the CPT Appendix to locate modifiers.

2. Assign the modifier that describes the special circumstances associated with a procedural statement.

INSTRUCTIONS

Assign the CPT code and appropriate modifier to the following procedural statements. (Refer to Tables 7-1A and 7-1B in the textbook for assistance in assigning modifiers.)

1. Vasovasostomy discontinued after anesthesia due to heart arrhythmia, hospital outpatient _____

2. Decision for surgery during initial office visit, comprehensive _____

3. Expanded office visit for follow-up of mastectomy; new onset diabetes was discovered and treatment initiated _____

4. Cholecystectomy, postoperative management only _____

5. Hospital outpatient hemorrhoidectomy by simple ligature discontinued prior to anesthesia due to severe drop in blood pressure _____

6. Total urethrectomy including cystotomy, female, surgical care only _____

7. Simple repair of 2-inch laceration of the right foot, discontinued due to near-syncope, physician's office _____

8. Tonsillectomy and adenoidectomy, age 10, and wart removal from the patient's neck while in the operating room _____

9. Repeat left medial collateral ligament repair, same surgeon _____

10. At the patient's request, bilateral Silver procedures were performed for correction of bunion deformity _____

ASSIGNMENT 7.9 Coding Case Studies

OBJECTIVES

At the conclusion of this assignment, the student should be able to:

1. Use the CPT Index to locate Procedure and Service codes.
2. Verify codes in the appropriate section of CPT.
3. Assign modifier(s) when special circumstances are documented in a case study.

INSTRUCTIONS

Code the following case studies using the CPT Index. Be sure to verify the code(s) in the appropriate section of CPT. (Assign just the Procedure and Service codes for each case study. Do not code diagnoses.) Refer to textbook Figures 7-10A through 7-10D for assistance with E/M code selection and Tables 7-1A and 7-1B for assistance with assigning modifiers.

1. ### PATIENT CASE #1

   HISTORY OF PRESENT ILLNESS: The patient is a 37-year-old female who has complaints of severe fatigue, sore throat, headache, and acute bilateral ear pain. The symptoms have been gradually increasing over the past 7 to 10 days, to the point where she is not able to sleep at night due to coughing and intense bilateral ear pain. She was referred to me for further evaluation and medical treatment.

PHYSICAL EXAMINATION: GENERAL: The patient appears tired and ill. HEENT: Eyes are within normal limits. Bilateral otoscopic examination shows erythematous, inflamed tympanic membranes with question of perforation on the right. Throat is red and tonsils appear mildly swollen. NECK: There is mild cervical lymphadenopathy. HEART: Within normal limits. LUNGS: Generally clear. The rest of the exam was within normal limits. LABORATORY: Rapid strep was negative. Poly Stat Mono test was positive.

ASSESSMENT: Mononucleosis, pharyngitis, bilateral otitis media, and probable sinusitis.

PLAN: CBC with differential. Sinus X-ray to rule out sinusitis. The patient will be placed on a Z-Pak and prednisone taper. Tussionex for cough. The patient is to be off work for the next 10 days, and is to return to this office in 7 days; sooner if she does not begin to feel better or if symptoms worsen.

2. **PATIENT CASE #2**

OPERATIVE PROCEDURE: Cystoscopy.

PREOPERATIVE DIAGNOSES:

1. Benign prostatic hypertrophy.

2. Rule out stricture of the urethra.

3. Rule out bladder lesions.

POSTOPERATIVE DIAGNOSIS:

1. Benign prostatic hypertrophy.

2. Cystitis.

POSTOPERATIVE CONDITION: Satisfactory.

OPERATIVE PROCEDURE AND FINDINGS: The patient was placed in the lithotomy position. Genital area was prepped with Betadine and draped in the usual sterile fashion. About 10 cc of 2% Xylocaine jelly was introduced into the urethra and a cystoscopy was performed using a #16 French flexible cystoscope. The urethra was grossly normal. The prostate gland was moderately enlarged. There was mild inflammation of the bladder mucosa, but there were no gross tumors or calculi seen in the bladder at this time. Cystoscope was removed. The patient tolerated the procedure well and left the procedure room in good condition.

3. **PATIENT CASE #3**

S: Chronic fatigue. No acute complaints. The patient purchased an Advantage BG and sugars are 97 to 409; no pattern. (She did not bring copies of her sugars as requested.) Eats two meals a day; history of noncompliance. The patient was seen in GYN Clinic this morning. Has GI upset with oral estrogen and doctor recommended estrogen patch. Seen in ophthalmology in July; no retinopathy. Last mammography was in June. Noncompliant with 6-month follow-up of calcified cluster in the right breast, upper outer quadrant. Four-year history of small, tender irregularity in the right breast 5 o'clock position. Feet: The patient still has occasional pain with over-the-counter B12 pills. No change in respiration; refuses to attempt to quit smoking. Self catheterizes neurogenic bladder.

O: Obese white female in no acute distress. Lump found on breast self-exam, right. Left breast reveals no mass, no nodes, nipple okay. Right breast reveals tender spots at 8 and 10 o'clock, mobile. Patient believes this has been the same for the past 4 years. Patient routinely does breast self-exam. Heart reveals regular sinus rhythm.

A: Diabetes mellitus on oral therapy, poorly controlled. Chronic small airway disease. Nicotine dependent. Obesity. Menopause. Rule out breast disease.

P: Hemoglobin today. Fasting lipid profile today. Repeat both labs in three months. Schedule mammogram today. Counseled patient on the importance of keeping the mammography appointment and close watch of the masses. Return to clinic in 6 weeks if mammogram is okay. Will start estrogen patch 0.5 mg/24 hours, #8. All other meds refilled today.

4. PATIENT CASE #4

HISTORY: The patient presented today for evaluation of ulcers of the lower left leg, in the region of the tibia and also in the calf area. The patient reports discomfort with these areas. The patient agreed to be seen at the insistence of his wife and because of increasing pain in the areas of the ulcerations. The patient is a known diabetic with poor compliance and sugars are usually high. We discussed his blood sugar monitoring schedule and his wife indicates that the patient is very stubborn about monitoring his blood sugars. The patient could benefit from an intensive education session regarding diabetes, diabetic care, and preventing or slowing diabetes disease progression. He is either in complete denial of his diagnosis or is simply not making the effort to take care of himself; either way, the situation needs to be addressed.

PHYSICAL EXAMINATION: The exam was limited to the lower extremities. The left lower leg shows stasis dermatitis with two ulcerations in the region of the calf. One is approximately 1 cm in diameter and the other is approximately 1.5 cm in diameter. There are varicosities present as well as mild edema noted. There is a small, shallow ulcer in the mid-tibia region as well. The right lower leg has mild edema but is free of ulcers at this time.

DIAGNOSES:

1. Stasis dermatitis with ulcerations.

2. Dependent edema.

3. Diabetes mellitus, uncontrolled.

PLAN: The patient underwent wound irrigation and application of Silvadene cream to the ulcerations. Wounds were dressed with sterile gauze and wrapped with Kerlix. The patient will return in one week for reevaluation. If there is no improvement in the ulcerations, an Unna boot will be the next step. Additionally, we will arrange for intensive diabetic education for this patient.

5. PATIENT CASE #5

PREOPERATIVE DIAGNOSIS: Pilonidal cyst.

POSTOPERATIVE DIAGNOSIS: Pilonidal cyst, cellulitis.

OPERATION: Pilonidal cystectomy, cyst tract exploration and irrigation.

HISTORY: The patient is a 42-year-old white male who has had intermittent flare-ups of the pilonidal cyst. He was seen in the office 2 days ago with an acute flare-up with acute pain, pressure, and he reported he was running a fever. He was scheduled for office surgery for removal and presents today for the above.

OPERATION: The patient was premedicated with 10 mg of Versed. The patient was brought to the procedure room and placed in the jackknife position. The lower sacrum and coccygeal areas were prepped with Betadine and the operative field was draped in a sterile fashion. Local anesthetic was administered with topical Hurricane spray, and 1% Xylocaine was then injected into the margins of the wound. An incision was made into the area of the obvious pilonidal cyst formation and approximately 15 cc of foul, purulent drainage was expressed from the wound. The contents of the cyst were excised, labeled, and sent for pathology. There was cellulitis extending circumferentially around the cyst, extending approximately 1.5 cm outside the area of the cyst. Exploration of the sinus tract was performed and the tract extended down approximately 2.5 cm. It was felt at this time that no sutures would be required, and the tract was irrigated with normal saline and flushed with antibiotic solution. The wound was then packed and dressed. The patient tolerated the procedure well. The patient was observed for 30 minutes following the procedure, after which was instructed on wound care and signs of infection. The patient was released to the care of his wife. He was given a prescription for Keflex 500 mg p.o. b.i.d. and Darvocet N-100, #20, 1 p.o. q.4h. as needed for pain. He will return to the office in 2 days for reevaluation.

ASSIGNMENT 7.10 Multiple Choice Review

1. How many body systems are included in the Surgery section of CPT?
   a. six
   c. eight
   b. seven
   d. nine

2. Instructions provided at the beginning of each section, which define terms particular to that section and provide explanation for codes and services that apply to that section, are called _____.
   a. guidelines
   c. qualifiers
   b. instructional notes
   d. special reports

3. Rather than using unlisted procedure or service CPT codes, Medicare and other third-party payers require providers to
   a. assign ICD-9 procedure codes.
   c. perform a known procedure.
   b. attach a special report.
   d. report HCPCS level II codes.

4. CPT modifiers are used to indicate that
   a. a special report need not be attached to the claim.
   b. the description of the procedure performed has been altered.
   c. the provider should receive a higher reimbursement rate.
   d. the technique of the procedure was performed differently.

5. Which component is included in the surgical package?
   a. assistant surgeon services
   b. epidural or spinal anesthesia
   c. prescription pain medications
   d. uncomplicated postoperative care

6. Which modifier is reported if a third-party payer requires a second opinion for a surgical procedure?
   a. -26 professional component
   c. -59 distinct procedural service
   b. -32 mandated services
   d. -62 two surgeons

7. The time frame during which all postoperative services are included in the surgical package is the global _____.
   a. billing
   b. package
   c. period
   d. surgery

8. The technique for removing a skin lesion that involves transverse incision or horizontal slicing to remove epidermal or dermal lesions is called
   a. destruction.
   b. excision.
   c. repair.
   d. shaving.

9. The proper way to report the repair of multiple lacerations at the same anatomic site is to
   a. add together the length of each laceration and report a single code.
   b. code each individual laceration based on the length of each wound.
   c. code each individual laceration based on the most complicated repair.
   d. report individual codes for each laceration if they involved trauma.

10. Which term does CPT use to indicate "manipulation of a fracture"?
    a. fixation
    b. reduction
    c. traction
    d. treatment

11. CPT codes that are optional and are used for tracking performance measurements are called _____ codes.
    a. Category I
    b. Category II
    c. Category III
    d. Category IV

12. A bullet located to the left of a code number identifies
    a. a revised code description.
    b. codes exempt from modifier -51.
    c. new procedures and services.
    d. revised guidelines and notes.

13. A patient undergoes an "office toenail avulsion procedure." Which is the main term that you locate in the Index to identify the CPT code?
    a. avulsion
    b. evacuation
    c. excision
    d. repair

14. A series of very specific blood chemistry studies ordered at one time is called a(n)
    a. assay.
    b. panel.
    c. report.
    d. study.

15. The CPT definition of *counseling* as it relates to E/M coding includes
    a. coordination of care by the provider.
    b. discussing diagnostic tests with a patient.
    c. providing psychotherapy to the patient.
    d. reviewing care instructions with the family.

16. If a patient is seen by the provider for a presenting problem that runs a definite and prescribed course, is transient in nature, and is not likely to alter the patient's permanent health status, the problem is considered
    a. low severity.
    b. minimal.
    c. minor.
    d. moderate severity.

17. A patient admitted to the hospital through the emergency department for treatment and who is held for a period of 8 hours to be monitored receives hospital _____ services.

    a. critical care

    b. inpatient

    c. observation

    d. outpatient

18. A patient was urgently admitted to the hospital and undergoes excisional biopsy of the left breast for suspected high-grade malignancy. The pathologist was requested to be available for immediate analysis of the specimen. Which service will the pathologist report on the CMS-1500 claim form?

    a. assistant surgeon

    b. critical care

    c. operative standby

    d. prolonged services

19. Which service is reported for the care of patients who live in a boarding home?

    a. consultation services

    b. domiciliary care

    c. home services

    d. nursing facility services

20. Which codes are reported by all physician specialties?

    a. Evaluation and Management

    b. Laboratory

    c. Medicine

    d. Surgery

CHAPTER 8

HCPCS Coding

INTRODUCTION

This chapter familiarizes students with coding procedures, services, and supplies according to HCPCS. Students will code procedural statements and case studies by applying HCPCS coding conventions, principles, and rules.

ASSIGNMENT 8.1 HCPCS Index

OBJECTIVES

At the conclusion of the assignment, the student should be able to:

1. Identify the word in a service or procedural statement that would be considered the main term in the HCPCS Index.

2. Locate main terms in the HCPCS Index.

INSTRUCTIONS

In each of the following statements, underline the word that would be considered the main term in the HCPCS Index.

1. Breast pump

2. Cardiac output assessment

3. Diasylate solution

4. External defibrillator electrode

5. Fracture orthosis

6. Liquid gas system

7. Oral antiemetic

8. Pneumatic nebulizer administration set

9. Pneumococcal vaccination administration

10. Wheelchair shock absorber

OBJECTIVES

At the conclusion of this assignment, the student should be able to:

1. Locate main terms in the HCPCS Index.

2. Identify codes in the HCPCS Index and verify them in the tabular section.

INSTRUCTIONS

Assign HCPCS codes to the following procedures and services:

Transport Services Including Ambulance (A0000–A0999)

1. Advanced life support, Level 2 _____

2. Ambulance transport of newborn from rural hospital to a children's specialty hospital _____

3. Patient received basic life support (BLS) during emergency transport via ambulance _____

4. Patient received life-sustaining oxygen in ambulance during transport to hospital _____

5. Wheelchair van transporting patient from assisted living facility to doctor's office _____

Medical and Surgical Supplies (A4000–A8999)

6. Physician gave patient injection using a sterile 3 cc syringe with needle _____

7. One pint of pHisoHex solution _____

8. Contraception implant system (including implants and supplies) _____

9. Replacement adapter for breast pump _____

10. One pound of paraffin _____

11. Male external catheter with adhesive coating _____

12. Two-way indwelling Foley catheter _____

13. Ostomy belt _____

14. Reusable enema bag with tubing _____

15. One pair of apnea monitor electrodes _____

16. Rubber pessary _____

17. Tracheostomy care kit for new tracheostomy _____

18. Automatic blood pressure monitor _____

19. Ammonia test strips for dialysis (50 count) _____

20. Patient with diabetes was fitted with a pair of shoes custom-molded from casts of the patient's feet _____

Administrative, Miscellaneous, and Investigational (A9000–A9999)

21. DME delivery and setup _____

22. Exercise equipment _____

23. I-131 sodium iodide capsule as radiopharmaceutical diagnostic agent (1 millicurie) _____

24. Injectable contrast material for use in echocardiography, one study _____

25. One dose technetium Tc99m sestamibi _____

Enteral and Parenteral Therapy (B4000–B9999)

26. 500 cc of 10% lipids parenteral nutrition solution _____

27. Category V enteral formula via feeding tube (100 calories/1 unit) _____

28. Enteral infusion pump with alarm _____

29. Gravity-fed enteral feeding supply kit (one day) _____

30. Parenteral nutrition administration kit (2 days) _____

C Codes for Use under the Hospital Outpatient Prospective Payment System (C1000–C9999)

31. Brachytherapy seed, high-dose rate iridium 192 _____

32. Cardiac event recorder (implantable) _____

33. Injection of 1 ml of hepatitis B immunoglobulin _____

34. Patient underwent left breast MRI without contrast, followed by left breast MRI with contrast _____

35. Short-term hemodialysis catheter _____

36. Single-chamber implantable cardioverter-defibrillator _____

Durable Medical Equipment (E0100–E9999)

37. "Patient helper" trapeze bars (attached to bed) _____

38. Adult oxygen tent _____

39. Bilirubin light with photometer _____

40. Dispensing fee for DME nebulizer drug _____

41. Folding walker with adjustable height _____

42. Four-lead TENS unit _____

43. Free-standing cervical traction stand _____

44. Heavy-duty, extra-wide hospital bed with mattress to accommodate patient who weighs 460 pounds _____

45. Heparin infusion pump for hemodialysis _____

46. Jug urinal (male) _____

47. Lambswool sheepskin heel pad for decubitus prevention _____

48. Low-intensity ultrasound osteogenesis stimulator _____

49. Metal bed pan _____

50. Non-electronic communication board   _____

51. Patient was fitted with a pair of underarm wooden crutches
    with pads, tips, and handgrips   _____

52. Portable paraffin bath (unit)   _____

53. Portable sitz bath   _____

54. Quad cane with tips   _____

55. Raised toilet seat   _____

56. Remote joystick power wheelchair accessory including
    all electronics and fixed mounting hardware   _____

57. Replacement brake attachment for wheeled walker   _____

58. Ultraviolet light therapy 6-foot panel, with bulbs, timer, and eye
    protection   _____

59. Variable height hospital bed with mattress and side rails   _____

60. Wheelchair anti-tipping device   _____

Procedures/Professional Services (Temporary) (G0000–G9999)

61. Automated CBC (complete) with automated WBC differential
    count   _____

62. End-stage renal disease (ESRD) services for 16-year-old
    patient, 3 physician visits per month   _____

63. Individual smoking cessation counseling (10 minutes)   _____

64. Initial E/M evaluation for patient with LOPS   _____

65. PET imaging for initial diagnosis of breast cancer   _____

Alcohol and/or Drug Abuse Treatment Services (H0001–H2037)

66. Behavioral health counseling and therapy, 30 minutes   _____

67. Partial hospitalization for mental health crisis, 18 hours   _____

68. Psychiatric health facility services (one day)   _____

69. Respite care services, not in the home (per diem)   _____

70. Thirty minutes of activity therapy   _____

Temporary Durable Medical Equipment (K0000–K9999)

71. Complete front caster assembly for wheelchair with two
    semi-pneumatic tires   _____

72. IV hanger (each)   _____

73. Leg strap (for wheelchair)   _____

74. Lightweight portable motorized wheelchair   _____

75. Replacement alkaline battery, 1.5 volt, for patient-owned
    external infusion pump   _____

Orthotic Procedures (L0000–L4999)

76. Cervical wire frame, semi-rigid, for occipital/mandibular support _____

77. Custom-fabricated thoracic rib belt _____

78. HALO procedure; cervical halo incorporated into Milwaukee orthosis _____

79. Neoprene heel and sole elevation lift (one inch) _____

80. Posterior solid ankle plastic AFO, custom fabricated _____

81. Spenco foot insert _____

Prosthetic Procedures (L5000–L9999)

82. Below-knee disarticulation prosthesis, molded socket, shin, with SACH foot _____

83. Electric hand, myoelectrically controlled, Otto Bock _____

84. Partial foot prosthesis, shoe insert with longitudinal arch, toe filler _____

85. Preparatory prosthesis for hip disarticulation-hemipelvectomy; pylon, no cover, solid ankle cushion heel foot, thermoplastic, molded to patient model _____

86. Silicone breast prosthesis _____

Medical Services (M0000–M0399)

87. Brief office visit to change prescription medication used for treating the patient's personality disorder _____

88. Cellular therapy _____

89. Chemical endarterectomy (IV chelation therapy) _____

90. Fabric wrapping of abdominal aneurysm _____

91. Prolotherapy _____

Pathology and Laboratory Services (P0000–P2999)

92. Catheterization for collection of specimen (one patient) _____

93. Congo red, blood _____

94. Pinworm examination _____

95. Platelets, each unit _____

96. Two units whole blood for transfusion _____

Q Codes: Temporary Codes (Q0000–Q9999)

97. Chemotherapy administration by push _____

98. Collagen skin test _____

99. Elliott's B solution injection, 1 ml _____

100. Injection hepatitis B vaccination, pediatric dose _____

101. KOH preparation _____

Diagnostic Radiology Services (R0000–R5999)

102. Portable X-ray service transportation to nursing home, one trip, one patient seen _____

103. Transportation of portable ECG to nursing facility, one patient seen _____

104. Transportation of portable X-ray service to patient's home, 2 patients seen (husband and wife) _____

Temporary National Codes (Non-Medicare) (S0000–S9999)

105. Allogenic cord-blood-derived stem cell transplant _____

106. Echosclerotherapy _____

107. Gastrointestinal fat absorption study _____

108. Global fee for extracorporeal shock wave lithotripsy (ESWL) treatment of kidney stone _____

109. Harvesting of multivisceral organs from cadaver with preparation and maintenance of allografts _____

110. Vaginal birth after Cesarean (VBAC) classes _____

National T Codes Established for State Medicaid Agencies (T1000–T9999)

111. Family training and counseling for child development, 15 minutes _____

112. Human breast milk processing, storage, and distribution _____

113. Intramuscular medication administration by home health LPN _____

114. Private-duty nursing, 30 minutes _____

115. Waiver for utility services to support medical equipment _____

Vision Services (V0000–V2999)

116. Bifocal lenses, bilateral, 5.25 sphere, 2.12 cylinder _____

117. Deluxe frame _____

118. Photochromatic tint for 2 lenses _____

119. Processing, preserving, and transporting corneal tissue _____

120. Reduction of ocular prosthesis _____

Hearing Services (V5000–V5999)

121. Assessment for hearing aid _____

122. Binaural behind-the-ear hearing aid _____

123. Digitally programmable monaural hearing aid, analog _____

124. Dispensing fee, BICROS _____

125. Telephone amplifier _____

ASSIGNMENT 8.3 Coding Drugs in HCPCS

OBJECTIVES

At the conclusion of this assignment, the student should be able to:

1. Interpret the HCPCS Table of Drugs.

2. Assign HCPCS codes to procedure or service statements that contain drugs.

INSTRUCTIONS

Code the following statements using the Table of Drugs in HCPCS. Be sure to verify the code(s) in the HCPCS tabular section.

NOTE: Drugs in the HCPCS Table of Drugs are listed by the generic or chemical name. (Drugs are listed by the trade name only if no generic or chemical name is available.) If you search for a drug by its trade name in the table, you are instructed to "see" the generic or chemical name. For assistance with identifying generic or chemical drug names, go to http://www.rxlist.com.

1. Tetracycline 250 mg IV

2. Ancef 500 mg IV

3. Clonidine HCl, 1 mg

4. Botulinum toxin type B, 100 units

5. Duramorph 100 mg SC

6. Kenalog-40 20 mg

7. Streptokinase 250,000 IU IV

8. Ranitidine HCl injection, 25 mg

9. NPH insulin 50 units SC

10. Lasix 10 mg IM

ASSIGNMENT 8.4 HCPCS Level II National Modifiers

OBJECTIVES

At the conclusion of this assignment, the student should be able to:

1. Locate HCPCS level II national modifiers in the coding manual.

2. Assign HCPCS level II national modifiers to special circumstances associated with procedures, services, and supplies.

INSTRUCTIONS

Match the modifier in the left column to its appropriate description in the right column.

_____ 1. AH   a. Left hand, thumb

_____ 2. E4   b. Technical component

_____ 3. FA   c. Four patients served

91

_____	**4.** NU	d. Registered (RN)
_____	**5.** RC	e. Lower right eyelid
_____	**6.** SB	f. New equipment
_____	**7.** TA	g. Clinical psychologist
_____	**8.** TC	h. Right coronary artery
_____	**9.** TD	i. Left foot, great toe
_____	**10.** UQ	j. Nurse midwife

ASSIGNMENT 8.5 Coding Case Studies

OBJECTIVES

At the conclusion of this assignment, the student should be able to:

1. Use the HCPCS Index to locate procedure and service codes.
2. Verify codes in the appropriate section of HCPCS.
3. Assign modifier(s) when special circumstances are documented in a case study.

INSTRUCTIONS

Code the following case studies using the HCPCS Index. Be sure to verify the code(s) in the appropriate section of HCPCS. (Assign just the HCPCS procedure and service codes for each case study. Do not code diagnoses or assign CPT codes.)

1. ### PATIENT CASE #1

   S: The patient is an 89-year-old white female resident of the county nursing facility. I was asked to see her today because the nursing staff had noticed the patient having difficulty breathing and was coughing up purulent material. A chest X-ray was ordered, and the mobile X-ray service arrived and took the X-ray while I was seeing my other patients.

   O: The patient appears ill. Temperature is 100.7. CHEST: Scattered rhonchi throughout all lung fields, with severely diminished breath sounds in the left lower lung. Expiratory and inspiratory wheezes present. HEART: Within normal limits. ABDOMEN: No tenderness on palpation. EXTREMITIES: Mild dependent edema is noted; otherwise within normal limits.

   A: The chest X-ray revealed a density consistent with left lower lobe pneumonia.

   P: The patient was given Zithromax 500 mg. The cough does not seem to be bothersome to the patient right now, so the nursing staff will wait and watch. The nursing staff is to monitor her for any signs of increased fever, lethargy, or medication reaction. They are to encourage fluids and keep the patient up in a chair as much as possible when she is not sleeping. They are to contact me immediately if the patient's symptoms worsen.

2. ### PATIENT CASE #2

   S: This 45-year-old construction worker was seen in the office today on an emergency basis because he stepped on a sharp edge of steel and lacerated his right foot. He states he cannot recall his last tetanus shot.

O: Examination of the right foot reveals a laceration of approximately 3.5 cm at the lateral edge of the foot which extends medially across the heel. PROCEDURE: The right heel was cleansed with pHisoHex and prepped with Betadine. The wound edges were infiltrated with 1% Xylocaine. After adequate anesthesia was obtained, the laceration was repaired with 3-0 nylon sutures. The wound was dressed with gauze and secured with paper tape.

A: Laceration of right heel, repaired in the office.

P: The patient was given a tetanus shot today. He was given instructions on wound care and signs of infection, and was also given reference sheets on the same. He is to be non-weightbearing for the next 3 days, and was given a pair of wooden crutches. He will return to the office in 3 days for reevaluation. The patient was also reminded to call immediately if pain increases or if he shows any signs of fever.

3. *PATIENT CASE #3*

MAMMOGRAPHY CLINIC NOTE: The patient is a 72-year-old female who presented today for mammogram. She states she has remained up-to-date with her mammograms, and her record shows compliance with yearly screening exams. The patient stated that when performing her self-breast exam about 5 days ago, she felt a lump in the upper outer quadrant of the left breast. The technician asked her to identify the location of the lump and it was marked with a BB for mammography. The patient was asked to wait until the radiologist had read the initial X-rays. Upon interpretation, there indeed was a suspicious lesion in the upper outer quadrant of the left breast, approximately 1.5 cm. The patient was then asked to undergo additional radiographic views of the left breast for further investigation of the lesion. It is felt that the lesion is consistent with malignancy, and the patient was counseled by the nurse practitioner regarding the results of the mammography. We contacted the surgeon's office and the patient was scheduled tomorrow for biopsy and further evaluation as needed.

4. *PATIENT CASE #4*

S: The patient presents today for annual physical exam with Pap. She is now 34, has two healthy children, and is doing well except for some complaints of fatigue and recent weight gain.

O: VITAL SIGNS: Blood pressure is 124/72. Pulse is 64 and regular. Respiratory rate is 20. Temperature is 98.8. Weight is 156, which is up 12 pounds since her last visit. HEENT: Within normal limits. The patient wears glasses. NECK: No thyromegaly or lymphadenopathy. HEART: Regular sinus rhythm. CHEST: Clear breath sounds throughout all lung fields. ABDOMEN: No tenderness or organomegaly. PELVIC: Normal external genitalia. Vagina is pink and rugated. Pap specimen was obtained without difficulty. RECTAL: Exam was deferred. EXTREMITIES: Pulses were full and equal. Neurologic: No complaints; exam within normal limits. LABORATORY: Lab performed in the office today included a CBC with differential, thyroid panel, and complete metabolic panel.

A: Fatigue and weight gain in an otherwise healthy 34-year-old female.

P: Will await the results of the blood work and call the patient to discuss them. Instructed the patient to take a daily multivitamin and drink at least 2 glasses of milk daily. Discussed dietary modifications to help stop weight gain. If the patient's blood work indicates abnormal thyroid function, will refer to Endocrinology.

5. **PATIENT CASE #5**

   PROSTHESIS CLINIC NOTE: The patient presents today because of complaints of discomfort from his right ocular prosthesis. The prosthesis is relatively new and may need some modification. Upon examination, the patient appeared otherwise generally well. The right eye prosthesis was removed and given to the technician for evaluation. The right eye socket had a very small patch of irritated tissue in the upper medial wall. The technician resurfaced and polished the prosthesis, and after refitting, the patient reported a noticeable improvement in his level of comfort. The patient and I then discussed the psychological struggles he has had with the loss of his eye, but overall he feels more optimistic and states he believes he will be able to fully resume his normal level of activity.

ASSIGNMENT 8.6 Multiple Choice Review

1. Which HCPCS codes were phased out in December 2003?
   a. level I
   b. level II
   c. level III
   d. level IV

2. Which organization is responsible for annual updates to HCPCS level II codes?
   a. AMA
   b. CMS
   c. HHS
   d. WHO

3. Which is a member of the HCPCS National Panel?
   a. American Hospital Association
   b. American Medical Association
   c. Centers for Disease Control and Prevention
   d. Centers for Medicare and Medicaid Services

4. Which organization is responsible for providing suppliers and manufacturers with assistance in determining HCPCS codes to be used?
   a. BCBSA
   b. DMEPOS
   c. DMERC
   d. SADMERC

5. Which HCPCS codes are used by state Medicaid agencies and mandated by state law to separately identify mental health services?
   a. G
   b. H
   c. K
   d. S

6. The first alphabetic character in a HCPCS code identifies the code
   a. as one established for Medicare.
   b. as one unique to Medicaid.
   c. section of HCPCS level I.
   d. section of HCPCS level II.

7. Drugs are listed in the HCPCS Table of Drugs according to
   a. dosage to be used.
   b. generic or chemical name.
   c. route of administration.
   d. trade or brand name.

8. A regional MAC will receive claims that contain which HCPCS codes?
   a. A, J, Q, V
   b. B, E, K, L
   c. C, F, H, N, S
   d. D, G, M, P, R

9. If a provider is not registered with a regional MAC, a patient will receive medical equipment when the
   a. local hospital dispenses the equipment.
   b. patient places an order for the equipment.
   c. physician refers the patient to another doctor.
   d. provider writes a prescription to be filled.

10. If a particular service has both a CPT code and a HCPCS code, the provider will
    a. assign only the CPT code.
    b. follow instructions provided by the payer.
    c. report both codes on the CMS-1500 claim form.
    d. report only the HCPCS code.

11. If a HCPCS drug code description states "per 50 mg" and is administered in an 80 mg dose, which quantity (e.g., units) is reported on the CMS-1500 claim form?
    a. 1   c. 50
    b. 2   d. 80

12. HCPCS level II is considered a _____ system.
    a. coding   c. payment
    b. nomenclature   d. reimbursement

13. Which professional organization maintains level II "D" codes?
    a. American Billers Association   c. American Hospital Association
    b. American Dental Association   d. American Medical Association

14. How many regional MACs are assigned by CMS to process DME claims?
    a. two   c. four
    b. three   d. five

15. Which is an example of durable medical equipment (DME)?
    a. blood glucose monitor   c. IV pain medication
    b. irrigation solution   d. liquid oxygen

16. New HCPCS codes are implemented on
    a. January 1 and July 1.   c. June 1 and December 1.
    b. March 1 and September 1.   d. October 1 and April 1.

17. Which code range is assigned to "Administrative, Miscellaneous, and Investigational" HCPCS procedures or services?
    a. A4000–A8999   c. E0100–E9999
    b. A9000–A9999   d. S0000–S9999

18. Which modifier is used to describe a second surgical opinion?
    a. -SM   c. -SV
    b. -SN   d. -SW

19. Which modifier is used to describe basic life support (BLS) transport by a volunteer ambulance provider?
    a. -TK   c. -TQ
    b. -TP   d. -TS

20. HCPCS level II manuals are published by
    a. the American Medical Association.
    b. the Blue Cross/Blue Shield Association of America.
    c. the Centers for Medicare and Medicaid Services.
    d. various private publishing organizations.

## CHAPTER 9

CMS Reimbursement Methodologies

ASSIGNMENT 9.1 Outpatient Prospective Payment System (OPPS)

OBJECTIVES

At the completion of this assignment, the student should be able to:

1. Explain the difference between coinsurance and copayment.

2. Calculate the patient's share of charges for an outpatient service.

INSTRUCTIONS

Under the OPPS, Medicare allows patients to pay either a coinsurance amount (20% of the charge for procedures and services) *or* a fixed copayment amount, whichever is less. For each of the following cases, calculate the amount the patient is required to pay to the hospital for the outpatient service provided.

NOTE: In each of the following cases, the patient has already met the annual deductible required by the payer.

1. Sally Jones underwent outpatient surgery to have one mole removed from her upper back. The charge was $65. The fixed copayment amount for this type of procedure, adjusted for wages in the geographic area, is $15.

2. Cherie Brown underwent an outpatient chest X-ray that cost $75. The fixed copayment for this type of procedure, adjusted for wages in the geographic area, is $25.

3. James Hill underwent an outpatient oral glucose tolerance test. The charge for this procedure was $122. The fixed copayment for this type of procedure, adjusted for wages in the geographic area, is $20.

4. Scott Wills underwent toenail removal as an outpatient. The charge was $81. The fixed copayment for this type of procedure, adjusted for wages in the geographic area, is $25.

5. George Harris had a suspicious lesion removed from his left temple as an outpatient. The charge was $78. The fixed copayment amount for this type of procedure, adjusted for wages in the geographic area, is $15.

ASSIGNMENT 9.2 Diagnosis-Related Groups

OBJECTIVES

At the conclusion of this assignment, the student should be able to:

1. Interpret a diagnosis-related group (DRG) decision tree.

2. Differentiate between medical partitioning and surgical partitioning DRG decision trees.

3. Determine which DRG is assigned when a secondary diagnosis such as a complication or comorbidity is documented in the patient record.

INSTRUCTIONS

Diagnoses and procedures are grouped according to a particular DRG, and DRG decision trees (Figures 9-1 and 9-2) visually represent the process of assigning a DRG within a medical diagnostic category (MDC). The decision trees use a flowchart design to facilitate the decision-making logic for assigning a DRG. (Only ICD-9-CM diagnosis codes are grouped according to a medical partitioning DRG decision tree. ICD-9-CM surgical procedure codes are grouped according to a surgical partitioning DRG decision tree.)

1. Interpret the DRG decision tree in Figure 9-1 to answer the following questions.

EXAMPLE: Which neoplasm DRG is assigned to a patient whose provider has documented a complication and/or comorbidity? ANSWER: DRG 10.

---

    a. Which DRG is assigned when the provider documents "transient ischemia" as the patient's principal diagnosis?

    b. For a patient who has cranial and peripheral nerve disorders and a documented comorbidity, which DRG is assigned?

    c. Which DRG is assigned for a patient whose principal diagnosis is multiple sclerosis?

    d. A patient was diagnosed with trigeminal neuralgia. This is the only diagnosis reported in the record. Which DRG is assigned?

    e. For a patient with cardiovascular disease that is classified as nonspecific, which DRG is assigned when the patient has a secondary diagnosis of insulin-dependent diabetes mellitus?

2. Interpret the DRG decision tree in Figure 9-2 to answer the following questions.

    a. For a patient who undergoes craniotomy for implantation of a chemotherapeutic agent, which DRG is assigned?

    b. Which DRG is assigned to a 5-year-old patient who underwent a procedure for a ventricular shunt?

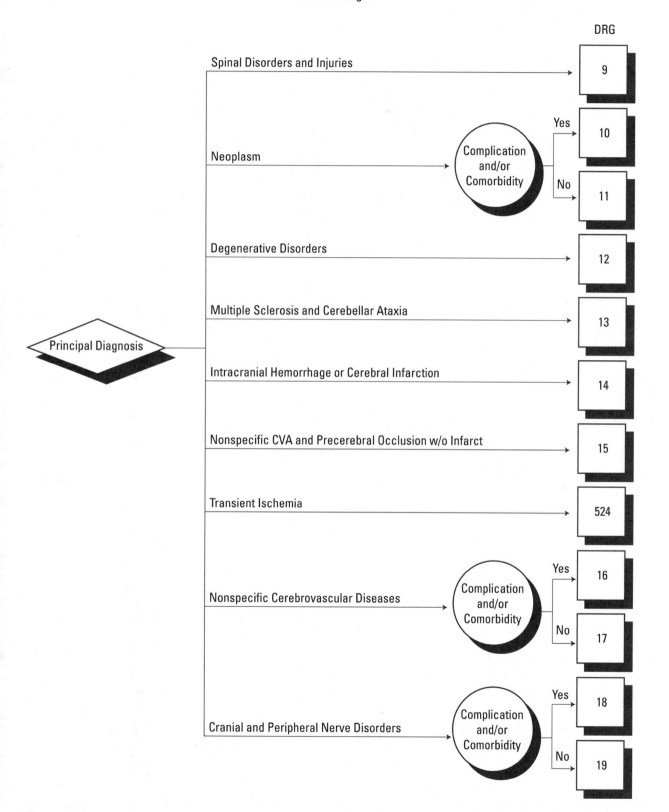

Figure 9-1 *Major Diagnostic Category 1: Diseases and Disorders of the Nervous System (Medical Partitioning)*

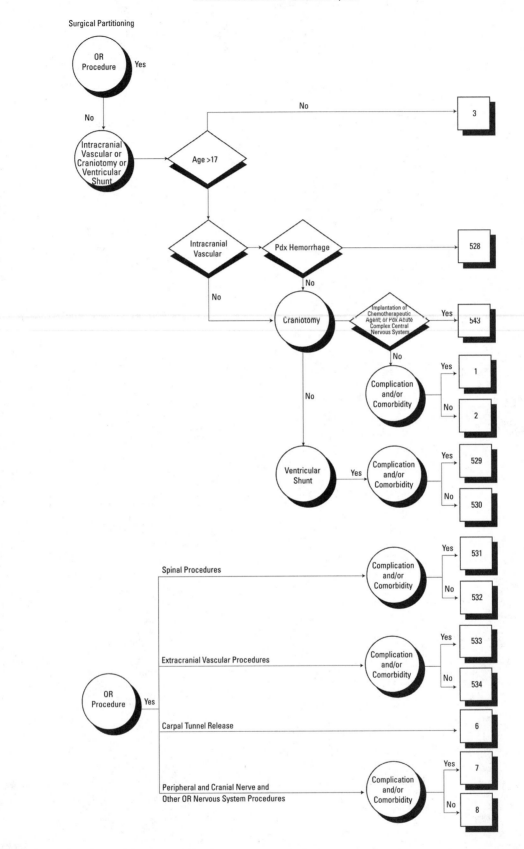

Figure 9-2 *Major Diagnostic Category 1: Diseases and Disorders of the Nervous System (Surgical Partitioning)*

c. A 56-year-old patient underwent a craniotomy and suffered a cerebrovascular accident after the procedure. Which DRG is assigned?

d. Which DRG is assigned for an otherwise healthy patient who underwent sciatic nerve biopsy?

e. A patient underwent lumbar laminectomy because of injury from a fall. The patient recently completed a course of chemotherapy for non-Hodgkin's lymphoma. Which DRG is assigned?

ASSIGNMENT 9.3 Multiple Choice Review

1. The Resource-Based Relative Value Scale (RBRVS) system is also known as
   a. Clinical Laboratory Fee Schedule.
   b. Long-Term Care Diagnosis Related Groups.
   c. Medicare Physician Fee Schedule.
   d. Resource Utilization Groups.

2. Which reimbursement system establishes rates in advance of services and is based on reported charges from which a per diem rate is determined?
   a. fee-for-service cost-based   c. prospective cost-based
   b. prospective price-based   d. retrospective reasonable cost

3. Review the following ambulance fee schedule and calculate the Medicare payment rate in the year 2006 (for an ambulance company reasonable charge of $600).

AMBULANCE FEE SCHEDULE

YEAR	AMBULANCE COMPANY (REASONABLE) CHARGE (a)	% OF REASONABLE CHARGE (b)	AMOUNT (c)	AMBULANCE FEE SCHEDULE RATE (d)	PHASE IN % (e)	AMOUNT (f)	MEDICARE PAYMENT (g)
		Formula: [(a) × (b) = (c)] + [(d) × (e) = (f)] = Medicare payment (g)					
2001	$600	80%	$480	n/a	n/a	n/a	
2002	$600	80%	$480	$425	20%	$85	
2003	$600	60%	$360	$425	40%	$170	
2004	$600	40%	$240	$425	60%	$255	
2005	$600	20%	$120	$425	80%	$340	
2006	$600	0%	$0	$425	100%	$425	

a. $425   c. $480
b. $460   d. $495

4. Review the following ambulance fee schedule and calculate the amount Medicare paid in the year 2005 (for an ambulance company reasonable charge of $720).

AMBULANCE FEE SCHEDULE

YEAR	AMBULANCE COMPANY (REASONABLE) (a)	% OF REASONABLE CHARGE (b)	AMOUNT (c)	AMBULANCE FEE SCHEDULE RATE (d)	PHASE IN % (e)	AMOUNT (f)	MEDICARE PAYMENT (g)
	Formula: [(a) × (b) = (c)] + [(d) × (e) = (f)] = Medicare payment (g)						
2001	$720	80%	$480	n/a	n/a	n/a	
2002	$720	80%	$480	$425	20%	$85	
2003	$720	60%	$360	$425	40%	$170	
2004	$720	40%	$240	$425	60%	$255	
2005	$720	20%	$120	$425	80%	$340	
2006	$720	0%	$0	$425	100%	$425	

a. $425
b. $460
c. $484
d. $576

5. Review the following ambulatory surgery center payment (ASC) groups and rates and select the reimbursement rate for a Group 6 procedure.

ASC PAYMENT GROUPS AND RATES

ASC GROUP	REIMBURSEMENT RATE
Group 1 Procedure	$333
Group 2 Procedure	$446
Group 3 Procedure	$510
Group 4 Procedure	$630
Group 5 Procedure	$717
Group 6 Procedure	$826 ($676 + $150 for intraocular lenses)
Group 7 Procedure	$995
Group 8 Procedure	$1,339 ($823 + $150 for intraocular lenses)

a. $676
b. $826
c. $973
d. $995

6. Sally Brown registered as an outpatient at the hospital for three encounters: chest X-ray, gait training physical therapy, and excision of lesion from right upper arm. Ambulatory patient classification (APC) reimbursement will be based on the

a. APC that provides the hospital with the highest reimbursement amount possible.

b. assignment of multiple APCs that reflect all services provided, with discounting.

c. calculation of four APC rates after codes are assigned to calculate the payment.

d. reimbursement determined by the APC that the primary care provider documents.

7. An *episode of care* in the home health prospective payment system (HHPPS) is _____ days.
   - a. 21
   - b. 30
   - c. 60
   - d. 90

8. In which year was the inpatient prospective payment system implemented?
   - a. 1973
   - b. 1976
   - c. 1983
   - d. 1986

9. Which type of hospital is excluded from the inpatient prospective payment system?
   - a. cancer
   - b. coronary
   - c. osteopathic
   - d. university

10. Which is the unit of payment for the inpatient prospective payment system?
    - a. episode of care
    - b. hospital admission
    - c. outpatient encounter
    - d. outpatient visit

11. Which is a relative value unit (RVU) in the Medicare physician fee schedule payment system?
    - a. geographic location
    - b. payroll expenditures
    - c. physician experience
    - d. practice expense

12. Medicare Part B radiology services payments are based on the
    - a. cost of supplies.
    - b. place of service.
    - c. relative value units.
    - d. time with the patient.

13. The physician fee schedule for CPT code 99214 is $75. Calculate the nonPAR *limiting charge* for this service.
    - a. $56.25
    - b. $71.25
    - c. $75.00
    - d. $81.94

14. The physician fee schedule for CPT code 99214 is $75. Calculate the nonPAR *allowed charge* for this service.
    - a. $56.25
    - b. $71.25
    - c. $75.00
    - d. $81.94

15. The intent of establishing a limiting charge for nonPARs is to
    - a. increase the patient case load of Medicare PARs.
    - b. offer financial protection for Medicare enrollees.
    - c. penalize providers who do not participate in Medicare.
    - d. reduce fraud and abuse of the Medicare system.

16. Jeffrey Border received care from his physician, who charged $300 for her services. (Mr. Border has already met his Medicare Part B deductible.) Mr. Border has primary coverage with his employer group health plan (EGHP). The EGHP's allowed charge for the service was $260, of which 80% was paid by the EGHP ($192). The Medicare physician fee schedule for the procedure is $240. Using the rules to determine the amount of Medicare secondary benefits, calculate the Medicare secondary payment.
    - a. $36
    - b. $48
    - c. $84
    - d. $108

17. Which is classified as a nonphysician practitioner?
    - a. laboratory technician
    - b. medical assistant
    - c. physician assistant
    - d. radiologic technologist

18. Which publication communicates new or changed policies and procedures that are being incorporated into a specific CMS manual?
    a. benefit policy manual
    b. coverage determinations manual
    c. program transmittal
    d. quarterly provider update

19. When an office-based service is performed in a health care facility, payment is affected by the use of
    a. additional CPT modifier(s).
    b. a case-mix adjustment.
    c. ICD9-CM procedure code(s).
    d. a site of service differential.

20. Medicare is primary to which insurance plan?
    a. BCBS EGHP
    b. homeowner liability insurance
    c. Medicaid
    d. workers' compensation

## CHAPTER 10

Coding for Medical Necessity

ASSIGNMENT 10.1 Choosing the First-Listed Diagnosis

OBJECTIVES

At the conclusion of this assignment, the student should be able to:

1. Define *first-listed diagnosis* as it is reported on the CMS-1500 claim.

2. Identify the first-listed diagnosis upon review of conditions, diagnoses, and signs or symptoms.

INSTRUCTIONS

Review each case and underline the first-listed diagnosis.

EXAMPLE: Patient was seen in the office to rule out cervical radiculopathy. Patient has a recent history of pain in both scapular regions along with spasms of the left upper trapezius muscle. Patient has limited range of motion, neck and left arm. X-rays reveal significant cervical osteoarthritis. FIRST-LISTED DIAGNOSIS: <u>Cervical osteoarthritis.</u>

NOTE: Do not select differentiated diagnoses, such as "rule out cervical radiculopathy," as the answer because such diagnoses are not coded and reported on the CMS-1500 claim for outpatient cases. Also, do not report symptoms such as spasms of the left upper trapezius muscle and limited range of motion, neck and left arm, because they are due to the cervical osteoarthritis that is reported as the first-listed diagnosis in block 21, #1, of the CMS-1500 claim.

1. Pain, left knee. History of injury to left knee 20 years ago. Patient underwent arthroscopic surgery and medial meniscectomy, right knee (10 years ago). Probable arthritis, left knee.

2. Patient admitted to the emergency department (ED) with complaints of severe chest pain. Possible myocardial infarction. EKG and cardiac enzymes revealed normal findings. Diagnosis upon discharge was gastroesophageal reflux disease.

3. Female patient seen in the office for follow-up of hypertension. The nurse noticed upper arm bruising on the patient and asked how she sustained the bruising. The physician renewed the patient's hypertension prescription, hydrochlorothiazide.

4. 10-year-old male seen in the office for sore throat. Nurse swabbed patient's throat and sent swabs to the hospital lab for strep test. Physician documented "likely strep throat" on the patient's record.

5. Patient was seen in the outpatient department to have a lump in his abdomen evaluated and removed. Surgeon removed the lump and pathology report revealed that the lump was a lipoma.

ASSIGNMENT 10.2 Linking Diagnoses with Procedures/Services

OBJECTIVES

At the conclusion of this assignment, the student should be able to:

1. Define *medical necessity*.
2. Link diagnoses with procedures/services to justify medical necessity.

INSTRUCTIONS

Match the diagnosis in the right-hand column with the procedure/service in the left-hand column that justifies medical necessity.

_____	1. allergy test	a. bronchial asthma
_____	2. EKG	b. chest pain
_____	3. inhalation treatment	c. family history, cervical cancer
_____	4. Pap smear	d. fractured wrist
_____	5. removal of ear wax	e. hay fever
_____	6. sigmoidoscopy	f. hematuria
_____	7. strep test	g. impacted cerumen
_____	8. urinalysis	h. jaundice
_____	9. venipuncture	i. rectal bleeding
_____	10. X-ray, radius and ulna	j. sore throat

ASSIGNMENT 10.3 National Coverage Determinations

OBJECTIVES

At the conclusion of this assignment, the student should be able to:

1. Define *national coverage determinations*.
2. Locate national coverage determination policies at the CMS Web site.
3. Interpret national coverage determination policies to determine whether Medicare will reimburse for procedures/services provided.

INSTRUCTIONS

Assign ICD (diagnosis) and CPT or HCPCS (procedure/service) codes to the following outpatient scenarios. (Do *not* assign ICD procedure codes.) Go to http://www.cms.hhs.gov/mcd, click the **Indexes** link, and click on the National Coverage Determinations (NCDs) alphabetical listing link to determine whether medical necessity requirements were met for each case.

1. A 65-year-old white female underwent apheresis of red blood cells for the treatment of Guillain-Barré syndrome.

2. A 70-year-old male underwent blood glucose testing to monitor his diabetes mellitus.

3. A 45-year-old disabled female underwent gastric bypass surgery for severe obesity. The patient also has hypertension and uncontrolled diabetes mellitus.

4. A 75-year-old female participated in a cardiac rehabilitation program for three months immediately following inpatient hospital discharge for an initial acute myocardial infarction. (Cardiac rehabilitation was provided by a nurse practitioner.)

5. A 72-year-old female underwent her annual screening mammogram, bilateral.

ASSIGNMENT 10.4 Coding from Case Scenarios

OBJECTIVES

At the conclusion of this assignment, the student should be able to:

1. Select diagnoses, procedures, and services upon review of case scenarios.

2. Assign ICD-9-CM, CPT, and HCPCS level II national codes (and appropriate modifiers) to diagnoses, procedures, and services.

INSTRUCTIONS

Assign ICD codes to diagnoses and CPT or HCPCS level II national codes to procedures and services in each case scenario. Be sure to report CPT and HCPCS modifiers where appropriate.

1. A 35-year-old established patient came to the office for excessive menstruation and irregular menstrual cycle. The physician performed an expanded problem focused evaluation and cervical biopsy.

   CPT Codes   **ICD-9 Codes**

   _____   _____

2. Patient was referred to me by his primary care physician, Dr. Pearson, because of severe back pain. Dr. Pearson feels he should have surgery, but the patient states the pain is relieved by regular chiropractic care and doesn't want to have back surgery. After a problem focused examination and a complete radiologic examination of the lumbosacral spine, including bending views, I consulted with Dr. Pearson and concluded the patient's degenerative disc disease is probably doing as well with a chiropractor as with orthopedic treatment. I did not recommend surgery at this time.

   CPT Codes   **ICD-9 Codes**

   _____   _____

3. Patient underwent a barium enema which included air contrast. The request form noted severe abdominal pain and diarrhea for the past two weeks. The radiology impression was diverticulitis of the colon.

CPT Codes   ICD-9 Codes

_____   _____

4. Patient presented for follow-up of COPD. At this time the patient is experiencing no significant cough, no sputum, no fever, and no respiratory distress. However, there is dyspnea only with exertion, which is accompanied by angina. A detailed examination was performed and the physician spent approximately 25 minutes with the patient. Chest is clear, no wheeze or rales. Chest X-rays, frontal and lateral, were taken to determine status of COPD. No additional treatment is required at this time.

CPT Codes   ICD-9 Codes

_____   _____

5. A surgeon is called to the hospital by the emergency department physician to see a 59-year-old male who presented with an abdominal mass, left lower quadrant. The surgeon performed a comprehensive examination, admitted the patient, and scheduled an exploratory laparotomy.

CPT Codes   ICD-9 Codes

_____   _____

ASSIGNMENT 10.5 Coding from SOAP Notes and Operative Reports

OBJECTIVES

At the conclusion of this assignment, the student should be able to:

1. Interpret SOAP notes and the contents of operative reports to identify diagnoses, procedures, and services that should be reported on the CMS-1500 claim.

2. Assign ICD-9-CM, CPT, and HCPCS level II national codes to diagnoses, procedures, and services.

INSTRUCTIONS

Review the following SOAP notes and operative reports to select the diagnoses, procedures, and services that should be reported on the CMS-1500 claim. Then assign ICD-9-CM codes to diagnoses and CPT or HCPCS codes (and appropriate modifiers) to procedures and services. (The level of service is indicated for each visit.)

1. **CASE STUDY #1**

   S: This new patient was seen today in the GI clinic for a level 2 visit. She complains of one week of severe epigastric pain and burning, especially after eating.

   O: On examination there is extreme guarding and tenderness, epigastric region, with no rebound. Bowel sounds are normal. BP 110/70.

   A: R/O gastric ulcer.

   P: Patient is to have upper gastrointestinal series. Start on Zantac and eliminate alcohol, fried foods, and caffeine. Return to clinic in one week.

   CPT Code(s)   ICD-9 Code(s)

   _____   _____

2. CASE STUDY #2

S: Patient returns to the clinic for a level 2 visit after undergoing an upper gastrointestinal series. She states she is still experiencing epigastric pain.

O: Upper gastrointestinal series revealed areas of ulceration.

A: Acute gastric ulcer.

P: Omeprazole 10 mg q.d. Return for follow-up visit in 3 weeks.

CPT Code(s)   **ICD-9 Code(s)**

_____   _____

3. CASE STUDY #3

S: Patient was seen in the orthopedic clinic today for an urgent level 3 visit. Patient was walking up his driveway when he slipped and fell, landing on his left arm and striking his head against the car. He was unconscious for less than 10 minutes, experienced dizziness and vomiting, and felt severe pain in his left arm. The patient's wife was actually coming here today for follow-up of her rheumatoid arthritis, and asked that we evaluate her husband's injuries.

O: Examination of the head reveals a 2.5-cm superficial laceration of the scalp, temporal region, left side. Examination of the left arm reveals restriction of motion and acute pain upon palpation and with attempted range of motion of the upper arm and shoulder. The patient underwent a skull X-ray to rule out fracture and X-ray of the left arm and shoulder for evaluation of the pain. The patient was taken to the radiography department where X-ray was negative for skull fracture, revealing only swelling in the area of the laceration. An X-ray of the left arm and shoulder, however, revealed an undisplaced fracture of the proximal left humerus at the greater tuberosity.

A: Concussion. Superficial laceration of scalp, 2.5 cm. Undisplaced fracture proximal left humerus at the greater tuberosity.

P: The patient underwent simple repair of the scalp laceration with sutures. The left arm was manipulated slightly to achieve proper anatomic alignment of the proximal humerus. The arm and shoulder were immobilized with sling and binder. The patient was given pain medication, and the patient's wife was instructed on how to perform neuro checks every 2 hours on the patient for the next 24 hours. The patient will be seen back in the clinic in 2 days. The patient and wife were instructed to contact the office if any problems arise in the meantime.

CPT Code(s)   **ICD-9 Code(s)**

_____   _____

4. CASE STUDY #4

S: This established patient was seen today for a level 2 visit. The patient complains of rectal discomfort, rectal bleeding, and severe itching.

O: Rectal examination reveals multiple soft external hemorrhoids.

A: Multiple soft, thrombosed external hemorrhoids.

P: Suppositories are to be used after each bowel movement. The patient will return to the office in four weeks for reevaluation.

CPT Code(s)   **ICD-9 Code(s)**

_____   _____

          109

5. **CASE STUDY #5**

S: This 53-year-old new patient was seen today for a level 2 visit. The patient presents with complaints of polyuria, polydipsia, and weight loss.

O: Urinalysis by dip, automated, with microscopy reveals elevated glucose.

A: Possible diabetes.

P: The patient is to have a glucose tolerance test and return in three days for blood work results and applicable management of care.

CPT Code(s)	ICD-9 Code(s)

6. **CASE STUDY #6**

PREOPERATIVE DIAGNOSIS: Pterygium of the right eye

POSTOPERATIVE DIAGNOSIS: Pterygium of the right eye

PROCEDURE PERFORMED: Pterygium excision with conjunctival autograft of the right eye

ANESTHESIA: General endotracheal anesthesia

PROCEDURE: After the patient was prepped and draped in the usual sterile fashion, attention was directed to his right eye under the operating microscope. The area of the pterygium was viewed and an injection of lidocaine with Marcaine was placed subconjunctivally to infiltrate area of the pterygium and surrounding conjunctiva. Then, using a combination of sharp and blunt dissection with 57 Beaver blade Westcott scissors, the pterygium was lifted away from the cornea, making a plane to the cornea to achieve clarity to the cornea. Next, an area was marked with a hand-held cautery nasally through the conjunctiva. A muscle hook was inserted to identify the medial rectus muscle. Then, using Westcott scissors and .12, the head and body of the pterygium were removed noting where the medial rectus muscle was at all times. Cautery was used to achieve hemostasis. An area of conjunctiva superior to the area of the prior pterygium under the lid was isolated and an incision was made through the conjunctiva. This section of conjunctiva was then transposed and placed into position over the area of the prior pterygium, thus forming an autograft. This was sutured into place with multiple single 8-0 Vicryl sutures. The autograft was noted to be in good position. Hemostasis was noted to be well achieved. The cornea was noted to be smooth and clear in the area of the prior pterygium with the epithelial defect secondary to removal of the pterygium. Maxitrol drops were placed. The patient's eye was patched. The patient tolerated the procedure well without complications and is to follow up in our office tomorrow.

CPT Codes	ICD-9 Codes

7. **CASE STUDY #7**

PREOPERATIVE DIAGNOSIS: Subcutaneous mass, posterior scalp

POSTOPERATIVE DIAGNOSIS: Subcutaneous mass, posterior scalp

PROCEDURE PERFORMED: Excision, subcutaneous mass, posterior scalp

ANESTHESIA: General

PROCEDURE: After instillation of 1% Xylocaine, a transverse incision was made directly over this elongated posterior scalp lesion. Hemostasis was obtained with electrocautery and suture ligature. A fatty tumor was encountered and sharp dissection used in completely excising this lesion. Hemostasis was obtained with ties, suture ligatures, and electrocautery. The 3-cm lesion was removed in its entirety. The wound was irrigated and the incision closed in layers. The skin was closed with a running nylon suture for hemostasis.

CPT Codes   **ICD-9 Codes**

---

8. CASE STUDY #8

PREOPERATIVE DIAGNOSIS: Ventral hernia

POSTOPERATIVE DIAGNOSIS: Ventral hernia

PROCEDURE PERFORMED: Repair of ventral hernia with mesh

ANESTHESIA: General

PROCEDURE: The vertical midline incision was opened. Sharp and blunt dissection was used in defining the hernia sac. The hernia sac was opened and the fascia examined. The hernia defect was sizable. Careful inspection was utilized to uncover any additional adjacent fascial defects. Small defects were observed on both sides of the major hernia and were incorporated into the main hernia. The hernia sac was dissected free of the surrounding subcutaneous tissues and retained. Prolene mesh was then fashioned to size and sutured to one side with running #0 Prolene suture. Interrupted Prolene sutures were placed on the other side and tagged untied. The hernia sac was then sutured to the opposite side of the fascia with Vicryl suture. The Prolene sutures were passed through the interstices of the Prolene mesh and tied into place, insuring that the Prolene mesh was not placed under tension. Excess mesh was excised. Jackson-Pratt drains were placed, one on each side. Running subcutaneous suture utilizing Vicryl was placed, after which the skin was stapled.

CPT Codes   **ICD-9 Codes**

---

9. CASE STUDY #9

PREOPERATIVE DIAGNOSIS: Intermittent exotropia, alternating

fusion with decreased stereopsis

POSTOPERATIVE DIAGNOSIS: Intermittent exotropia, alternating

fusion with decreased stereopsis

PROCEDURE PERFORMED: Bilateral lateral rectus recession of 7.0 mm

ANESTHESIA: General endotracheal anesthesia

PROCEDURE: The patient was brought to the operating room and placed in supine position where she was prepped and draped in the usual sterile fashion for strabismus surgery. Both eyes were exposed to the surgical field. After adequate anesthesia, one drop of 2.5% Neosynephrine was placed in each eye for vasoconstriction. Forced ductions were performed on both eyes and the lateral rectus was found to be normal. An eye speculum was placed in the right eye and surgery was begun on the right eye. An inferotemporal fornix incision was performed. The right lateral rectus muscle was isolated on a muscle hook. The muscle insertion was isolated and checked ligaments were dissected back. After a series of muscle hook passes using the Steven's hook and finishing with two passes of a Green's hook, the right lateral rectus was isolated. The epimesium, as well as Tenon's capsule, was dissected from the muscle insertion and the checked ligaments were lysed. The muscle was imbricated on a 6-0 Vicryl suture with an S29 needle with locking bites at either end. The muscle was detached from the globe and a distance of 7.0 mm posterior to the insertion of the muscle was marked. The muscle was then reattached 7.0 mm posterior to the original insertion using a cross-swords technique. The conjunctiva was closed using two buried sutures. Attention was then turned to the left eye where an identical procedure was performed. At the end of the case the eyes seemed slightly exotropic in position in the anesthetized state. Bounce back tests were normal. Both eyes were dressed with Tetracaine drops and Maxitrol ointment. There were no complications. The patient tolerated the procedure well, was awakened from anesthesia without difficulty, and sent to the recovery room. The patient was instructed in the use of topical antibiotics and detailed postoperative instructions were provided. The patient will be followed up within a 48-hour period in my office.

CPT Codes   **ICD-9 Codes**

_____   _____

10. **CASE STUDY #10**

PREOPERATIVE DIAGNOSIS: Right trigger thumb

POSTOPERATIVE DIAGNOSIS: Right trigger thumb

OPERATION: Right trigger thumb release, midlateral incision technique

ANESTHESIA: Local digital block

ESTIMATED BLOOD LOSS: Minimal

DESCRIPTION OF PROCEDURE: A local digital block anesthetic was administered to allow the patient to actively flex the thumb after release. After exsanguination of the extremity, a tourniquet cuff on the right upper arm was inflated. A longitudinal skin incision was marked along the radial side of the metacarpophalangeal crease, approximately 1 cm from the midline and measuring 2.5 cm in length.

The skin incision was made with a # 15 blade scalpel. Care was taken to extend the incision only through the dermal layer, and skin hooks were used for retraction. Blunt dissection was performed to identify the radial digital nerve. The nerve was retracted away from the flexor tendon and protected throughout the procedure. Blunt dissection was continued to expose the first annular pulley and its boundaries. Retraction allowed full visualization of the pulley to perform the longitudinal release. The patient was asked to flex and extend the thumb to confirm the absence of triggering. The wound was irrigated, and the skin was closed with nonabsorbable suture. The patient tolerated the procedure well, and was discharged to the outpatient observation area in good condition.

CPT Codes   **ICD-9 Codes**

_____   _____

ASSIGNMENT 10.6 Multiple Choice Review

1. A physician documented a patient's history of pneumonia four months ago. How is this reported on the CMS-1500 claim?
   a. as the ICD-9-CM code for "status post pneumonia"
   b. by reporting modifier -25 with the appropriate E/M code
   c. the pneumonia history is not documented on the claim
   d. using an E/M code that reflects an extended evaluation

2. A secondary diagnosis is also known as a _____ condition.
   a. coexisting
   b. complicating
   c. reference
   d. verified

3. An acceptable reason to delay a documentation entry in the patient record is to
   a. authenticate provided services.
   b. change an erroneous entry.
   c. provide additional information.
   d. substantiate medical necessity.

4. Local coverage determinations (LCDs) contain
   a. auditing instructions.
   b. coding guidelines.
   c. noncovered codes.
   d. reimbursement rates.

5. For any procedure that is medically unnecessary, the patient must sign a(n)
   a. Advance Beneficiary Notice.
   b. Medicare Summary Notice.
   c. Release of Medical Information.
   d. Statement of Confidentiality.

6. The objective section of a SOAP note includes the
   a. chief complaint and the patient's description of the presenting problem.
   b. diagnostic statement and the physician's rationale for the diagnosis.
   c. documentation of measurable observations made during a physical exam.
   d. statement of the physician's future plans for work-up and management.

7. Which of the following belongs in the "review of systems" section of the history and physical examination report?
   a. Blood pressure 113/70; pulse 80 and regular; temperature 97.9; respiratory rate 18.
   b. No complaints of nausea, vomiting, diarrhea, bloody stools, reflux, or constipation.
   c. Patient has a long-standing history of atrial fibrillation and is on Coumadin therapy.
   d. The patient's mother died from leukemia when the patient was 25; father is living and well.

8. After a fall at home, a 77-year-old woman was brought to the emergency department by her daughter. The patient sustained a 2 cm laceration of the thigh and a small, 0.5 cm laceration of the wrist. The thigh wound was closed with sutures and the wrist laceration underwent butterfly closure. The patient was discharged from the emergency department in satisfactory condition.

   Select the appropriate CPT and HCPCS procedure code(s) and modifier(s) for this case.
   a. 12001, G0168-59
   b. 99281-25, 12001
   c. 99281-25, 12001, G0168-59
   d. 99281-25, 12001-59, G0168-59

9. A patient was seen in the physician's office with complaints of rapid heartbeat. The patient has no known history of cardiac problems. The physician ordered an electrolyte panel. After receiving the results, the physician ordered a repeat potassium level.

   Select the appropriate CPT code(s) and modifier(s) for this case.
   a. 80051, 84132
   b. 80051, 84132, 84132
   c. 80051, 84132-59
   d. 80051, 84132-91

10. A 42-year-old male was referred to an ophthalmologist for evaluation of two lesions of his left eye, and was scheduled for surgery a week after the evaluation. The patient presented for surgery, and was prepped and draped in the usual sterile fashion. The patient underwent two separate procedures: the first was excision of a chelazion of the left lower eyelid. The second procedure performed was biopsy of a lesion of the left upper eyelid.

Select the appropriate CPT code(s) and modifier(s) for this case.

a. 67800, 67810

b. 67800, 67810-59

c. 67800-E1, 67810-59-E2

d. 67800-E1, 67810-E2

11. A 58-year-old male presented for screening colonoscopy. The patient received premedication per protocol. The scope was inserted and advanced, but despite multiple attempts, could not pass beyond the splenic flexure. For the patient's comfort, the procedure was terminated.

Select the appropriate CPT code(s) and modifier(s) for this case.

a. 45330

b. 45330-21

c. 45378

d. 45378-52

12. A patient was admitted to the day surgery unit to undergo a laparoscopic cholecystectomy. The patient was prepped and draped in the usual sterile fashion for laparoscopy. Upon laparoscopic examination, the patient's gallbladder was noted to be extremely friable, and there was also question of obstruction or torsion of the common bile duct. The decision was made to perform an open cholecystectomy. The patient still had excellent general anesthetic response and the open procedure was begun. The gallbladder was removed without much difficulty. The surgeon also performed exploration of the common bile duct and although it had appeared abnormal under laparoscopic viewing, the common bile duct was normal and free of stone or obstruction. The patient tolerated the procedure well.

Select the appropriate CPT code for this case.

a. 47562-57

b. 47562

c. 47600

d. 47610

13. The patient was seen by General Surgery and scheduled for removal of a worrisome lump behind the right knee. The patient stated he had no idea how long it had been there; he noticed it while trying to "rub out" a cramp of his calf muscle. The patient underwent excision of what was identified as a Baker's cyst of the left popliteal fossa. The patient tolerated the procedure well, and was understandably relieved by the definitive benign diagnosis.

Select the appropriate CPT code for this case.

a. 27334

b. 27345

c. 27347

d. 27360

14. HISTORY: The patient is a very vibrant 82-year-old woman seen today for routine physical examination. She states she has been very busy with local travel with her seniors group and also with spending time with her grandchildren and great-grandchildren. She is status post CABG six years ago and is doing wonderfully. Her only complaint today is that of arthritis of the left hip, which she manages with an over-the-counter anti-inflammatory. She is conscientious about taking the tablets with food or milk to prevent stomach irritation. Otherwise, she is well. REVIEW OF SYSTEMS: Essentially unchanged since last visit. EXAMINATION:

HEENT: PERRLA. Neck: Clear. Chest: No wheezes, rubs, or rhonchi. Heart: Regular rate and rhythm, with no murmurs. Abdomen: Soft, flat, without hepatosplenomegaly or tenderness. Pelvic: Not performed today. Rectal: Not performed today. Extremities: There are varicosities of both lower extremities which are nontender, otherwise unremarkable. Neurologic: Cranial nerves II through XII are intact. The patient amazingly does not require glasses and has good hearing. ASSESSMENT: Delightful, healthy 82-year-old female with osteoarthritis of the left hip, essentially unchanged. PLAN: The patient will return in six months for routine evaluation; sooner if problems arise.

Select the appropriate CPT code for this case.

a. 99201   c. 99211

b. 99202   d. 99212

15. The patient is a 40-year-old male who is known to me and was seen in the office today on an urgent basis because he believed he had collapsed his right lung. He has a history of collapsed lung and was confident it had happened again. On examination, the patient's breath sounds on the right were nonexistent. An emergency two-view (frontal and lateral) chest X-ray was performed which demonstrated the collapsed lung on the right. The patient was sent to the local hospital emergency department. The on-call surgeon was contacted and met the patient in the emergency department, where she performed a right tube thoracoscopy.

Select the appropriate CPT code(s) and modifier(s) for the office visit only for this case.

a. 99212-57, 71020   c. 99241, 71020

b. 99213-57, 71020   d. 99281, 71020

16. The patient presents to the office after a five-year absence with complaints of abdominal pain, diarrhea, and rectal bleeding which began three weeks ago. A detailed examination revealed a tense abdomen with some guarding in the right upper quadrant. The patient is to be scheduled for a flexible sigmoidoscopy to rule out colon cancer.

Select the appropriate CPT code(s) and modifier(s) for this case.

a. 99202   c. 99203

b. 99202-57   d. 99203-57

17. On 08/12/YY, a patient underwent an exploratory laparotomy, left partial hepatic resection for malignant hepatoma, and a cholecystectomy.

Select the CPT code for the first-listed procedure in this case.

a. 47120   c. 47125

b. 47122   d. 47141

18. A 65-year-old patient underwent bronchoscopy and biopsy for a left lower lobe lung mass. The biopsy was sent to pathology immediately and revealed adenocarcinoma of the left lower lobe. The patient then underwent a left lower lobectomy and thoracic lymphadenopathy.

Select the CPT code for the first-listed procedure in this case.

a. 31625   c. 32663

b. 32480   d. 38746

19. A 33-year-old patient with a strong family history of breast cancer underwent excision of a right breast mass in the outpatient surgery center. The pathology report was returned immediately and revealed a malignant neoplasm, central portion of the right breast. The patient then underwent a right modified radical mastectomy.

Select the CPT code for the first-listed procedure in this case.

a. 19160

b. 19160-58

c. 19240

d. 19240-78

20. An 80-year-old patient was admitted to the outpatient surgery center for dilation of a urethral stricture with insertion of urethral stent. A cystourethroscope was inserted through the urethral meatus and advanced through the urethra into the bladder. It was able to pass through the site of stricture successfully, although with some difficulty. Examination of the urethra showed the area of stricture. Examination of the bladder revealed the bladder appeared to be essentially unremarkable. A urethral stent was introduced into the urethra and placed at the point of stricture. Improved urinary flow was immediately noted. The procedure was concluded and the patient tolerated the procedure well.

Select the CPT code for the first-listed procedure in this case.

a. 52000

b. 52005

c. 52281

d. 52282

## CHAPTER 11

Essential CMS-1500 Claim Instructions

INTRODUCTION

This chapter familiarizes students with special instructions that apply to completion of CMS-1500 claim forms.

ASSIGNMENT 11.1 Optical Scanning Guidelines

OBJECTIVES

At the conclusion of this assignment, the student should be able to:

1. List and explain optical scanning guidelines used when completing CMS-1500 claim forms.

2. Apply optical scanning guidelines to the completion of CMS-1500 claim forms.

INSTRUCTIONS

Circle the optical scanning errors found on the Stanley L. Fruit, Jr., CMS-1500 claim found on the next page. Go to the back of the workbook for removable blank CMS-1500 claim forms, or print blank CMS-1500 claim forms using the textbook CD-ROM, and enter the Stanley L. Fruit, Jr., claims data correctly.

ASSIGNMENT 11.2 Entering Diagnoses and Procedures on the CMS-1500 Claim Form

OBJECTIVES

At the conclusion of this assignment, the student should be able to:

1. Assign ICD-9-CM diagnosis and CPT or HCPCS procedure/service codes.

2. Enter diagnosis and procedure/service codes on a CMS-1500 claim form using optical scanning guidelines.

PLEASE
DO NOT
STAPLE
IN THIS
AREA

Case Study 11-a

CARRIER

PICA	**HEALTH INSURANCE CLAIM FORM**	PICA

1. MEDICARE	MEDICAID	CHAMPUS	CHAMPVA	GROUP HEALTH PLAN	FECA BLK LUNG	OTHER	1a. INSURED'S I.D. NUMBER	(FOR PROGRAM IN ITEM 1)
☐ (Medicare #)	☐ (Medicaid #)	☐ (Sponsor's SSN)	☐ (VA File #)	☐ (SSN or ID)	☐ (SSN)	☒ (ID)	017-09-1234	

2. PATIENT'S NAME (Last Name, First Name, Middle Initial)	3. PATIENT'S BIRTH DATE	SEX	4. INSURED'S NAME (Last Name, First Name, Middle Initial)
STANLEY L. FRUIT JR.	MM 7 DD 15 YY 1954	M ☒ F ☐	SAME

5. PATIENT'S ADDRESS (No. Street)	6. PATIENT RELATIONSHIP TO INSURED	7. INSURED'S ADDRESS (No. Street)
25 S. HANSON ST.	Self ☒ Spouse ☐ Child ☐ Other ☐	SAME

CITY	STATE	8. PATIENT STATUS	CITY	STATE
ANYWHERE	US	Single ☒ Married ☐ Other ☐		

ZIP CODE	TELEPHONE (Include Area Code)		ZIP CODE	TELEPHONE (INCLUDE AREA CODE)
12345	(101) 112-2222	Employed ☒ Full-Time Student ☐ Part-Time Student ☐		( )

9. OTHER INSURED'S NAME (Last Name, First Name, Middle Initial)	10. IS PATIENT'S CONDITION RELATED TO:	11. INSURED'S POLICY GROUP OR FECA NUMBER
None		FED 101

a. OTHER INSURED'S POLICY OR GROUP NUMBER	a. EMPLOYMENT? (CURRENT OR PREVIOUS)	a. INSURED'S DATE OF BIRTH MM DD YY	SEX
	☐ YES ☒ NO		M ☐ F ☐

b. OTHER INSURED'S DATE OF BIRTH MM DD YY	SEX	b. AUTO ACCIDENT? PLACE (State)	b. EMPLOYER'S NAME OR SCHOOL NAME
	M ☐ F ☐	☐ YES ☒ NO	U.S. POSTAL SERVICE

c. EMPLOYER'S NAME OR SCHOOL NAME	c. OTHER ACCIDENT?	c. INSURANCE PLAN NAME OR PROGRAM NAME
	☐ YES ☒ NO	MAILHANDLERS

d. INSURANCE PLAN NAME OR PROGRAM NAME	10d. RESERVED FOR LOCAL USE	d. IS THERE ANOTHER HEALTH BENEFIT PLAN?
		☐ YES ☒ NO If yes, return to and complete item 9 a – d.

READ BACK OF FORM BEFORE COMPLETING & SIGNING THIS FORM.

12. PATIENT'S OR AUTHORIZED PERSON'S SIGNATURE I authorize the release of any medical or other information necessary to process this claim. I also request payment of government benefits either to myself or to the party who accepts assignment below.

SIGNED **SIGNATURE ON FILE**   DATE _____

13. INSURED'S OR AUTHORIZED PERSON'S SIGNATURE I authorize payment of medical benefits to the undersigned physician or supplier for services described below.

SIGNED **SIGNATURE ON FILE**

PATIENT AND INSURED INFORMATION

14. DATE OF CURRENT: MM DD YY ILLNESS (First symptom) OR INJURY (Accident) OR PREGNANCY (LMP)	15. IF PATIENT HAS HAD SAME OR SIMILAR ILLNESS, GIVE FIRST DATE MM DD YY	16. DATES PATIENT UNABLE TO WORK IN CURRENT OCCUPATION FROM MM DD YY TO MM DD YY

17. NAME OF REFERRING PHYSICIAN OR OTHER SOURCE	17a. I.D. NUMBER OF REFERRING PHYSICIAN	18. HOSPITALIZATION DATES RELATED TO CURRENT SERVICES FROM MM DD YY TO MM DD YY

19. RESERVED FOR LOCAL USE	20. OUTSIDE LAB? $ CHARGES
	☐ YES ☒ NO

21. DIAGNOSIS OR NATURE OF ILLNESS OR INJURY. (RELATE ITEMS 1, 2, 3, OR 4 TO ITEM 24E BY LINE)	22. MEDICAID RESUBMISSION CODE ORIGINAL REF. NO.
1. 782.0 3. ___ . ___	
2. 788.41 4. ___ . ___	23. PRIOR AUTHORIZATION NUMBER

24. A. DATE(S) OF SERVICE From MM DD YY To MM DD YY	B. Place of Service	C. Type of Service	D. PROCEDURES, SERVICES, OR SUPPLIES (Explain Unusual Circumstances) CPT/HCPCS MODIFIER	E. DIAGNOSIS CODE	F. $ CHARGES	G. DAYS OR UNITS	H. EPSDT Family Plan	I. EMG	J. COB	K. RESERVED FOR LOCAL USE
1	6 7 YYYY		11	99213	782.0	$ 60 00	1				
2											
3	6 7 YYYY		11	81001	788.41	$ 10 00	1				
4											
5											
6											

25. FEDERAL TAX I.D. NUMBER	SSN	EIN	26. PATIENT'S ACCOUNT NO.	27. ACCEPT ASSIGNMENT? (For govt. claims, see back)	28. TOTAL CHARGE	29. AMOUNT PAID	30. BALANCE DUE
11-1234567	☐	☒	11-a	☐ YES ☒ NO	$ 70 00	$	$ 70 00

31. SIGNATURE OF PHYSICIAN OR SUPPLIER INCLUDING DEGREES OR CREDENTIALS (I certify that the statements on the reverse apply to this bill and are made a part thereof.)	32. NAME AND ADDRESS OF FACILITY WHERE SERVICES WERE RENDERED (If other than home or office)	33. PHYSICIAN'S, SUPPLIER'S BILLING NAME, ADDRESS, ZIP CODE & PHONE #
R.K. PAINFREE, M.D. SIGNED DATE MMDDYYYY		GOODMEDICINE CLINIC PIN# GRP#

PHYSICIAN OR SUPPLIER INFORMATION

INSTRUCTIONS

Refer to the optical scanning guidelines in the textbook to complete blocks 21 and 24A through 24G of the CMS-1500 claim for case studies 11-b and 11-c. Go to the back of the workbook for removable blank CMS-1500 claim forms, or print blank CMS-1500 claim forms using the textbook CD-ROM, and enter the data correctly.

NOTE: Complete only blocks 21 and 24A through 24G of the CMS–1500 claim form.

DONALD L. GIVINGS, M.D.

11350 Medical Drive ■ Anywhere US 12345 ■ (101) 111-5555
EIN: 11-1234562

Case Study 11-b

PATIENT INFORMATION:

Name:	Jane Normal
Address:	534 Robin St.
City:	Anywhere
State:	US
Zip Code:	12345
Telephone:	(410) 123-1234
Gender:	Female
Date of Birth:	02-07-1953
Occupation:	
Employer:	Dress Barn
Spouse's Employer:	

INSURANCE INFORMATION:

Patient Number:	11-b
Place of Service:	Office
Primary Insurance Plan:	Metropolitan
Primary Insurance Plan ID #:	121-01-2179
Group #:	C26
Primary Policyholder:	Jane Normal
Policyholder Date of Birth:	02-07-1953
Relationship to Patient:	Self
Secondary Insurance Plan:	
Secondary Insurance Plan ID #:	
Secondary Policyholder:	

Patient Status ☒ Married ☐ Divorced ☐ Single ☐ Student ☐ Other

---

DIAGNOSIS INFORMATION

Diagnosis	Code	Diagnosis	Code
1. Sinusitis, frontal		5.	
2.		6.	
3.		7.	
4.		8.	

PROCEDURE INFORMATION

Description of Procedure or Service	Date	Code	Charge
1. Established patient OV level II	02-05-YYYY		$65.00
2.			
3.			
4.			
5.			

SPECIAL NOTES:

Return visit: PRN

DONALD L. GIVINGS, M.D.

11350 Medical Drive ■ Anywhere US 12345 ■ (101) 111-5555

EIN: 11-1234562

Case Study 11-c

PATIENT INFORMATION:

Name:	Thomas J. Meekes
Address:	39567 Aliceville Rd.
City:	Anywhere
State:	US
Zip Code:	12345
Telephone:	(101) 333-4444
Gender:	Male
Date of Birth:	12-10-1949
Occupation:	
Employer:	Western Auto
Spouse's Employer:	

INSURANCE INFORMATION:

Patient Number:	11-c
Place of Service:	Mercy Hospital
Primary Insurance Plan:	Atlantic Plus
Primary Insurance Plan ID #:	411-44-1111
Group #:	J276
Primary Policyholder:	Thomas J. Meekes
Policyholder Date of Birth:	12-10-1949
Relationship to Patient:	Self
Secondary Insurance Plan:	
Secondary Insurance Plan ID #:	
Secondary Policyholder:	

Patient Status ☒ Married ☐ Divorced ☐ Single ☐ Student ☐ Other

DIAGNOSIS INFORMATION

Diagnosis	Code	Diagnosis	Code
1. Bronchial Pneumonia		5.	
2.		6.	
3.		7.	
4.		8.	

PROCEDURE INFORMATION

Description of Procedure or Service	Date	Code	Charge
1. Initial Hospital Care Level I	08-09-YYYY		$75.00
2. Subsequent Hospital Care Level I	08-10-YYYY		50.00
3. Subsequent Hospital Care Level I	08-11-YYYY		50.00
4. Subsequent Hospital Care Level I	08-12-YYYY		50.00
5. Discharge, 30 min.	08-13-YYYY		75.00

SPECIAL NOTES:

Pt will call to set up appointment within one week

1. HIPAA privacy standards require providers to notify patients about their right to
   a. appeal.
   b. care.
   c. confidentiality.
   d. privacy.

2. Development of an insurance claim begins when the
   a. health insurance specialist reviews the encounter form for CPT codes.
   b. patient contacts the provider's office and schedules an appointment.
   c. patient pays his or her share of the treatment costs (e.g., the coinsurance).
   d. provider completes the patient's history and physical examination.

3. Which of the following is true?
   a. An inpatient admission can be converted to outpatient observation care.
   b. If a patient is admitted after observation, the charges are billed separately.
   c. Outpatient observation care can be converted to inpatient admission.
   d. Outpatient observation services are the same as critical care services.

4. When a fee submitted to an insurance company is higher than the health care provider's normal fee for the coded procedure, the provider must
   a. attach a letter to the claim explaining the rationale for the higher charge.
   b. report modifier -59 to the administrative contractor for appropriate payment.
   c. request documentation from the patient to prove consent for the procedure.
   d. submit the claim directly to CMS for review and payment consideration.

5. Optical character reader (OCR) guidelines were established when the
   a. Balanced Budget Act was passed.
   b. CMS-1500 claim form was developed.
   c. HCFA changed to CMS in 2001.
   d. HIPAA legislation was passed.

6. When typewritten data in a CMS-1500 claim form runs over into adjacent blocks, the claim will be
   a. corrected by the payer and processed.
   b. rejected and returned to the provider.
   c. reviewed manually and sent to the payer.
   d. sent to the patient with a denial letter.

7. Which is the correct way to enter the amount of $125.75 on the CMS-1500 claim form?
   a. $125.75
   b. 125.75
   c. $125 75
   d. 125 75

8. A patient's name on the insurance card reads Marvin L. Blue III. How is this entered on the CMS-1500 claim form?
   a. BLUE III MARVIN L
   b. BLUE MARVIN L III
   c. MARVIN BLUE L III
   d. MARVIN L BLUE III

9. Which is the proper way to report a patient's birth date of June 16, 1967, on the CMS-1500 claim form?
   a. 06-16-67
   c. 06-16-1967
   b. 06 16 67
   d. 06 16 1967

10. Which is the proper way to prepare a rejected claim for resubmission?
    a. Correct the error and submit a photocopy of the corrected claim.
    b. Create the corrected claim on an original (red-print) claim form.
    c. Use whiteout on the original returned claim and resubmit the claim.
    d. Write the correction on the original claim and submit it manually.

11. You are a health insurance specialist and have printed a batch of claims from your computer onto pin-fed paper. Which is the next step to take before placing the claims in the envelope?
    a. Credit each patient account as paid in full.
    b. Make photocopies of the claims for payment.
    c. Remove page borders and separate each claim.
    d. Sign each claim for identification purposes.

12. Secondary diagnosis codes are reported on the CMS-1500 claim form if they
    a. justify the procedures/services listed in block 24.
    b. reflect a remote history of a costly medical condition.
    c. were not treated but provided for additional information.
    d. will result in a higher reimbursement rate for the claim.

13. Data is required by all payers in which block of the CMS-1500 claim form?
    a. block 24B
    c. block 9C
    b. block 24C
    d. block 9D

14. When more than one diagnosis reference number is reported on a CMS-1500 claim form, the first-listed code is the
    a. condition that has been treated most regularly.
    b. diagnosis with the highest reimbursement rate.
    c. illness most likely to require hospital admission.
    d. reason the patient sought care from the provider.

15. On 02/14/YYYY, a patient was sent to the radiology department for a three-view ankle X-ray. Which number is reported in block 24G?
    a. 1
    c. 3
    b. 2
    d. 4

16. A patient's nickname was entered as the first name on the CMS-1500 claim form. How is this handled by the health insurance specialist?
    a. Correct the nickname to the patient's full name and submit a new claim.
    b. Cross out the nickname, write in the full first name, and submit the claim.
    c. Erase the nickname, write in the full first name, and submit the claim.
    d. Submit the claim to the insurance company; nicknames are acceptable.

17. Remittance advice forms that are organized and filed according to month and payer are
    a. batched and fully paid claims.
    b. closed assigned cases.
    c. open assigned cases.
    d. unassigned/nonparticipating claims.

18. Which form is considered a source document?
    a. encounter form (or superbill)
    c. release of medical information
    b. patient registration form
    d. signed copy of privacy policy

19. The purpose of reporting the diagnosis reference numbers in block 24E is to
    a. conserve space on the CMS-1500 claim form in order to save paper.
    b. justify the medical necessity of the procedures/services performed.
    c. offer the payer a way to keep treatment statistics data for patients.
    d. provide the claims examiner with additional patient information.

20. What does an X in the YES box of block 27 indicate?
    a. The patient agrees to pay the charges in full.
    b. The patient will only see that provider for care.
    c. The payer will send reimbursement to the patient.
    d. The provider agrees to accept assignment.

CHAPTER 12

Commercial Insurance

INTRODUCTION

This chapter familiarizes students with completion of the CMS-1500 claim form for primary and secondary commercial payers.

ASSIGNMENT 12.1 Commercial Primary CMS-1500 Claims Completion

OBJECTIVES

At the conclusion of this assignment, the student should be able to:

1. Assign ICD-9-CM diagnosis and CPT or HCPCS procedure/service codes.
2. Prepare a commercial insurance primary payer CMS-1500 claim form.

INSTRUCTIONS

Use optical scanning guidelines to complete CMS-1500 claim forms for case studies 12-a through 12-e. Go to the back of the workbook for removable blank CMS-1500 claim forms or print blank CMS-1500 claim forms using the textbook CD-ROM. Refer to the CMS-1500 claims completion instructions (primary) in the textbook.

ASSIGNMENT 12.2 Commercial Secondary CMS-1500 Claims Completion

OBJECTIVES

At the conclusion of this assignment, the student should be able to:

1. Assign ICD-9-CM diagnosis and CPT or HCPCS procedure/service codes.
2. Prepare a commercial insurance secondary payer CMS-1500 claim form.

DONALD L. GIVINGS, M.D.

11350 Medical Drive ■ Anywhere US 12345 ■ (101) 111-5555

EIN: 11-1234562

Case Study 12-a

PATIENT INFORMATION:

Name:	Dawn L. Zapp
Address:	663 Hilltop Drive
City:	Anywhere
State:	US
Zip Code:	12345
Telephone:	(101) 333-4445
Gender:	Female
Date of Birth:	02-12-1967
Occupation:	
Employer:	Superfresh Foods
Spouse's Employer:	

INSURANCE INFORMATION:

Patient Number:	12-a
Place of Service:	Office
Primary Insurance Plan:	North West Health
Primary Insurance Plan ID #:	444-55-6666
Group #:	SF123
Primary Policyholder:	Dawn L. Zapp
Policyholder Date of Birth:	02-12-1967
Relationship to Patient:	Self
Secondary Insurance Plan:	
Secondary Insurance Plan ID #:	
Secondary Policyholder:	

Patient Status   ☐ Married   ☐ Divorced   ☒ Single   ☐ Student   ☐ Other

DIAGNOSIS INFORMATION

Diagnosis	Code	Diagnosis	Code
1. Headache, facial pain		5.	
2. Cough		6.	
3.		7.	
4.		8.	

PROCEDURE INFORMATION

Description of Procedure or Service	Date	Code	Charge
1. Est. patient OV level II	05-10-YYYY		$65.00
2.			
3.			
4.			
5.			

SPECIAL NOTES:

Return visit: 2 weeks

DONALD L. GIVINGS, M.D.

11350 Medical Drive ■ Anywhere US 12345 ■ (101) 111-5555
EIN: 11-1234562

Case Study 12-b

PATIENT INFORMATION:

Name:	Bethany L. Branch
Address:	401 Cartvalley Court
City:	Anywhere
State:	US
Zip Code:	12345
Telephone:	(101) 333-4466
Gender:	Female
Date of Birth:	05-03-1986
Occupation:	
Employer:	Gateway Computers Inc.
Spouse's Employer:	

INSURANCE INFORMATION:

Patient Number:	12-b
Place of Service:	Office
Primary Insurance Plan:	Metropolitan
Primary Insurance Plan ID #:	212-22-4545
Group #:	GW292
Primary Policyholder:	John L. Branch
Policyholder Date of Birth:	10-10-54
Relationship to Patient:	Father
Secondary Insurance Plan:	
Secondary Insurance Plan ID #:	
Secondary Policyholder:	

Patient Status   ☐ Married   ☐ Divorced   ☒ Single   ☐ Student   ☐ Other

DIAGNOSIS INFORMATION

Diagnosis	Code	Diagnosis	Code
1. Bronchitis		5.	
2. Strep throat		6.	
3.		7.	
4.		8.	

PROCEDURE INFORMATION

Description of Procedure or Service	Date	Code	Charge
1. Office consult level II	12-04-YYYY		$75.00
2. Quick strep test	12-04-YYYY		12.00
3.			
4.			
5.			

SPECIAL NOTES:
Return visit: PRN
Referring physician: James R. Feltbetter, M.D.
EIN: 77-7887878

DONALD L. GIVINGS, M.D.

11350 Medical Drive ■ Anywhere US 12345 ■ (101) 111-5555
EIN: 11-1234562

Case Study 12-c

PATIENT INFORMATION:

Name:	Laurie P. Reed
Address:	579 Vacation Drive
City:	Anywhere
State:	US
Zip Code:	12345
Telephone:	(101) 333-5555
Gender:	Female
Date of Birth:	06-05-1964
Occupation:	
Employer:	The Learning Center
Spouse's Employer:	

INSURANCE INFORMATION:

Patient Number:	12-c
Place of Service:	Office
Primary Insurance Plan:	US Health
Primary Insurance Plan ID #:	C748593
Group #:	TLC45
Primary Policyholder:	Laurie P. Reed
Policyholder Date of Birth:	06-05-1964
Relationship to Patient:	Self
Secondary Insurance Plan:	
Secondary Insurance Plan ID #:	
Secondary Policyholder:	

Patient Status   ☐ Married   ☐ Divorced   ☒ Single   ☐ Student   ☐ Other

DIAGNOSIS INFORMATION

Diagnosis	Code	Diagnosis	Code
1. Allergic rhinitis		5.	
2.		6.	
3.		7.	
4.		8.	

PROCEDURE INFORMATION

Description of Procedure or Service	Date	Code	Charge
1. Est. patient OV level II	10/28/YYYY		$55.00
2.			
3.			
4.			
5.			

SPECIAL NOTES:

Return visit: PRN

DONALD L. GIVINGS, M.D.

11350 Medical Drive ■ Anywhere US 12345 ■ (101) 111-5555
EIN: 11-1234562

Case Study 12-d

PATIENT INFORMATION:

Name:	Pamela Sharp
Address:	678 Heather Ave.
City:	Anywhere
State:	US
Zip Code:	12345
Telephone:	(101) 333-5559
Gender:	Female
Date of Birth:	05-09-1970
Occupation:	
Employer:	Design Consultants
Spouse's Employer:	

INSURANCE INFORMATION:

Patient Number:	12-d
Place of Service:	Inpatient hospital
Primary Insurance Plan:	Cigna
Primary Insurance Plan ID #:	123-66-6666
Group #:	DC22
Primary Policyholder:	Pamela Sharp
Policyholder Date of Birth:	05-09-1970
Relationship to Patient:	Self
Secondary Insurance Plan:	
Secondary Insurance Plan ID #:	
Secondary Policyholder:	

Patient Status	☐ Married	☐ Divorced	☒ Single	☐ Student	☐ Other

DIAGNOSIS INFORMATION

Diagnosis	Code	Diagnosis	Code
1. Chronic obstructive asthma		5.	
2. Bronchial pneumonia		6.	
3.		7.	
4.		8.	

PROCEDURE INFORMATION

Description of Procedure or Service	Date	Code	Charge
1. Initial hospital level I	06-28-YYYY		$75.00
2. Subsequent hospital level I	06-29-YYYY		50.00
3. Subsequent hospital level I	06-30-YYYY		50.00
4. Subsequent hospital level I	07-01-YYYY		50.00
5. Subsequent hospital level I	07-02-YYYY		50.00
6. Discharge, 30 min.	07-03-YYYY		75.00

SPECIAL NOTES:

Inpatient care provided at Mercy Hospital, Anywhere St., Anywhere US 12345.
Referring physician: Ledger Masters, M.D.
EIN: 59-5334959

DONALD L. GIVINGS, M.D.

11350 Medical Drive ■ Anywhere US 12345 ■ (101) 111-5555
EIN: 11-1234562

Case Study 12-e

PATIENT INFORMATION:

Name:	James R. Brandt
Address:	95 Commission Circle
City:	Anywhere
State:	US
Zip Code:	12345
Telephone:	(101) 223-5555
Gender:	Male
Date of Birth:	12-05-1948
Occupation:	
Employer:	The Yard Guard
Spouse's Employer:	

INSURANCE INFORMATION:

Patient Number:	12-e
Place of Service:	Office
Primary Insurance Plan:	Prudential
Primary Insurance Plan ID #:	555-66-7777
Group #:	YG4
Primary Policyholder:	James R. Brandt
Policyholder Date of Birth:	12-05-1948
Relationship to Patient:	Self
Secondary Insurance Plan:	
Secondary Insurance Plan ID #:	
Secondary Policyholder:	

Patient Status   ☐ Married   ☐ Divorced   ☒ Single   ☐ Student   ☐ Other

DIAGNOSIS INFORMATION

Diagnosis	Code	Diagnosis	Code
1. Diabetes, type II		5.	
2. Hypertension, benign		6.	
3. Gout		7.	
4.		8.	

PROCEDURE INFORMATION

Description of Procedure or Service	Date	Code	Charge
1. New patient OV level IV	02-02-YYYY		$100.00
2. EKG	02-02-YYYY		50.00
3. Blood glucose level	02-02-YYYY		10.00
4. Est. patient OV level III	02-03-YYYY		75.00
5. Blood glucose level	02-03-YYYY		10.00

SPECIAL NOTES:
Referring physician: Rita M. Michaels, M.D., EIN: 34-3547979
Onset 02/02/YYYY
Return visit: 2 weeks

INSTRUCTIONS

Use optical scanning guidelines to complete CMS-1500 claim forms for case studies 12-f through 12-j. Go to the back of the workbook for removable blank CMS-1500 claim forms or print blank CMS-1500 claim forms using the textbook CD-ROM. Refer to the CMS-1500 claims completion instructions (secondary) in the textbook.

ASSIGNMENT 12.3 Multiple Choice Review

1. Which is considered a commercial health insurance company?
   a. Medicaid
   b. Medicare
   c. Prudential
   d. TRICARE

2. Commercial insurance claims are generally paid on a _____ basis.
   a. capitated
   b. fee-for-service
   c. prepaid
   d. sliding-scale

3. A significant way in which commercial payers differ from Blue Cross/Blue Shield plans is that commercial payers
   a. do not make their billing manuals available.
   b. do not require use of the CMS-1500 claim form.
   c. have a higher physician reimbursement rate.
   d. will reimburse liability and auto insurance claims.

4. Logan is the daughter of Amy (DOB 3/29/68) and Bill (DOB 11/15/70), and is covered by both parents' health insurance plans. According to the birthday rule, a medical claim for Logan will be submitted to
   a. Amy's plan as primary payer and Bill's plan as secondary payer.
   b. Amy's plan only, as she is two years older than her husband.
   c. Bill's plan as primary payer and Amy's plan as secondary payer.
   d. Bill's plan only, as he has been employed with his company longer.

5. When the patient is the domestic partner of the primary policyholder, this is indicated on the CMS-1500 claim form by
   a. entering "DP" after the patient's name in block 2.
   b. entering the patient's full name in block 9.
   c. placing an X in the OTHER box of block 6.
   d. placing an X in the SINGLE box of block 8.

6. What must be submitted with the CMS-1500 claim in order for the commercial payer to consider payment on a liability claim?
   a. a copy of the patient's insurance card proving coverage for emergency care
   b. a remittance advice from the liable party indicating that the claim was denied
   c. a written report from the patient's primary care provider detailing the accident
   d. an explanation of benefits from the patient indicating that the claim was not paid

DONALD L. GIVINGS, M.D.

11350 Medical Drive ■ Anywhere US 12345 ■ (101) 111-5555
EIN: 11-1234562

Case Study 12-f

PATIENT INFORMATION:

Name:	Judy R. Hudnet
Address:	548 Dayton Terr.
City:	Anywhere
State:	US
Zip Code:	12345
Telephone:	(101) 333-5555
Gender:	Female
Date of Birth:	03-28-1950
Occupation:	Clerk
Employer:	Printers "R" Us
Spouse's Employer:	Alfred State College

INSURANCE INFORMATION:

Patient Number:	12-f
Place of Service:	Office
Primary Insurance Plan:	Great West
Primary Insurance Plan ID #:	21785
Group #:	
Primary Policyholder:	Judy R. Hudnet
Policyholder Date of Birth:	03-28-1950
Relationship to Patient:	Self
Secondary Insurance Plan:	Great West
Secondary Insurance Plan ID #:	57890
Secondary Policyholder:	Sam Hudnet

Patient Status ☒ Married ☐ Divorced ☐ Single ☐ Student ☐ Other

DIAGNOSIS INFORMATION

Diagnosis	Code	Diagnosis	Code
1. Incontinence of urine		5.	
2. Polyuria		6.	
3.		7.	
4.		8.	

PROCEDURE INFORMATION

Description of Procedure or Service	Date	Code	Charge
1. Est. patient OV level II	04-23-YYYY		$65.00
2. Urinalysis	04-23-YYYY		10.00
3.			
4.			
5.			

SPECIAL NOTES:

Patient referred to Dr. Stream.

Patient paid $10.00 toward today's bill.

PAUL R. STREAM, M.D., UROLOGY

456 Hospital Drive ■ Anywhere US 12345 ■ (101) 111-5555

EIN: 11-2233442

Case Study 12-g

PATIENT INFORMATION:

Name:	Judy R. Hudnet
Address:	548 Dayton Terr.
City:	Anywhere
State:	US
Zip Code:	12345
Telephone:	(101) 333-5555
Gender:	Female
Date of Birth:	03-28-1950
Occupation:	Clerk
Employer:	Printers "R" US
Spouse's Employer:	Alfred State College

INSURANCE INFORMATION:

Patient Number:	12-g
Place of Service:	Office
Primary Insurance Plan:	Great West
Primary Insurance Plan ID #:	21785
Group #:	
Primary Policyholder:	Judy R. Hudnet
Policyholder Date of Birth:	03-28-1950
Relationship to Patient:	Self
Secondary Insurance Plan:	Great West
Secondary Insurance Plan ID #:	57890
Secondary Policyholder:	Sam Hudnet

Patient Status ☒ Married   ☐ Divorced   ☐ Single   ☐ Student   ☐ Other

---

DIAGNOSIS INFORMATION

Diagnosis	Code	Diagnosis	Code
1. Incontinence of urine		5.	
2. Polyuria		6.	
3.		7.	
4.		8.	

PROCEDURE INFORMATION

Description of Procedure or Service	Date	Code	Charge
1. Office consultation level III	05-12-YYYY		$85.00
2. Urinalysis, with microscopy	05-12-YYYY		10.00
3.			
4.			
5.			

SPECIAL NOTES:
Referring physician: Donald L. Givings, M.D., SSN: 123-12-1234
Patient to be scheduled at St. John's Hospital for surgery.
Onset of symptoms 4/23/YYYY

PAUL R. STREAM, M.D., UROLOGY

456 Hospital Drive ■ Anywhere US 12345 ■ (101) 111-5555

EIN: 11-2233442

Case Study 12-h

PATIENT INFORMATION:

Name:	Judy R. Hudnet
Address:	548 Dayton Terr.
City:	Anywhere
State:	US
Zip Code:	12345
Telephone:	(101) 333-5555
Gender:	Female
Date of Birth:	03-28-1950
Occupation:	Clerk
Employer:	Printers "R" US
Spouse's Employer:	Alfred State College

INSURANCE INFORMATION:

Patient Number:	12-h
Place of Service:	St. John's Hospital (Outpatient)
Primary Insurance Plan:	Great West
Primary Insurance Plan ID #:	21785
Group #:	
Primary Policyholder:	Judy R. Hudnet
Policyholder Date of Birth:	03-28-1950
Relationship to Patient:	Self
Secondary Insurance Plan:	Great West
Secondary Insurance Plan ID #:	57890
Secondary Policyholder:	Sam Hudnet

Patient Status   ☒ Married   ☐ Divorced   ☐ Single   ☐ Student   ☐ Other

DIAGNOSIS INFORMATION

Diagnosis	Code	Diagnosis	Code
1. Bladder tumor, anterior wall		5.	
2.		6.	
3.		7.	
4.		8.	

PROCEDURE INFORMATION

Description of Procedure or Service	Date	Code	Charge
1. Cystourethroscopy w/ fulguration of 3.0 cm bladder tumor	05-19-YYYY		$1200.00
2.			
3.			
4.			
5.			

SPECIAL NOTES:
St. John's Hospital, 456 Hospital Drive, Anywhere US 12345.
Referring physician: Donald L. Givings, M.D., EIN: 11-1234562.
Onset of symptoms: 05-01-YYYY.

DONALD L. GIVINGS, M.D.

11350 Medical Drive ■ Anywhere US 12345 ■ (101) 111-5555
EIN: 11-1234562

Case Study 12-i

PATIENT INFORMATION:

Name:	Ben A. Hanson
Address:	632 Greenvalley Ct.
City:	Anywhere
State:	US
Zip Code:	12345
Telephone:	(101) 223-5555
Gender:	Male
Date of Birth:	08-09-1975
Occupation:	Plumber
Employer:	Ace Plumbing Service
Spouse's Employer:	Dew Drop Inn

INSURANCE INFORMATION:

Patient Number:	12-i
Place of Service:	Office
Primary Insurance Plan:	Guardian
Primary Insurance Plan ID #:	334-55-8686
Group #:	4596
Primary Policyholder:	Ben A. Hanson
Policyholder Date of Birth:	08-09-1975
Relationship to Patient:	Self
Secondary Insurance Plan:	Liberty Mutual
Secondary Insurance Plan ID #:	334-88-7788 #DD12
Secondary Policyholder:	Joy M. Hanson
Secondary Policyholder DOB:	10-10-1977

Patient Status   ☒ Married   ☐ Divorced   ☐ Single   ☐ Student   ☐ Other

DIAGNOSIS INFORMATION

Diagnosis	Code	Diagnosis	Code
1. Painful respiration		5.	
2. Chest tightness		6.	
3.		7.	
4.		8.	

PROCEDURE INFORMATION

Description of Procedure or Service	Date	Code	Charge
1. Est. patient OV level III	09-03-YYYY		$75.00
2. EKG	09-03-YYYY		50.00
3.			
4.			
5.			

SPECIAL NOTES:

Return visit: 2 weeks after seeing Dr. Hart

STANLEY M. HART, M.D. CARDIOLOGY

316 Grace Way, Suite 102 ■ Anywhere US 12345 ■ (101) 111-5555

EIN: 11-7856782

Case Study 12-j

PATIENT INFORMATION:

Name:	Ben A. Hanson
Address:	632 Greenvalley Ct.
City:	Anywhere
State:	US
Zip Code:	12345
Telephone:	(101) 223-5555
Gender:	Male
Date of Birth:	08-09-1975
Occupation:	
Employer:	Ace Plumbing Service
Spouse's Employer:	Dew Drop Inn

INSURANCE INFORMATION:

Patient Number:	12-j
Place of Service:	Office
Primary Insurance Plan:	Guardian
Primary Insurance Plan ID #:	334-55-8686
Group #:	4596
Primary Policyholder:	Ben A. Hanson
Policyholder Date of Birth:	08-09-1975
Relationship to Patient:	Self
Secondary Insurance Plan:	Liberty Mutual
Secondary Insurance Plan ID #:	334-88-7788 #DD12
Secondary Policyholder:	Joy M. Hanson
Secondary Policyholder DOB:	10-10-1977

Patient Status   ☒ Married   ☐ Divorced   ☐ Single   ☐ Student   ☐ Other

DIAGNOSIS INFORMATION

Diagnosis	Code	Diagnosis	Code
1. Painful respiration		5.	
2. Chest tightness		6.	
3. Abnormal chest sounds		7.	
4.		8.	

PROCEDURE INFORMATION

Description of Procedure or Service	Date	Code	Charge
1. Office consult level II	09-04-YYYY		$ 75.00
2. Cardiovascular stress test, with interpretation and report	09-04-YYYY		150.00
3.			
4.			
5.			

SPECIAL NOTES:

Referring physician: Donald L. Givings, M.D. SSN: 123-12-1234.
Return visit: PRN

7. The patient was seen in the provider's office on 12/03/YYYY. The patient's history reflects that the patient was injured four months earlier. What is entered in block 14 of the CMS-1500 claim form?

    a. 04 03 2006
    b. 08 03 2006
    c. 11 03 2006
    d. 12 03 2006

8. What is entered in block 17a of the CMS-1500 when the payer is a participating provider (PAR)?

    a. Medicare UPIN
    b. National Provider Identifier (NPI)
    c. provider identification number (PIN)
    d. provider's Social Security number

9. Which describes an intensive outpatient program (IOP)?

    a. a comprehensive outpatient treatment program for patients diagnosed with Alzheimer's disease
    b. a highly regulated outpatient program for developmentally disabled patients integrated into the community
    c. a multifaceted program designed to help individuals with chemical dependencies and/or abuse issues
    d. an intensive outpatient physical rehabilitation program that includes physical and speech therapy

10. If another payer has already paid on the claim being submitted, this is indicated on the CMS-1500 claim form by entering the

    a. amount paid in block 19.
    b. amount paid in block 24K.
    c. letter Y in block 24J.
    d. letter Y in block 27.

11. The patient was required to obtain an authorization number before being treated by a specialist. Where is the authorization number entered in the CMS-1500 claim form?

    a. block 10d
    b. block 17a
    c. block 19
    d. block 23

12. Which is the correct way to enter multiple diagnosis reference numbers in block 24E?

    a. 1 2 3
    b. 1, 2, 3
    c. 1/2/3
    d. 1-2-3

13. Beatrice Blue wishes to have payment from the health insurance company sent directly to her provider. How is this reported on the CMS-1500 claim form?

    a. Beatrice Blue will sign block 12.
    b. Beatrice Blue will sign block 13.
    c. The provider will sign block 12.
    d. The provider will sign block 13.

14. Which is the correct way to enter the provider's name and credentials in block 31?

    a. DR JOHN BROWN
    b. DR. JOHN BROWN
    c. JOHN BROWN MD
    d. JOHN BROWN, M.D.

15. A balance of $12.55 is due to the patient for services provided by Dr. Brown. Which is entered in block 17a of the CMS-1500 claim form when the payer is a PAR provider?

    a. 0 00
    b. 12 55
    c. −12 55
    d. CREDIT

16. A secondary health insurance plan generally provides coverage that is
    a. available for outpatient services only.
    b. intended for copayments and coinsurance only.
    c. less comprehensive than the primary plan.
    d. similar to that of a primary health insurance plan.

17. Benefits such as coverage for copayments, deductibles, and coinsurance are offered by which type of insurance plan?
    a. liability
    b. primary
    c. secondary
    d. supplemental

18. James Rivers was evaluated and treated by his provider for a total charge of $72.80. How much will Mr. Rivers be required to pay for his visit if his coinsurance is 20%?
    a. $14.56
    b. $20.00
    c. $58.24
    d. $72.80

19. Mr. Rivers's copayment amount is entered in which block of the CMS-1500 claim form?
    a. block 20
    b. block 28
    c. block 29
    d. block 30

20. Another term for "outside lab" is _____ lab.
    a. insurance
    b. physician
    c. reference
    d. secondary

CHAPTER 13

Blue Cross and Blue Shield Plans

INTRODUCTION

This chapter familiarizes students with completion of CMS-1500 claim forms for primary and secondary Blue Cross and Blue Shield (BCBS) payers.

ASSIGNMENT 13.1 BCBS Primary CMS-1500 Claims Completion

OBJECTIVES

At the conclusion of this assignment, the student should be able to:

1. Assign ICD-9-CM diagnosis and CPT or HCPCS procedure/service codes.
2. Prepare a BCBS insurance primary payer CMS-1500 claim form.

INSTRUCTIONS

Use optical scanning guidelines to complete a CMS-1500 for case studies 13-a through 13-d. Go to the back of the workbook for removable blank CMS-1500 claim forms or print blank CMS-1500 claim forms using the textbook CD-ROM. Refer to the CMS-1500 claims completion instructions (primary) in the textbook.

ASSIGNMENT 13.2 BCBS Secondary CMS-1500 Claims Completion

OBJECTIVES

At the conclusion of this assignment, the student should be able to:

1. Assign ICD-9-CM diagnosis and CPT or HCPCS procedure/service codes.
2. Prepare a BCBS insurance secondary payer CMS-1500 claim form.

DONALD L. GIVINGS, M.D.

11350 Medical Drive ■ Anywhere US 12345 ■ (101) 111-5555
EIN: 11-1234562
BCBS PIN: 12345

Case Study 13-a

PATIENT INFORMATION:

Name:	Monty L. Booker
Address:	47 Snowflake Road
City:	Anywhere
State:	US
Zip Code:	12345
Telephone:	(101) 333-5555
Gender:	Male
Date of Birth:	12-25-1966
Occupation:	Editor
Employer:	Atlanta Publisher
Spouse's Employer:	

INSURANCE INFORMATION:

Patient Number:	13-a
Place of Service:	Office
Primary Insurance Plan:	BCBS US
Primary Insurance Plan ID #:	NXY 678-22-3434
Group #:	678
Primary Policyholder:	Monty L. Booker
Policyholder Date of Birth:	12-25-1966
Relationship to Patient:	Self
Secondary Insurance Plan:	
Secondary Insurance Plan ID #:	
Secondary Policyholder:	

Patient Status ☒ Married ☐ Divorced ☐ Single ☐ Student ☐ Other

DIAGNOSIS INFORMATION

Diagnosis	Code	Diagnosis	Code
1. Abnormal loss of weight		5.	
2. Polydipsia		6.	
3. Polyphagia		7.	
4.		8.	

PROCEDURE INFORMATION

Description of Procedure or Service	Date	Code	Charge
1. New patient OV level IV	01-19-YYYY		$100.00
2. Urinalysis, with microscopy	01-19-YYYY		10.00
3.			
4.			
5.			

SPECIAL NOTES:
    Return visit: 3 weeks

INSTRUCTIONS

Use optical scanning guidelines to complete a CMS-1500 for case studies 13-e through 13-h. Go to the back of the workbook for removable blank CMS-1500 claim forms or

DONALD L. GIVINGS, M.D.

11350 Medical Drive ■ Anywhere US 12345 ■ (101) 111-5555
EIN: 11-1234562
BCBS PIN: 12345

Case Study 13-b

PATIENT INFORMATION:

Name:	Anita B. Strong
Address:	124 Prosper Way
City:	Anywhere
State:	US
Zip Code:	12345
Telephone:	(101) 333-5555
Gender:	Female
Date of Birth:	04-25-1959
Occupation:	Author
Employer:	Self
Spouse's Employer:	

INSURANCE INFORMATION:

Patient Number:	13-b
Place of Service:	Office
Primary Insurance Plan:	BCBS US
Primary Insurance Plan ID #:	XWG 214-55-6666
Group #:	1357
Primary Policyholder:	Anita B. Strong
Policyholder Date of Birth:	04-25-1959
Relationship to Patient:	Self
Secondary Insurance Plan:	
Secondary Insurance Plan ID #:	
Secondary Policyholder:	

Patient Status ☒ Married ☐ Divorced ☐ Single ☐ Student ☐ Other

DIAGNOSIS INFORMATION

Diagnosis	Code	Diagnosis	Code
1. Migraine, classical		5.	
2.		6.	
3.		7.	
4.		8.	

PROCEDURE INFORMATION

Description of Procedure or Service	Date	Code	Charge
1. Est. patient OV level I	11-07-YYYY		$55.00
2.			
3.			
4.			
5.			

SPECIAL NOTES:
   Return visit: PRN
   Patient paid $20.00 toward today's bill.

print blank CMS-1500 claim forms using the textbook CD-ROM. Refer to the CMS-1500 claims completion instructions (secondary) in the textbook.

DONALD L. GIVINGS, M.D.

11350 Medical Drive ■ Anywhere US 12345 ■ (101) 111-5555
EIN: 11-1234562
BCBS PIN: 12345

Case Study 13-c

PATIENT INFORMATION:

Name:	Virginia A. Love
Address:	61 Isaiah Circle
City:	Anywhere
State:	US
Zip Code:	12345
Telephone:	(101) 333-5555
Gender:	Female
Date of Birth:	07-04-1962
Occupation:	
Employer:	None
Spouse's Employer:	Imperial Bayliners

INSURANCE INFORMATION:

Patient Number:	13-c
Place of Service:	Office
Primary Insurance Plan:	BCBS POS
Primary Insurance Plan ID #:	XWN 212-56-7972
Group #:	123
Primary Policyholder:	Charles L. Love
Policyholder Date of Birth:	10-06-60
Relationship to Patient:	Spouse
Secondary Insurance Plan:	
Secondary Insurance Plan ID #:	
Secondary Policyholder:	

Patient Status ☒ Married ☐ Divorced ☐ Single ☐ Student ☐ Other

DIAGNOSIS INFORMATION

Diagnosis	Code	Diagnosis	Code
1. Chronic conjunctivitis		5.	
2. Contact dermatitis		6.	
3.		7.	
4.		8.	

PROCEDURE INFORMATION

Description of Procedure or Service	Date	Code	Charge
1. Est. patient OV level I	07-03-YYYY		$55.00
2.			
3.			
4.			
5.			

SPECIAL NOTES:

If conjunctivitis does not clear within one week refer to Dr. Glance.

Return visit: PRN

IRIS A. GLANCE, M.D. OPHTHALMOLOGIST

66 Granite Drive ■ Anywhere US 12345 ■ (101) 111-5555
EIN: 11-6161612
BCBS PIN: 45678

Case Study 13-d

PATIENT INFORMATION:

Name:	Virginia A. Love
Address:	61 Isaiah Circle
City:	Anywhere
State:	US
Zip Code:	12345
Telephone:	(101) 333-5555
Gender:	Female
Date of Birth:	07-04-1962
Occupation:	
Employer:	None
Spouse's Employer:	Imperial Bayliners

INSURANCE INFORMATION:

Patient Number:	13-d
Place of Service:	Office
Primary Insurance Plan:	BCBS POS
Primary Insurance Plan ID #:	XWN 212-56-7972
Group #:	123
Primary Policyholder:	Charles L. Love
Policyholder Date of Birth:	10-06-60
Relationship to Patient:	Spouse
Secondary Insurance Plan:	
Secondary Insurance Plan ID #:	
Secondary Policyholder:	

Patient Status   ☒ Married   ☐ Divorced   ☐ Single   ☐ Student   ☐ Other

---

DIAGNOSIS INFORMATION

Diagnosis	Code	Diagnosis	Code
1. Chronic conjunctivitis		5.	
2. Conjunctival degeneration		6.	
3.		7.	
4.		8.	

PROCEDURE INFORMATION

Description of Procedure or Service	Date	Code	Charge
1. Office consult level I	07-04-YYYY		$65.00
2.			
3.			
4.			
5.			

SPECIAL NOTES:

Referring physician: Donald L. Givings, M.D. EIN: 11-1234562.
Onset of symptoms: 07-03-YYYY.

DONALD L. GIVINGS, M.D.

11350 Medical Drive ■ Anywhere US 12345 ■ (101) 111-5555
EIN: 11-1234562
BCBS PIN: 12345

Case Study 13-e

PATIENT INFORMATION:

Name:	Keith S. Kutter
Address:	22 Pinewood Avenue
City:	Anywhere
State:	US
Zip Code:	12345
Telephone:	(101) 333-5555
Gender:	Male
Date of Birth:	12-01-1955
Occupation:	Manager
Employer:	First League
Spouse's Employer:	Anderson Music & Sound

INSURANCE INFORMATION:

Patient Number:	13-e
Place of Service:	Office
Primary Insurance Plan:	BCBS US
Primary Insurance Plan ID #:	FLX 313-99-7777
Group #:	567
Primary Policyholder:	Keith S. Kutter
Policyholder Date of Birth:	12-01-1955
Relationship to Patient:	Self
Secondary Insurance Plan:	Aetna
Secondary Insurance Plan ID #:	212-44-0808
Secondary Policyholder:	Linda Kutter
Secondary Policyholder DOB:	05-22-1956

Patient Status   ☒ Married   ☐ Divorced   ☐ Single   ☐ Student   ☐ Other

DIAGNOSIS INFORMATION

Diagnosis	Code	Diagnosis	Code
1. Muscle spasms		5.	
2.		6.	
3.		7.	
4.		8.	

PROCEDURE INFORMATION

Description of Procedure or Service	Date	Code	Charge
1. Est. patient OV level II	09-03-YYYY		$65.00
2.			
3.			
4.			
5.			

SPECIAL NOTES:
     Refer to a chiropractor

ROBERT STRAIN, D.C. CHIROPRACTOR

234 Winding Bend Road ■ Anywhere US 12345 ■ (101) 111-5555
EIN: 11-4466882
BCBS PIN: 98765

Case Study 13-f

PATIENT INFORMATION:

Name:	Keith S. Kutter
Address:	22 Pinewood Avenue
City:	Anywhere
State:	US
Zip Code:	12345
Telephone:	(101) 333-5555
Gender:	Male
Date of Birth:	12-01-1955
Occupation:	Manager
Employer:	First League
Spouse's Employer:	Anderson Music & Sound

INSURANCE INFORMATION:

Patient Number:	13-f
Place of Service:	Office
Primary Insurance Plan:	BCBS US
Primary Insurance Plan ID #:	FLX 313-99-7777
Group #:	567
Primary Policyholder:	Keith S. Kutter
Policyholder Date of Birth:	12-01-1955
Relationship to Patient:	Self
Secondary Insurance Plan:	Aetna
Secondary Insurance Plan ID #:	212-44-6868
Secondary Policyholder:	Linda Kutter
Secondary Policyholder DOB:	05-22-1956

Patient Status ☒ Married ☐ Divorced ☐ Single ☐ Student ☐ Other

DIAGNOSIS INFORMATION

Diagnosis	Code	Diagnosis	Code
1. Cervical lesion		5.	
2. Rib cage lesion		6.	
3. Disorder of soft tissue		7.	
4. Muscle spasms		8.	

PROCEDURE INFORMATION

Description of Procedure or Service	Date	Code	Charge
1. Manipulation, 3-4 regions	09-10-YYYY		$55.00
2. Manipulation, extraspinal	09-10-YYYY		35.00
3. Massage	09-10-YYYY		30.00
4. Mechanical traction	09-10-YYYY		27.00
5. Electrical stimulation	09-10-YYYY		25.00

SPECIAL NOTES:

Referring physician: Donald L. Givings, M.D. EIN: 11-1234562
Return visit: PRN

DONALD L. GIVINGS, M.D.

11350 Medical Drive ■ Anywhere US 12345 ■ (101) 111-5555
EIN: 11-1234562
BCBS PIN: 12345

Case Study 13-g

PATIENT INFORMATION:

Name:	Kristen A. Wonder
Address:	1654 Willow Tree Dr.
City:	Anywhere
State:	US
Zip Code:	12345
Telephone:	(101) 333-5555
Gender:	Female
Date of Birth:	04-16-1999
Occupation:	
Employer:	None
Spouse's Employer:	

INSURANCE INFORMATION:

Patient Number:	13-g
Place of Service:	Office
Primary Insurance Plan:	BCBS US
Primary Insurance Plan ID #:	NYV 415-55-6767
Group #:	678
Primary Policyholder:	John F. Wonder
Policyholder Date of Birth:	05-22-1975
Relationship to Patient:	Father
Secondary Insurance Plan:	BCBS Empire
Secondary Insurance Plan ID #:	69234689
Secondary Policyholder:	Kristen A. Wonder

Patient Status: ☐ Married ☐ Divorced ☒ Single ☐ Student ☐ Other

DIAGNOSIS INFORMATION

Diagnosis	Code	Diagnosis	Code
1. Impacted wax		5.	
2.		6.	
3.		7.	
4.		8.	

PROCEDURE INFORMATION

Description of Procedure or Service	Date	Code	Charge
1. Est. patient OV level II	10-23-YYYY		$65.00
2. Removal, impacted cerumen	10-23-YYYY		25.00
3.			
4.			
5.			

SPECIAL NOTES:

Return visit: PRN

DONALD L. GIVINGS, M.D.

11350 Medical Drive ■ Anywhere US 12345 ■ (101) 111-5555
EIN: 11-1234562
BCBS PIN: 12345

Case Study 13-h

PATIENT INFORMATION:

Name:	Edward R. Turtle
Address:	68 North Street
City:	Anywhere
State:	US
Zip Code:	12345
Telephone:	(101) 333-5555
Gender:	Male
Date of Birth:	09-15-1949
Occupation:	
Employer:	Carpet Pro
Spouse's Employer:	

INSURANCE INFORMATION:

Patient Number:	13-h
Place of Service:	Inpatient hospital
Primary Insurance Plan:	BCBS Federal
Primary Insurance Plan ID #:	R12345678
Group #:	105
Primary Policyholder:	Edward R. Turtle
Policyholder Date of Birth:	09-15-1949
Relationship to Patient:	Self
Secondary Insurance Plan:	BCBS Empire
Secondary Insurance Plan ID #:	234789011
Secondary Policyholder:	Sally Turtle

Patient Status   ☒ Married   ☐ Divorced   ☐ Single   ☐ Student   ☐ Other

DIAGNOSIS INFORMATION

Diagnosis	Code	Diagnosis	Code
1. Rectal bleeding		5.	
2. Irritable bowel		6.	
3. Abdominal pain		7.	
4.		8.	

PROCEDURE INFORMATION

Description of Procedure or Service	Date	Code	Charge
1. Init. hospital level IV	4-14-YYYY		$175.00
2. Subsq. hospital level III	4-15-YYYY		85.00
3. Hospital discharge 30 min.	4-16-YYYY		75.00
4.			
5.			

SPECIAL NOTES:

Mercy Hospital, Anywhere Street, Anywhere US 12345.
Return visit: 4 weeks

1. Prior to the joint venture between Blue Cross and Blue Shield, the Blue Shield plans covered only
   a. hospital charges.
   b. physician services.
   c. prescription costs.
   d. therapy services.

2. Blue Cross facilities that had signed contracts to provide services to subscribers for special rates were known as _____ hospitals.
   a. benefit
   b. member
   c. plan
   d. subscriber

3. In what year was the BlueCross BlueShield Association (BCBSA) created?
   a. 1929
   b. 1938
   c. 1977
   d. 1986

4. Which is a function of the BlueCross BlueShield Association (BCBSA)?
   a. hiring local personnel
   b. membership enrollment
   c. national advertising
   d. processing Medicaid claims

5. The difference between for-profit status and nonprofit status is that
   a. for-profit corporations pay taxes on profits generated by the business.
   b. for-profit corporations pay their shareholders with before-tax profits.
   c. nonprofit corporations do not have stocks, shareholders, or officers.
   d. nonprofit corporations return earned profits to stock shareholders.

6. When a policyholder moves into an area served by a different BCBS corporation than the policyholder previously used, the plan must
   a. guarantee transfer of the membership.
   b. immediately cancel the individual's policy.
   c. locate a primary provider for the member.
   d. prohibit the member from seeking urgent care.

7. The preferred provider network (PPN) allowed rate is generally
   a. 10% higher than the participating provider rate.
   b. 10% lower than the participating provider rate.
   c. based on the Medicare Physician Fee Schedule.
   d. equal to the participating provider payment.

8. Which is an incentive for a provider to sign a PPN contract?
   a. higher reimbursement rates than those of participating providers
   b. no quality assurance or cost-containment program requirements
   c. PPN providers are not held to any managed care provisions
   d. written notification of new PPN members and employer groups

9. Small businesses are likely to select which BCBS coverage?
   a. fee-for-service
   b. indemnity
   c. managed care
   d. supplemental

10. An example of a benefit provided by BCBS basic coverage is
    a. assistant surgeon fees.
    b. mental health visits.
    c. occupational therapy.
    d. private-duty nursing.

11. The BCBS plan type that offers the most flexibility for subscribers is
    a. Healthcare Anywhere.
    b. indemnity coverage.
    c. major medical coverage.
    d. managed care.

12. A special accidental injury rider provides which benefit?
    a. Chronic conditions are covered if treatment is sought within the contract's established guidelines.
    b. Medical care is paid at 100% if treatment is received within the contract's established time frame.
    c. Nonsurgical care is paid at 100% if treatment is received within the contract's established time frame.
    d. Surgical care is paid at 100% if treatment is received within the contract's established time frame.

13. What special handling is required for BCBS claims filed under the medical emergency care rider?
    a. The claim will require all six procedure/service codes to be entered in block 24D.
    b. The CPT codes must reflect critical care services provided to the patient.
    c. The health insurance specialist must enter four diagnosis codes in block 21.
    d. The ICD-9-CM codes must reflect a condition that requires immediate care.

14. The outpatient pretreatment authorization plan (OPAP) is also known as
    a. preapproval.
    b. preauthorization.
    c. precertification.
    d. prevention.

15. Which title is listed on the BCBS identification cards for federal employees?
    a. BCBS Federal Employee Program
    b. BCBS National Account for Federal Employees
    c. Federal Employee Health Benefits Program
    d. Government-Wide Service Benefit Plan

16. BCBS Medicare supplemental plans are also known as _____ plans.
    a. MediBlue
    b. Medicare
    c. Medigap
    d. MediSup

17. The BlueCard Program allows members to obtain health services while in another BCBS service area. The patient will also
    a. pay a higher copayment or coinsurance for care.
    b. pay a higher premium for the flexible coverage.
    c. receive the benefits of the other BCBS contract.
    d. receive the benefits of his or her home plan contract.

18. Which BCBS program or plan would be most appropriate for a student who is attending school out of state?
    a. Away from Home Care Program
    b. BlueCard Program
    c. indemnity plan
    d. point-of-service plan

19. What information is entered in block 13 of a BCBS CMS-1500 claim form?
   a. nothing; the box is left blank
   c. the patient's signature
   b. SIGNATURE ON FILE
   d. the provider's signature

20. When submitting a BCBS claim for assistant surgeon services, the name of the _____ is entered in block 17.
   a. assistant surgeon
   c. primary care physician
   b. attending surgeon
   d. surgical facility

## CHAPTER 14

Medicare

INTRODUCTION

This chapter familiarizes students with completion of CMS-1500 claim forms for primary Medicare, Medicare as Secondary Payer (MSP), Medicare/Medigap, and Medicare/Medicaid.

ASSIGNMENT 14.1 Medicare Primary CMS-1500 Claims Completion

OBJECTIVES

At the conclusion of this assignment, the student should be able to:

1. Assign ICD-9-CM diagnosis and CPT or HCPCS procedure/service codes.
2. Prepare a Medicare insurance primary payer CMS-1500 claim form.

INSTRUCTIONS

Use optical scanning guidelines to complete a CMS-1500 for case studies 14-a through 14-d. Go to the back of the workbook for removable blank CMS-1500 claim forms, or print blank CMS-1500 claim forms using the textbook CD-ROM. Refer to the CMS-1500 claims completion instructions (primary) in the textbook.

ASSIGNMENT 14.2 Medicare as Secondary Payer CMS-1500 Claims Completion

OBJECTIVES

At the conclusion of this assignment, the student should be able to:

1. Assign ICD-9-CM diagnosis and CPT or HCPCS procedure/service codes.
2. Prepare a Medicare as Secondary Payer (MSP) CMS-1500 claim form.

DONALD L. GIVINGS, M.D.

11350 Medical Drive ■ Anywhere US 12345 ■ (101) 111-5555

EIN: 11-1234562

NPI: 123ABC4567

Case Study 14-a

PATIENT INFORMATION:

Name:	Alice E. Worthington
Address:	3301 Sunny Day Dr.
City:	Anywhere
State:	US
Zip Code:	12345
Telephone:	(101) 333-5555
Gender:	Female
Date of Birth:	02-16-1926
Occupation:	
Employer:	None
Spouse's Employer:	

INSURANCE INFORMATION:

Patient Number:	14-a
Place of Service:	Office
Primary Insurance Plan:	Medicare
Primary Insurance Plan ID #:	444-22-3333A
Group #:	
Primary Policyholder:	Alice E. Worthington
Policyholder Date of Birth:	02-16-1926
Relationship to Patient:	Self
Secondary Insurance Plan:	
Secondary Insurance Plan ID #:	
Secondary Policyholder:	

Patient Status ☐ Married   ☐ Divorced   ☒ Single   ☐ Student   ☐ Other

DIAGNOSIS INFORMATION

Diagnosis	Code	Diagnosis	Code
1. Breast lump		5.	
2. Breast pain		6.	
3. Family history of breast cancer		7.	
4.		8.	

PROCEDURE INFORMATION

Description of Procedure or Service	Date	Code	Charge
1. Est. patient OV level II	07-12-YYYY		$65.00
2.			
3.			
4.			
5.			

SPECIAL NOTES:

Refer to Dr. Kutter

INSTRUCTIONS

Use optical scanning guidelines to complete a CMS-1500 for case studies 14-e through 14-g. Go to the back of the workbook for removable blank CMS-1500 claim forms, or

JONATHAN B. KUTTER, M.D. SURGERY

339 Woodland Place ■ Anywhere US 12345 ■ (101) 111-5555

EIN: 11-5566772

NPI: 234ABC5678

Case Study 14-b

PATIENT INFORMATION:

Name:	Alice E. Worthington
Address:	3301 Sunny Day Dr.
City:	Anywhere
State:	US
Zip Code:	12345
Telephone:	(101) 333-5555
Gender:	Female
Date of Birth:	02-16-1926
Occupation:	
Employer:	None
Spouse's Employer:	

INSURANCE INFORMATION:

Patient Number:	14-b
Place of Service:	Office
Primary Insurance Plan:	Medicare
Primary Insurance Plan ID #:	444-22-3333A
Group #:	
Primary Policyholder:	Alice E. Worthington
Policyholder Date of Birth:	02-16-1926
Relationship to Patient:	Self
Secondary Insurance Plan:	
Secondary Insurance Plan ID #:	
Secondary Policyholder:	

Patient Status   ☐ Married   ☐ Divorced   ☒ Single   ☐ Student   ☐ Other

DIAGNOSIS INFORMATION

Diagnosis	Code	Diagnosis	Code
1. Breast lump		5.	
2. Breast pain		6.	
3. Family history of breast cancer		7.	
4.		8.	

PROCEDURE INFORMATION

Description of Procedure or Service	Date	Code	Charge
1. Office consult level II	07-15-YYYY		$75.00
2.			
3.			
4.			
5.			

SPECIAL NOTES:

Referring physician: Donald L. Givings, M.D., NPI: 123ABC4567.
Onset of symptoms: 07-12-YYYY.

print blank CMS-1500 claim forms using the textbook CD-ROM. Refer to the CMS-1500 claims completion instructions (secondary) in the textbook.

JONATHAN B. KUTTER, M.D. SURGERY

339 Woodland Place ■ Anywhere US 12345 ■ (101) 111-5555

EIN: 11-5566772

NPI: 234ABC5678

Case Study 14-c

PATIENT INFORMATION:

Name:	Alice E. Worthington
Address:	3301 Sunny Day Dr.
City:	Anywhere
State:	US
Zip Code:	12345
Telephone:	(101) 333-5555
Gender:	Female
Date of Birth:	02-16-1926
Occupation:	
Employer:	None
Spouse's Employer:	

INSURANCE INFORMATION:

Patient Number:	14-c
Place of Service:	Inpatient hospital
Primary Insurance Plan:	Medicare
Primary Insurance Plan ID #:	444-22-3333A
Group #:	
Primary Policyholder:	Alice E. Worthington
Policyholder Date of Birth:	02-16-1926
Relationship to Patient:	Self
Secondary Insurance Plan:	
Secondary Insurance Plan ID #:	
Secondary Policyholder:	

Patient Status   ☐ Married   ☐ Divorced   ☒ Single   ☐ Student   ☐ Other

DIAGNOSIS INFORMATION

Diagnosis	Code	Diagnosis	Code
1. Breast cancer		5.	
2.		6.	
3.		7.	
4.		8.	

PROCEDURE INFORMATION

Description of Procedure or Service	Date	Code	Charge
1. Mastectomy, simple, complete	07-22-YYYY		$1,200.00
2.			
3.			
4.			
5.			

SPECIAL NOTES:
Mercy Hospital, Anywhere St, Anywhere US 12345. NPI: 987XYZ6543.
Referring physician: Donald L. Givings, M.D., NPI: 123ABC4567.
Onset of symptoms: 07-12-YYYY.

JONATHAN B. KUTTER, M.D. SURGERY

339 Woodland Place ■ Anywhere US 12345 ■ (101) 111-5555

EIN: 11-5566772

NPI: 234ABC5678

Case Study 14-d

PATIENT INFORMATION:

Name:	Alice E. Worthington
Address:	3301 Sunny Day Dr.
City:	Anywhere
State:	US
Zip Code:	12345
Telephone:	(101) 333-5555
Gender:	Female
Date of Birth:	02-16-1926
Occupation:	
Employer:	None
Spouse's Employer:	

INSURANCE INFORMATION:

Patient Number:	14-d
Place of Service:	Office
Primary Insurance Plan:	Medicare
Primary Insurance Plan ID #:	444-22-3333A
Group #:	
Primary Policyholder:	Alice E. Worthington
Policyholder Date of Birth:	02-16-1926
Relationship to Patient:	Self
Secondary Insurance Plan:	
Secondary Insurance Plan ID #:	
Secondary Policyholder:	

Patient Status   ☐ Married   ☐ Divorced   ☒ Single   ☐ Student   ☐ Other

DIAGNOSIS INFORMATION

Diagnosis	Code	Diagnosis	Code
1. Breast cancer		5.	
2.		6.	
3.		7.	
4.		8.	

PROCEDURE INFORMATION

Description of Procedure or Service	Date	Code	Charge
1. Postoperative follow-up visit	08-12-YYYY		$0.00
2.			
3.			
4.			
5.			

SPECIAL NOTES:

Referring physician: Donald L. Givings, M.D., NPI: 123ABC4567.

DONALD L. GIVINGS, M.D.

11350 Medical Drive ■ Anywhere US 12345 ■ (101) 111-5555
EIN: 11-1234562
NPI: 123ABC4567

Case Study 14-e

PATIENT INFORMATION:

Name:	Rebecca Nichols
Address:	384 Dean Street
City:	Anywhere
State:	US
Zip Code:	12345
Telephone:	(101) 333-5555
Gender:	Female
Date of Birth:	10-12-1925
Occupation:	
Employer:	Retired
Spouse's Employer:	

INSURANCE INFORMATION:

Patient Number:	14-e
Place of Service:	Inpatient hospital
Primary Insurance Plan:	BCBS
Primary Insurance Plan ID #:	667-14-3344
Group #:	
Primary Policyholder:	Rebecca Nichols
Policyholder Date of Birth:	10-12-1925
Relationship to Patient:	Self
Secondary Insurance Plan:	Medicare
Secondary Insurance Plan ID #:	667 14 3344A
Secondary Policyholder:	Rebecca Nichols

Patient Status ☐ Married ☐ Divorced ☒ Single ☐ Student ☐ Other

DIAGNOSIS INFORMATION

Diagnosis	Code	Diagnosis	Code
1. Rectal bleeding		5.	
2. Diarrhea		6.	
3. Abnormal loss of weight		7.	
4.		8.	

PROCEDURE INFORMATION

Description of Procedure or Service	Date	Code	Charge
1. Initial hosp. level IV	08-06-YYYY		$175.00
2. Subsq. hosp. level III	08-07-YYYY		85.00
3. Subsq. hosp. level III	08-08-YYYY		85.00
4. Subsq. hosp. level II	08-09-YYYY		75.00
5. Hosp. discharge, 30 min.	08-10-YYYY		75.00

SPECIAL NOTES:

Mercy Hospital, Anywhere St, Anywhere US 12345. NPI: 987XYZ6543.

Dr. Gestive saw the patient for a consult on August 7 & August 8.

COLIN D. GESTIVE, M.D. GASTROENTEROLOGY

35 Ulcer Place ■ Anywhere US 12345 ■ (101) 111-5555

EIN: 11-4477662

NPI: 345ABC6789

Case Study 14-f

PATIENT INFORMATION:

Name:	Rebecca Nichols
Address:	384 Dean Street
City:	Anywhere
State:	US
Zip Code:	12345
Telephone:	(101) 333-5555
Gender:	Female
Date of Birth:	10-12-1925
Occupation:	
Employer:	Retired
Spouse's Employer:	

INSURANCE INFORMATION:

Patient Number:	14-f
Place of Service:	Inpatient hospital
Primary Insurance Plan:	BCBS
Primary Insurance Plan ID #:	667-14-3344
Group #:	
Primary Policyholder:	Rebecca Nichols
Policyholder Date of Birth:	10-12-1925
Relationship to Patient:	Self
Secondary Insurance Plan:	Medicare
Secondary Insurance Plan ID #:	667-14-3344A
Secondary Policyholder:	Rebecca Nichols

Patient Status   ☐ Married   ☐ Divorced   ☒ Single   ☐ Student   ☐ Other

---

DIAGNOSIS INFORMATION

Diagnosis	Code	Diagnosis	Code
1. Diverticulitis of the colon with hemorrhage		5.	
2.		6.	
3.		7.	
4.		8.	

PROCEDURE INFORMATION

Description of Procedure or Service	Date	Code	Charge
1. Initial inpatient consult level IV	08-07-YYYY		$220.00
2. Follow-up inpatient consult level III	08-08-YYYY		80.00
3.			
4.			
5.			

SPECIAL NOTES:

Mercy Hospital, Anywhere St, Anywhere US 12345. NPI: 987XYZ6543.

Referring physician: Donald L. Givings, M.D.   NPI: 123ABC4567.

LISA M. MASON, M.D., FAMILY PRACTICE

547 Antigua Road ■ Anywhere US 12345 ■ (101) 111-5555

EIN: 11-4958672

NPI: 456ABC7890

Case Study 14-g

PATIENT INFORMATION:

Name:	Samuel T. Mahoney Jr.
Address:	498 Meadow Lane
City:	Anywhere
State:	US
Zip Code:	12345
Telephone:	(101) 333-5555
Gender:	Male
Date of Birth:	09-04-1930
Occupation:	
Employer:	None
Spouse's Employer:	

INSURANCE INFORMATION:

Patient Number:	14-g
Place of Service:	Office
Primary Insurance Plan:	Aetna
Primary Insurance Plan ID #:	312-78-5894
Group #:	
Primary Policyholder:	Samuel T. Mahoney Jr.
Policyholder Date of Birth:	09-04-1930
Relationship to Patient:	Self
Secondary Insurance Plan:	Medicare
Secondary Insurance Plan ID #:	312 78 5894A
Secondary Policyholder:	Samuel T. Mahoney Jr.

Patient Status   ☒ Married   ☐ Divorced   ☐ Single   ☐ Student   ☐ Other

DIAGNOSIS INFORMATION

Diagnosis	Code	Diagnosis	Code
1. Asthma, unspecified		5.	
2. URI		6.	
3.		7.	
4.		8.	

PROCEDURE INFORMATION

Description of Procedure or Service	Date	Code	Charge
1. Est. patient OV level II	10-03-YYYY		$25.16
2.			
3.			
4.			
5.			

SPECIAL NOTES:

Dr. Mason is nonPAR with Medicare
Onset of disease: 01-01-YYYY

ASSIGNMENT 14.3 Medicare/Medigap CMS-1500 Claims Completion

OBJECTIVES

At the conclusion of this assignment, the student should be able to:

1. Assign ICD-9-CM diagnosis and CPT or HCPCS procedure/service codes.
2. Prepare a Medicare/Medigap CMS-1500 claim form.

INSTRUCTIONS

Use optical scanning guidelines to complete a CMS-1500 for case studies 14-h through 14-j. Go to the back of the workbook for removable blank CMS-1500 claim forms, or print blank CMS-1500 claim forms using the textbook CD-ROM. Refer to the CMS-1500 claims completion instructions (secondary) in the textbook.

ASSIGNMENT 14.4 Medicare/Medicaid CMS-1500 Claims Completion

OBJECTIVES

At the conclusion of this assignment, the student should be able to:

1. Assign ICD-9-CM diagnosis and CPT or HCPCS procedure/service codes.
2. Prepare a Medicare/Medicaid CMS-1500 claim form.

INSTRUCTIONS

Use optical scanning guidelines to complete a CMS-1500 for case studies 14-k through 14-m. Go to the back of the workbook for removable blank CMS-1500 claim forms, or print blank CMS-1500 claim forms using the textbook CD-ROM. Refer to the CMS-1500 claims completion instructions (secondary) in the textbook.

ASSIGNMENT 14.5 Multiple Choice Review

1. Medicare Part A coverage is available to individuals under the age of 65 who
   a. are kidney dialysis or kidney transplant patients.
   b. are not disabled and are willing to pay the premium.
   c. have received RRB disability benefits for one year.
   d. have received SSA disability benefits for one year.

DONALD L. GIVINGS, M.D.

11350 Medical Drive ■ Anywhere US 12345 ■ (101) 111-5555

EIN: 11-1234562

NPI: 123ABC4567

Case Study 14-h

PATIENT INFORMATION:

Name:	Abraham N. Freed
Address:	12 Nottingham Circle
City:	Anywhere
State:	US
Zip Code:	12345
Telephone:	(101) 333-5555
Gender:	Male
Date of Birth:	10-03-1922
Occupation:	
Employer:	Retired Johnson Steel
Spouse's Employer:	

INSURANCE INFORMATION:

Patient Number:	14-h
Place of Service:	Office
Primary Insurance Plan:	Medicare
Primary Insurance Plan ID #:	645-45-4545A
Group #:	
Primary Policyholder:	Abraham N. Freed
Policyholder Date of Birth:	10-03-1922
Relationship to Patient:	Self
Secondary Insurance Plan:	BCBS Medigap
Secondary Insurance Plan ID #:	NXY645-45-4545 987
Secondary Policyholder:	Abraham N. Freed

Patient Status   ☒ Married   ☐ Divorced   ☐ Single   ☐ Student   ☐ Other

DIAGNOSIS INFORMATION

Diagnosis	Code	Diagnosis	Code
1. Hypertension, malignant		5.	
2. Dizziness		6.	
3.		7.	
4.		8.	

PROCEDURE INFORMATION

Description of Procedure or Service	Date	Code	Charge
1. New patient OV level IV	03-07-YYYY		$100.00
2. EKG	03-07-YYYY		50.00
3. Venipuncture	03-07-YYYY		8.00
4.			
5.			

SPECIAL NOTES:

Return visit: 2 weeks

DONALD L. GIVINGS, M.D.

11350 Medical Drive ■ Anywhere US 12345 ■ (101) 111-5555
EIN: 11-1234562
NPI: 123ABC4567

Case Study 14-i

PATIENT INFORMATION:

Name:	Esther K. Freed
Address:	12 Nottingham Circle
City:	Anywhere
State:	US
Zip Code:	12345
Telephone:	(101) 333-5555
Gender:	Female
Date of Birth:	03-26-1925
Occupation:	
Employer:	
Spouse's Employer:	Retired Johnson Steel

INSURANCE INFORMATION:

Patient Number:	14-i
Place of Service:	Office
Primary Insurance Plan:	Medicare
Primary Insurance Plan ID #:	777-66-4444A
Group #:	
Primary Policyholder:	Abraham N. Freed
Policyholder Date of Birth:	10-03-1922
Relationship to Patient:	Spouse
Secondary Insurance Plan:	BCBS Medigap
Secondary Insurance Plan ID #:	NXY645-45-4545 987
Secondary Policyholder:	Abraham N. Freed

Patient Status   ☒ Married   ☐ Divorced   ☐ Single   ☐ Student   ☐ Other

DIAGNOSIS INFORMATION

Diagnosis	Code	Diagnosis	Code
1. Bronchopneumonia		5.	
2. Hemoptysis		6.	
3. Hematuria		7.	
4.		8.	

PROCEDURE INFORMATION

Description of Procedure or Service	Date	Code	Charge
1. New patient OV level IV	03-07-YYYY		$100.00
2. Chest X-ray 2 views	03-07-YYYY		50.00
3. Urinalysis, with microscopy	03-07-YYYY		10.00
4.			
5.			

SPECIAL NOTES:

Return visit: 2 weeks

DONALD L. GIVINGS, M.D.

11350 Medical Drive ■ Anywhere US 12345 ■ (101) 111-5555
EIN: 11-1234562
NPI: 123ABC4567

Case Study 14-j

PATIENT INFORMATION:

Name:	Mary R. Booth
Address:	1007 Bond Avenue
City:	Anywhere
State:	US
Zip Code:	12345
Telephone:	(101) 333-5555
Gender:	Female
Date of Birth:	10-14-1933
Occupation:	
Employer:	Retired Mt. Royal Drugs
Spouse's Employer:	

INSURANCE INFORMATION:

Patient Number:	14-j
Place of Service:	Office
Primary Insurance Plan:	Medicare
Primary Insurance Plan ID #:	212-77-4444A
Group #:	
Primary Policyholder:	Mary R. Booth
Policyholder Date of Birth:	10-14-1933
Relationship to Patient:	Self
Secondary Insurance Plan:	AARP Medigap
Secondary Insurance Plan ID #:	212-77-4444
Secondary Policyholder:	Self

Patient Status ☐ Married ☐ Divorced ☒ Single ☐ Student ☐ Other

DIAGNOSIS INFORMATION

Diagnosis	Code	Diagnosis	Code
1. Hypertension, benign		5.	
2.		6.	
3.		7.	
4.		8.	

PROCEDURE INFORMATION

Description of Procedure or Service	Date	Code	Charge
1. Est. patient OV level I	03-17-YYYY		$55.00
2.			
3.			
4.			
5.			

SPECIAL NOTES:

Return visit: 3 months

DONALD L. GIVINGS, M.D.

11350 Medical Drive ■ Anywhere US 12345 ■ (101) 111-5555
EIN: 11-1234562
NPI: 123ABC4567

Case Study 14-k

PATIENT INFORMATION:

Name:	Patricia S. Delaney
Address:	485 Garden Lane
City:	Anywhere
State:	US
Zip Code:	12345
Telephone:	(101) 333-5555
Gender:	Female
Date of Birth:	04-12-1931
Occupation:	
Employer:	
Spouse's Employer:	

INSURANCE INFORMATION:

Patient Number:	14-k
Place of Service:	Office
Primary Insurance Plan:	Medicare
Primary Insurance Plan ID #:	485375869A
Group #:	
Primary Policyholder:	Patricia S. Delaney
Policyholder Date of Birth:	04-12-1931
Relationship to Patient:	Self
Secondary Insurance Plan:	Medicaid
Secondary Insurance Plan ID #:	22886644XT
Secondary Policyholder:	Self

Patient Status   ☐ Married   ☐ Divorced   ☒ Single   ☐ Student   ☐ Other

DIAGNOSIS INFORMATION

Diagnosis	Code	Diagnosis	Code
1. Rosacea		5.	
2.		6.	
3.		7.	
4.		8.	

PROCEDURE INFORMATION

Description of Procedure or Service	Date	Code	Charge
1. Est. patient OV level I	12-15-YYYY		$55.00
2.			
3.			
4.			
5.			

SPECIAL NOTES:

Refer patient to dermatologist
Return visit: PRN

CLAIRE M. SKINNER, M.D. DERMATOLOGY

50 Clear View Drive ∎ Anywhere US 12345 ∎ (101) 111-5555

EIN: 11-5555552

NPI: 567ABC8901

Case Study 14-I

PATIENT INFORMATION:

Name:	Patricia S. Delaney
Address:	485 Garden Lane
City:	Anywhere
State:	US
Zip Code:	12345
Telephone:	(101) 333-5555
Gender:	Female
Date of Birth:	04-12-1931
Occupation:	
Employer:	
Spouse's Employer:	

INSURANCE INFORMATION:

Patient Number:	14-I
Place of Service:	Office
Primary Insurance Plan:	Medicare
Primary Insurance Plan ID #:	485375869A
Group #:	
Primary Policyholder:	Patricia S. Delaney
Policyholder Date of Birth:	04-12-1931
Relationship to Patient:	Self
Secondary Insurance Plan:	Medicaid
Secondary Insurance Plan ID #:	22080044XT
Secondary Policyholder:	Self

Patient Status   ☐ Married   ☐ Divorced   ☒ Single   ☐ Student   ☐ Other

DIAGNOSIS INFORMATION

Diagnosis	Code	Diagnosis	Code
1. Rosacea		5.	
2.		6.	
3.		7.	
4.		8.	

PROCEDURE INFORMATION

Description of Procedure or Service	Date	Code	Charge
1. Office consult level III	12-18-YYYY		$85.00
2.			
3.			
4.			
5.			

SPECIAL NOTES:
Referred by Donald L. Givings, M.D. NPI: 123ABC4567.
Return visit: PRN
Onset of symptoms: 12-15-YYYY

DONALD L. GIVINGS, M.D.

11350 Medical Drive ■ Anywhere US 12345 ■ (101) 111-5555
EIN: 11-1234562
NPI: 123ABC4567

Case Study 14-m

PATIENT INFORMATION:

Name:	Danielle H. Ford
Address:	28 Delightful Drive
City:	Anywhere
State:	US
Zip Code:	12345
Telephone:	(101) 333-5555
Gender:	Female
Date of Birth:	12-10-1922
Occupation:	
Employer:	
Spouse's Employer:	

INSURANCE INFORMATION:

Patient Number:	14-m
Place of Service:	Office
Primary Insurance Plan:	Medicare
Primary Insurance Plan ID #:	756-66-7878W
Group #:	
Primary Policyholder:	Danielle H. Ford
Policyholder Date of Birth:	12-10-1922
Relationship to Patient:	Self
Secondary Insurance Plan:	Medicaid
Secondary Insurance Plan ID #:	756-66-7878
Secondary Policyholder:	Danielle H. Ford

Patient Status ☐ Married ☐ Divorced ☒ Single ☐ Student ☐ Other

DIAGNOSIS INFORMATION

Diagnosis	Code	Diagnosis	Code
1. Routine examination		5.	
2.		6.	
3.		7.	
4.		8.	

PROCEDURE INFORMATION

Description of Procedure or Service	Date	Code	Charge
1. Preventive medicine, 65 years and over	08-09-YYYY		$65.00
2.			
3.			
4.			
5.			

SPECIAL NOTES:
   Return visit: PRN

2. Which information must be obtained about the beneficiary to confirm Medicare eligibility over the phone?
   a. date of birth
   b. mailing address
   c. marital status
   d. social security number

3. What length of time is the Medicare initial enrollment period (IEP)?
   a. 1 year
   b. 12 months
   c. 7 months
   d. 90 days

4. The Medicare "spell of illness" is also known as the
   a. benefit period.
   b. elective days.
   c. reserve days.
   d. sickness period.

5. Patients may elect to use their Medicare lifetime reserve days after how many continuous days of hospitalization?
   a. 14
   b. 45
   c. 60
   d. 90

6. For a beneficiary to qualify for Medicare's skilled nursing benefit, the individual must have
   a. enrolled in Medicare Part B in addition to Medicare Part A.
   b. had a 90-day hospitalization in an acute care facility.
   c. had at least three inpatient days of an acute hospital stay.
   d. lifetime reserve days available for nursing facility care.

7. Temporary hospitalization of a patient for the purpose of providing relief from duty for the nonpaid primary caregiver of a patient is called _____ care.
   a. boarding
   b. hospice
   c. relief
   d. respite

8. All terminally ill Medicare patients qualify for _____ care.
   a. home health
   b. hospice
   c. private-duty
   d. respite

9. Medicare Part B will cover some home health care services if the patient
   a. has been disabled more than two years.
   b. has enrolled in Medicare Advantage.
   c. has not enrolled in Medicare Part A.
   d. is terminally ill and at the end of life.

10. How much is a beneficiary with Medicare Part B expected to pay for durable medical equipment (DME)?
    a. 20% of the Medicare-approved amount
    b. 50% of the retail cost of the equipment
    c. a copay of $20 per each DME item
    d. the full Medicare-approved amount

11. Which component of the Medicare Modernization Act of 2003 was created to provide tax-favored treatment for individuals covered by a high-deductible health plan?
    a. extra coverage plans
    b. health savings accounts
    c. Medicare Part D
    d. Medicare savings accounts

12. Dr. Cummings has been practicing in town for nearly 30 years. As a courtesy to his loyal Medicare patients, he does not charge the coinsurance. How can this affect Dr. Cummings' practice?

    a. It will increase the doctor's patient base because new residents will want the savings.

    b. The billing process will be smoother for the doctor's health insurance specialists.

    c. The doctor may be subject to large fines and exclusion from the Medicare program.

    d. This will only affect the doctor's bottom line; he will earn less profit with this practice.

13. One of the benefits of becoming a Medicare participating provider (PAR) is

    a. faster processing and payment of assigned claims.

    b. that providers can balance-bill the beneficiaries.

    c. that there is no Advance Beneficiary Notice requirement.

    d. that there is no limit on fees or charges for services.

14. The maximum fee a nonPAR may charge for a covered service is called the

    a. allowed fee.   c. maximum benefit.

    b. limiting charge.   d. usual fee.

15. An example of a limited license practitioner (LLP) is a

    a. clinical psychologist.   c. nurse practitioner.

    b. nurse midwife.   d. physician assistant.

16. Dr. Taylor has instructed you, as the health insurance specialist, to obtain an Advance Beneficiary Notice (ABN) on all surgical cases in the practice just in case Medicare denies the claim. How should you handle this situation?

    a. At the next practice meeting, solicit ideas on how best to obtain signatures from each Medicare patient.

    b. Discuss the ABN with every Medicare surgical patient and, persuade the patient to sign the form.

    c. Explain to Dr. Taylor that the practice cannot do this, as Medicare considers this activity fraudulent.

    d. Print out a list of all Medicare patients in the practice and send each an ABN to sign.

17. What is entered in block 11 of the CMS-1500 claim form when a reference lab provides services to a Medicare patient in the absence of a face-to-face encounter?

    a. MSP CLAIM   c. ON FILE

    b. NONE   d. SAME

18. How often are providers required to collect or verify Medicare as Secondary Payer (MSP) information?

    a. after a primary Medicare claim has been denied

    b. at the time of the initial beneficiary encounter only

    c. each time the beneficiary is seen by the provider

    d. each time the patient re-registers with the practice

19. Under which circumstance will Medicare assign a claim conditional primary payer status?
    a. A patient who is mentally impaired failed to file a claim with the primary carrier.
    b. A workers' compensation claim was denied and has been successfully appealed.
    c. The patient did not provide MSP information and the provider submits a request.
    d. The liability carrier has not provided a response within 60 days of filing the claim.

20. If a service was performed on June 30, the Medicare claim must be submitted for payment and postmarked no later than
    a. December 31 of the same year.
    b. January 1 of the next year.
    c. June 30 of the next year.
    d. December 31 of the next year.

## CHAPTER 15

Medicaid

INTRODUCTION

This chapter familiarizes students with completion of CMS-1500 claim forms for primary and mother/baby Medicaid payers.

ASSIGNMENT 15.1 Medicaid Primary CMS-1500 Claims Completion

OBJECTIVES

At the conclusion of this assignment, the student should be able to:

1. Assign ICD-9-CM diagnosis and CPT or HCPCS procedure/service codes.
2. Prepare a Medicaid insurance primary payer CMS-1500 claim form.

INSTRUCTIONS

Use optical scanning guidelines to complete a CMS-1500 for case studies 15-a through 15-d. Go to the back of the workbook for removable blank CMS-1500 claim forms, or print blank CMS-1500 claim forms using the textbook CD-ROM. Refer to the CMS-1500 claims completion instructions (primary) in the textbook.

ASSIGNMENT 15.2 Medicaid Mother/Baby CMS-1500 Claims Completion

OBJECTIVES

At the conclusion of this assignment, the student should be able to:

1. Assign ICD-9-CM diagnosis and CPT or HCPCS procedure/service codes.
2. Prepare a Medicaid mother/baby CMS-1500 claim form.

INSTRUCTIONS

Use optical scanning guidelines to complete a CMS-1500 for case studies 15-e through 15-f. Go to the back of the workbook for removable blank CMS-1500 claim forms, or

DONALD L. GIVINGS, M.D.

11350 Medical Drive ■ Anywhere US 12345 ■ (101) 111-5555

EIN: 11-1234562

NPI: 123ABC4567

Case Study 15-a

PATIENT INFORMATION:

Name:	Sharon W. Casey
Address:	483 Oakdale Avenue
City:	Anywhere
State:	US
Zip Code:	12345
Telephone:	(101) 333-5555
Gender:	Female
Date of Birth:	10-06-1970
Occupation:	
Employer:	
Spouse's Employer:	

INSURANCE INFORMATION:

Patient Number:	15-a
Place of Service:	Office
Primary Insurance Plan:	Medicaid
Primary Insurance Plan ID #:	22334455
Group #:	
Primary Policyholder:	Sharon W. Casey
Policyholder Date of Birth:	10-06-1970
Relationship to Patient:	Self
Secondary Insurance Plan:	
Secondary Insurance Plan ID #:	
Secondary Policyholder:	

Patient Status ☐ Married ☐ Divorced ☒ Single ☐ Student ☐ Other

DIAGNOSIS INFORMATION

Diagnosis	Code	Diagnosis	Code
1. Excessive menstruation		5.	
2. Irregular menstrual cycle		6.	
3.		7.	
4.		8.	

PROCEDURE INFORMATION

Description of Procedure or Service	Date	Code	Charge
1. Est. patient OV level III	11-13-YYYY		$75.00
2.			
3.			
4.			
5.			

SPECIAL NOTES:

Refer patient to GYN

Return visit: PRN

print blank CMS-1500 claim forms using the textbook CD-ROM. Refer to the CMS-1500 claims completion instructions (mother/baby) in the textbook.

MARIA C. SECTION, M.D.   OB/GYN

11 Maden Lane ■ Anywhere US 12345 ■ (101) 111-5555

EIN: 11-6699772

NPI: 678ABC9012

Case Study 15-b

PATIENT INFORMATION:

Name:	Sharon W. Casey
Address:	483 Oakdale Avenue
City:	Anywhere
State:	US
Zip Code:	12345
Telephone:	(101) 333-5555
Gender:	Female
Date of Birth:	10-06-1970
Occupation:	
Employer:	
Spouse's Employer:	

INSURANCE INFORMATION:

Patient Number:	15-b
Place of Service:	Office
Primary Insurance Plan:	Medicaid
Primary Insurance Plan ID #:	22334455
Group #:	
Primary Policyholder:	Sharon W. Casey
Policyholder Date of Birth:	10-06-1970
Relationship to Patient:	Self
Secondary Insurance Plan:	
Secondary Insurance Plan ID #:	
Secondary Policyholder:	

Patient Status   ☐ Married   ☐ Divorced   ☒ Single   ☐ Student   ☐ Other

---

DIAGNOSIS INFORMATION

Diagnosis	Code	Diagnosis	Code
1. Excessive menstruation		5.	
2. Irregular menstrual cycle		6.	
3.		7.	
4.		8.	

PROCEDURE INFORMATION

Description of Procedure or Service	Date	Code	Charge
1. Office consult level III	11-20-YYYY		$85.00
2.			
3.			
4.			
5.			

SPECIAL NOTES:

Onset of symptoms: 11-13-YYYY.

Referred by Donald L. Givings, M.D.,   NPI: 123ABC4567

Return visit: One month

DONALD L. GIVINGS, M.D.

11350 Medical Drive ■ Anywhere US 12345 ■ (101) 111-5555
EIN: 11-1234562
NPI: 123ABC4567

Case Study 15-c

PATIENT INFORMATION:

Name:	Fred R. Jones
Address:	444 Taylor Avenue
City:	Anywhere
State:	US
Zip Code:	12345
Telephone:	(101) 333-5555
Gender:	Male
Date of Birth:	01-05-1949
Occupation:	
Employer:	
Spouse's Employer:	

INSURANCE INFORMATION:

Patient Number:	15-c
Place of Service:	Office
Primary Insurance Plan:	Medicaid
Primary Insurance Plan ID #:	55771122
Group #:	
Primary Policyholder:	Fred R. Jones
Policyholder Date of Birth:	01-05-1949
Relationship to Patient:	Self
Secondary Insurance Plan:	
Secondary Insurance Plan ID #:	
Secondary Policyholder:	

Patient Status ☐ Married ☒ Divorced ☐ Single ☐ Student ☐ Other

---

DIAGNOSIS INFORMATION

Diagnosis	Code	Diagnosis	Code
1. Difficulty in walking		5.	
2.		6.	
3.		7.	
4.		8.	

PROCEDURE INFORMATION

Description of Procedure or Service	Date	Code	Charge
1. Est. patient OV level III	06-19-YYYY		$75.00
2.			
3.			
4.			
5.			

SPECIAL NOTES:

Refer patient to a podiatrist
Return visit: 3 months

JOHN F. WALKER, D.P.M.   PODIATRY

546 Foothill Place ■ Anywhere US 12345 ■ (101) 111-5555

EIN: 11-9933772

NPI: 890ABC1234

Case Study 15-d

PATIENT INFORMATION:

Name:	Fred R. Jones
Address:	444 Taylor Avenue
City:	Anywhere
State:	US
Zip Code:	12345
Telephone:	(101) 333-5555
Gender:	Male
Date of Birth:	01-05-1949
Occupation:	
Employer:	
Spouse's Employer:	

INSURANCE INFORMATION:

Patient Number:	15-d
Place of Service:	Office
Primary Insurance Plan:	Medicaid
Primary Insurance Plan ID #:	55771122
Group #:	
Primary Policyholder:	Fred R. Jones
Policyholder Date of Birth:	01-05-1949
Relationship to Patient:	Self
Secondary Insurance Plan:	
Secondary Insurance Plan ID #:	
Secondary Policyholder:	

Patient Status   ☐ Married   ☒ Divorced   ☐ Single   ☐ Student   ☐ Other

---

DIAGNOSIS INFORMATION

Diagnosis	Code	Diagnosis	Code
1. Fracture, great toe		5.	
2.		6.	
3.		7.	
4.		8.	

PROCEDURE INFORMATION

Description of Procedure or Service	Date	Code	Charge
1. Office consult level II	06-23-YYYY		$75.00
2. Toe X-ray 2 views	06-23-YYYY		50.00
3. Closed treatment of fracture, great toe	06-23-YYYY		65.00
4.			
5.			

SPECIAL NOTES:

Onset of symptoms: 06-19-YYYY

Referred by Donald L. Givings, M.D.,   NPI: 123ABC4567.

DONALD L. GIVINGS, M.D.

11350 Medical Drive ■ Anywhere US 12345 ■ (101) 111-5555
EIN: 11-1234562
NPI: 123ABC4567

Case Study 15-e

PATIENT INFORMATION:

Name:	Jackson, Newborn
Address:	3764 Ravenwood Ave.
City:	Anywhere
State:	US
Zip Code:	12345
Telephone:	(101) 333-5555
Gender:	Male
Date of Birth:	03-10-2005
Occupation:	
Employer:	
Spouse's Employer:	

INSURANCE INFORMATION:

Patient Number:	15-e
Place of Service:	Inpatient hospital
Primary Insurance Plan:	Medicaid
Primary Insurance Plan ID #:	77557755 (mother)
Group #:	
Primary Policyholder:	Sandy Jackson
Policyholder Date of Birth:	02-15-1985
Relationship to Patient:	Mother
Secondary Insurance Plan:	
Secondary Insurance Plan ID #:	
Secondary Policyholder:	

Patient Status ☐ Married ☐ Divorced ☒ Single ☐ Student ☐ Other

DIAGNOSIS INFORMATION

Diagnosis	Code	Diagnosis	Code
1. Healthy single liveborn infant		5.	
2.		6.	
3.		7.	
4.		8.	

PROCEDURE INFORMATION

Description of Procedure or Service	Date	Code	Charge
1. History and examination of normal newborn	03-10-YYYY		$150.00
2. Attendance at delivery	03-10-YYYY		400.00
3. Subsequent care for normal newborn	03-11-YYYY		100.00
4.			
5.			

SPECIAL NOTES:

Inpatient care provided at Goodmedicine Hospital, Anywhere St, Anywhere US 12345. NPI: 112ABC3456.
Application for infant's Medicaid ID number has been submitted.

DONALD L. GIVINGS, M.D.

11350 Medical Drive ■ Anywhere US 12345 ■ (101) 111-5555
EIN: 11-1234562
NPI: 123ABC4567

Case Study 15-f

PATIENT INFORMATION:

Name:	Giovanni, Newborn
Address:	384 Beverly Avenue
City:	Anywhere
State:	US
Zip Code:	12345
Telephone:	(101) 333-5555
Gender:	Female
Date of Birth:	10-22-2005
Occupation:	
Employer:	
Spouse's Employer:	

INSURANCE INFORMATION:

Patient Number:	15-f
Place of Service:	Inpatient hospital
Primary Insurance Plan:	Medicaid
Primary Insurance Plan ID #:	88776655 (mother)
Group #:	
Primary Policyholder:	Kristin Giovanni
Policyholder Date of Birth:	03-10-1990
Relationship to Patient:	Mother
Secondary Insurance Plan:	
Secondary Insurance Plan ID #:	
Secondary Policyholder:	

Patient Status ☐ Married ☐ Divorced ☒ Single ☐ Student ☐ Other

DIAGNOSIS INFORMATION

Diagnosis	Code	Diagnosis	Code
1. Healthy single liveborn infant		5.	
2.		6.	
3.		7.	
4.		8.	

PROCEDURE INFORMATION

Description of Procedure or Service	Date	Code	Charge
1. History and examination of normal newborn	10-22-YYYY		$150.00
2. Attendance at delivery	10-22-YYYY		400.00
3. Subsequent care for normal newborn	10-23-YYYY		100.00
4.			
5.			

SPECIAL NOTES:

Inpatient care provided at Goodmedicine Hospital, Anywhere St, Anywhere US 12345. NPI: 112ABC3456.
Application for infant's Medicaid ID number has been submitted.

1. The Medicaid program is
   a. federally funded and state mandated.
   b. federally mandated and state administered.
   c. state funded and federally administered.
   d. state mandated and federally administered.

2. The Temporary Assistance to Needy Families (TANF) program provides
   a. cash assistance on a limited-time basis for children deprived of support.
   b. cash assistance to low-income families who need to purchase groceries.
   c. financial assistance for food, utilities, health care, and school expenses.
   d. temporary financial support for housing and household-related costs.

3. Which resource is included in the Protected Resource Amount (PRA), according to the Spousal Impoverishment Protection legislation?
   a. automobile
   b. burial funds
   c. family home
   d. summer camp

4. When a patient has become retroactively eligible for Medicaid benefits, any payments made by the patient during the retroactive period must be
   a. applied toward future medical care.
   b. recorded as additional practice income.
   c. refunded to the patient by Medicaid.
   d. refunded to the patient by the practice.

5. To receive matching funds through Medicaid, states must offer which coverage?
   a. inpatient hospital services
   b. prescription drug benefits
   c. private-duty nursing care
   d. surgical dental services

6. Early and Periodic Screening, Diagnostic, and Treatment (EPSDT) services are offered for which Medicaid-enrolled population?
   a. home health patients
   b. infants and children
   c. persons over the age of 65
   d. rehabilitation facility inpatients

7. Programs of All-Inclusive Care for the Elderly (PACE) programs work to limit out-of-pocket costs to beneficiaries by
   a. limiting participants to care only from contract providers.
   b. providing only very basic medical and preventive care.
   c. requiring a flat $10 copayment for every service provided.
   d. waiving deductibles, copayments, or other cost-sharing.

8. Which is subject to Medicaid preauthorization guidelines?
   a. any minor surgery performed in the provider's procedure room
   b. medically necessary inpatient admission with documentation
   c. outpatient admission on the morning of the day prior to surgery
   d. patient hospitalization that exceeds the expected length of stay

9. Which services are exempt from Medicaid copayments?
   a. family planning services
   b. inpatient hospitalization
   c. outpatient urgent care
   d. prescription drug costs

10. An individual whose income is below 100% of the FPL and has resources at or below twice the standard allowed under the SSI program may receive Medicare benefits as a
    a. qualified disabled and working individual (QDWI).
    b. qualified Medicare beneficiary (QMB).
    c. qualifying individual (QI).
    d. specified low-income Medicare beneficiary (SLMB).

11. A primary care provider in a Medicaid primary care case management (PCCM) plan differs from an HMO primary care provider in that the Medicaid primary care provider is
    a. at higher risk for the cost of care provided.
    b. never permitted to authorize specialty care.
    c. not at risk for the cost of care provided.
    d. responsible for coordinating patient care.

12. A Medicaid voided claim
    a. has an additional payment to the provider.
    b. is in suspense and awaiting approval.
    c. must be corrected and resubmitted.
    d. should not have been paid originally.

13. One way the federal government verifies receipt of Medicaid services by a patient is by use of
    a. an annual audit of each state's Medicaid offices to validate expenditures.
    b. a monthly audit of all the provider's remittance advice notices and receipts.
    c. a monthly survey sent to a sample of Medicaid recipients requesting verification.
    d. a survey provided to each Medicaid recipient upon completion of treatment.

14. Medicaid reimbursement may be denied if the provider neglects to
    a. authenticate each CMS-1500 claim form filed with a manual signature.
    b. check the YES box in block 27 to accept assignment on the claim.
    c. enter the required insurance information in blocks 11 through 11d.
    d. enter the required insurance information in blocks 9 through 9d.

15. A Medicaid card issued for the "unborn child of . . ." is good for
    a. hospitalization services for the newborn child and the mother
    b. medical care rendered to the mother, such as for a back strain
    c. physician office visits for the mother for care other than prenatal
    d. services that promote the life and health of the unborn child

16. What is required in block 32 if an X is entered in the YES box of block 20?
    a. name and address of the outside laboratory
    b. name and address of the referring provider
    c. the same information as was entered in block 31
    d. the same information as was entered in block 33

17. How are diagnosis reference numbers reported in block 24E of a Medicaid claim?
    a. One diagnosis reference number is allowed per line.
    b. Separate each diagnosis reference number with a comma.
    c. Separate each diagnosis reference number with a dash.
    d. Separate each diagnosis reference number with a space.

18. What is entered in block 24I of a Medicare claim?
    a. the letter B, if the service was for both EPSDT and family planning
    b. the letter E, if the service provided was for a medical emergency
    c. the number of days the Medicaid patient was treated for the current problem
    d. the number of times the Medicare patient has been treated for the problem

19. When a Medicaid patient has third-party payer coverage and a claim has been rejected, the rejection code is recorded in which block of the Medicaid CMS-1500 claim?
    a. block 11   c. block 22
    b. block 19   d. block 24K

20. When payment has been received by a primary payer, the payment amount is recorded in which block of the Medicaid CMS-1500 claim?
    a. block 19   c. block 29
    b. block 20   d. block 30

## CHAPTER 16

TRICARE

INTRODUCTION

This chapter familiarizes students with completion of CMS-1500 claim forms for primary TRICARE payers.

ASSIGNMENT 16.1 TRICARE Primary CMS-1500 Claims Completion

OBJECTIVES

At the conclusion of this assignment, the student should be able to:

1. Assign ICD-9-CM diagnosis and CPT or HCPCS procedure/service codes.
2. Prepare a TRICARE insurance primary payer CMS-1500 claim form.

INSTRUCTIONS

Use optical scanning guidelines to complete a CMS-1500 for case studies 16-a through 16-e. Go to the back of the workbook for removable blank CMS-1500 claim forms, or print blank CMS-1500 claim forms using the textbook CD-ROM. Refer to the CMS-1500 claims completion instructions (primary) in the textbook.

ASSIGNMENT 16.2 Multiple Choice Review

1. The conversion of CHAMPUS to TRICARE was the result of a(n)
   a. act of legislation that was passed in 1967 by request of the military.
   b. need to limit the amount of money paid for military dependents' care.
   c. reorganization of each of the United States uniformed services.
   d. successful demonstration project conducted in California and Hawaii.

DONALD L. GIVINGS, M.D.

11350 Medical Drive ■ Anywhere US 12345 ■ (101) 111-5555
EIN: 11-1234562

Case Study 16-a

PATIENT INFORMATION:

Name:	Jeffrey D. Heem
Address:	333 Heavenly Place
City:	Anywhere
State:	US
Zip Code:	12345
Telephone:	(101) 333-5555
Gender:	Male
Date of Birth:	05-05-1964
Occupation:	
Employer:	US Army
Spouse's Employer:	

INSURANCE INFORMATION:

Patient Number:	16-a
Place of Service:	Office
Primary Insurance Plan:	TRICARE Standard
Primary Insurance Plan ID #:	234-55-6789
Group #:	
Primary Policyholder:	Jeffrey D. Heem
Policyholder Date of Birth:	05-05-1964
Relationship to Patient:	Self
Secondary Insurance Plan:	
Secondary Insurance Plan ID #:	
Secondary Policyholder:	

Patient Status   ☒ Married   ☐ Divorced   ☐ Single   ☐ Student   ☐ Other

---

DIAGNOSIS INFORMATION

Diagnosis	Code	Diagnosis	Code
1. Acute sinusitis, frontal		5.	
2. Sore throat		6.	
3.		7.	
4.		8.	

PROCEDURE INFORMATION

Description of Procedure or Service	Date	Code	Charge
1. New patient OV, level II	11-05-YYYY		$70.00
2.			
3.			
4.			
5.			

SPECIAL NOTES:

DONALD L. GIVINGS, M.D.

11350 Medical Drive ■ Anywhere US 12345 ■ (101) 111-5555
EIN: 11-1234562

Case Study 16-b

PATIENT INFORMATION:

Name:	Dana S. Bright
Address:	28 Upton Circle
City:	Anywhere
State:	US
Zip Code:	12345
Telephone:	(101) 333-5555
Gender:	Female
Date of Birth:	07-05-1971
Occupation:	
Employer:	
Spouse's Employer:	US Navy (See duty address below)

INSURANCE INFORMATION:

Patient Number:	16-b
Place of Service:	Office
Primary Insurance Plan:	TRICARE Extra
Primary Insurance Plan ID #:	567-56-5757
Group #:	
Primary Policyholder:	Ron L. Bright
Policyholder Date of Birth:	08-12-70
Relationship to Patient:	Spouse
Secondary Insurance Plan:	
Secondary Insurance Plan ID #:	
Secondary Policyholder:	

Patient Status ☒ Married   ☐ Divorced   ☐ Single   ☐ Student   ☐ Other

DIAGNOSIS INFORMATION

Diagnosis	Code	Diagnosis	Code
1. Chronic cholecystitis		5.	
2.		6.	
3.		7.	
4.		8.	

PROCEDURE INFORMATION

Description of Procedure or Service	Date	Code	Charge
1. Est. patient OV level IV	06-22-YYYY		$85.00
2.			
3.			
4.			
5.			

SPECIAL NOTES:

Spouse's Employer's Address: Duty Station Address Dept. 21 Naval Station, Anywhere US 23456

Refer patient to Dr. Kutter

JONATHAN B. KUTTER, M.D. SURGERY

339 Woodland Place ■ Anywhere US 12345 ■ (101) 111-5555
EIN: 11-5566772

Case Study 16-c

PATIENT INFORMATION:

Name:	Dana S. Bright
Address:	28 Upton Circle
City:	Anywhere
State:	US
Zip Code:	12345
Telephone:	(101) 333-5555
Gender:	Female
Date of Birth:	07-05-1971
Occupation:	
Employer:	
Spouse's Employer:	US Navy (See duty address below)

INSURANCE INFORMATION:

Patient Number:	16-c
Place of Service:	Mercy Hospital (Outpatient)
Primary Insurance Plan:	TRICARE Extra
Primary Insurance Plan ID #:	567-56-5757
Group #:	
Primary Policyholder:	Ron L. Bright
Policyholder Date of Birth:	08-12-70
Relationship to Patient:	Spouse
Secondary Insurance Plan:	
Secondary Insurance Plan ID #:	
Secondary Policyholder:	

Patient Status   ☒ Married   ☐ Divorced   ☐ Single   ☐ Student   ☐ Other

DIAGNOSIS INFORMATION

Diagnosis	Code	Diagnosis	Code
1. Chronic cholecystitis		5.	
2.		6.	
3.		7.	
4.		8.	

PROCEDURE INFORMATION

Description of Procedure or Service	Date	Code	Charge
1. Laparoscopic cholecystectomy	06-29-YYYY		$2,300.00
2.			
3.			
4.			
5.			

SPECIAL NOTES:
Referred by Donald L. Givings, M.D.,   EIN: 111234562
Onset of symptoms: 06-22-YYYY.

DONALD L. GIVINGS, M.D.

11350 Medical Drive ■ Anywhere US 12345 ■ (101) 111-5555
EIN: 11-1234562

Case Study 16-d

PATIENT INFORMATION:

Name:	Odel M. Ryer, Jr.
Address:	484 Pinewood Ave.
City:	Anywhere
State:	US
Zip Code:	12345
Telephone:	(101) 333-5555
Gender:	Male
Date of Birth:	04-28-1949
Occupation:	
Employer:	US Air Force Retired
Spouse's Employer:	

INSURANCE INFORMATION:

Patient Number:	16-d
Place of Service:	Office
Primary Insurance Plan:	TRICARE Standard
Primary Insurance Plan ID #:	464-44-4646
Group #:	
Primary Policyholder:	Odel M. Ryer, Jr.
Policyholder Date of Birth:	04-28-1949
Relationship to Patient:	Self
Secondary Insurance Plan:	
Secondary Insurance Plan ID #:	
Secondary Policyholder:	

Patient Status   ☒ Married   ☐ Divorced   ☐ Single   ☐ Student   ☐ Other

DIAGNOSIS INFORMATION

Diagnosis	Code	Diagnosis	Code
1. Heartburn		5.	
2.		6.	
3.		7.	
4.		8.	

PROCEDURE INFORMATION

Description of Procedure or Service	Date	Code	Charge
1. Est. patient OV level I	04-12-YYYY		$55.00
2.			
3.			
4.			
5.			

SPECIAL NOTES:
   Return visit: PRN

DONALD L. GIVINGS, M.D.

11350 Medical Drive ■ Anywhere US 12345 ■ (101) 111-5555
EIN: 11-1234562

Case Study 16-e

PATIENT INFORMATION:

Name:	Annalisa M. Faris
Address:	394 Myriam Court
City:	Anywhere
State:	US
Zip Code:	12345
Telephone:	(101) 333-5555
Gender:	Female
Date of Birth:	04-04-1999
Occupation:	
Employer:	
Spouse's Employer:	

INSURANCE INFORMATION:

Patient Number:	16-e
Place of Service:	Inpatient hospital
Primary Insurance Plan:	TRICARE Prime
Primary Insurance Plan ID #:	323-23-3333
Group #:	
Primary Policyholder:	Nacir R. Faris
Policyholder Date of Birth:	06-21-1975
Relationship to Patient:	Father
Secondary Insurance Plan:	
Secondary Insurance Plan ID #:	
Secondary Policyholder:	

Patient Status ☐ Married ☐ Divorced ☒ Single ☐ Student ☐ Other

DIAGNOSIS INFORMATION

Diagnosis	Code	Diagnosis	Code
1. Chills with fever		5.	
2. Lethargy		6.	
3. Loss of appetite		7.	
4. Loss of weight		8.	

PROCEDURE INFORMATION

Description of Procedure or Service	Date	Code	Charge
1. Initial hosp. level IV	06-02-YYYY		$200.00
2. Subsq. hosp. level III	06-03-YYYY		$85.00
3. Subsq. hosp. level III	06-04-YYYY		$85.00
4. Subsq. hosp. level III	06-06-YYYY		$85.00
5. Subsq. hosp. level II	06-07-YYYY		$75.00
6. Subsq. hosp. level II	06-09-YYYY		$75.00
7. Subsq. hosp. level II	06-10-YYYY		$75.00

SPECIAL NOTES:
Mercy Hospital, Anywhere Street, Anywhere US 12345.
Father is stationed at 555 Regiment Way, Anywhere US 12345
Patient was discharged 06/11/YYYY but not seen

2. Lead Agents of selected military treatment facilities (MTFs) hold which rank?
   a. captain
   b. commander
   c. lieutenant
   d. major

3. The entire health care system of the U.S. uniformed services is known as the
   a. CHAMPUS Reform Initiative (CRI).
   b. Department of Defense Health System.
   c. Military Health Services System (MHSS).
   d. TRICARE Demonstration Project.

4. The organization responsible for coordinating and administering the TRICARE program is the
   a. Military Health Services System.
   b. TRICARE Management Activity.
   c. U.S. Department of Defense.
   d. U.S. Office of Health Affairs.

5. The term *sponsor* is used to describe
   a. active duty military personnel.
   b. beneficiaries of military personnel.
   c. dependents of military personnel.
   d. remarried former spouses of military personnel.

6. Claims are submitted to the TRICARE
   a. Management Activity.
   b. Program Integrity Office.
   c. regional contractors.
   d. service centers.

7. TRICARE plans are primary to
   a. employer-sponsored HMOs.
   b. liability insurance claims.
   c. Medicaid.
   d. workers' compensation.

8. TRICARE nurse advisors are available 24/7 to assist with
   a. preauthorizations and referrals for health care services.
   b. providing information to beneficiaries about TRICARE.
   c. rendering emergency care to TRICARE beneficiaries.
   d. treatment alternatives and recommendations for care.

9. The entity responsible for the prevention, detection, investigation, and control of TRICARE fraud, waste, and abuse is the
   a. Military Health Services System.
   b. Program Integrity Office.
   c. TRICARE Management Activity.
   d. TRICARE Service Center.

10. Which TRICARE option is a fee-for-service plan?
    a. TRICARE Extra
    b. TRICARE Premium
    c. TRICARE Prime
    d. TRICARE Standard

11. In which TRICARE option are active military personnel required to enroll?
    a. TRICARE Extra
    b. TRICARE Premium
    c. TRICARE Prime
    d. TRICARE Standard

12. A military treatment facility (MTF) *catchment area* is
    a. also known as a TRICARE Region, and is managed by Lead Agents.
    b. defined by code boundaries within a 40-mile radius of an MTF.
    c. an area where health care services are not available to military personnel.
    d. an area that contains civilian health care professionals to render care.

13. If a TRICARE Prime beneficiary seeks care from a facility outside of the treatment area without prior approval, the point-of-service option is activated. This will result in what cost(s) to the beneficiary?
    a. a coinsurance payment of 50% for each service or treatment and no deductible
    b. an annual deductible plus 50% or more of visit or treatment fees
    c. beneficiary payment for all services out-of-pocket
    d. the same annual deductible as TRICARE Extra and Standard

14. Which TRICARE option has the highest out-of-pocket costs of all the TRICARE plans?
    a. TRICARE Extra
    b. TRICARE Premium
    c. TRICARE Prime
    d. TRICARE Standard

15. TRICARE outpatient claims will be denied if they are filed more than
    a. one year after the patient's discharge.
    b. one year from the date of service.
    c. six months after the date of service.
    d. 30 days after the date of service.

16. If physician's charges for care of a TRICARE beneficiary, as the result of an accidental injury, are $500 or higher, the insurance specialist must submit a
    a. DD Form 2527 that was completed by the patient.
    b. DD Form 2527 that was completed by the provider.
    c. DD Form 2642 that was completed by the patient.
    d. DD Form 2642 that was completed by the provider.

17. TRICARE has established a good-faith policy for assigned claims to protect the provider when
    a. a claim submitted to TRICARE contains charges for a noncovered service.
    b. a patient presented an invalid ID card when treatment was rendered and billed.
    c. the health insurance specialist entered an incorrect charge on the claim.
    d. the provider has abused the TRICARE program and is under investigation.

18. What special handling is required for TRICARE hospice claims?
    a. Enter the words HOSPICE CLAIM at the top of the CMS-1500 claim form.
    b. Enter the words HOSPICE CLAIMS on the envelope.
    c. Hospice claims can only be submitted every four weeks.
    d. No special handling is required; processing is the same.

19. What information is entered in block 13 of the TRICARE CMS-1500 claim form?
    a. SEE AUTHORIZATION FORM
    b. SIGNATURE ON FILE
    c. the patient's full signature
    d. the provider's full signature

20. When the TRICARE patient has been referred by a military treatment facility, attach a(n) _____ to the CMS-1500 claim form.
    a. DD Form 2527
    b. DD Form 2161
    c. DD Form 2642
    d. MTF referral form

CHAPTER 17

Workers' Compensation

INTRODUCTION

This chapter familiarizes students with completion of CMS-1500 claim forms for primary workers' compensation payers.

ASSIGNMENT 17.1 Workers' Compensation Primary CMS-1500 Claims Completion

OBJECTIVES

At the conclusion of this assignment, the student should be able to:

1. Assign ICD-9-CM diagnosis and CPT or HCPCS procedure/service codes.
2. Prepare a workers' compensation insurance primary payer CMS-1500 claim form.

INSTRUCTIONS

Use optical scanning guidelines to complete a CMS-1500 for case studies 17-a through 17-f. Go to the back of the workbook for removable blank CMS-1500 claim forms, or print blank CMS-1500 claim forms using the textbook CD-ROM. Refer to the CMS-1500 claims completion instructions (primary) in the textbook.

ASSIGNMENT 17.2 Multiple Choice Review

1. Which federal workers' compensation program is administered by the Office of Workers' Compensation Programs?
   a. Federal Black Lung Program
   b. Federal Employees' Compensation Act Program
   c. Federal Employment Liability Act
   d. Longshore and Harbor Workers' Compensation Program

DONALD L. GIVINGS, M.D.

11350 Medical Drive ■ Anywhere US 12345 ■ (101) 111-5555
EIN: 11-1234562

Case Study 17-a

PATIENT INFORMATION:

Name:	Sandy S. Grand
Address:	109 Darling Road
City:	Anywhere
State:	US
Zip Code:	12345
Telephone:	(101) 333-5555
Gender:	Female
Date of Birth:	12-03-1972
Occupation:	
Employer:	Starport Fitness Center
Spouse's Employer:	

INSURANCE INFORMATION:

Patient Number:	17-a
Place of Service:	Office
Primary Insurance Plan:	Workers Trust
Primary Insurance Plan ID #:	CLR5457 (claim ID #)
Group #:	
Primary Policyholder:	
Policyholder Date of Birth:	
Relationship to Patient:	
Secondary Insurance Plan:	
Secondary Insurance Plan ID #:	
Secondary Policyholder:	

Patient Status ☐ Married ☐ Divorced ☒ Single ☐ Student ☐ Other

DIAGNOSIS INFORMATION

Diagnosis	Code	Diagnosis	Code
1. Wrist fracture, closed		5.	
2. Fall from chair on 02-03-YYYY		6.	
3.		7.	
4.		8.	

PROCEDURE INFORMATION

Description of Procedure or Service	Date	Code	Charge
1. New patient OV level IV	02-03-YYYY		$100.00
2.			
3.			
4.			
5.			

SPECIAL NOTES:
   Patient cannot return to work until cleared by the orthopedist, Dr. Breaker.

ELLIOT A. BREAKER, M.D. ORTHOPEDIST

5124 Pharmacy Drive ■ Anywhere US 12345 ■ (101) 111-5555
EIN: 11-9977552

Case Study 17-b

PATIENT INFORMATION:

Name:	Sandy S. Grand
Address:	109 Darling Road
City:	Anywhere
State:	US
Zip Code:	12345
Telephone:	(101) 333-5555
Gender:	Female
Date of Birth:	12-03-1972
Occupation:	
Employer:	Starport Fitness Center
Spouse's Employer:	

INSURANCE INFORMATION:

Patient Number:	17-b
Place of Service:	Office
Primary Insurance Plan:	Workers Trust
Primary Insurance Plan ID #:	CLR5457 (claim ID #)
Group #:	
Primary Policyholder:	
Policyholder Date of Birth:	
Relationship to Patient:	
Secondary Insurance Plan:	
Secondary Insurance Plan ID #:	
Secondary Policyholder:	

Patient Status   ☐ Married   ☐ Divorced   ☒ Single   ☐ Student   ☐ Other

DIAGNOSIS INFORMATION

Diagnosis	Code	Diagnosis	Code
1. Wrist fracture, closed		5.	
2. Fall from chair		6.	
3.		7.	
4.		8.	

PROCEDURE INFORMATION

Description of Procedure or Service	Date	Code	Charge
1. Office consult level IV	02-05-YYYY		$95.00
2. X-ray wrist, complete	02-05-YYYY		75.00
3. Application of cast, hand and lower forearm	02-05-YYYY		50.00
4.			
5.			

SPECIAL NOTES:

Date of injury: 02-03-YYYY. Return to work 02-12-YYYY.
Referred by Donald L. Givings, M.D. EIN 11-1234562
Return visit: 2 weeks

DONALD L. GIVINGS, M.D.

11350 Medical Drive ■ Anywhere US 12345 ■ (101) 111-5555

EIN: 11-1234562

Case Study 17-c

PATIENT INFORMATION:

Name:	Marianna D. Holland
Address:	509 Dutch Street
City:	Anywhere
State:	US
Zip Code:	12345
Telephone:	(101) 333-5555
Gender:	Female
Date of Birth:	11-05-1977
Occupation:	
Employer:	Hair Etc.
Spouse's Employer:	

INSURANCE INFORMATION:

Patient Number:	17-c
Place of Service:	Office
Primary Insurance Plan:	Workers Shield
Primary Insurance Plan ID #:	BA6788 (claim ID #)
Group #:	
Primary Policyholder:	
Policyholder Date of Birth:	
Relationship to Patient:	
Secondary Insurance Plan:	
Secondary Insurance Plan ID #:	
Secondary Policyholder:	

Patient Status ☒ Married   ☐ Divorced   ☐ Single   ☐ Student   ☐ Other

DIAGNOSIS INFORMATION

Diagnosis	Code	Diagnosis	Code
1. Fracture, nasal bones, closed		5.	
2.		6.	
3.		7.	
4.		8.	

PROCEDURE INFORMATION

Description of Procedure or Service	Date	Code	Charge
1. New patient OV level III	05-12-YYYY		$80.00
2.			
3.			
4.			
5.			

SPECIAL NOTES:

Patient may return to work 5/16/YYYY.
Return visit: PRN

DONALD L. GIVINGS, M.D.

11350 Medical Drive ■ Anywhere US 12345 ■ (101) 111-5555
EIN: 11-1234562

Case Study 17-d

PATIENT INFORMATION:

Name:	Thomas J. Buffet
Address:	12 Hauser Drive
City:	Anywhere
State:	US
Zip Code:	12345
Telephone:	(101) 333-5555
Gender:	Male
Date of Birth:	12-03-1965
Occupation:	
Employer:	Start Packing Real Estate
Spouse's Employer:	

INSURANCE INFORMATION:

Patient Number:	17-d
Place of Service:	Office
Primary Insurance Plan:	Workers Guard
Primary Insurance Plan ID #:	WC4958 (claim ID #)
Group #:	
Primary Policyholder:	
Policyholder Date of Birth:	
Relationship to Patient:	
Secondary Insurance Plan:	
Secondary Insurance Plan ID #:	
Secondary Policyholder:	

Patient Status ☒ Married ☐ Divorced ☐ Single ☐ Student ☐ Other

DIAGNOSIS INFORMATION

Diagnosis	Code	Diagnosis	Code
1. Ankle sprain, deltoid		5.	
2.		6.	
3.		7.	
4.		8.	

PROCEDURE INFORMATION

Description of Procedure or Service	Date	Code	Charge
1. New patient OV level II	10-10-YYYY		$70.00
2.			
3.			
4.			
5.			

SPECIAL NOTES:
   Date of injury: 10-09-YYYY.
   Patient may return to work tomorrow.
   Return visit: PRN

DONALD L. GIVINGS, M.D.

11350 Medical Drive ■ Anywhere US 12345 ■ (101) 111-5555
EIN: 11-1234562

Case Study 17-e

PATIENT INFORMATION:

Name:	Priscilla R. Shepard
Address:	23 Easy Street
City:	Anywhere
State:	US
Zip Code:	12345
Telephone:	(101) 333-5555
Gender:	Female
Date of Birth:	07-15-1956
Occupation:	
Employer:	Ultimate Cleaners
Spouse's Employer:	

INSURANCE INFORMATION:

Patient Number:	17-e
Place of Service:	Emergency hospital
Primary Insurance Plan:	Workers Prompt
Primary Insurance Plan ID #:	MA4958 (claim ID #)
Group #:	
Primary Policyholder:	
Policyholder Date of Birth:	
Relationship to Patient:	
Secondary Insurance Plan:	
Secondary Insurance Plan ID #:	
Secondary Policyholder:	

Patient Status ☐ Married   ☐ Divorced   ☒ Single   ☐ Student   ☐ Other

---

DIAGNOSIS INFORMATION

Diagnosis	Code	Diagnosis	Code
1. Open wound, shoulder		5.	
2.		6.	
3.		7.	
4.		8.	

PROCEDURE INFORMATION

Description of Procedure or Service	Date	Code	Charge
1. ER visit level III	07-16-YYYY		$150.00
2.			
3.			
4.			
5.			

SPECIAL NOTES:

Mercy Hospital, Anywhere St, Anywhere US 12345.
Patient was seen in the ER today. Injury occurred at work this morning.

DONALD L. GIVINGS, M.D.

11350 Medical Drive ■ Anywhere US 12345 ■ (101) 111-5555
EIN: 11-1234562

Case Study 17-f

PATIENT INFORMATION:

Name:	Priscilla R. Shepard
Address:	23 Easy Street
City:	Anywhere
State:	US
Zip Code:	12345
Telephone:	(101) 333-5555
Gender:	Female
Date of Birth:	07-15-1956
Occupation:	
Employer:	Ultimate Cleaners
Spouse's Employer:	

INSURANCE INFORMATION:

Patient Number:	17-f
Place of Service:	Inpatient hospital
Primary Insurance Plan:	Workers Prompt
Primary Insurance Plan ID #:	MA4958 (claim ID #)
Group #:	
Primary Policyholder:	
Policyholder Date of Birth:	
Relationship to Patient:	
Secondary Insurance Plan:	
Secondary Insurance Plan ID #:	
Secondary Policyholder:	

Patient Status ☐ Married ☐ Divorced ☒ Single ☐ Student ☐ Other

DIAGNOSIS INFORMATION

Diagnosis	Code	Diagnosis	Code
1. Open wound, shoulder, complicated		5.	
2.		6.	
3.		7.	
4.		8.	

PROCEDURE INFORMATION

Description of Procedure or Service	Date	Code	Charge
1. Initial visit level III	07-20-YYYY		$150.00
2. Subsq. hosp. level II	07-21-YYYY		$75.00
3. Subsq. hosp. level II	07-22-YYYY		$75.00
4. Hosp. discharge, 45 min.	07-23-YYYY		$75.00
5.			

SPECIAL NOTES:

Mercy Hospital, Anywhere St, Anywhere US 12345.
Date of injury 07/16/YYYY.

2. State workers' compensation laws are applicable to
   a. companies with a history of occupational deaths.
   b. employers who are able to afford coverage.
   c. most large and small employers in each state.
   d. only companies with high-risk occupations.

3. The medical term for black lung disease is
   a. pneumoconiosis.
   b. pneumocystitis.
   c. pneumonia.
   d. pneumothorax.

4. The Mine Safety and Health Administration (MSHA) is similar in purpose and intent to the
   a. Energy Employees Occupational Illness Compensation Program.
   b. Federal Occupational Illness Compensation Program.
   c. Longshore and Harbor Workers' Compensation Program.
   d. Occupational Safety and Health Administration (OSHA).

5. Material Safety Data Sheets (MSDS) contain data regarding
   a. chemical and hazardous substances used at a worksite.
   b. how to implement an effective safety program at work.
   c. medicinal and therapeutic substances used at a worksite.
   d. the yearly number of occupational injuries and illness.

6. How long must records of employee vaccinations and accidental exposure incidents be retained?
   a. 10 years
   b. 20 years
   c. 7 years
   d. 5 years

7. The Federal Employment Liability Act (FELA) and the Merchant Marine Act were designed to
   a. develop a compensation fund for occupational injuries and deaths.
   b. increase the salaries of persons in certain high-risk occupations.
   c. offer medical and health care benefits to federal employees.
   d. provide employees with protection from employer negligence.

8. Which agency is responsible for handling appeals for denied workers' compensation claims?
   a. Occupational Safety and Health Administration
   b. Office of Workers' Compensation Programs
   c. State Insurance Commissioner
   d. State Workers' Compensation Commission

9. In which scenario would an employee be eligible for workers' compensation benefits?
   a. An angry worker was injured in the warehouse when he tried to attack a coworker.
   b. An employee broke her ankle while walking with a coworker during their lunch hour.
   c. An employee was injured in a car accident while delivering X-ray films to a specialist.
   d. The employee was injured in a fall after drinking too much alcohol at a dinner meeting.

10. Workers' compensation survivor benefits are calculated according to the
    a. degree of risk that was involved in the employee's occupation.
    b. employee's earning capacity at the time of illness or injury.
    c. number of survivors in the household under the age of 18.
    d. period of time the employee was disabled before death.

11. A patient was treated by his primary care physician on 01/25/YYYY for a wrist fracture that occurred on the job. On 02/02/YYYY, the patient was evaluated for symptoms of severe high blood pressure and a recheck of the wrist fracture. Where should the provider document treatment from the visit on 02/02/YYYY?
    a. Both services should be recorded in the patient's medical record.
    b. Both services should be recorded in the workers' compensation record.
    c. Only the fracture recheck is to be recorded in the workers' compensation record.
    d. Only the visit from 01/25/YYYY is to be recorded in the workers' compensation record.

12. The First Report of Injury form is completed by the
    a. employer.   c. provider.
    b. patient.   d. witness.

13. The treating physician's personal signature is required
    a. if the patient has requested report copies.
    b. on all original reports and photocopies.
    c. only on original reports.
    d. only on photocopied reports.

14. After the claim has been acknowledged, the information that must be included on all correspondence to the employer, carrier, billings, and the Commission Board is the
    a. file/case number assigned to the claim.
    b. patient's employee number.
    c. patient's social security number.
    d. treating physician's provider EIN number.

15. When an appeals board renders a final determination on a claim, this is known as
    a. adjudication.   c. deposition.
    b. arbitration.   d. mediation.

16. Which of the following can be a designated state workers' compensation fiscal agent?
    a. a private, commercial insurance company
    b. the Office of Workers' Compensation Programs
    c. the state's compensation board
    d. the state's Department of Labor

17. Workers' compensation plans that allow an employer to set aside a state-mandated percentage of capital funds to cover employee compensation and benefits are
    a. combination programs.   c. self-insurance plans.
    b. commercial insurance.   d. state-funded plans.

18. If a patient fails to alert the provider that an injury was work-related, and then changes his mind later and tries to receive workers' compensation benefits, the claim will most likely be
    a. denied by the workers' compensation payer, and the patient will have to appeal.
    b. held in suspense for an indefinite period of time until documentation is reviewed.
    c. paid by workers' compensation beginning with the date of the most recent treatment.
    d. paid out-of-pocket by the patient first, then reimbursed by workers' compensation.

19. Which box is marked in block 6 of the workers' compensation CMS-1500 claim form?
    a. CHILD
    b. OTHER
    c. SELF
    d. SPOUSE

20. What is entered in block 17a of the workers' compensation CMS-1500 claim form?
    a. nothing; the block is left blank
    b. the provider's EIN number
    c. the provider's PlanID number
    d. the provider's social security number

(SAMPLE ONLY - NOT APPROVED FOR USE)

CARRIER

PICA

HEALTH INSURANCE CLAIM FORM

PICA

1. MEDICARE ☐ (Medicare #) MEDICAID ☐ (Medicaid #) CHAMPUS ☐ (Sponsor's SSN) CHAMPVA ☐ (VA File #) GROUP HEALTH PLAN ☐ (SSN or ID) FECA BLK LUNG ☐ (SSN) OTHER ☐ (ID)

1a. INSURED'S I.D. NUMBER (FOR PROGRAM IN ITEM 1)

2. PATIENT'S NAME (Last Name, First Name, Middle Initial)

3. PATIENT'S BIRTH DATE MM | DD | YY   SEX M ☐ F ☐

4. INSURED'S NAME (Last Name, First Name, Middle Initial)

5. PATIENT'S ADDRESS (No. Street)

6. PATIENT RELATIONSHIP TO INSURED Self ☐ Spouse ☐ Child ☐ Other ☐

7. INSURED'S ADDRESS (No. Street)

CITY   STATE

8. PATIENT STATUS Single ☐ Married ☐ Other ☐ Employed ☐ Full-Time Student ☐ Part-Time Student ☐

CITY   STATE

ZIP CODE   TELEPHONE (Include Area Code) (   )

ZIP CODE   TELEPHONE (INCLUDE AREA CODE) (   )

9. OTHER INSURED'S NAME (Last Name, First Name, Middle Initial)

10. IS PATIENT'S CONDITION RELATED TO:

11. INSURED'S POLICY GROUP OR FECA NUMBER

a. OTHER INSURED'S POLICY OR GROUP NUMBER

a. EMPLOYMENT? (CURRENT OR PREVIOUS) ☐ YES ☐ NO

a. INSURED'S DATE OF BIRTH MM | DD | YY   SEX M ☐ F ☐

b. OTHER INSURED'S DATE OF BIRTH MM | DD | YY   SEX M ☐ F ☐

b. AUTO ACCIDENT?   PLACE (State) ☐ YES ☐ NO

b. EMPLOYER'S NAME OR SCHOOL NAME

c. EMPLOYER'S NAME OR SCHOOL NAME

c. OTHER ACCIDENT? ☐ YES ☐ NO

c. INSURANCE PLAN NAME OR PROGRAM NAME

d. INSURANCE PLAN NAME OR PROGRAM NAME

10d. RESERVED FOR LOCAL USE

d. IS THERE ANOTHER HEALTH BENEFIT PLAN? ☐ YES ☐ NO If yes, return to and complete item 9 a – d.

READ BACK OF FORM BEFORE COMPLETING & SIGNING THIS FORM.
12. PATIENT'S OR AUTHORIZED PERSON'S SIGNATURE I authorize the release of any medical or other information necessary to process this claim. I also request payment of government benefits either to myself or to the party who accepts assignment below.

SIGNED   DATE

13. INSURED'S OR AUTHORIZED PERSON'S SIGNATURE I authorize payment of medical benefits to the undersigned physician or supplier for services described below.

SIGNED

PATIENT AND INSURED INFORMATION

14. DATE OF CURRENT: ILLNESS (First symptom) OR INJURY (Accident) OR PREGNANCY (LMP) MM | DD | YY

15. IF PATIENT HAS HAD SAME OR SIMILAR ILLNESS, GIVE FIRST DATE MM | DD | YY

16. DATES PATIENT UNABLE TO WORK IN CURRENT OCCUPATION FROM MM | DD | YY TO MM | DD | YY

17. NAME OF REFERRING PHYSICIAN OR OTHER SOURCE

17a. I.D. NUMBER OF REFERRING PHYSICIAN

18. HOSPITALIZATION DATES RELATED TO CURRENT SERVICES FROM MM | DD | YY TO MM | DD | YY

19. RESERVED FOR LOCAL USE

20. OUTSIDE LAB? ☐ YES ☐ NO $ CHARGES

21. DIAGNOSIS OR NATURE OF ILLNESS OR INJURY. (RELATE ITEMS 1, 2, 3, OR 4 TO ITEM 24E BY LINE)

1. |___.___| 3. |___.___|

2. |___.___| 4. |___.___|

22. MEDICAID RESUBMISSION CODE   ORIGINAL REF. NO.

23. PRIOR AUTHORIZATION NUMBER

24. A DATE(S) OF SERVICE						B Place of Service	C Type of Service	D PROCEDURES, SERVICES, OR SUPPLIES (Explain Unusual Circumstances)		E DIAGNOSIS CODE	F $ CHARGES	G DAYS OR UNITS	H EPSDT Family Plan	I EMG	J COB	K RESERVED FOR LOCAL USE
From MM	DD	YY	To MM	DD	YY			CPT/HCPCS	MODIFIER							
1																
2																
3																
4																
5																
6																

25. FEDERAL TAX I.D. NUMBER SSN ☐ EIN ☐

26. PATIENT'S ACCOUNT NO.

27. ACCEPT ASSIGNMENT? (For govt. claims, see back) ☐ YES ☐ NO

28. TOTAL CHARGE $

29. AMOUNT PAID $

30. BALANCE DUE $

31. SIGNATURE OF PHYSICIAN OR SUPPLIER INCLUDING DEGREES OR CREDENTIALS (I certify that the statements on the reverse apply to this bill and are made a part thereof.)

SIGNED   DATE

32. NAME AND ADDRESS OF FACILITY WHERE SERVICES WERE RENDERED (If other than home or office)

33. PHYSICIAN'S, SUPPLIER'S BILLING NAME, ADDRESS, ZIP CODE & PHONE #

PIN#   GRP#

PHYSICIAN OR SUPPLIER INFORMATION

(SAMPLE ONLY - NOT APPROVED FOR USE)   PLEASE PRINT OR TYPE

SAMPLE FORM 1500
SAMPLE FORM 1500 SAMPLE FORM 1500

197

PLEASE
DO NOT
STAPLE
IN THIS
AREA

CARRIER

☐☐ PICA

HEALTH INSURANCE CLAIM FORM

PICA ☐☐

1. MEDICARE	MEDICAID	CHAMPUS	CHAMPVA	GROUP HEALTH PLAN	FECA BLK LUNG	OTHER	1a. INSURED'S I.D. NUMBER	(FOR PROGRAM IN ITEM 1)
☐ (Medicare #)	☐ (Medicaid #)	☐ (Sponsor's SSN)	☐ (VA File #)	☐ (SSN or ID)	☐ (SSN)	☐ (ID)		

2. PATIENT'S NAME (Last Name, First Name, Middle Initial)

3. PATIENT'S BIRTH DATE MM | DD | YY   SEX   M ☐ F ☐

4. INSURED'S NAME (Last Name, First Name, Middle Initial)

5. PATIENT'S ADDRESS (No. Street)

6. PATIENT RELATIONSHIP TO INSURED   Self ☐ Spouse ☐ Child ☐ Other ☐

7. INSURED'S ADDRESS (No. Street)

CITY   STATE

8. PATIENT STATUS   Single ☐   Married ☐   Other ☐
Employed ☐   Full-Time Student ☐   Part-Time Student ☐

CITY   STATE

ZIP CODE   TELEPHONE (Include Area Code) (   )

ZIP CODE   TELEPHONE (INCLUDE AREA CODE) (   )

9. OTHER INSURED'S NAME (Last Name, First Name, Middle Initial)

10. IS PATIENT'S CONDITION RELATED TO:

11. INSURED'S POLICY GROUP OR FECA NUMBER

a. OTHER INSURED'S POLICY OR GROUP NUMBER

a. EMPLOYMENT? (CURRENT OR PREVIOUS)   ☐ YES   ☐ NO

a. INSURED'S DATE OF BIRTH MM | DD | YY   SEX   M ☐ F ☐

b. OTHER INSURED'S DATE OF BIRTH MM | DD | YY   SEX   M ☐ F ☐

b. AUTO ACCIDENT?   PLACE (State)   ☐ YES   ☐ NO

b. EMPLOYER'S NAME OR SCHOOL NAME

c. EMPLOYER'S NAME OR SCHOOL NAME

c. OTHER ACCIDENT?   ☐ YES   ☐ NO

c. INSURANCE PLAN NAME OR PROGRAM NAME

d. INSURANCE PLAN NAME OR PROGRAM NAME

10d. RESERVED FOR LOCAL USE

d. IS THERE ANOTHER HEALTH BENEFIT PLAN?   ☐ YES   ☐ NO   If yes, return to and complete item 9 a – d.

READ BACK OF FORM BEFORE COMPLETING & SIGNING THIS FORM.
12. PATIENT'S OR AUTHORIZED PERSON'S SIGNATURE I authorize the release of any medical or other information necessary to process this claim. I also request payment of government benefits either to myself or to the party who accepts assignment below.

SIGNED _____   DATE _____

13. INSURED'S OR AUTHORIZED PERSON'S SIGNATURE I authorize payment of medical benefits to the undersigned physician or supplier for services described below.

SIGNED _____

PATIENT AND INSURED INFORMATION

14. DATE OF CURRENT: MM | DD | YY   ◄ ILLNESS (First symptom) OR INJURY (Accident) OR PREGNANCY (LMP)

15. IF PATIENT HAS HAD SAME OR SIMILAR ILLNESS, GIVE FIRST DATE   MM | DD | YY

16. DATES PATIENT UNABLE TO WORK IN CURRENT OCCUPATION   MM | DD | YY   FROM   TO   MM | DD | YY

17. NAME OF REFERRING PHYSICIAN OR OTHER SOURCE

17a. I.D. NUMBER OF REFERRING PHYSICIAN

18. HOSPITALIZATION DATES RELATED TO CURRENT SERVICES   MM | DD | YY FROM   TO   MM | DD | YY

19. RESERVED FOR LOCAL USE

20. OUTSIDE LAB?   ☐ YES   ☐ NO $ CHARGES

21. DIAGNOSIS OR NATURE OF ILLNESS OR INJURY. (RELATE ITEMS 1, 2, 3, OR 4 TO ITEM 24E BY LINE)

1. |___|___.___| 3. |___|___.___|

2. |___|___.___| 4. |___|___.___|

22. MEDICAID RESUBMISSION CODE   ORIGINAL REF. NO.

23. PRIOR AUTHORIZATION NUMBER

24. A DATE(S) OF SERVICE						B Place of Service	C Type of Service	D PROCEDURES, SERVICES, OR SUPPLIES (Explain Unusual Circumstances)		E DIAGNOSIS CODE	F $ CHARGES	G DAYS OR UNITS	H EPSDT Family Plan	I EMG	J COB	K RESERVED FOR LOCAL USE
From MM	DD	YY	To MM	DD	YY			CPT/HCPCS	MODIFIER							
1																
2																
3																
4																
5																
6																

25. FEDERAL TAX I.D. NUMBER   SSN ☐ EIN ☐

26. PATIENT'S ACCOUNT NO.

27. ACCEPT ASSIGNMENT? (For govt. claims, see back)   ☐ YES   ☐ NO

28. TOTAL CHARGE $

29. AMOUNT PAID $

30. BALANCE DUE $

31. SIGNATURE OF PHYSICIAN OR SUPPLIER INCLUDING DEGREES OR CREDENTIALS (I certify that the statements on the reverse apply to this bill and are made a part thereof.)

SIGNED _____   DATE _____

32. NAME AND ADDRESS OF FACILITY WHERE SERVICES WERE RENDERED (If other than home or office)

33. PHYSICIAN'S, SUPPLIER'S BILLING NAME, ADDRESS, ZIP CODE & PHONE #

PIN#   GRP#

PHYSICIAN OR SUPPLIER INFORMATION

PLEASE PRINT OR TYPE

SAMPLE FORM 1500
SAMPLE FORM 1500 SAMPLE FORM 1500

(SAMPLE ONLY - NOT APPROVED FOR USE)

CARRIER

| | PICA |

HEALTH INSURANCE CLAIM FORM

PICA | |

1. MEDICARE	MEDICAID	CHAMPUS	CHAMPVA	GROUP HEALTH PLAN	FECA BLK LUNG	OTHER	1a. INSURED'S I.D. NUMBER	(FOR PROGRAM IN ITEM 1)
☐ (Medicare #)	☐ (Medicaid #)	☐ (Sponsor's SSN)	☐ (VA File #)	☐ (SSN or ID)	☐ (SSN)	☐ (ID)		

2. PATIENT'S NAME (Last Name, First Name, Middle Initial)

3. PATIENT'S BIRTH DATE MM | DD | YY   SEX M ☐ F ☐

4. INSURED'S NAME (Last Name, First Name, Middle Initial)

5. PATIENT'S ADDRESS (No. Street)

6. PATIENT RELATIONSHIP TO INSURED
Self ☐ Spouse ☐ Child ☐ Other ☐

7. INSURED'S ADDRESS (No. Street)

CITY | STATE

8. PATIENT STATUS
Single ☐ Married ☐ Other ☐
Employed ☐ Full-Time Student ☐ Part-Time Student ☐

CITY | STATE

ZIP CODE | TELEPHONE (Include Area Code) ( )

ZIP CODE | TELEPHONE (INCLUDE AREA CODE) ( )

9. OTHER INSURED'S NAME (Last Name, First Name, Middle Initial)

10. IS PATIENT'S CONDITION RELATED TO:

11. INSURED'S POLICY GROUP OR FECA NUMBER

a. OTHER INSURED'S POLICY OR GROUP NUMBER

a. EMPLOYMENT? (CURRENT OR PREVIOUS)
☐ YES ☐ NO

a. INSURED'S DATE OF BIRTH MM | DD | YY   SEX M ☐ F ☐

b. OTHER INSURED'S DATE OF BIRTH MM | DD | YY   SEX M ☐ F ☐

b. AUTO ACCIDENT?   PLACE (State)
☐ YES ☐ NO

b. EMPLOYER'S NAME OR SCHOOL NAME

c. EMPLOYER'S NAME OR SCHOOL NAME

c. OTHER ACCIDENT?
☐ YES ☐ NO

c. INSURANCE PLAN NAME OR PROGRAM NAME

d. INSURANCE PLAN NAME OR PROGRAM NAME

10d. RESERVED FOR LOCAL USE

d. IS THERE ANOTHER HEALTH BENEFIT PLAN?
☐ YES ☐ NO   If yes, return to and complete item 9 a – d.

READ BACK OF FORM BEFORE COMPLETING & SIGNING THIS FORM.
12. PATIENT'S OR AUTHORIZED PERSON'S SIGNATURE I authorize the release of any medical or other information necessary to process this claim. I also request payment of government benefits either to myself or to the party who accepts assignment below.

SIGNED _____ DATE _____

13. INSURED'S OR AUTHORIZED PERSON'S SIGNATURE I authorize payment of medical benefits to the undersigned physician or supplier for services described below.

SIGNED _____

14. DATE OF CURRENT: ILLNESS (First symptom) OR INJURY (Accident) OR PREGNANCY (LMP) MM | DD | YY

15. IF PATIENT HAS HAD SAME OR SIMILAR ILLNESS, GIVE FIRST DATE MM | DD | YY

16. DATES PATIENT UNABLE TO WORK IN CURRENT OCCUPATION MM | DD | YY FROM ___ TO ___ MM | DD | YY

17. NAME OF REFERRING PHYSICIAN OR OTHER SOURCE

17a. I.D. NUMBER OF REFERRING PHYSICIAN

18. HOSPITALIZATION DATES RELATED TO CURRENT SERVICES MM | DD | YY FROM ___ TO ___ MM | DD | YY

19. RESERVED FOR LOCAL USE

20. OUTSIDE LAB? $ CHARGES
☐ YES ☐ NO

21. DIAGNOSIS OR NATURE OF ILLNESS OR INJURY. (RELATE ITEMS 1, 2, 3, OR 4 TO ITEM 24E BY LINE)

1. |___ . ___   3. |___ . ___

2. |___ . ___   4. |___ . ___

22. MEDICAID RESUBMISSION CODE | ORIGINAL REF. NO.

23. PRIOR AUTHORIZATION NUMBER

24.	A DATE(S) OF SERVICE						B Place of Service	C Type of Service	D PROCEDURES, SERVICES, OR SUPPLIES (Explain Unusual Circumstances)		E DIAGNOSIS CODE	F $ CHARGES	G DAYS OR UNITS	H EPSDT Family Plan	I EMG	J COB	K RESERVED FOR LOCAL USE
	From MM	DD	YY	To MM	DD	YY			CPT/HCPCS	MODIFIER							
1																	
2																	
3																	
4																	
5																	
6																	

25. FEDERAL TAX I.D. NUMBER   SSN ☐ EIN ☐

26. PATIENT'S ACCOUNT NO.

27. ACCEPT ASSIGNMENT? (For govt. claims, see back) ☐ YES ☐ NO

28. TOTAL CHARGE $

29. AMOUNT PAID $

30. BALANCE DUE $

31. SIGNATURE OF PHYSICIAN OR SUPPLIER INCLUDING DEGREES OR CREDENTIALS (I certify that the statements on the reverse apply to this bill and are made a part thereof.)

SIGNED _____ DATE _____

32. NAME AND ADDRESS OF FACILITY WHERE SERVICES WERE RENDERED (If other than home or office)

33. PHYSICIAN'S, SUPPLIER'S BILLING NAME, ADDRESS, ZIP CODE & PHONE #

PIN# _____   GRP# _____

PATIENT AND INSURED INFORMATION

PHYSICIAN OR SUPPLIER INFORMATION

(SAMPLE ONLY - NOT APPROVED FOR USE)

PLEASE PRINT OR TYPE

SAMPLE FORM 1500
SAMPLE FORM 1500 SAMPLE FORM 1500

PLEASE
DO NOT
STAPLE
IN THIS
AREA

CARRIER

HEALTH INSURANCE CLAIM FORM PICA

PICA

1. MEDICARE MEDICAID CHAMPUS CHAMPVA GROUP HEALTH PLAN FECA BLK LUNG OTHER	1a. INSURED'S I.D. NUMBER (FOR PROGRAM IN ITEM 1)
(Medicare #) (Medicaid #) (Sponsor's SSN) (VA File #) (SSN or ID) (SSN) (ID)	

2. PATIENT'S NAME (Last Name, First Name, Middle Initial)	3. PATIENT'S BIRTH DATE MM DD YY SEX M F	4. INSURED'S NAME (Last Name, First Name, Middle Initial)

5. PATIENT'S ADDRESS (No. Street)	6. PATIENT RELATIONSHIP TO INSURED Self Spouse Child Other	7. INSURED'S ADDRESS (No. Street)
CITY STATE	8. PATIENT STATUS Single Married Other	CITY STATE
ZIP CODE TELEPHONE (Include Area Code) ( )	Employed Full-Time Student Part-Time Student	ZIP CODE TELEPHONE (INCLUDE AREA CODE) ( )

9. OTHER INSURED'S NAME (Last Name, First Name, Middle Initial)	10. IS PATIENT'S CONDITION RELATED TO:	11. INSURED'S POLICY GROUP OR FECA NUMBER
a. OTHER INSURED'S POLICY OR GROUP NUMBER	a. EMPLOYMENT? (CURRENT OR PREVIOUS) YES NO	a. INSURED'S DATE OF BIRTH MM DD YY SEX M F
b. OTHER INSURED'S DATE OF BIRTH MM DD YY SEX M F	b. AUTO ACCIDENT? PLACE (State) YES NO	b. EMPLOYER'S NAME OR SCHOOL NAME
c. EMPLOYER'S NAME OR SCHOOL NAME	c. OTHER ACCIDENT? YES NO	c. INSURANCE PLAN NAME OR PROGRAM NAME
d. INSURANCE PLAN NAME OR PROGRAM NAME	10d. RESERVED FOR LOCAL USE	d. IS THERE ANOTHER HEALTH BENEFIT PLAN? YES NO If yes, return to and complete item 9 a – d.

READ BACK OF FORM BEFORE COMPLETING & SIGNING THIS FORM.
12. PATIENT'S OR AUTHORIZED PERSON'S SIGNATURE I authorize the release of any medical or other information necessary to process this claim. I also request payment of government benefits either to myself or to the party who accepts assignment below.

SIGNED _____   DATE _____

13. INSURED'S OR AUTHORIZED PERSON'S SIGNATURE I authorize payment of medical benefits to the undersigned physician or supplier for services described below.

SIGNED _____

PATIENT AND INSURED INFORMATION

14. DATE OF CURRENT: ILLNESS (First symptom) OR INJURY (Accident) OR PREGNANCY (LMP) MM DD YY	15. IF PATIENT HAS HAD SAME OR SIMILAR ILLNESS, GIVE FIRST DATE MM DD YY	16. DATES PATIENT UNABLE TO WORK IN CURRENT OCCUPATION MM DD YY MM DD YY FROM TO
17. NAME OF REFERRING PHYSICIAN OR OTHER SOURCE	17a. I.D. NUMBER OF REFERRING PHYSICIAN	18. HOSPITALIZATION DATES RELATED TO CURRENT SERVICES MM DD YY MM DD YY FROM TO
19. RESERVED FOR LOCAL USE		20. OUTSIDE LAB? YES NO $ CHARGES

21. DIAGNOSIS OR NATURE OF ILLNESS OR INJURY. (RELATE ITEMS 1, 2, 3, OR 4 TO ITEM 24E BY LINE)	22. MEDICAID RESUBMISSION CODE ORIGINAL REF. NO.
1. |___.___| 3. |___.___|	
2. |___.___| 4. |___.___|	23. PRIOR AUTHORIZATION NUMBER

24. A DATE(S) OF SERVICE		B PLACE of Service	C Type of Service	D PROCEDURES, SERVICES, OR SUPPLIES (Explain Unusual Circumstances)		E DIAGNOSIS CODE	F $ CHARGES	G DAYS OR UNITS	H EPSDT Family Plan	I EMG	J COB	K RESERVED FOR LOCAL USE
From MM DD YY	To MM DD YY			CPT/HCPCS	MODIFIER							
1												
2												
3												
4												
5												
6												

25. FEDERAL TAX I.D. NUMBER SSN EIN	26. PATIENT'S ACCOUNT NO.	27. ACCEPT ASSIGNMENT? (For govt. claims, see back) YES NO	28. TOTAL CHARGE $	29. AMOUNT PAID $	30. BALANCE DUE $
31. SIGNATURE OF PHYSICIAN OR SUPPLIER INCLUDING DEGREES OR CREDENTIALS (I certify that the statements on the reverse apply to this bill and are made a part thereof.) SIGNED _____ DATE _____	32. NAME AND ADDRESS OF FACILITY WHERE SERVICES WERE RENDERED (If other than home or office)	33. PHYSICIAN'S, SUPPLIER'S BILLING NAME, ADDRESS, ZIP CODE & PHONE # PIN# GRP#

PHYSICIAN OR SUPPLIER INFORMATION

200

(SAMPLE ONLY - NOT APPROVED FOR USE)

CARRIER

| | PICA | | **HEALTH INSURANCE CLAIM FORM** | PICA | | |

| 1. MEDICARE | MEDICAID | CHAMPUS | CHAMPVA | GROUP HEALTH PLAN | FECA BLK LUNG | OTHER | 1a. INSURED'S I.D. NUMBER | (FOR PROGRAM IN ITEM 1) |
| (Medicare #) | (Medicaid #) | (Sponsor's SSN) | (VA File #) | (SSN or ID) | (SSN) | (ID) | | |

2. PATIENT'S NAME (Last Name, First Name, Middle Initial)

3. PATIENT'S BIRTH DATE MM | DD | YY   SEX M   F

4. INSURED'S NAME (Last Name, First Name, Middle Initial)

5. PATIENT'S ADDRESS (No. Street)

6. PATIENT RELATIONSHIP TO INSURED Self   Spouse   Child   Other

7. INSURED'S ADDRESS (No. Street)

CITY | STATE

8. PATIENT STATUS Single   Married   Other
Employed   Full-Time Student   Part-Time Student

CITY | STATE

ZIP CODE | TELEPHONE (Include Area Code) ( )

ZIP CODE | TELEPHONE (INCLUDE AREA CODE) ( )

9. OTHER INSURED'S NAME (Last Name, First Name, Middle Initial)

10. IS PATIENT'S CONDITION RELATED TO:

11. INSURED'S POLICY GROUP OR FECA NUMBER

a. OTHER INSURED'S POLICY OR GROUP NUMBER

a. EMPLOYMENT? (CURRENT OR PREVIOUS) YES   NO

a. INSURED'S DATE OF BIRTH MM | DD | YY   SEX M   F

b. OTHER INSURED'S DATE OF BIRTH MM | DD | YY   SEX M   F

b. AUTO ACCIDENT?   PLACE (State) YES   NO

b. EMPLOYER'S NAME OR SCHOOL NAME

c. EMPLOYER'S NAME OR SCHOOL NAME

c. OTHER ACCIDENT? YES   NO

c. INSURANCE PLAN NAME OR PROGRAM NAME

d. INSURANCE PLAN NAME OR PROGRAM NAME

10d. RESERVED FOR LOCAL USE

d. IS THERE ANOTHER HEALTH BENEFIT PLAN? YES   NO   If yes, return to and complete item 9 a – d.

READ BACK OF FORM BEFORE COMPLETING & SIGNING THIS FORM.
12. PATIENT'S OR AUTHORIZED PERSON'S SIGNATURE I authorize the release of any medical or other information necessary to process this claim. I also request payment of government benefits either to myself or to the party who accepts assignment below.

SIGNED _____ DATE _____

13. INSURED'S OR AUTHORIZED PERSON'S SIGNATURE I authorize payment of medical benefits to the undersigned physician or supplier for services described below.

SIGNED _____

PATIENT AND INSURED INFORMATION

14. DATE OF CURRENT: ILLNESS (First symptom) OR INJURY (Accident) OR PREGNANCY (LMP) MM | DD | YY

15. IF PATIENT HAS HAD SAME OR SIMILAR ILLNESS, GIVE FIRST DATE MM | DD | YY

16. DATES PATIENT UNABLE TO WORK IN CURRENT OCCUPATION MM | DD | YY FROM   TO MM | DD | YY

17. NAME OF REFERRING PHYSICIAN OR OTHER SOURCE

17a. I.D. NUMBER OF REFERRING PHYSICIAN

18. HOSPITALIZATION DATES RELATED TO CURRENT SERVICES MM | DD | YY FROM   TO MM | DD | YY

19. RESERVED FOR LOCAL USE

20. OUTSIDE LAB? YES   NO $ CHARGES

21. DIAGNOSIS OR NATURE OF ILLNESS OR INJURY. (RELATE ITEMS 1, 2, 3, OR 4 TO ITEM 24E BY LINE)

1. ____ 3. ____
2. ____ 4. ____

22. MEDICAID RESUBMISSION CODE   ORIGINAL REF. NO.

23. PRIOR AUTHORIZATION NUMBER

24. A DATE(S) OF SERVICE			B Place of Service	C Type of Service	D PROCEDURES, SERVICES, OR SUPPLIES (Explain Unusual Circumstances) CPT/HCPCS MODIFIER	E DIAGNOSIS CODE	F $ CHARGES	G DAYS OR UNITS	H EPSDT Family Plan	I EMG	J COB	K RESERVED FOR LOCAL USE
From MM DD YY	To MM DD YY											
1												
2												
3												
4												
5												
6												

25. FEDERAL TAX I.D. NUMBER SSN EIN

26. PATIENT'S ACCOUNT NO.

27. ACCEPT ASSIGNMENT? (For govt. claims, see back) YES   NO

28. TOTAL CHARGE $

29. AMOUNT PAID $

30. BALANCE DUE $

31. SIGNATURE OF PHYSICIAN OR SUPPLIER INCLUDING DEGREES OR CREDENTIALS (I certify that the statements on the reverse apply to this bill and are made a part thereof.)

SIGNED _____ DATE _____

32. NAME AND ADDRESS OF FACILITY WHERE SERVICES WERE RENDERED (If other than home or office)

33. PHYSICIAN'S, SUPPLIER'S BILLING NAME, ADDRESS, ZIP CODE & PHONE #

PIN# | GRP#

PHYSICIAN OR SUPPLIER INFORMATION

(SAMPLE ONLY - NOT APPROVED FOR USE)

PLEASE PRINT OR TYPE

SAMPLE FORM 1500
SAMPLE FORM 1500 SAMPLE FORM 1500

201

(SAMPLE ONLY - NOT APPROVED FOR USE)

CARRIER

[ ] [ ] PICA

HEALTH INSURANCE CLAIM FORM

PICA [ ] [ ]

1. MEDICARE MEDICAID CHAMPUS CHAMPVA GROUP HEALTH PLAN FECA BLK LUNG OTHER
[ ] (Medicare #) [ ] (Medicaid #) [ ] (Sponsor's SSN) [ ] (VA File #) [ ] (SSN or ID) [ ] (SSN) [ ] (ID)

1a. INSURED'S I.D. NUMBER	(FOR PROGRAM IN ITEM 1)

2. PATIENT'S NAME (Last Name, First Name, Middle Initial)

3. PATIENT'S BIRTH DATE MM | DD | YY   SEX M [ ] F [ ]

4. INSURED'S NAME (Last Name, First Name, Middle Initial)

5. PATIENT'S ADDRESS (No. Street)

6. PATIENT RELATIONSHIP TO INSURED
Self [ ] Spouse [ ] Child [ ] Other [ ]

7. INSURED'S ADDRESS (No. Street)

CITY   STATE

8. PATIENT STATUS
Single [ ] Married [ ] Other [ ]

CITY   STATE

ZIP CODE   TELEPHONE (Include Area Code)
(   )

Employed [ ] Full-Time Student [ ] Part-Time Student [ ]

ZIP CODE   TELEPHONE (INCLUDE AREA CODE)
(   )

9. OTHER INSURED'S NAME (Last Name, First Name, Middle Initial)

10. IS PATIENT'S CONDITION RELATED TO:

11. INSURED'S POLICY GROUP OR FECA NUMBER

a. OTHER INSURED'S POLICY OR GROUP NUMBER

a. EMPLOYMENT? (CURRENT OR PREVIOUS)
[ ] YES [ ] NO

a. INSURED'S DATE OF BIRTH MM | DD | YY   SEX M [ ] F [ ]

b. OTHER INSURED'S DATE OF BIRTH MM | DD | YY   SEX M [ ] F [ ]

b. AUTO ACCIDENT?   PLACE (State)
[ ] YES [ ] NO [ ]

b. EMPLOYER'S NAME OR SCHOOL NAME

c. EMPLOYER'S NAME OR SCHOOL NAME

c. OTHER ACCIDENT?
[ ] YES [ ] NO

c. INSURANCE PLAN NAME OR PROGRAM NAME

d. INSURANCE PLAN NAME OR PROGRAM NAME

10d. RESERVED FOR LOCAL USE

d. IS THERE ANOTHER HEALTH BENEFIT PLAN?
[ ] YES [ ] NO If yes, return to and complete item 9 a – d.

READ BACK OF FORM BEFORE COMPLETING & SIGNING THIS FORM.
12. PATIENT'S OR AUTHORIZED PERSON'S SIGNATURE I authorize the release of any medical or other information necessary to process this claim. I also request payment of government benefits either to myself or to the party who accepts assignment below.

SIGNED _____ DATE _____

13. INSURED'S OR AUTHORIZED PERSON'S SIGNATURE I authorize payment of medical benefits to the undersigned physician or supplier for services described below.

SIGNED _____

14. DATE OF CURRENT: MM | DD | YY ◄ ILLNESS (First symptom) OR INJURY (Accident) OR PREGNANCY (LMP)

15. IF PATIENT HAS HAD SAME OR SIMILAR ILLNESS, GIVE FIRST DATE MM | DD | YY

16. DATES PATIENT UNABLE TO WORK IN CURRENT OCCUPATION
FROM MM | DD | YY   TO MM | DD | YY

17. NAME OF REFERRING PHYSICIAN OR OTHER SOURCE

17a. I.D. NUMBER OF REFERRING PHYSICIAN

18. HOSPITALIZATION DATES RELATED TO CURRENT SERVICES
FROM MM | DD | YY   TO MM | DD | YY

19. RESERVED FOR LOCAL USE

20. OUTSIDE LAB? $ CHARGES
[ ] YES [ ] NO

21. DIAGNOSIS OR NATURE OF ILLNESS OR INJURY. (RELATE ITEMS 1, 2, 3, OR 4 TO ITEM 24E BY LINE) ──────

1. |___|.___| 3. |___|.___|
2. |___|.___| 4. |___|.___|

22. MEDICAID RESUBMISSION
CODE   ORIGINAL REF. NO.

23. PRIOR AUTHORIZATION NUMBER

24. A DATE(S) OF SERVICE		B Place of Service	C Type of Service	D PROCEDURES, SERVICES, OR SUPPLIES (Explain Unusual Circumstances)		E DIAGNOSIS CODE	F $ CHARGES	G DAYS OR UNITS	H EPSDT Family Plan	I EMG	J COB	K RESERVED FOR LOCAL USE
From MM DD YY	To MM DD YY			CPT/HCPCS	MODIFIER							
1												
2												
3												
4												
5												
6												

25. FEDERAL TAX I.D. NUMBER   SSN EIN [ ] [ ]

26. PATIENT'S ACCOUNT NO.

27. ACCEPT ASSIGNMENT?
(For govt. claims, see back)
[ ] YES [ ] NO

28. TOTAL CHARGE
$

29. AMOUNT PAID
$

30. BALANCE DUE
$

31. SIGNATURE OF PHYSICIAN OR SUPPLIER INCLUDING DEGREES OR CREDENTIALS
(I certify that the statements on the reverse apply to this bill and are made a part thereof.)

SIGNED _____ DATE _____

32. NAME AND ADDRESS OF FACILITY WHERE SERVICES WERE RENDERED (If other than home or office)

33. PHYSICIAN'S, SUPPLIER'S BILLING NAME, ADDRESS, ZIP CODE & PHONE #

PIN#   GRP#

(SAMPLE ONLY - NOT APPROVED FOR USE)

PLEASE PRINT OR TYPE

SAMPLE FORM 1500
SAMPLE FORM 1500 SAMPLE FORM 1500

PLEASE
DO NOT
STAPLE
IN THIS
AREA

CARRIER

| | PICA

HEALTH INSURANCE CLAIM FORM

PICA | |

1. MEDICARE	MEDICAID	CHAMPUS	CHAMPVA	GROUP HEALTH PLAN	FECA BLK LUNG	OTHER	1a. INSURED'S I.D. NUMBER	(FOR PROGRAM IN ITEM 1)
(Medicare #)	(Medicaid #)	(Sponsor's SSN)	(VA File #)	(SSN or ID)	(SSN)	(ID)		

2. PATIENT'S NAME (Last Name, First Name, Middle Initial)

3. PATIENT'S BIRTH DATE
MM | DD | YY   SEX
M [ ]   F [ ]

4. INSURED'S NAME (Last Name, First Name, Middle Initial)

5. PATIENT'S ADDRESS (No. Street)

6. PATIENT RELATIONSHIP TO INSURED
Self [ ]   Spouse [ ]   Child [ ]   Other [ ]

7. INSURED'S ADDRESS (No. Street)

CITY   STATE

8. PATIENT STATUS
Single [ ]   Married [ ]   Other [ ]
Employed [ ]   Full-Time Student [ ]   Part-Time Student [ ]

CITY   STATE

ZIP CODE   TELEPHONE (Include Area Code)
(   )

ZIP CODE   TELEPHONE (INCLUDE AREA CODE)
(   )

9. OTHER INSURED'S NAME (Last Name, First Name, Middle Initial)

10. IS PATIENT'S CONDITION RELATED TO:

11. INSURED'S POLICY GROUP OR FECA NUMBER

a. OTHER INSURED'S POLICY OR GROUP NUMBER

a. EMPLOYMENT? (CURRENT OR PREVIOUS)
[ ] YES   [ ] NO

a. INSURED'S DATE OF BIRTH
MM | DD | YY   SEX
M [ ]   F [ ]

b. OTHER INSURED'S DATE OF BIRTH
MM | DD | YY   SEX
M [ ]   F [ ]

b. AUTO ACCIDENT?   PLACE (State)
[ ] YES   [ ] NO

b. EMPLOYER'S NAME OR SCHOOL NAME

c. EMPLOYER'S NAME OR SCHOOL NAME

c. OTHER ACCIDENT?
[ ] YES   [ ] NO

c. INSURANCE PLAN NAME OR PROGRAM NAME

d. INSURANCE PLAN NAME OR PROGRAM NAME

10d. RESERVED FOR LOCAL USE

d. IS THERE ANOTHER HEALTH BENEFIT PLAN?
[ ] YES   [ ] NO   If yes, return to and complete item 9 a – d.

READ BACK OF FORM BEFORE COMPLETING & SIGNING THIS FORM.
12. PATIENT'S OR AUTHORIZED PERSON'S SIGNATURE I authorize the release of any medical or other information necessary to process this claim. I also request payment of government benefits either to myself or to the party who accepts assignment below.

SIGNED _____   DATE _____

13. INSURED'S OR AUTHORIZED PERSON'S SIGNATURE I authorize payment of medical benefits to the undersigned physician or supplier for services described below.

SIGNED _____

PATIENT AND INSURED INFORMATION

14. DATE OF CURRENT: ILLNESS (First symptom) OR INJURY (Accident) OR PREGNANCY (LMP)
MM | DD | YY

15. IF PATIENT HAS HAD SAME OR SIMILAR ILLNESS, GIVE FIRST DATE   MM | DD | YY

16. DATES PATIENT UNABLE TO WORK IN CURRENT OCCUPATION
FROM MM | DD | YY   TO MM | DD | YY

17. NAME OF REFERRING PHYSICIAN OR OTHER SOURCE

17a. I.D. NUMBER OF REFERRING PHYSICIAN

18. HOSPITALIZATION DATES RELATED TO CURRENT SERVICES
FROM MM | DD | YY   TO MM | DD | YY

19. RESERVED FOR LOCAL USE

20. OUTSIDE LAB? $ CHARGES
[ ] YES   [ ] NO

21. DIAGNOSIS OR NATURE OF ILLNESS OR INJURY. (RELATE ITEMS 1, 2, 3, OR 4 TO ITEM 24E BY LINE)
1. |___ . ___|
2. |___ . ___|
3. |___ . ___|
4. |___ . ___|

22. MEDICAID RESUBMISSION
CODE   ORIGINAL REF. NO.

23. PRIOR AUTHORIZATION NUMBER

24. A						B	C	D		E	F	G	H	I	J	K
DATE(S) OF SERVICE						Place of Service	Type of Service	PROCEDURES, SERVICES, OR SUPPLIES (Explain Unusual Circumstances)		DIAGNOSIS CODE	$ CHARGES	DAYS OR UNITS	EPSDT Family Plan	EMG	COB	RESERVED FOR LOCAL USE
From			To					CPT/HCPCS	MODIFIER							
MM	DD	YY	MM	DD	YY											
1																
2																
3																
4																
5																
6																

25. FEDERAL TAX I.D. NUMBER   SSN [ ] EIN [ ]

26. PATIENT'S ACCOUNT NO.

27. ACCEPT ASSIGNMENT? (For govt. claims, see back)
[ ] YES   [ ] NO

28. TOTAL CHARGE
$

29. AMOUNT PAID
$

30. BALANCE DUE
$

31. SIGNATURE OF PHYSICIAN OR SUPPLIER INCLUDING DEGREES OR CREDENTIALS
(I certify that the statements on the reverse apply to this bill and are made a part thereof.)

SIGNED _____   DATE _____

32. NAME AND ADDRESS OF FACILITY WHERE SERVICES WERE RENDERED (If other than home or office)

33. PHYSICIAN'S, SUPPLIER'S BILLING NAME, ADDRESS, ZIP CODE & PHONE #

PIN# _____   GRP# _____

PHYSICIAN OR SUPPLIER INFORMATION

PLEASE PRINT OR TYPE

SAMPLE FORM 1500
SAMPLE FORM 1500 SAMPLE FORM 1500

(SAMPLE ONLY - NOT APPROVED FOR USE)

CARRIER

HEALTH INSURANCE CLAIM FORM

| | PICA |

PICA | | | |

1. MEDICARE ☐ (Medicare #)   MEDICAID ☐ (Medicaid #)   CHAMPUS ☐ (Sponsor's SSN)   CHAMPVA ☐ (VA File #)   GROUP HEALTH PLAN ☐ (SSN or ID)   FECA BLK LUNG ☐ (SSN)   OTHER ☐ (ID)

1a. INSURED'S I.D. NUMBER   (FOR PROGRAM IN ITEM 1)

2. PATIENT'S NAME (Last Name, First Name, Middle Initial)

3. PATIENT'S BIRTH DATE   MM | DD | YY   SEX   M ☐   F ☐

4. INSURED'S NAME (Last Name, First Name, Middle Initial)

5. PATIENT'S ADDRESS (No. Street)

6. PATIENT RELATIONSHIP TO INSURED
Self ☐   Spouse ☐   Child ☐   Other ☐

7. INSURED'S ADDRESS (No. Street)

CITY   STATE

8. PATIENT STATUS
Single ☐   Married ☐   Other ☐
Employed ☐   Full-Time Student ☐   Part-Time Student ☐

CITY   STATE

ZIP CODE   TELEPHONE (Include Area Code) ( )

ZIP CODE   TELEPHONE (INCLUDE AREA CODE) ( )

9. OTHER INSURED'S NAME (Last Name, First Name, Middle Initial)

10. IS PATIENT'S CONDITION RELATED TO:

11. INSURED'S POLICY GROUP OR FECA NUMBER

a. OTHER INSURED'S POLICY OR GROUP NUMBER

a. EMPLOYMENT? (CURRENT OR PREVIOUS) YES ☐   NO ☐

a. INSURED'S DATE OF BIRTH   MM | DD | YY   SEX   M ☐   F ☐

b. OTHER INSURED'S DATE OF BIRTH   MM | DD | YY   SEX   M ☐   F ☐

b. AUTO ACCIDENT?   PLACE (State)   YES ☐   NO ☐

b. EMPLOYER'S NAME OR SCHOOL NAME

c. EMPLOYER'S NAME OR SCHOOL NAME

c. OTHER ACCIDENT?   YES ☐   NO ☐

c. INSURANCE PLAN NAME OR PROGRAM NAME

d. INSURANCE PLAN NAME OR PROGRAM NAME

10d. RESERVED FOR LOCAL USE

d. IS THERE ANOTHER HEALTH BENEFIT PLAN?
YES ☐   NO ☐   If yes, return to and complete item 9 a – d.

READ BACK OF FORM BEFORE COMPLETING & SIGNING THIS FORM.
12. PATIENT'S OR AUTHORIZED PERSON'S SIGNATURE I authorize the release of any medical or other information necessary to process this claim. I also request payment of government benefits either to myself or to the party who accepts assignment below.

SIGNED _____   DATE _____

13. INSURED'S OR AUTHORIZED PERSON'S SIGNATURE I authorize payment of medical benefits to the undersigned physician or supplier for services described below.

SIGNED _____

14. DATE OF CURRENT: ◄ ILLNESS (First symptom) OR INJURY (Accident) OR PREGNANCY (LMP)   MM | DD | YY

15. IF PATIENT HAS HAD SAME OR SIMILAR ILLNESS, GIVE FIRST DATE   MM | DD | YY

16. DATES PATIENT UNABLE TO WORK IN CURRENT OCCUPATION
FROM   MM | DD | YY   TO   MM | DD | YY

17. NAME OF REFERRING PHYSICIAN OR OTHER SOURCE

17a. I.D. NUMBER OF REFERRING PHYSICIAN

18. HOSPITALIZATION DATES RELATED TO CURRENT SERVICES
FROM   MM | DD | YY   TO   MM | DD | YY

19. RESERVED FOR LOCAL USE

20. OUTSIDE LAB? $ CHARGES
YES ☐   NO ☐

21. DIAGNOSIS OR NATURE OF ILLNESS OR INJURY. (RELATE ITEMS 1, 2, 3, OR 4 TO ITEM 24E BY LINE)
1. _____   3. _____
2. _____   4. _____

22. MEDICAID RESUBMISSION CODE   ORIGINAL REF. NO.

23. PRIOR AUTHORIZATION NUMBER

24. A DATE(S) OF SERVICE						B Place of Service	C Type of Service	D PROCEDURES, SERVICES, OR SUPPLIES (Explain Unusual Circumstances) CPT/HCPCS	MODIFIER	E DIAGNOSIS CODE	F $ CHARGES	G DAYS OR UNITS	H EPSDT Family Plan	I EMG	J COB	K RESERVED FOR LOCAL USE
From MM	DD	YY	To MM	DD	YY											
1																
2																
3																
4																
5																
6																

25. FEDERAL TAX I.D. NUMBER   SSN ☐   EIN ☐

26. PATIENT'S ACCOUNT NO.

27. ACCEPT ASSIGNMENT? (For govt. claims, see back)   YES ☐   NO ☐

28. TOTAL CHARGE $

29. AMOUNT PAID $

30. BALANCE DUE $

31. SIGNATURE OF PHYSICIAN OR SUPPLIER INCLUDING DEGREES OR CREDENTIALS
(I certify that the statements on the reverse apply to this bill and are made a part thereof.)

SIGNED _____   DATE _____

32. NAME AND ADDRESS OF FACILITY WHERE SERVICES WERE RENDERED (If other than home or office)

33. PHYSICIAN'S, SUPPLIER'S BILLING NAME, ADDRESS, ZIP CODE & PHONE #

PIN#   GRP#

(SAMPLE ONLY - NOT APPROVED FOR USE)

PLEASE PRINT OR TYPE

SAMPLE FORM 1500
SAMPLE FORM 1500 SAMPLE FORM 1500

(SAMPLE ONLY - NOT APPROVED FOR USE)

CARRIER

| | PICA |

HEALTH INSURANCE CLAIM FORM

PICA | | |

1. MEDICARE ☐ (Medicare #) MEDICAID ☐ (Medicaid #) CHAMPUS ☐ (Sponsor's SSN) CHAMPVA ☐ (VA File #) GROUP HEALTH PLAN ☐ (SSN or ID) FECA BLK LUNG ☐ (SSN) OTHER ☐ (ID)

1a. INSURED'S I.D. NUMBER (FOR PROGRAM IN ITEM 1)

2. PATIENT'S NAME (Last Name, First Name, Middle Initial)

3. PATIENT'S BIRTH DATE MM | DD | YY SEX M ☐ F ☐

4. INSURED'S NAME (Last Name, First Name, Middle Initial)

5. PATIENT'S ADDRESS (No. Street)

6. PATIENT RELATIONSHIP TO INSURED Self ☐ Spouse ☐ Child ☐ Other ☐

7. INSURED'S ADDRESS (No. Street)

CITY STATE

8. PATIENT STATUS Single ☐ Married ☐ Other ☐ Employed ☐ Full-Time Student ☐ Part-Time Student ☐

CITY STATE

ZIP CODE TELEPHONE (Include Area Code) (   )

ZIP CODE TELEPHONE (INCLUDE AREA CODE) (   )

9. OTHER INSURED'S NAME (Last Name, First Name, Middle Initial)

10. IS PATIENT'S CONDITION RELATED TO:

11. INSURED'S POLICY GROUP OR FECA NUMBER

a. OTHER INSURED'S POLICY OR GROUP NUMBER

a. EMPLOYMENT? (CURRENT OR PREVIOUS) YES ☐ NO ☐

a. INSURED'S DATE OF BIRTH MM | DD | YY SEX M ☐ F ☐

b. OTHER INSURED'S DATE OF BIRTH MM | DD | YY SEX M ☐ F ☐

b. AUTO ACCIDENT? PLACE (State) YES ☐ NO ☐

b. EMPLOYER'S NAME OR SCHOOL NAME

c. EMPLOYER'S NAME OR SCHOOL NAME

c. OTHER ACCIDENT? YES ☐ NO ☐

c. INSURANCE PLAN NAME OR PROGRAM NAME

d. INSURANCE PLAN NAME OR PROGRAM NAME

10d. RESERVED FOR LOCAL USE

d. IS THERE ANOTHER HEALTH BENEFIT PLAN? YES ☐ NO ☐ If yes, return to and complete item 9 a – d.

READ BACK OF FORM BEFORE COMPLETING & SIGNING THIS FORM.
12. PATIENT'S OR AUTHORIZED PERSON'S SIGNATURE I authorize the release of any medical or other information necessary to process this claim. I also request payment of government benefits either to myself or to the party who accepts assignment below.

SIGNED _____ DATE _____

13. INSURED'S OR AUTHORIZED PERSON'S SIGNATURE I authorize payment of medical benefits to the undersigned physician or supplier for services described below.

SIGNED _____

PATIENT AND INSURED INFORMATION

14. DATE OF CURRENT: MM | DD | YY ◄ ILLNESS (First symptom) OR INJURY (Accident) OR PREGNANCY (LMP)

15. IF PATIENT HAS HAD SAME OR SIMILAR ILLNESS, GIVE FIRST DATE MM | DD | YY

16. DATES PATIENT UNABLE TO WORK IN CURRENT OCCUPATION MM | DD | YY FROM TO MM | DD | YY

17. NAME OF REFERRING PHYSICIAN OR OTHER SOURCE

17a. I.D. NUMBER OF REFERRING PHYSICIAN

18. HOSPITALIZATION DATES RELATED TO CURRENT SERVICES MM | DD | YY FROM TO MM | DD | YY

19. RESERVED FOR LOCAL USE

20. OUTSIDE LAB? YES ☐ NO ☐ $ CHARGES

21. DIAGNOSIS OR NATURE OF ILLNESS OR INJURY. (RELATE ITEMS 1, 2, 3, OR 4 TO ITEM 24E BY LINE)

1. |___.___| 3. |___.___|
2. |___.___| 4. |___.___|

22. MEDICAID RESUBMISSION CODE ORIGINAL REF. NO.

23. PRIOR AUTHORIZATION NUMBER

24. A DATE(S) OF SERVICE						B Place of Service	C Type of Service	D PROCEDURES, SERVICES, OR SUPPLIES (Explain Unusual Circumstances)		E DIAGNOSIS CODE	F $ CHARGES	G DAYS OR UNITS	H EPSDT Family Plan	I EMG	J COB	K RESERVED FOR LOCAL USE
From MM	DD	YY	To MM	DD	YY			CPT/HCPCS	MODIFIER							
1																
2																
3																
4																
5																
6																

25. FEDERAL TAX I.D. NUMBER SSN ☐ EIN ☐

26. PATIENT'S ACCOUNT NO.

27. ACCEPT ASSIGNMENT? (For govt. claims, see back) YES ☐ NO ☐

28. TOTAL CHARGE $

29. AMOUNT PAID $

30. BALANCE DUE $

31. SIGNATURE OF PHYSICIAN OR SUPPLIER INCLUDING DEGREES OR CREDENTIALS (I certify that the statements on the reverse apply to this bill and are made a part thereof.)

SIGNED _____ DATE _____

32. NAME AND ADDRESS OF FACILITY WHERE SERVICES WERE RENDERED (If other than home or office)

33. PHYSICIAN'S, SUPPLIER'S BILLING NAME, ADDRESS, ZIP CODE & PHONE #

PIN# _____ GRP# _____

PHYSICIAN OR SUPPLIER INFORMATION

(SAMPLE ONLY - NOT APPROVED FOR USE) *PLEASE PRINT OR TYPE*

SAMPLE FORM 1500
SAMPLE FORM 1500 SAMPLE FORM 1500

PLEASE
DO NOT
STAPLE
IN THIS
AREA

CARRIER

☐☐ PICA

HEALTH INSURANCE CLAIM FORM

PICA ☐☐☐

1.
MEDICARE	MEDICAID	CHAMPUS	CHAMPVA	GROUP HEALTH PLAN	FECA BLK LUNG	OTHER
☐ (Medicare #)	☐ (Medicaid #)	☐ (Sponsor's SSN)	☐ (VA File #)	☐ (SSN or ID)	☐ (SSN)	☐ (ID)

1a. INSURED'S I.D. NUMBER   (FOR PROGRAM IN ITEM 1)

2. PATIENT'S NAME (Last Name, First Name, Middle Initial)

3. PATIENT'S BIRTH DATE
MM DD YY   SEX
M ☐   F ☐

4. INSURED'S NAME (Last Name, First Name, Middle Initial)

5. PATIENT'S ADDRESS (No. Street)

6. PATIENT RELATIONSHIP TO INSURED
Self ☐   Spouse ☐   Child ☐   Other ☐

7. INSURED'S ADDRESS (No. Street)

CITY   STATE

8. PATIENT STATUS
Single ☐   Married ☐   Other ☐

Employed ☐   Full-Time Student ☐   Part-Time Student ☐

CITY   STATE

ZIP CODE   TELEPHONE (Include Area Code)
(   )

ZIP CODE   TELEPHONE (INCLUDE AREA CODE)
(   )

9. OTHER INSURED'S NAME (Last Name, First Name, Middle Initial)

10. IS PATIENT'S CONDITION RELATED TO:

11. INSURED'S POLICY GROUP OR FECA NUMBER

a. OTHER INSURED'S POLICY OR GROUP NUMBER

a. EMPLOYMENT? (CURRENT OR PREVIOUS)
☐ YES   ☐ NO

a. INSURED'S DATE OF BIRTH
MM DD YY   SEX
M ☐   F ☐

b. OTHER INSURED'S DATE OF BIRTH
MM DD YY   SEX
M ☐   F ☐

b. AUTO ACCIDENT?   PLACE (State)
☐ YES   ☐ NO

b. EMPLOYER'S NAME OR SCHOOL NAME

c. EMPLOYER'S NAME OR SCHOOL NAME

c. OTHER ACCIDENT?
☐ YES   ☐ NO

c. INSURANCE PLAN NAME OR PROGRAM NAME

d. INSURANCE PLAN NAME OR PROGRAM NAME

10d. RESERVED FOR LOCAL USE

d. IS THERE ANOTHER HEALTH BENEFIT PLAN?
☐ YES   ☐ NO   If yes, return to and complete item 9 a – d.

READ BACK OF FORM BEFORE COMPLETING & SIGNING THIS FORM.
12. PATIENT'S OR AUTHORIZED PERSON'S SIGNATURE I authorize the release of any medical or other information necessary to process this claim. I also request payment of government benefits either to myself or to the party who accepts assignment below.

SIGNED _____   DATE _____

13. INSURED'S OR AUTHORIZED PERSON'S SIGNATURE I authorize payment of medical benefits to the undersigned physician or supplier for services described below.

SIGNED _____

PATIENT AND INSURED INFORMATION

14. DATE OF CURRENT: ◄ ILLNESS (First symptom) OR
MM DD YY   INJURY (Accident) OR
                  PREGNANCY (LMP)

15. IF PATIENT HAS HAD SAME OR SIMILAR ILLNESS,
GIVE FIRST DATE   MM DD YY

16. DATES PATIENT UNABLE TO WORK IN CURRENT OCCUPATION
MM DD YY   MM DD YY
FROM   TO

17. NAME OF REFERRING PHYSICIAN OR OTHER SOURCE

17a. I.D. NUMBER OF REFERRING PHYSICIAN

18. HOSPITALIZATION DATES RELATED TO CURRENT SERVICES
MM DD YY   MM DD YY
FROM   TO

19. RESERVED FOR LOCAL USE

20. OUTSIDE LAB? $ CHARGES
☐ YES   ☐ NO

21. DIAGNOSIS OR NATURE OF ILLNESS OR INJURY. (RELATE ITEMS 1, 2, 3, OR 4 TO ITEM 24E BY LINE)
1. └___ . ___   3. └___ . ___
2. └___ . ___   4. └___ . ___

22. MEDICAID RESUBMISSION
CODE   ORIGINAL REF. NO.

23. PRIOR AUTHORIZATION NUMBER

24. A DATE(S) OF SERVICE						B Place of Service	C Type of Service	D PROCEDURES, SERVICES, OR SUPPLIES (Explain Unusual Circumstances)		E DIAGNOSIS CODE	F $ CHARGES	G DAYS OR UNITS	H EPSDT Family Plan	I EMG	J COB	K RESERVED FOR LOCAL USE
From			To					CPT/HCPCS	MODIFIER							
MM	DD	YY	MM	DD	YY											
1																
2																
3																
4																
5																
6																

25. FEDERAL TAX I.D. NUMBER   SSN ☐ EIN ☐

26. PATIENT'S ACCOUNT NO.

27. ACCEPT ASSIGNMENT?
(For govt. claims, see back)
☐ YES   ☐ NO

28. TOTAL CHARGE
$

29. AMOUNT PAID
$

30. BALANCE DUE
$

31. SIGNATURE OF PHYSICIAN OR SUPPLIER INCLUDING DEGREES OR CREDENTIALS
(I certify that the statements on the reverse apply to this bill and are made a part thereof.)

SIGNED _____ DATE _____

32. NAME AND ADDRESS OF FACILITY WHERE SERVICES WERE RENDERED (If other than home or office)

33. PHYSICIAN'S, SUPPLIER'S BILLING NAME, ADDRESS, ZIP CODE & PHONE #

PIN#   GRP#

PHYSICIAN OR SUPPLIER INFORMATION

(SAMPLE ONLY - NOT APPROVED FOR USE)

PLEASE PRINT OR TYPE

SAMPLE FORM 1500
SAMPLE FORM 1500 SAMPLE FORM 1500

206

(SAMPLE ONLY - NOT APPROVED FOR USE)

CARRIER

☐☐ PICA

HEALTH INSURANCE CLAIM FORM   PICA ☐☐

1.	MEDICARE	MEDICAID	CHAMPUS	CHAMPVA	GROUP HEALTH PLAN	FECA BLK LUNG	OTHER	1a. INSURED'S I.D. NUMBER	(FOR PROGRAM IN ITEM 1)
	☐ (Medicare #)	☐ (Medicaid #)	☐ (Sponsor's SSN)	☐ (VA File #)	☐ (SSN or ID)	☐ (SSN)	☐ (ID)		

2. PATIENT'S NAME (Last Name, First Name, Middle Initial)

3. PATIENT'S BIRTH DATE   MM   DD   YY   SEX   M ☐   F ☐

4. INSURED'S NAME (Last Name, First Name, Middle Initial)

5. PATIENT'S ADDRESS (No. Street)

6. PATIENT RELATIONSHIP TO INSURED
Self ☐   Spouse ☐   Child ☐   Other ☐

7. INSURED'S ADDRESS (No. Street)

CITY   STATE

8. PATIENT STATUS
Single ☐   Married ☐   Other ☐
Employed ☐   Full-Time Student ☐   Part-Time Student ☐

CITY   STATE

ZIP CODE   TELEPHONE (Include Area Code)
(   )

ZIP CODE   TELEPHONE (INCLUDE AREA CODE)
(   )

9. OTHER INSURED'S NAME (Last Name, First Name, Middle Initial)

10. IS PATIENT'S CONDITION RELATED TO:

11. INSURED'S POLICY GROUP OR FECA NUMBER

a. OTHER INSURED'S POLICY OR GROUP NUMBER

a. EMPLOYMENT? (CURRENT OR PREVIOUS)
☐ YES   ☐ NO

a. INSURED'S DATE OF BIRTH   MM   DD   YY   SEX   M ☐   F ☐

b. OTHER INSURED'S DATE OF BIRTH   MM   DD   YY   SEX   M ☐   F ☐

b. AUTO ACCIDENT?   PLACE (State)
☐ YES   ☐ NO

b. EMPLOYER'S NAME OR SCHOOL NAME

c. EMPLOYER'S NAME OR SCHOOL NAME

c. OTHER ACCIDENT?
☐ YES   ☐ NO

c. INSURANCE PLAN NAME OR PROGRAM NAME

d. INSURANCE PLAN NAME OR PROGRAM NAME

10d. RESERVED FOR LOCAL USE

d. IS THERE ANOTHER HEALTH BENEFIT PLAN?
☐ YES   ☐ NO   If yes, return to and complete item 9 a – d.

READ BACK OF FORM BEFORE COMPLETING & SIGNING THIS FORM.
12. PATIENT'S OR AUTHORIZED PERSON'S SIGNATURE I authorize the release of any medical or other information necessary to process this claim. I also request payment of government benefits either to myself or to the party who accepts assignment below.

SIGNED _____   DATE _____

13. INSURED'S OR AUTHORIZED PERSON'S SIGNATURE I authorize payment of medical benefits to the undersigned physician or supplier for services described below.

SIGNED _____

PATIENT AND INSURED INFORMATION

14. DATE OF CURRENT: ILLNESS (First symptom) OR   MM   DD   YY   INJURY (Accident) OR   PREGNANCY (LMP)

15. IF PATIENT HAS HAD SAME OR SIMILAR ILLNESS, GIVE FIRST DATE   MM   DD   YY

16. DATES PATIENT UNABLE TO WORK IN CURRENT OCCUPATION   MM   DD   YY   FROM   TO   MM   DD   YY

17. NAME OF REFERRING PHYSICIAN OR OTHER SOURCE

17a. I.D. NUMBER OF REFERRING PHYSICIAN

18. HOSPITALIZATION DATES RELATED TO CURRENT SERVICES   MM   DD   YY   FROM   TO   MM   DD   YY

19. RESERVED FOR LOCAL USE

20. OUTSIDE LAB? $ CHARGES
☐ YES   ☐ NO

21. DIAGNOSIS OR NATURE OF ILLNESS OR INJURY. (RELATE ITEMS 1, 2, 3, OR 4 TO ITEM 24E BY LINE)
1. _____   3. _____
2. _____   4. _____

22. MEDICAID RESUBMISSION CODE   ORIGINAL REF. NO.

23. PRIOR AUTHORIZATION NUMBER

24. A DATE(S) OF SERVICE							B Place of Service	C Type of Service	D PROCEDURES, SERVICES, OR SUPPLIES (Explain Unusual Circumstances) CPT/HCPCS MODIFIER	E DIAGNOSIS CODE	F $ CHARGES	G DAYS OR UNITS	H EPSDT Family Plan	I EMG	J COB	K RESERVED FOR LOCAL USE
	From MM	DD	YY	To MM	DD	YY										
1																
2																
3																
4																
5																
6																

25. FEDERAL TAX I.D. NUMBER   SSN ☐ EIN ☐

26. PATIENT'S ACCOUNT NO.

27. ACCEPT ASSIGNMENT? (For govt. claims, see back)   YES ☐   NO ☐

28. TOTAL CHARGE $

29. AMOUNT PAID $

30. BALANCE DUE $

31. SIGNATURE OF PHYSICIAN OR SUPPLIER INCLUDING DEGREES OR CREDENTIALS (I certify that the statements on the reverse apply to this bill and are made a part thereof.)

SIGNED _____   DATE _____

32. NAME AND ADDRESS OF FACILITY WHERE SERVICES WERE RENDERED (If other than home or office)

33. PHYSICIAN'S, SUPPLIER'S BILLING NAME, ADDRESS, ZIP CODE & PHONE #

PIN#   GRP#

PHYSICIAN OR SUPPLIER INFORMATION

(SAMPLE ONLY - NOT APPROVED FOR USE)

PLEASE PRINT OR TYPE

SAMPLE FORM 1500
SAMPLE FORM 1500 SAMPLE FORM 1500

CARRIER

PICA

HEALTH INSURANCE CLAIM FORM

PICA

1. MEDICARE	MEDICAID	CHAMPUS	CHAMPVA	GROUP HEALTH PLAN	FECA BLK LUNG	OTHER	1a. INSURED'S I.D. NUMBER	(FOR PROGRAM IN ITEM 1)
(Medicare #)	(Medicaid #)	(Sponsor's SSN)	(VA File #)	(SSN or ID)	(SSN)	(ID)		

2. PATIENT'S NAME (Last Name, First Name, Middle Initial)

3. PATIENT'S BIRTH DATE   MM   DD   YY   SEX   M ☐   F ☐

4. INSURED'S NAME (Last Name, First Name, Middle Initial)

5. PATIENT'S ADDRESS (No. Street)

6. PATIENT RELATIONSHIP TO INSURED   Self ☐ Spouse ☐ Child ☐ Other ☐

7. INSURED'S ADDRESS (No. Street)

CITY   STATE

8. PATIENT STATUS   Single ☐   Married ☐   Other ☐

CITY   STATE

ZIP CODE   TELEPHONE (Include Area Code) ( )

Employed ☐   Full-Time Student ☐   Part-Time Student ☐

ZIP CODE   TELEPHONE (INCLUDE AREA CODE) ( )

9. OTHER INSURED'S NAME (Last Name, First Name, Middle Initial)

10. IS PATIENT'S CONDITION RELATED TO:

11. INSURED'S POLICY GROUP OR FECA NUMBER

a. OTHER INSURED'S POLICY OR GROUP NUMBER

a. EMPLOYMENT? (CURRENT OR PREVIOUS)   YES ☐   NO ☐

a. INSURED'S DATE OF BIRTH   MM   DD   YY   SEX   M ☐   F ☐

b. OTHER INSURED'S DATE OF BIRTH   MM   DD   YY   SEX   M ☐   F ☐

b. AUTO ACCIDENT?   PLACE (State)   YES ☐   NO ☐

b. EMPLOYER'S NAME OR SCHOOL NAME

c. EMPLOYER'S NAME OR SCHOOL NAME

c. OTHER ACCIDENT?   YES ☐   NU ☐

c. INSURANCE PLAN NAME OR PROGRAM NAME

d. INSURANCE PLAN NAME OR PROGRAM NAME

10d. RESERVED FOR LOCAL USE

d. IS THERE ANOTHER HEALTH BENEFIT PLAN?   YES ☐   NO ☐   If yes, return to and complete item 9 a – d.

READ BACK OF FORM BEFORE COMPLETING & SIGNING THIS FORM.
12. PATIENT'S OR AUTHORIZED PERSON'S SIGNATURE I authorize the release of any medical or other information necessary to process this claim. I also request payment of government benefits either to myself or to the party who accepts assignment below.

SIGNED _____   DATE _____

13. INSURED'S OR AUTHORIZED PERSON'S SIGNATURE I authorize payment of medical benefits to the undersigned physician or supplier for services described below.

SIGNED _____

14. DATE OF CURRENT: ILLNESS (First symptom) OR   MM   DD   YY   INJURY (Accident) OR   PREGNANCY (LMP)

15. IF PATIENT HAS HAD SAME OR SIMILAR ILLNESS,   GIVE FIRST DATE   MM   DD   YY

16. DATES PATIENT UNABLE TO WORK IN CURRENT OCCUPATION   MM   DD   YY   MM   DD   YY   FROM   TO

17. NAME OF REFERRING PHYSICIAN OR OTHER SOURCE

17a. I.D. NUMBER OF REFERRING PHYSICIAN

18. HOSPITALIZATION DATES RELATED TO CURRENT SERVICES   MM   DD   YY   MM   DD   YY   FROM   TO

19. RESERVED FOR LOCAL USE

20. OUTSIDE LAB?   YES ☐   NO ☐ $ CHARGES

21. DIAGNOSIS OR NATURE OF ILLNESS OR INJURY. (RELATE ITEMS 1, 2, 3, OR 4 TO ITEM 24E BY LINE)

1. |___.___   3. |___.___

2. |___.___   4. |___.___

22. MEDICAID RESUBMISSION CODE   ORIGINAL REF. NO.

23. PRIOR AUTHORIZATION NUMBER

24. A DATE(S) OF SERVICE						B Place of Service	C Type of Service	D PROCEDURES, SERVICES, OR SUPPLIES (Explain Unusual Circumstances) CPT/HCPCS	MODIFIER	E DIAGNOSIS CODE	F $ CHARGES	G DAYS OR UNITS	H EPSDT Family Plan	I EMG	J COB	K RESERVED FOR LOCAL USE
From MM	DD	YY	To MM	DD	YY											
1																
2																
3																
4																
5																
6																

25. FEDERAL TAX I.D. NUMBER   SSN ☐ EIN ☐

26. PATIENT'S ACCOUNT NO.

27. ACCEPT ASSIGNMENT? (For govt. claims, see back)   YES ☐   NO ☐

28. TOTAL CHARGE $

29. AMOUNT PAID $

30. BALANCE DUE $

31. SIGNATURE OF PHYSICIAN OR SUPPLIER INCLUDING DEGREES OR CREDENTIALS (I certify that the statements on the reverse apply to this bill and are made a part thereof.)

SIGNED _____   DATE _____

32. NAME AND ADDRESS OF FACILITY WHERE SERVICES WERE RENDERED (If other than home or office)

33. PHYSICIAN'S, SUPPLIER'S BILLING NAME, ADDRESS, ZIP CODE & PHONE #

PIN# _____   GRP# _____

PATIENT AND INSURED INFORMATION

PHYSICIAN OR SUPPLIER INFORMATION

PLEASE PRINT OR TYPE

SAMPLE FORM 1500
SAMPLE FORM 1500 SAMPLE FORM 1500

(SAMPLE ONLY - NOT APPROVED FOR USE)

CARRIER

◻◻ PICA

HEALTH INSURANCE CLAIM FORM

PICA ◻◻

1. ◻ MEDICARE ◻ MEDICAID ◻ CHAMPUS ◻ CHAMPVA ◻ GROUP HEALTH PLAN ◻ FECA BLK LUNG ◻ OTHER
(Medicare #) (Medicaid #) (Sponsor's SSN) (VA File #) (SSN or ID) (SSN) (ID)

1a. INSURED'S I.D. NUMBER (FOR PROGRAM IN ITEM 1)

2. PATIENT'S NAME (Last Name, First Name, Middle Initial)

3. PATIENT'S BIRTH DATE
MM | DD | YY   SEX   M ◻   F ◻

4. INSURED'S NAME (Last Name, First Name, Middle Initial)

5. PATIENT'S ADDRESS (No. Street)

6. PATIENT RELATIONSHIP TO INSURED
Self ◻   Spouse ◻   Child ◻   Other ◻

7. INSURED'S ADDRESS (No. Street)

CITY | STATE

8. PATIENT STATUS
Single ◻   Married ◻   Other ◻

CITY | STATE

ZIP CODE | TELEPHONE (Include Area Code) ( )

Employed ◻   Full-Time Student ◻   Part-Time Student ◻

ZIP CODE | TELEPHONE (INCLUDE AREA CODE) ( )

9. OTHER INSURED'S NAME (Last Name, First Name, Middle Initial)

10. IS PATIENT'S CONDITION RELATED TO:

11. INSURED'S POLICY GROUP OR FECA NUMBER

a. OTHER INSURED'S POLICY OR GROUP NUMBER

a. EMPLOYMENT? (CURRENT OR PREVIOUS)
◻ YES ◻ NO

a. INSURED'S DATE OF BIRTH
MM | DD | YY   SEX   M ◻   F ◻

b. OTHER INSURED'S DATE OF BIRTH
MM | DD | YY   SEX   M ◻   F ◻

b. AUTO ACCIDENT?   PLACE (State)
◻ YES ◻ NO

b. EMPLOYER'S NAME OR SCHOOL NAME

c. EMPLOYER'S NAME OR SCHOOL NAME

c. OTHER ACCIDENT?
◻ YES ◻ NO

c. INSURANCE PLAN NAME OR PROGRAM NAME

d. INSURANCE PLAN NAME OR PROGRAM NAME

10d. RESERVED FOR LOCAL USE

d. IS THERE ANOTHER HEALTH BENEFIT PLAN?
◻ YES ◻ NO   If yes, return to and complete item 9 a – d.

READ BACK OF FORM BEFORE COMPLETING & SIGNING THIS FORM.
12. PATIENT'S OR AUTHORIZED PERSON'S SIGNATURE I authorize the release of any medical or other information necessary to process this claim. I also request payment of government benefits either to myself or to the party who accepts assignment below.

SIGNED _____ DATE _____

13. INSURED'S OR AUTHORIZED PERSON'S SIGNATURE I authorize payment of medical benefits to the undersigned physician or supplier for services described below.

SIGNED _____

PATIENT AND INSURED INFORMATION

14. DATE OF CURRENT: ◻ ILLNESS (First symptom) OR ◻ INJURY (Accident) OR ◻ PREGNANCY (LMP)
MM | DD | YY

15. IF PATIENT HAS HAD SAME OR SIMILAR ILLNESS, GIVE FIRST DATE MM | DD | YY

16. DATES PATIENT UNABLE TO WORK IN CURRENT OCCUPATION
FROM MM | DD | YY TO MM | DD | YY

17. NAME OF REFERRING PHYSICIAN OR OTHER SOURCE

17a. I.D. NUMBER OF REFERRING PHYSICIAN

18. HOSPITALIZATION DATES RELATED TO CURRENT SERVICES
FROM MM | DD | YY TO MM | DD | YY

19. RESERVED FOR LOCAL USE

20. OUTSIDE LAB? $ CHARGES
◻ YES ◻ NO

21. DIAGNOSIS OR NATURE OF ILLNESS OR INJURY. (RELATE ITEMS 1, 2, 3, OR 4 TO ITEM 24E BY LINE)

1. ⌐__ . __
2. ⌐__ . __
3. ⌐__ . __
4. ⌐__ . __

22. MEDICAID RESUBMISSION
CODE   ORIGINAL REF. NO.

23. PRIOR AUTHORIZATION NUMBER

24. A DATE(S) OF SERVICE						B Place of Service	C Type of Service	D PROCEDURES, SERVICES, OR SUPPLIES (Explain Unusual Circumstances)		E DIAGNOSIS CODE	F $ CHARGES	G DAYS OR UNITS	H EPSDT Family Plan	I EMG	J COB	K RESERVED FOR LOCAL USE
From MM	DD	YY	To MM	DD	YY			CPT/HCPCS	MODIFIER							
1																
2																
3																
4																
5																
6																

25. FEDERAL TAX I.D. NUMBER   SSN ◻ EIN ◻

26. PATIENT'S ACCOUNT NO.

27. ACCEPT ASSIGNMENT? (For govt. claims, see back)
◻ YES ◻ NO

28. TOTAL CHARGE $

29. AMOUNT PAID $

30. BALANCE DUE $

31. SIGNATURE OF PHYSICIAN OR SUPPLIER INCLUDING DEGREES OR CREDENTIALS (I certify that the statements on the reverse apply to this bill and are made a part thereof.)

SIGNED _____ DATE _____

32. NAME AND ADDRESS OF FACILITY WHERE SERVICES WERE RENDERED (If other than home or office)

33. PHYSICIAN'S, SUPPLIER'S BILLING NAME, ADDRESS, ZIP CODE & PHONE #

PIN# _____ GRP# _____

PHYSICIAN OR SUPPLIER INFORMATION

(SAMPLE ONLY - NOT APPROVED FOR USE)

PLEASE PRINT OR TYPE

SAMPLE FORM 1500
SAMPLE FORM 1500 SAMPLE FORM 1500

PLEASE
DO NOT
STAPLE
IN THIS
AREA

CARRIER

[ ][ ] PICA

HEALTH INSURANCE CLAIM FORM

PICA [ ][ ]

1. MEDICARE	MEDICAID	CHAMPUS	CHAMPVA	GROUP HEALTH PLAN	FECA BLK LUNG	OTHER	1a. INSURED'S I.D. NUMBER	(FOR PROGRAM IN ITEM 1)
[ ] (Medicare #)	[ ] (Medicaid #)	[ ] (Sponsor's SSN)	[ ] (VA File #)	[ ] (SSN or ID)	[ ] (SSN)	[ ] (ID)		

2. PATIENT'S NAME (Last Name, First Name, Middle Initial)

3. PATIENT'S BIRTH DATE MM | DD | YY SEX M [ ] F [ ]

4. INSURED'S NAME (Last Name, First Name, Middle Initial)

5. PATIENT'S ADDRESS (No. Street)

6. PATIENT RELATIONSHIP TO INSURED Self [ ] Spouse [ ] Child [ ] Other [ ]

7. INSURED'S ADDRESS (No. Street)

CITY   STATE

8. PATIENT STATUS Single [ ] Married [ ] Other [ ]

CITY   STATE

ZIP CODE   TELEPHONE (Include Area Code) (   )

Employed [ ] Full-Time Student [ ] Part-Time Student [ ]

ZIP CODE   TELEPHONE (INCLUDE AREA CODE) (   )

9. OTHER INSURED'S NAME (Last Name, First Name, Middle Initial)

10. IS PATIENT'S CONDITION RELATED TO:

11. INSURED'S POLICY GROUP OR FECA NUMBER

a. OTHER INSURED'S POLICY OR GROUP NUMBER

a. EMPLOYMENT? (CURRENT OR PREVIOUS) [ ] YES [ ] NO

a. INSURED'S DATE OF BIRTH MM | DD | YY SEX M [ ] F [ ]

b. OTHER INSURED'S DATE OF BIRTH MM | DD | YY SEX M [ ] F [ ]

b. AUTO ACCIDENT? PLACE (State) [ ] YES [ ] NO

b. EMPLOYER'S NAME OR SCHOOL NAME

c. EMPLOYER'S NAME OR SCHOOL NAME

c. OTHER ACCIDENT? [ ] YES [ ] NO

c. INSURANCE PLAN NAME OR PROGRAM NAME

d. INSURANCE PLAN NAME OR PROGRAM NAME

10d. RESERVED FOR LOCAL USE

d. IS THERE ANOTHER HEALTH BENEFIT PLAN? [ ] YES [ ] NO If yes, return to and complete item 9 a – d.

READ BACK OF FORM BEFORE COMPLETING & SIGNING THIS FORM.
12. PATIENT'S OR AUTHORIZED PERSON'S SIGNATURE I authorize the release of any medical or other information necessary to process this claim. I also request payment of government benefits either to myself or to the party who accepts assignment below.

SIGNED _____   DATE _____

13. INSURED'S OR AUTHORIZED PERSON'S SIGNATURE I authorize payment of medical benefits to the undersigned physician or supplier for services described below.

SIGNED _____

14. DATE OF CURRENT: MM | DD | YY ILLNESS (First symptom) OR INJURY (Accident) OR PREGNANCY (LMP)

15. IF PATIENT HAS HAD SAME OR SIMILAR ILLNESS, GIVE FIRST DATE MM | DD | YY

16. DATES PATIENT UNABLE TO WORK IN CURRENT OCCUPATION MM | DD | YY FROM   TO MM | DD | YY

17. NAME OF REFERRING PHYSICIAN OR OTHER SOURCE

17a. I.D. NUMBER OF REFERRING PHYSICIAN

18. HOSPITALIZATION DATES RELATED TO CURRENT SERVICES MM | DD | YY FROM   TO MM | DD | YY

19. RESERVED FOR LOCAL USE

20. OUTSIDE LAB? [ ] YES [ ] NO $ CHARGES

21. DIAGNOSIS OR NATURE OF ILLNESS OR INJURY. (RELATE ITEMS 1, 2, 3, OR 4 TO ITEM 24E BY LINE)

1. |___.___   3. |___.___

2. |___.___   4. |___.___

22. MEDICAID RESUBMISSION CODE   ORIGINAL REF. NO.

23. PRIOR AUTHORIZATION NUMBER

24. A DATE(S) OF SERVICE						B Place of Service	C Type of Service	D PROCEDURES, SERVICES, OR SUPPLIES (Explain Unusual Circumstances) CPT/HCPCS	MODIFIER	E DIAGNOSIS CODE	F $ CHARGES	G DAYS OR UNITS	H EPSDT Family Plan	I EMG	J COB	K RESERVED FOR LOCAL USE
From MM	DD	YY	To MM	DD	YY											
1																
2																
3																
4																
5																
6																

25. FEDERAL TAX I.D. NUMBER SSN [ ] EIN [ ]

26. PATIENT'S ACCOUNT NO.

27. ACCEPT ASSIGNMENT? (For govt. claims, see back) [ ] YES [ ] NO

28. TOTAL CHARGE $

29. AMOUNT PAID $

30. BALANCE DUE $

31. SIGNATURE OF PHYSICIAN OR SUPPLIER INCLUDING DEGREES OR CREDENTIALS (I certify that the statements on the reverse apply to this bill and are made a part thereof.)

SIGNED _____ DATE _____

32. NAME AND ADDRESS OF FACILITY WHERE SERVICES WERE RENDERED (If other than home or office)

33. PHYSICIAN'S, SUPPLIER'S BILLING NAME, ADDRESS, ZIP CODE & PHONE #

PIN#   GRP#

PLEASE PRINT OR TYPE

SAMPLE FORM 1500
SAMPLE FORM 1500 SAMPLE FORM 1500

PATIENT AND INSURED INFORMATION

PHYSICIAN OR SUPPLIER INFORMATION

(SAMPLE ONLY - NOT APPROVED FOR USE)

CARRIER

| | PICA | | **HEALTH INSURANCE CLAIM FORM** | PICA | | |

1.
MEDICARE   MEDICAID   CHAMPUS   CHAMPVA   GROUP HEALTH PLAN   FECA BLK LUNG   OTHER
(Medicare #)   (Medicaid #)   (Sponsor's SSN)   (VA File #)   (SSN or ID)   (SSN)   (ID)

1a. INSURED'S I.D. NUMBER   (FOR PROGRAM IN ITEM 1)

2. PATIENT'S NAME (Last Name, First Name, Middle Initial)

3. PATIENT'S BIRTH DATE
MM   DD   YY   SEX
M   F

4. INSURED'S NAME (Last Name, First Name, Middle Initial)

5. PATIENT'S ADDRESS (No. Street)

6. PATIENT RELATIONSHIP TO INSURED
Self   Spouse   Child   Other

7. INSURED'S ADDRESS (No. Street)

CITY   STATE

8. PATIENT STATUS
Single   Married   Other

CITY   STATE

ZIP CODE   TELEPHONE (Include Area Code)
(   )

Employed   Full-Time Student   Part-Time Student

ZIP CODE   TELEPHONE (INCLUDE AREA CODE)
(   )

9. OTHER INSURED'S NAME (Last Name, First Name, Middle Initial)

10. IS PATIENT'S CONDITION RELATED TO:

11. INSURED'S POLICY GROUP OR FECA NUMBER

a. OTHER INSURED'S POLICY OR GROUP NUMBER

a. EMPLOYMENT? (CURRENT OR PREVIOUS)
YES   NO

a. INSURED'S DATE OF BIRTH
MM   DD   YY   SEX
M   F

b. OTHER INSURED'S DATE OF BIRTH
MM   DD   YY   SEX
M   F

b. AUTO ACCIDENT?   PLACE (State)
YES   NO

b. EMPLOYER'S NAME OR SCHOOL NAME

c. EMPLOYER'S NAME OR SCHOOL NAME

c. OTHER ACCIDENT?
YES   NO

c. INSURANCE PLAN NAME OR PROGRAM NAME

d. INSURANCE PLAN NAME OR PROGRAM NAME

10d. RESERVED FOR LOCAL USE

d. IS THERE ANOTHER HEALTH BENEFIT PLAN?
YES   NO   If yes, return to and complete item 9 a – d.

READ BACK OF FORM BEFORE COMPLETING & SIGNING THIS FORM.
12. PATIENT'S OR AUTHORIZED PERSON'S SIGNATURE I authorize the release of any medical or other information necessary to process this claim. I also request payment of government benefits either to myself or to the party who accepts assignment below.

SIGNED _____   DATE _____

13. INSURED'S OR AUTHORIZED PERSON'S SIGNATURE I authorize payment of medical benefits to the undersigned physician or supplier for services described below.

SIGNED _____

PATIENT AND INSURED INFORMATION

14. DATE OF CURRENT: ILLNESS (First symptom) OR INJURY (Accident) OR PREGNANCY (LMP)
MM   DD   YY

15. IF PATIENT HAS HAD SAME OR SIMILAR ILLNESS, GIVE FIRST DATE   MM   DD   YY

16. DATES PATIENT UNABLE TO WORK IN CURRENT OCCUPATION
MM   DD   YY   MM   DD   YY
FROM   TO

17. NAME OF REFERRING PHYSICIAN OR OTHER SOURCE

17a. I.D. NUMBER OF REFERRING PHYSICIAN

18. HOSPITALIZATION DATES RELATED TO CURRENT SERVICES
MM   DD   YY   MM   DD   YY
FROM   TO

19. RESERVED FOR LOCAL USE

20. OUTSIDE LAB? $ CHARGES
YES   NO

21. DIAGNOSIS OR NATURE OF ILLNESS OR INJURY. (RELATE ITEMS 1, 2, 3, OR 4 TO ITEM 24E BY LINE)

1. ___ . ___   3. ___ . ___

2. ___ . ___   4. ___ . ___

22. MEDICAID RESUBMISSION
CODE   ORIGINAL REF. NO.

23. PRIOR AUTHORIZATION NUMBER

24. A DATE(S) OF SERVICE						B Place of Service	C Type of Service	D PROCEDURES, SERVICES, OR SUPPLIES (Explain Unusual Circumstances)		E DIAGNOSIS CODE	F $ CHARGES	G DAYS OR UNITS	H EPSDT Family Plan	I EMG	J COB	K RESERVED FOR LOCAL USE
From MM	DD	YY	To MM	DD	YY			CPT/HCPCS	MODIFIER							
1																
2																
3																
4																
5																
6																

25. FEDERAL TAX I.D. NUMBER   SSN   EIN

26. PATIENT'S ACCOUNT NO.

27. ACCEPT ASSIGNMENT? (For govt. claims, see back)
YES   NO

28. TOTAL CHARGE
$

29. AMOUNT PAID
$

30. BALANCE DUE
$

31. SIGNATURE OF PHYSICIAN OR SUPPLIER INCLUDING DEGREES OR CREDENTIALS
(I certify that the statements on the reverse apply to this bill and are made a part thereof.)

SIGNED _____   DATE _____

32. NAME AND ADDRESS OF FACILITY WHERE SERVICES WERE RENDERED (If other than home or office)

33. PHYSICIAN'S, SUPPLIER'S BILLING NAME, ADDRESS, ZIP CODE & PHONE #

PIN#   GRP#

PHYSICIAN OR SUPPLIER INFORMATION

PLEASE PRINT OR TYPE

SAMPLE FORM 1500
SAMPLE FORM 1500 SAMPLE FORM 1500

PLEASE
DO NOT
STAPLE
IN THIS
AREA

CARRIER

HEALTH INSURANCE CLAIM FORM

☐☐ PICA | PICA ☐☐☐

| 1. MEDICARE ☐ (Medicare #) MEDICAID ☐ (Medicaid #) CHAMPUS ☐ (Sponsor's SSN) CHAMPVA ☐ (VA File #) GROUP HEALTH PLAN ☐ (SSN or ID) FECA BLK LUNG ☐ (SSN) OTHER ☐ (ID) | 1a. INSURED'S I.D. NUMBER (FOR PROGRAM IN ITEM 1) |

2. PATIENT'S NAME (Last Name, First Name, Middle Initial) | 3. PATIENT'S BIRTH DATE MM | DD | YY   SEX M ☐ F ☐ | 4. INSURED'S NAME (Last Name, First Name, Middle Initial)

5. PATIENT'S ADDRESS (No. Street) | 6. PATIENT RELATIONSHIP TO INSURED Self ☐ Spouse ☐ Child ☐ Other ☐ | 7. INSURED'S ADDRESS (No. Street)

CITY | STATE | 8. PATIENT STATUS Single ☐ Married ☐ Other ☐ | CITY | STATE

ZIP CODE | TELEPHONE (Include Area Code) (   ) | Employed ☐ Full-Time Student ☐ Part-Time Student ☐ | ZIP CODE | TELEPHONE (INCLUDE AREA CODE) (   )

9. OTHER INSURED'S NAME (Last Name, First Name, Middle Initial) | 10. IS PATIENT'S CONDITION RELATED TO: | 11. INSURED'S POLICY GROUP OR FECA NUMBER

a. OTHER INSURED'S POLICY OR GROUP NUMBER | a. EMPLOYMENT? (CURRENT OR PREVIOUS) ☐ YES ☐ NO | a. INSURED'S DATE OF BIRTH MM | DD | YY   SEX M ☐ F ☐

b. OTHER INSURED'S DATE OF BIRTH MM | DD | YY   SEX M ☐ F ☐ | b. AUTO ACCIDENT?   PLACE (State) ☐ YES ☐ NO | b. EMPLOYER'S NAME OR SCHOOL NAME

c. EMPLOYER'S NAME OR SCHOOL NAME | c. OTHER ACCIDENT? ☐ YES ☐ NO | c. INSURANCE PLAN NAME OR PROGRAM NAME

d. INSURANCE PLAN NAME OR PROGRAM NAME | 10d. RESERVED FOR LOCAL USE | d. IS THERE ANOTHER HEALTH BENEFIT PLAN? ☐ YES ☐ NO If yes, return to and complete item 9 a – d.

READ BACK OF FORM BEFORE COMPLETING & SIGNING THIS FORM.
12. PATIENT'S OR AUTHORIZED PERSON'S SIGNATURE I authorize the release of any medical or other information necessary to process this claim. I also request payment of government benefits either to myself or to the party who accepts assignment below.

SIGNED _____ DATE _____

13. INSURED'S OR AUTHORIZED PERSON'S SIGNATURE I authorize payment of medical benefits to the undersigned physician or supplier for services described below.

SIGNED _____

PATIENT AND INSURED INFORMATION

14. DATE OF CURRENT: MM | DD | YY ILLNESS (First symptom) OR INJURY (Accident) OR PREGNANCY (LMP) | 15. IF PATIENT HAS HAD SAME OR SIMILAR ILLNESS, GIVE FIRST DATE MM | DD | YY | 16. DATES PATIENT UNABLE TO WORK IN CURRENT OCCUPATION MM | DD | YY   MM | DD | YY FROM _____ TO _____

17. NAME OF REFERRING PHYSICIAN OR OTHER SOURCE | 17a. I.D. NUMBER OF REFERRING PHYSICIAN | 18. HOSPITALIZATION DATES RELATED TO CURRENT SERVICES MM | DD | YY   MM | DD | YY FROM _____ TO _____

19. RESERVED FOR LOCAL USE | 20. OUTSIDE LAB? ☐ YES ☐ NO | $ CHARGES

21. DIAGNOSIS OR NATURE OF ILLNESS OR INJURY. (RELATE ITEMS 1, 2, 3, OR 4 TO ITEM 24E BY LINE)
1. |___.___| 3. |___.___|
2. |___.___| 4. |___.___|

22. MEDICAID RESUBMISSION CODE | ORIGINAL REF. NO.

23. PRIOR AUTHORIZATION NUMBER

24. A DATE(S) OF SERVICE			B Place of Service	C Type of Service	D PROCEDURES, SERVICES, OR SUPPLIES (Explain Unusual Circumstances) CPT/HCPCS	MODIFIER	E DIAGNOSIS CODE	F $ CHARGES	G DAYS OR UNITS	H EPSDT Family Plan	I EMG	J COB	K RESERVED FOR LOCAL USE
From MM DD YY	To MM DD YY												
1													
2													
3													
4													
5													
6													

25. FEDERAL TAX I.D. NUMBER   SSN ☐ EIN ☐ | 26. PATIENT'S ACCOUNT NO. | 27. ACCEPT ASSIGNMENT? (For govt. claims, see back) ☐ YES ☐ NO | 28. TOTAL CHARGE $ | 29. AMOUNT PAID $ | 30. BALANCE DUE $

31. SIGNATURE OF PHYSICIAN OR SUPPLIER INCLUDING DEGREES OR CREDENTIALS (I certify that the statements on the reverse apply to this bill and are made a part thereof.)

SIGNED _____ DATE _____

32. NAME AND ADDRESS OF FACILITY WHERE SERVICES WERE RENDERED (If other than home or office)

33. PHYSICIAN'S, SUPPLIER'S BILLING NAME, ADDRESS, ZIP CODE & PHONE #

PIN# | GRP#

PHYSICIAN OR SUPPLIER INFORMATION

PLEASE PRINT OR TYPE

SAMPLE FORM 1500
SAMPLE FORM 1500 SAMPLE FORM 1500

(SAMPLE ONLY - NOT APPROVED FOR USE)

CARRIER

| | PICA |

HEALTH INSURANCE CLAIM FORM

PICA | |

1. MEDICARE MEDICAID CHAMPUS CHAMPVA GROUP HEALTH PLAN FECA BLK LUNG OTHER
(Medicare #) (Medicaid #) (Sponsor's SSN) (VA File #) (SSN or ID) (SSN) (ID)

1a. INSURED'S I.D. NUMBER (FOR PROGRAM IN ITEM 1)

2. PATIENT'S NAME (Last Name, First Name, Middle Initial)

3. PATIENT'S BIRTH DATE
MM   DD   YY   SEX   M   F

4. INSURED'S NAME (Last Name, First Name, Middle Initial)

5. PATIENT'S ADDRESS (No. Street)

6. PATIENT RELATIONSHIP TO INSURED
Self   Spouse   Child   Other

7. INSURED'S ADDRESS (No. Street)

CITY   STATE

8. PATIENT STATUS
Single   Married   Other
Employed   Full-Time Student   Part-Time Student

CITY   STATE

ZIP CODE   TELEPHONE (Include Area Code) ( )

ZIP CODE   TELEPHONE (INCLUDE AREA CODE) ( )

9. OTHER INSURED'S NAME (Last Name, First Name, Middle Initial)

10. IS PATIENT'S CONDITION RELATED TO:

11. INSURED'S POLICY GROUP OR FECA NUMBER

a. OTHER INSURED'S POLICY OR GROUP NUMBER

a. EMPLOYMENT? (CURRENT OR PREVIOUS)   YES   NO

a. INSURED'S DATE OF BIRTH
MM   DD   YY   SEX   M   F

b. OTHER INSURED'S DATE OF BIRTH
MM   DD   YY   SEX   M   F

b. AUTO ACCIDENT?   PLACE (State)   YES   NO

b. EMPLOYER'S NAME OR SCHOOL NAME

c. EMPLOYER'S NAME OR SCHOOL NAME

c. OTHER ACCIDENT?   YES   NO

c. INSURANCE PLAN NAME OR PROGRAM NAME

d. INSURANCE PLAN NAME OR PROGRAM NAME

10d. RESERVED FOR LOCAL USE

d. IS THERE ANOTHER HEALTH BENEFIT PLAN?   YES   NO   If yes, return to and complete item 9 a – d.

READ BACK OF FORM BEFORE COMPLETING & SIGNING THIS FORM.
12. PATIENT'S OR AUTHORIZED PERSON'S SIGNATURE I authorize the release of any medical or other information necessary to process this claim. I also request payment of government benefits either to myself or to the party who accepts assignment below.

SIGNED _____   DATE _____

13. INSURED'S OR AUTHORIZED PERSON'S SIGNATURE I authorize payment of medical benefits to the undersigned physician or supplier for services described below.

SIGNED _____

PATIENT AND INSURED INFORMATION

14. DATE OF CURRENT: ILLNESS (First symptom) OR   INJURY (Accident) OR   PREGNANCY (LMP)
MM   DD   YY

15. IF PATIENT HAS HAD SAME OR SIMILAR ILLNESS, GIVE FIRST DATE   MM   DD   YY

16. DATES PATIENT UNABLE TO WORK IN CURRENT OCCUPATION
FROM   MM   DD   YY   TO   MM   DD   YY

17. NAME OF REFERRING PHYSICIAN OR OTHER SOURCE

17a. I.D. NUMBER OF REFERRING PHYSICIAN

18. HOSPITALIZATION DATES RELATED TO CURRENT SERVICES
FROM   MM   DD   YY   TO   MM   DD   YY

19. RESERVED FOR LOCAL USE

20. OUTSIDE LAB?   YES   NO $ CHARGES

21. DIAGNOSIS OR NATURE OF ILLNESS OR INJURY. (RELATE ITEMS 1, 2, 3, OR 4 TO ITEM 24E BY LINE)

1. ____ . ____   3. ____ . ____

2. ____ . ____   4. ____ . ____

22. MEDICAID RESUBMISSION CODE   ORIGINAL REF. NO.

23. PRIOR AUTHORIZATION NUMBER

24. A DATE(S) OF SERVICE					B Place of Service	C Type of Service	D PROCEDURES, SERVICES, OR SUPPLIES (Explain Unusual Circumstances)		E DIAGNOSIS CODE	F $ CHARGES	G DAYS OR UNITS	H EPSDT Family Plan	I EMG	J COB	K RESERVED FOR LOCAL USE
From MM	DD	YY	To MM	DD	YY			CPT/HCPCS	MODIFIER							
1															
2															
3															
4															
5															
6															

25. FEDERAL TAX I.D. NUMBER   SSN   EIN

26. PATIENT'S ACCOUNT NO.

27. ACCEPT ASSIGNMENT? (For govt. claims, see back)   YES   NO

28. TOTAL CHARGE $

29. AMOUNT PAID $

30. BALANCE DUE $

31. SIGNATURE OF PHYSICIAN OR SUPPLIER INCLUDING DEGREES OR CREDENTIALS
(I certify that the statements on the reverse apply to this bill and are made a part thereof.)

SIGNED _____   DATE _____

32. NAME AND ADDRESS OF FACILITY WHERE SERVICES WERE RENDERED (If other than home or office)

33. PHYSICIAN'S, SUPPLIER'S BILLING NAME, ADDRESS, ZIP CODE & PHONE #

PIN#   GRP#

PHYSICIAN OR SUPPLIER INFORMATION

(SAMPLE ONLY - NOT APPROVED FOR USE)

PLEASE PRINT OR TYPE

SAMPLE FORM 1500
SAMPLE FORM 1500 SAMPLE FORM 1500

PLEASE
DO NOT
STAPLE
IN THIS
AREA

CARRIER

[ ] [ ] [ ] PICA

HEALTH INSURANCE CLAIM FORM

PICA [ ] [ ] [ ]

1. MEDICARE MEDICAID CHAMPUS CHAMPVA GROUP HEALTH PLAN FECA BLK LUNG OTHER	1a. INSURED'S I.D. NUMBER (FOR PROGRAM IN ITEM 1)

[ ] (Medicare #) [ ] (Medicaid #) [ ] (Sponsor's SSN) [ ] (VA File #) [ ] (SSN or ID) [ ] (SSN) [ ] (ID)

2. PATIENT'S NAME (Last Name, First Name, Middle Initial)	3. PATIENT'S BIRTH DATE SEX MM DD YY M [ ] F [ ]	4. INSURED'S NAME (Last Name, First Name, Middle Initial)
5. PATIENT'S ADDRESS (No. Street)	6. PATIENT RELATIONSHIP TO INSURED Self [ ] Spouse [ ] Child [ ] Other [ ]	7. INSURED'S ADDRESS (No. Street)
CITY STATE	8. PATIENT STATUS Single [ ] Married [ ] Other [ ]	CITY STATE
ZIP CODE TELEPHONE (Include Area Code) ( )	Employed [ ] Full-Time Student [ ] Part-Time Student [ ]	ZIP CODE TELEPHONE (INCLUDE AREA CODE) ( )
9. OTHER INSURED'S NAME (Last Name, First Name, Middle Initial)	10. IS PATIENT'S CONDITION RELATED TO:	11. INSURED'S POLICY GROUP OR FECA NUMBER
a. OTHER INSURED'S POLICY OR GROUP NUMBER	a. EMPLOYMENT? (CURRENT OR PREVIOUS) [ ] YES [ ] NO	a. INSURED'S DATE OF BIRTH SEX MM DD YY M [ ] F [ ]
b. OTHER INSURED'S DATE OF BIRTH SEX MM DD YY M [ ] F [ ]	b. AUTO ACCIDENT? PLACE (State) [ ] YES [ ] NO	b. EMPLOYER'S NAME OR SCHOOL NAME
c. EMPLOYER'S NAME OR SCHOOL NAME	c. OTHER ACCIDENT? [ ] YES [ ] NO	c. INSURANCE PLAN NAME OR PROGRAM NAME
d. INSURANCE PLAN NAME OR PROGRAM NAME	10d. RESERVED FOR LOCAL USE	d. IS THERE ANOTHER HEALTH BENEFIT PLAN? [ ] YES [ ] NO If yes, return to and complete item 9 a – d.

READ BACK OF FORM BEFORE COMPLETING & SIGNING THIS FORM.

12. PATIENT'S OR AUTHORIZED PERSON'S SIGNATURE I authorize the release of any medical or other information necessary to process this claim. I also request payment of government benefits either to myself or to the party who accepts assignment below. SIGNED _____ DATE _____	13. INSURED'S OR AUTHORIZED PERSON'S SIGNATURE I authorize payment of medical benefits to the undersigned physician or supplier for services described below. SIGNED _____

PATIENT AND INSURED INFORMATION

14. DATE OF CURRENT: ILLNESS (First symptom) OR INJURY (Accident) OR PREGNANCY (LMP) MM DD YY	15. IF PATIENT HAS HAD SAME OR SIMILAR ILLNESS, GIVE FIRST DATE MM DD YY	16. DATES PATIENT UNABLE TO WORK IN CURRENT OCCUPATION MM DD YY TO MM DD YY FROM
17. NAME OF REFERRING PHYSICIAN OR OTHER SOURCE	17a. I.D. NUMBER OF REFERRING PHYSICIAN	18. HOSPITALIZATION DATES RELATED TO CURRENT SERVICES MM DD YY TO MM DD YY FROM
19. RESERVED FOR LOCAL USE		20. OUTSIDE LAB? $ CHARGES [ ] YES [ ] NO
21. DIAGNOSIS OR NATURE OF ILLNESS OR INJURY. (RELATE ITEMS 1, 2, 3, OR 4 TO ITEM 24E BY LINE) 1. ____.____ 3. ____.____ 2. ____.____ 4. ____.____		22. MEDICAID RESUBMISSION CODE ORIGINAL REF. NO. 23. PRIOR AUTHORIZATION NUMBER

24. A DATE(S) OF SERVICE From To MM DD YY MM DD YY	B Place of Service	C Type of Service	D PROCEDURES, SERVICES, OR SUPPLIES (Explain Unusual Circumstances) CPT/HCPCS MODIFIER	E DIAGNOSIS CODE	F $ CHARGES	G DAYS OR UNITS	H EPSDT Family Plan	I EMG	J COB	K RESERVED FOR LOCAL USE
1										
2										
3										
4										
5										
6										

25. FEDERAL TAX I.D. NUMBER SSN [ ] EIN [ ]	26. PATIENT'S ACCOUNT NO.	27. ACCEPT ASSIGNMENT? (For govt. claims, see back) [ ] YES [ ] NO	28. TOTAL CHARGE $	29. AMOUNT PAID $	30. BALANCE DUE $
31. SIGNATURE OF PHYSICIAN OR SUPPLIER INCLUDING DEGREES OR CREDENTIALS (I certify that the statements on the reverse apply to this bill and are made a part thereof.) SIGNED _____ DATE _____	32. NAME AND ADDRESS OF FACILITY WHERE SERVICES WERE RENDERED (If other than home or office)	33. PHYSICIAN'S, SUPPLIER'S BILLING NAME, ADDRESS, ZIP CODE & PHONE # PIN# GRP#			

PHYSICIAN OR SUPPLIER INFORMATION

PLEASE PRINT OR TYPE

SAMPLE FORM 1500
SAMPLE FORM 1500 SAMPLE FORM 1500

214

CARRIER

☐☐ PICA

HEALTH INSURANCE CLAIM FORM

PICA ☐☐

1. MEDICARE ☐ (Medicare #)	MEDICAID ☐ (Medicaid #)	CHAMPUS ☐ (Sponsor's SSN)	CHAMPVA ☐ (VA File #)	GROUP HEALTH PLAN ☐ (SSN or ID)	FECA BLK LUNG ☐ (SSN)	OTHER ☐ (ID)	1a. INSURED'S I.D. NUMBER	(FOR PROGRAM IN ITEM 1)

2. PATIENT'S NAME (Last Name, First Name, Middle Initial)

3. PATIENT'S BIRTH DATE
MM | DD | YY   SEX   M ☐   F ☐

4. INSURED'S NAME (Last Name, First Name, Middle Initial)

5. PATIENT'S ADDRESS (No. Street)

6. PATIENT RELATIONSHIP TO INSURED
Self ☐   Spouse ☐   Child ☐   Other ☐

7. INSURED'S ADDRESS (No. Street)

CITY | STATE

8. PATIENT STATUS
Single ☐   Married ☐   Other ☐
Employed ☐   Full-Time Student ☐   Part-Time Student ☐

CITY | STATE

ZIP CODE | TELEPHONE (Include Area Code)
(   )

ZIP CODE | TELEPHONE (INCLUDE AREA CODE)
(   )

9. OTHER INSURED'S NAME (Last Name, First Name, Middle Initial)

10. IS PATIENT'S CONDITION RELATED TO:

11. INSURED'S POLICY GROUP OR FECA NUMBER

a. OTHER INSURED'S POLICY OR GROUP NUMBER

a. EMPLOYMENT? (CURRENT OR PREVIOUS)
☐ YES   ☐ NO

a. INSURED'S DATE OF BIRTH
MM | DD | YY   SEX   M ☐   F ☐

b. OTHER INSURED'S DATE OF BIRTH
MM | DD | YY   SEX   M ☐   F ☐

b. AUTO ACCIDENT?   PLACE (State)
☐ YES   ☐ NO

b. EMPLOYER'S NAME OR SCHOOL NAME

c. EMPLOYER'S NAME OR SCHOOL NAME

c. OTHER ACCIDENT?
☐ YES   ☐ NO

c. INSURANCE PLAN NAME OR PROGRAM NAME

d. INSURANCE PLAN NAME OR PROGRAM NAME

10J. RESERVED FOR LOCAL USE

d. IS THERE ANOTHER HEALTH BENEFIT PLAN?
☐ YES   ☐ NO   If yes, return to and complete item 9 a – d.

READ BACK OF FORM BEFORE COMPLETING & SIGNING THIS FORM.
12. PATIENT'S OR AUTHORIZED PERSON'S SIGNATURE I authorize the release of any medical or other information necessary to process this claim. I also request payment of government benefits either to myself or to the party who accepts assignment below.

SIGNED _____   DATE _____

13. INSURED'S OR AUTHORIZED PERSON'S SIGNATURE I authorize payment of medical benefits to the undersigned physician or supplier for services described below.

SIGNED _____

PATIENT AND INSURED INFORMATION

14. DATE OF CURRENT: ILLNESS (First symptom) OR INJURY (Accident) OR PREGNANCY (LMP)
MM | DD | YY

15. IF PATIENT HAS HAD SAME OR SIMILAR ILLNESS, GIVE FIRST DATE   MM | DD | YY

16. DATES PATIENT UNABLE TO WORK IN CURRENT OCCUPATION
MM | DD | YY   FROM   MM | DD | YY   TO

17. NAME OF REFERRING PHYSICIAN OR OTHER SOURCE

17a. I.D. NUMBER OF REFERRING PHYSICIAN

18. HOSPITALIZATION DATES RELATED TO CURRENT SERVICES
MM | DD | YY   FROM   MM | DD | YY   TO

19. RESERVED FOR LOCAL USE

20. OUTSIDE LAB? $ CHARGES
☐ YES   ☐ NO

21. DIAGNOSIS OR NATURE OF ILLNESS OR INJURY. (RELATE ITEMS 1, 2, 3, OR 4 TO ITEM 24E BY LINE)
1. |___.___| 3. |___.___|
2. |___.___| 4. |___.___|

22. MEDICAID RESUBMISSION CODE   ORIGINAL REF. NO.

23. PRIOR AUTHORIZATION NUMBER

24. A DATE(S) OF SERVICE						B Place of Service	C Type of Service	D PROCEDURES, SERVICES, OR SUPPLIES (Explain Unusual Circumstances)		E DIAGNOSIS CODE	F $ CHARGES	G DAYS OR UNITS	H EPSDT Family Plan	I EMG	J COB	K RESERVED FOR LOCAL USE
From MM	DD	YY	To MM	DD	YY			CPT/HCPCS	MODIFIER							
1																
2																
3																
4																
5																
6																

25. FEDERAL TAX I.D. NUMBER   SSN ☐   EIN ☐

26. PATIENT'S ACCOUNT NO.

27. ACCEPT ASSIGNMENT? (For govt. claims, see back)
☐ YES   ☐ NO

28. TOTAL CHARGE $

29. AMOUNT PAID $

30. BALANCE DUE $

31. SIGNATURE OF PHYSICIAN OR SUPPLIER INCLUDING DEGREES OR CREDENTIALS
(I certify that the statements on the reverse apply to this bill and are made a part thereof.)

SIGNED _____   DATE _____

32. NAME AND ADDRESS OF FACILITY WHERE SERVICES WERE RENDERED (If other than home or office)

33. PHYSICIAN'S, SUPPLIER'S BILLING NAME, ADDRESS, ZIP CODE & PHONE #

PIN#   GRP#

PHYSICIAN OR SUPPLIER INFORMATION

PLEASE PRINT OR TYPE

SAMPLE FORM 1500
SAMPLE FORM 1500 SAMPLE FORM 1500

PLEASE
DO NOT
STAPLE
IN THIS
AREA

CARRIER

☐☐ PICA

HEALTH INSURANCE CLAIM FORM
PICA ☐☐

1. MEDICARE	MEDICAID	CHAMPUS	CHAMPVA	GROUP HEALTH PLAN	FECA BLK LUNG	OTHER	1a. INSURED'S I.D. NUMBER	(FOR PROGRAM IN ITEM 1)
☐ (Medicare #)	☐ (Medicaid #)	☐ (Sponsor's SSN)	☐ (VA File #)	☐ (SSN or ID)	☐ (SSN)	☐ (ID)		

2. PATIENT'S NAME (Last Name, First Name, Middle Initial)

3. PATIENT'S BIRTH DATE MM | DD | YY   SEX   M ☐   F ☐

4. INSURED'S NAME (Last Name, First Name, Middle Initial)

5. PATIENT'S ADDRESS (No. Street)

6. PATIENT RELATIONSHIP TO INSURED   Self ☐ Spouse ☐ Child ☐ Other ☐

7. INSURED'S ADDRESS (No. Street)

CITY   STATE

8. PATIENT STATUS   Single ☐   Married ☐   Other ☐

CITY   STATE

ZIP CODE   TELEPHONE (Include Area Code) (   )

Employed ☐   Full-Time Student ☐   Part-Time Student ☐

ZIP CODE   TELEPHONE (INCLUDE AREA CODE) (   )

9. OTHER INSURED'S NAME (Last Name, First Name, Middle Initial)

10. IS PATIENT'S CONDITION RELATED TO:

11. INSURED'S POLICY GROUP OR FECA NUMBER

a. OTHER INSURED'S POLICY OR GROUP NUMBER

a. EMPLOYMENT? (CURRENT OR PREVIOUS)   ☐ YES   ☐ NO

a. INSURED'S DATE OF BIRTH MM | DD | YY   SEX   M ☐   F ☐

b. OTHER INSURED'S DATE OF BIRTH MM | DD | YY   SEX   M ☐   F ☐

b. AUTO ACCIDENT?   PLACE (State)   ☐ YES   ☐ NO

b. EMPLOYER'S NAME OR SCHOOL NAME

c. EMPLOYER'S NAME OR SCHOOL NAME

c. OTHER ACCIDENT?   ☐ YES   ☐ NO

c. INSURANCE PLAN NAME OR PROGRAM NAME

d. INSURANCE PLAN NAME OR PROGRAM NAME

10d. RESERVED FOR LOCAL USE

d. IS THERE ANOTHER HEALTH BENEFIT PLAN?   ☐ YES   ☐ NO   If yes, return to and complete item 9 a – d.

READ BACK OF FORM BEFORE COMPLETING & SIGNING THIS FORM.
12. PATIENT'S OR AUTHORIZED PERSON'S SIGNATURE I authorize the release of any medical or other information necessary to process this claim. I also request payment of government benefits either to myself or to the party who accepts assignment below.

SIGNED _____   DATE _____

13. INSURED'S OR AUTHORIZED PERSON'S SIGNATURE I authorize payment of medical benefits to the undersigned physician or supplier for services described below.

SIGNED _____

14. DATE OF CURRENT: ILLNESS (First symptom) OR INJURY (Accident) OR PREGNANCY (LMP) MM | DD | YY

15. IF PATIENT HAS HAD SAME OR SIMILAR ILLNESS, GIVE FIRST DATE MM | DD | YY

16. DATES PATIENT UNABLE TO WORK IN CURRENT OCCUPATION MM | DD | YY FROM   TO   MM | DD | YY

17. NAME OF REFERRING PHYSICIAN OR OTHER SOURCE

17a. I.D. NUMBER OF REFERRING PHYSICIAN

18. HOSPITALIZATION DATES RELATED TO CURRENT SERVICES MM | DD | YY FROM   TO   MM | DD | YY

19. RESERVED FOR LOCAL USE

20. OUTSIDE LAB?   ☐ YES   ☐ NO $ CHARGES

21. DIAGNOSIS OR NATURE OF ILLNESS OR INJURY. (RELATE ITEMS 1, 2, 3, OR 4 TO ITEM 24E BY LINE)

1. |___.___| 3. |___.___|

2. |___.___| 4. |___.___|

22. MEDICAID RESUBMISSION CODE   ORIGINAL REF. NO.

23. PRIOR AUTHORIZATION NUMBER

24. A DATE(S) OF SERVICE						B Place of Service	C Type of Service	D PROCEDURES, SERVICES, OR SUPPLIES (Explain Unusual Circumstances) CPT/HCPCS MODIFIER	E DIAGNOSIS CODE	F $ CHARGES	G DAYS OR UNITS	H EPSDT Family Plan	I EMG	J COB	K RESERVED FOR LOCAL USE
From MM	DD	YY	To MM	DD	YY										
1															
2															
3															
4															
5															
6															

25. FEDERAL TAX I.D. NUMBER   SSN ☐ EIN ☐

26. PATIENT'S ACCOUNT NO.

27. ACCEPT ASSIGNMENT? (For govt. claims, see back)   ☐ YES   ☐ NO

28. TOTAL CHARGE $

29. AMOUNT PAID $

30. BALANCE DUE $

31. SIGNATURE OF PHYSICIAN OR SUPPLIER INCLUDING DEGREES OR CREDENTIALS (I certify that the statements on the reverse apply to this bill and are made a part thereof.)

SIGNED _____   DATE _____

32. NAME AND ADDRESS OF FACILITY WHERE SERVICES WERE RENDERED (If other than home or office)

33. PHYSICIAN'S, SUPPLIER'S BILLING NAME, ADDRESS, ZIP CODE & PHONE #

PIN#   GRP#

PLEASE PRINT OR TYPE

SAMPLE FORM 1500
SAMPLE FORM 1500 SAMPLE FORM 1500

PATIENT AND INSURED INFORMATION

PHYSICIAN OR SUPPLIER INFORMATION

PLEASE
DO NOT
STAPLE
IN THIS
AREA

CARRIER

☐☐ PICA

HEALTH INSURANCE CLAIM FORM

PICA ☐☐

| 1. MEDICARE ☐ (Medicare #) MEDICAID ☐ (Medicaid #) CHAMPUS ☐ (Sponsor's SSN) CHAMPVA ☐ (VA File #) GROUP HEALTH PLAN ☐ (SSN or ID) FECA BLK LUNG ☐ (SSN) OTHER ☐ (ID) | 1a. INSURED'S I.D. NUMBER (FOR PROGRAM IN ITEM 1) |

2. PATIENT'S NAME (Last Name, First Name, Middle Initial)

3. PATIENT'S BIRTH DATE MM ¦ DD ¦ YY   SEX M ☐ F ☐

4. INSURED'S NAME (Last Name, First Name, Middle Initial)

5. PATIENT'S ADDRESS (No. Street)

6. PATIENT RELATIONSHIP TO INSURED
Self ☐ Spouse ☐ Child ☐ Other ☐

7. INSURED'S ADDRESS (No. Street)

CITY   STATE

8. PATIENT STATUS
Single ☐ Married ☐ Other ☐
Employed ☐ Full-Time Student ☐ Part-Time Student ☐

CITY   STATE

ZIP CODE   TELEPHONE (Include Area Code)
(   )

ZIP CODE   TELEPHONE (INCLUDE AREA CODE)
(   )

9. OTHER INSURED'S NAME (Last Name, First Name, Middle Initial)

10. IS PATIENT'S CONDITION RELATED TO:

11. INSURED'S POLICY GROUP OR FECA NUMBER

a. OTHER INSURED'S POLICY OR GROUP NUMBER

a. EMPLOYMENT? (CURRENT OR PREVIOUS)
☐ YES ☐ NO

a. INSURED'S DATE OF BIRTH MM ¦ DD ¦ YY   SEX M ☐ F ☐

b. OTHER INSURED'S DATE OF BIRTH MM ¦ DD ¦ YY   SEX M ☐ F ☐

b. AUTO ACCIDENT?   PLACE (State)
☐ YES ☐ NO

b. EMPLOYER'S NAME OR SCHOOL NAME

c. EMPLOYER'S NAME OR SCHOOL NAME

c. OTHER ACCIDENT?
☐ YES ☐ NO

c. INSURANCE PLAN NAME OR PROGRAM NAME

d. INSURANCE PLAN NAME OR PROGRAM NAME

10d. RESERVED FOR LOCAL USE

d. IS THERE ANOTHER HEALTH BENEFIT PLAN?
☐ YES ☐ NO If yes, return to and complete item 9 a – d.

READ BACK OF FORM BEFORE COMPLETING & SIGNING THIS FORM.
12. PATIENT'S OR AUTHORIZED PERSON'S SIGNATURE I authorize the release of any medical or other information necessary to process this claim. I also request payment of government benefits either to myself or to the party who accepts assignment below.

SIGNED _____ DATE _____

13. INSURED'S OR AUTHORIZED PERSON'S SIGNATURE I authorize payment of medical benefits to the undersigned physician or supplier for services described below.

SIGNED _____

PATIENT AND INSURED INFORMATION

14. DATE OF CURRENT: ILLNESS (First symptom) OR INJURY (Accident) OR PREGNANCY (LMP)
MM ¦ DD ¦ YY

15. IF PATIENT HAS HAD SAME OR SIMILAR ILLNESS, GIVE FIRST DATE MM ¦ DD ¦ YY

16. DATES PATIENT UNABLE TO WORK IN CURRENT OCCUPATION
MM ¦ DD ¦ YY MM ¦ DD ¦ YY
FROM   TO

17. NAME OF REFERRING PHYSICIAN OR OTHER SOURCE

17a. I.D. NUMBER OF REFERRING PHYSICIAN

18. HOSPITALIZATION DATES RELATED TO CURRENT SERVICES
MM ¦ DD ¦ YY MM ¦ DD ¦ YY
FROM   TO

19. RESERVED FOR LOCAL USE

20. OUTSIDE LAB? $ CHARGES
☐ YES ☐ NO

21. DIAGNOSIS OR NATURE OF ILLNESS OR INJURY. (RELATE ITEMS 1, 2, 3, OR 4 TO ITEM 24E BY LINE)
1. |___.___| 3. |___.___|
2. |___.___| 4. |___.___|

22. MEDICAID RESUBMISSION CODE   ORIGINAL REF. NO.

23. PRIOR AUTHORIZATION NUMBER

24. A DATE(S) OF SERVICE From MM DD YY To MM DD YY	B Place of Service	C Type of Service	D PROCEDURES, SERVICES, OR SUPPLIES (Explain Unusual Circumstances) CPT/HCPCS MODIFIER	E DIAGNOSIS CODE	F $ CHARGES	G DAYS OR UNITS	H EPSDT Family Plan	I EMG	J COB	K RESERVED FOR LOCAL USE
1										
2										
3										
4										
5										
6										

25. FEDERAL TAX I.D. NUMBER   SSN ☐ EIN ☐

26. PATIENT'S ACCOUNT NO.

27. ACCEPT ASSIGNMENT? (For govt. claims, see back)
☐ YES ☐ NO

28. TOTAL CHARGE $

29. AMOUNT PAID $

30. BALANCE DUE $

31. SIGNATURE OF PHYSICIAN OR SUPPLIER INCLUDING DEGREES OR CREDENTIALS (I certify that the statements on the reverse apply to this bill and are made a part thereof.)

SIGNED _____ DATE _____

32. NAME AND ADDRESS OF FACILITY WHERE SERVICES WERE RENDERED (If other than home or office)

33. PHYSICIAN'S, SUPPLIER'S BILLING NAME, ADDRESS, ZIP CODE & PHONE #

PIN#   GRP#

PHYSICIAN OR SUPPLIER INFORMATION

PLEASE PRINT OR TYPE

SAMPLE FORM 1500
SAMPLE FORM 1500 SAMPLE FORM 1500

CARRIER

| | PICA | | **HEALTH INSURANCE CLAIM FORM** | PICA | |

| 1. MEDICARE ☐ (Medicare #) | MEDICAID ☐ (Medicaid #) | CHAMPUS ☐ (Sponsor's SSN) | CHAMPVA ☐ (VA File #) | GROUP HEALTH PLAN ☐ (SSN or ID) | FECA BLK LUNG ☐ (SSN) | OTHER ☐ (ID) | 1a. INSURED'S I.D. NUMBER (FOR PROGRAM IN ITEM 1) |

2. PATIENT'S NAME (Last Name, First Name, Middle Initial)

3. PATIENT'S BIRTH DATE MM | DD | YY   SEX M ☐   F ☐

4. INSURED'S NAME (Last Name, First Name, Middle Initial)

5. PATIENT'S ADDRESS (No. Street)

6. PATIENT RELATIONSHIP TO INSURED Self ☐ Spouse ☐ Child ☐ Other ☐

7. INSURED'S ADDRESS (No. Street)

CITY | STATE

8. PATIENT STATUS Single ☐ Married ☐ Other ☐ Employed ☐ Full-Time Student ☐ Part-Time Student ☐

CITY | STATE

ZIP CODE | TELEPHONE (Include Area Code) ( )

ZIP CODE | TELEPHONE (INCLUDE AREA CODE) ( )

9. OTHER INSURED'S NAME (Last Name, First Name, Middle Initial)

10. IS PATIENT'S CONDITION RELATED TO:

11. INSURED'S POLICY GROUP OR FECA NUMBER

a. OTHER INSURED'S POLICY OR GROUP NUMBER

a. EMPLOYMENT? (CURRENT OR PREVIOUS) ☐ YES ☐ NO

a. INSURED'S DATE OF BIRTH MM | DD | YY SEX M ☐ F ☐

b. OTHER INSURED'S DATE OF BIRTH MM | DD | YY SEX M ☐ F ☐

b. AUTO ACCIDENT? PLACE (State) ☐ YES ☐ NO

b. EMPLOYER'S NAME OR SCHOOL NAME

c. EMPLOYER'S NAME OR SCHOOL NAME

c. OTHER ACCIDENT? ☐ YES ☐ NO

c. INSURANCE PLAN NAME OR PROGRAM NAME

d. INSURANCE PLAN NAME OR PROGRAM NAME

10d. RESERVED FOR LOCAL USE

d. IS THERE ANOTHER HEALTH BENEFIT PLAN? ☐ YES ☐ NO If yes, return to and complete item 9 a – d.

READ BACK OF FORM BEFORE COMPLETING & SIGNING THIS FORM.
12. PATIENT'S OR AUTHORIZED PERSON'S SIGNATURE I authorize the release of any medical or other information necessary to process this claim. I also request payment of government benefits either to myself or to the party who accepts assignment below.

SIGNED _____ DATE _____

13. INSURED'S OR AUTHORIZED PERSON'S SIGNATURE I authorize payment of medical benefits to the undersigned physician or supplier for services described below.

SIGNED _____

PATIENT AND INSURED INFORMATION

14. DATE OF CURRENT: ILLNESS (First symptom) OR INJURY (Accident) OR PREGNANCY (LMP) MM | DD | YY

15. IF PATIENT HAS HAD SAME OR SIMILAR ILLNESS, GIVE FIRST DATE MM | DD | YY

16. DATES PATIENT UNABLE TO WORK IN CURRENT OCCUPATION MM | DD | YY FROM TO MM | DD | YY

17. NAME OF REFERRING PHYSICIAN OR OTHER SOURCE

17a. I.D. NUMBER OF REFERRING PHYSICIAN

18. HOSPITALIZATION DATES RELATED TO CURRENT SERVICES MM | DD | YY FROM TO MM | DD | YY

19. RESERVED FOR LOCAL USE

20. OUTSIDE LAB? $ CHARGES ☐ YES ☐ NO

21. DIAGNOSIS OR NATURE OF ILLNESS OR INJURY. (RELATE ITEMS 1, 2, 3, OR 4 TO ITEM 24E BY LINE)

1. _____ 3. _____

2. _____ 4. _____

22. MEDICAID RESUBMISSION CODE ORIGINAL REF. NO.

23. PRIOR AUTHORIZATION NUMBER

24. A DATE(S) OF SERVICE						B Place of Service	C Type of Service	D PROCEDURES, SERVICES, OR SUPPLIES (Explain Unusual Circumstances) CPT/HCPCS MODIFIER	E DIAGNOSIS CODE	F $ CHARGES	G DAYS OR UNITS	H EPSDT Family Plan	I EMG	J COB	K RESERVED FOR LOCAL USE
From MM	DD	YY	To MM	DD	YY										
1															
2															
3															
4															
5															
6															

25. FEDERAL TAX I.D. NUMBER SSN ☐ EIN ☐

26. PATIENT'S ACCOUNT NO.

27. ACCEPT ASSIGNMENT? (For govt. claims, see back) ☐ YES ☐ NO

28. TOTAL CHARGE $

29. AMOUNT PAID $

30. BALANCE DUE $

31. SIGNATURE OF PHYSICIAN OR SUPPLIER INCLUDING DEGREES OR CREDENTIALS (I certify that the statements on the reverse apply to this bill and are made a part thereof.)

SIGNED _____ DATE _____

32. NAME AND ADDRESS OF FACILITY WHERE SERVICES WERE RENDERED (If other than home or office)

33. PHYSICIAN'S, SUPPLIER'S BILLING NAME, ADDRESS, ZIP CODE & PHONE #

PIN# | GRP#

PHYSICIAN OR SUPPLIER INFORMATION

PLEASE PRINT OR TYPE

SAMPLE FORM 1500
SAMPLE FORM 1500 SAMPLE FORM 1500

CARRIER

| | PICA | | **HEALTH INSURANCE CLAIM FORM** | PICA | | |

1.

MEDICARE	MEDICAID	CHAMPUS	CHAMPVA	GROUP HEALTH PLAN	FECA BLK LUNG	OTHER	1a. INSURED'S I.D. NUMBER	(FOR PROGRAM IN ITEM 1)
(Medicare #)	(Medicaid #)	(Sponsor's SSN)	(VA File #)	(SSN or ID)	(SSN)	(ID)		

2. PATIENT'S NAME (Last Name, First Name, Middle Initial)

3. PATIENT'S BIRTH DATE MM | DD | YY   SEX M ☐ F ☐

4. INSURED'S NAME (Last Name, First Name, Middle Initial)

5. PATIENT'S ADDRESS (No. Street)

6. PATIENT RELATIONSHIP TO INSURED Self ☐ Spouse ☐ Child ☐ Other ☐

7. INSURED'S ADDRESS (No. Street)

CITY   STATE

8. PATIENT STATUS Single ☐ Married ☐ Other ☐

CITY   STATE

ZIP CODE   TELEPHONE (Include Area Code) ( )

Employed ☐ Full-Time Student ☐ Part-Time Student ☐

ZIP CODE   TELEPHONE (INCLUDE AREA CODE) ( )

9. OTHER INSURED'S NAME (Last Name, First Name, Middle Initial)

10. IS PATIENT'S CONDITION RELATED TO:

11. INSURED'S POLICY GROUP OR FECA NUMBER

a. OTHER INSURED'S POLICY OR GROUP NUMBER

a. EMPLOYMENT? (CURRENT OR PREVIOUS) YES ☐ NO ☐

a. INSURED'S DATE OF BIRTH MM | DD | YY   SEX M ☐ F ☐

b. OTHER INSURED'S DATE OF BIRTH MM | DD | YY   SEX M ☐ F ☐

b. AUTO ACCIDENT?   PLACE (State) YES ☐ NO ☐

b. EMPLOYER'S NAME OR SCHOOL NAME

c. EMPLOYER'S NAME OR SCHOOL NAME

c. OTHER ACCIDENT? YES ☐ NO ☐

c. INSURANCE PLAN NAME OR PROGRAM NAME

d. INSURANCE PLAN NAME OR PROGRAM NAME

10d. RESERVED FOR LOCAL USE

d. IS THERE ANOTHER HEALTH BENEFIT PLAN? YES ☐ NO ☐ If yes, return to and complete item 9 a – d.

READ BACK OF FORM BEFORE COMPLETING & SIGNING THIS FORM.
12. PATIENT'S OR AUTHORIZED PERSON'S SIGNATURE I authorize the release of any medical or other information necessary to process this claim. I also request payment of government benefits either to myself or to the party who accepts assignment below.

SIGNED _____   DATE _____

13. INSURED'S OR AUTHORIZED PERSON'S SIGNATURE I authorize payment of medical benefits to the undersigned physician or supplier for services described below.

SIGNED _____

PATIENT AND INSURED INFORMATION

14. DATE OF CURRENT: MM | DD | YY ◄ ILLNESS (First symptom) OR INJURY (Accident) OR PREGNANCY (LMP)

15. IF PATIENT HAS HAD SAME OR SIMILAR ILLNESS, GIVE FIRST DATE MM | DD | YY

16. DATES PATIENT UNABLE TO WORK IN CURRENT OCCUPATION MM | DD | YY FROM   MM | DD | YY TO

17. NAME OF REFERRING PHYSICIAN OR OTHER SOURCE

17a. I.D. NUMBER OF REFERRING PHYSICIAN

18. HOSPITALIZATION DATES RELATED TO CURRENT SERVICES MM | DD | YY FROM   MM | DD | YY TO

19. RESERVED FOR LOCAL USE

20. OUTSIDE LAB? YES ☐ NO ☐ $ CHARGES

21. DIAGNOSIS OR NATURE OF ILLNESS OR INJURY. (RELATE ITEMS 1, 2, 3, OR 4 TO ITEM 24E BY LINE) —

1. ____ . ____

3. ____ . ____

2. ____ . ____

4. ____ . ____

22. MEDICAID RESUBMISSION CODE   ORIGINAL REF. NO.

23. PRIOR AUTHORIZATION NUMBER

24. A DATE(S) OF SERVICE						B Place of Service	C Type of Service	D PROCEDURES, SERVICES, OR SUPPLIES (Explain Unusual Circumstances)		E DIAGNOSIS CODE	F $ CHARGES	G DAYS OR UNITS	H EPSDT Family Plan	I EMG	J COB	K RESERVED FOR LOCAL USE
From MM	DD	YY	To MM	DD	YY			CPT/HCPCS	MODIFIER							
1																
2																
3																
4																
5																
6																

25. FEDERAL TAX I.D. NUMBER   SSN ☐ EIN ☐

26. PATIENT'S ACCOUNT NO.

27. ACCEPT ASSIGNMENT? (For govt. claims, see back) YES ☐ NO ☐

28. TOTAL CHARGE $

29. AMOUNT PAID $

30. BALANCE DUE $

31. SIGNATURE OF PHYSICIAN OR SUPPLIER INCLUDING DEGREES OR CREDENTIALS (I certify that the statements on the reverse apply to this bill and are made a part thereof.)

SIGNED _____   DATE _____

32. NAME AND ADDRESS OF FACILITY WHERE SERVICES WERE RENDERED (If other than home or office)

33. PHYSICIAN'S, SUPPLIER'S BILLING NAME, ADDRESS, ZIP CODE & PHONE #

PIN#   GRP#

PHYSICIAN OR SUPPLIER INFORMATION

PLEASE PRINT OR TYPE

SAMPLE FORM 1500
SAMPLE FORM 1500 SAMPLE FORM 1500

CARRIER

| | PICA |

HEALTH INSURANCE CLAIM FORM

PICA | | |

| 1. MEDICARE ☐ (Medicare #) MEDICAID ☐ (Medicaid #) CHAMPUS ☐ (Sponsor's SSN) CHAMPVA ☐ (VA File #) GROUP HEALTH PLAN ☐ (SSN or ID) FECA BLK LUNG ☐ (SSN) OTHER ☐ (ID) | 1a. INSURED'S I.D. NUMBER (FOR PROGRAM IN ITEM 1) |

| 2. PATIENT'S NAME (Last Name, First Name, Middle Initial) | 3. PATIENT'S BIRTH DATE MM ¦ DD ¦ YY   SEX M ☐ F ☐ | 4. INSURED'S NAME (Last Name, First Name, Middle Initial) |

| 5. PATIENT'S ADDRESS (No. Street) | 6. PATIENT RELATIONSHIP TO INSURED Self ☐ Spouse ☐ Child ☐ Other ☐ | 7. INSURED'S ADDRESS (No. Street) |

| CITY | STATE | 8. PATIENT STATUS Single ☐ Married ☐ Other ☐ | CITY | STATE |

| ZIP CODE | TELEPHONE (Include Area Code) ( ) | Employed ☐ Full-Time Student ☐ Part-Time Student ☐ | ZIP CODE | TELEPHONE (INCLUDE AREA CODE) ( ) |

| 9. OTHER INSURED'S NAME (Last Name, First Name, Middle Initial) | 10. IS PATIENT'S CONDITION RELATED TO: | 11. INSURED'S POLICY GROUP OR FECA NUMBER |

| a. OTHER INSURED'S POLICY OR GROUP NUMBER | a. EMPLOYMENT? (CURRENT OR PREVIOUS) YES ☐ NO ☐ | a. INSURED'S DATE OF BIRTH MM ¦ DD ¦ YY SEX M ☐ F ☐ |

| b. OTHER INSURED'S DATE OF BIRTH MM ¦ DD ¦ YY SEX M ☐ F ☐ | b. AUTO ACCIDENT? PLACE (State) YES ☐ NO ☐ | b. EMPLOYER'S NAME OR SCHOOL NAME |

| c. EMPLOYER'S NAME OR SCHOOL NAME | c. OTHER ACCIDENT? YE3 ☐ NO ☐ | c. INSURANCE PLAN NAME OR PROGRAM NAME |

| d. INSURANCE PLAN NAME OR PROGRAM NAME | 10d. RESERVED FOR LOCAL USE | d. IS THERE ANOTHER HEALTH BENEFIT PLAN? YES ☐ NO ☐ If yes, return to and complete item 9 a – d. |

READ BACK OF FORM BEFORE COMPLETING & SIGNING THIS FORM.

12. PATIENT'S OR AUTHORIZED PERSON'S SIGNATURE I authorize the release of any medical or other information necessary to process this claim. I also request payment of government benefits either to myself or to the party who accepts assignment below.

SIGNED _____ DATE _____

13. INSURED'S OR AUTHORIZED PERSON'S SIGNATURE I authorize payment of medical benefits to the undersigned physician or supplier for services described below.

SIGNED _____

PATIENT AND INSURED INFORMATION

| 14. DATE OF CURRENT: ILLNESS (First symptom) OR INJURY (Accident) OR PREGNANCY (LMP) MM ¦ DD ¦ YY | 15. IF PATIENT HAS HAD SAME OR SIMILAR ILLNESS, GIVE FIRST DATE MM ¦ DD ¦ YY | 16. DATES PATIENT UNABLE TO WORK IN CURRENT OCCUPATION MM ¦ DD ¦ YY   MM ¦ DD ¦ YY FROM   TO |

| 17. NAME OF REFERRING PHYSICIAN OR OTHER SOURCE | 17a. I.D. NUMBER OF REFERRING PHYSICIAN | 18. HOSPITALIZATION DATES RELATED TO CURRENT SERVICES MM ¦ DD ¦ YY   MM ¦ DD ¦ YY FROM   TO |

| 19. RESERVED FOR LOCAL USE | 20. OUTSIDE LAB? $ CHARGES YES ☐ NO ☐ |

| 21. DIAGNOSIS OR NATURE OF ILLNESS OR INJURY. (RELATE ITEMS 1, 2, 3, OR 4 TO ITEM 24E BY LINE) 1. ⌐__ . __   3. ⌐__ . __ 2. ⌐__ . __   4. ⌐__ . __ | 22. MEDICAID RESUBMISSION CODE   ORIGINAL REF. NO. |
| | 23. PRIOR AUTHORIZATION NUMBER |

24. A. DATE(S) OF SERVICE			B. Place of Service	C. Type of Service	D. PROCEDURES, SERVICES, OR SUPPLIES (Explain Unusual Circumstances)		E. DIAGNOSIS CODE	F. $ CHARGES	G. DAYS OR UNITS	H. EPSDT Family Plan	I. EMG	J. COB	K. RESERVED FOR LOCAL USE
From MM DD YY	To MM DD YY				CPT/HCPCS	MODIFIER							
1													
2													
3													
4													
5													
6													

| 25. FEDERAL TAX I.D. NUMBER SSN ☐ EIN ☐ | 26. PATIENT'S ACCOUNT NO. | 27. ACCEPT ASSIGNMENT? (For govt. claims, see back) YES ☐ NO ☐ | 28. TOTAL CHARGE $ | 29. AMOUNT PAID $ | 30. BALANCE DUE $ |

| 31. SIGNATURE OF PHYSICIAN OR SUPPLIER INCLUDING DEGREES OR CREDENTIALS (I certify that the statements on the reverse apply to this bill and are made a part thereof.) SIGNED _____ DATE _____ | 32. NAME AND ADDRESS OF FACILITY WHERE SERVICES WERE RENDERED (If other than home or office) | 33. PHYSICIAN'S, SUPPLIER'S BILLING NAME, ADDRESS, ZIP CODE & PHONE # PIN#   GRP# |

PHYSICIAN OR SUPPLIER INFORMATION

PLEASE PRINT OR TYPE

SAMPLE FORM 1500
SAMPLE FORM 1500 SAMPLE FORM 1500

220

PLEASE
DO NOT
STAPLE
IN THIS
AREA

CARRIER

HEALTH INSURANCE CLAIM FORM

PICA ☐☐

PICA ☐☐

1.	MEDICARE	MEDICAID	CHAMPUS	CHAMPVA	GROUP HEALTH PLAN	FECA BLK LUNG	OTHER	1a. INSURED'S I.D. NUMBER (FOR PROGRAM IN ITEM 1)
	☐ (Medicare #)	☐ (Medicaid #)	☐ (Sponsor's SSN)	☐ (VA File #)	☐ (SSN or ID)	☐ (SSN)	☐ (ID)	

2. PATIENT'S NAME (Last Name, First Name, Middle Initial)

3. PATIENT'S BIRTH DATE
MM ┆ DD ┆ YY
SEX   M ☐   F ☐

4. INSURED'S NAME (Last Name, First Name, Middle Initial)

5. PATIENT'S ADDRESS (No. Street)

6. PATIENT RELATIONSHIP TO INSURED
Self ☐   Spouse ☐   Child ☐   Other ☐

7. INSURED'S ADDRESS (No. Street)

CITY   STATE

8. PATIENT STATUS
Single ☐   Married ☐   Other ☐

CITY   STATE

ZIP CODE   TELEPHONE (Include Area Code)
(   )

Employed ☐   Full-Time Student ☐   Part-Time Student ☐

ZIP CODE   TELEPHONE (INCLUDE AREA CODE)
(   )

9. OTHER INSURED'S NAME (Last Name, First Name, Middle Initial)

10. IS PATIENT'S CONDITION RELATED TO:

11. INSURED'S POLICY GROUP OR FECA NUMBER

a. OTHER INSURED'S POLICY OR GROUP NUMBER

a. EMPLOYMENT? (CURRENT OR PREVIOUS)
☐ YES   ☐ NO

a. INSURED'S DATE OF BIRTH
MM ┆ DD ┆ YY
SEX   M ☐   F ☐

b. OTHER INSURED'S DATE OF BIRTH
MM ┆ DD ┆ YY   SEX   M ☐   F ☐

b. AUTO ACCIDENT?   PLACE (State)
☐ YES   ☐ NO

b. EMPLOYER'S NAME OR SCHOOL NAME

c. EMPLOYER'S NAME OR SCHOOL NAME

c. OTHER ACCIDENT?
☐ YES   ☐ NO

c. INSURANCE PLAN NAME OR PROGRAM NAME

d. INSURANCE PLAN NAME OR PROGRAM NAME

10d. RESERVED FOR LOCAL USE

d. IS THERE ANOTHER HEALTH BENEFIT PLAN?
☐ YES   ☐ NO   If yes, return to and complete item 9 a – d.

READ BACK OF FORM BEFORE COMPLETING & SIGNING THIS FORM.
12. PATIENT'S OR AUTHORIZED PERSON'S SIGNATURE I authorize the release of any medical or other information necessary to process this claim. I also request payment of government benefits either to myself or to the party who accepts assignment below.

SIGNED _____ DATE _____

13. INSURED'S OR AUTHORIZED PERSON'S SIGNATURE I authorize payment of medical benefits to the undersigned physician or supplier for services described below.

SIGNED _____

PATIENT AND INSURED INFORMATION

14. DATE OF CURRENT: ILLNESS (First symptom) OR
MM ┆ DD ┆ YY   INJURY (Accident) OR
PREGNANCY (LMP)

15. IF PATIENT HAS HAD SAME OR SIMILAR ILLNESS,
GIVE FIRST DATE   MM ┆ DD ┆ YY

16. DATES PATIENT UNABLE TO WORK IN CURRENT OCCUPATION
MM ┆ DD ┆ YY   MM ┆ DD ┆ YY
FROM   TO

17. NAME OF REFERRING PHYSICIAN OR OTHER SOURCE

17a. I.D. NUMBER OF REFERRING PHYSICIAN

18. HOSPITALIZATION DATES RELATED TO CURRENT SERVICES
MM ┆ DD ┆ YY   MM ┆ DD ┆ YY
FROM   TO

19. RESERVED FOR LOCAL USE

20. OUTSIDE LAB? $ CHARGES
☐ YES   ☐ NO

21. DIAGNOSIS OR NATURE OF ILLNESS OR INJURY. (RELATE ITEMS 1, 2, 3, OR 4 TO ITEM 24E BY LINE)

1. └___ ___
2. └___ ___
3. └___ ___
4. └___ ___

22. MEDICAID RESUBMISSION
CODE   ORIGINAL REF. NO.

23. PRIOR AUTHORIZATION NUMBER

24. A DATE(S) OF SERVICE						B Place of Service	C Type of Service	D PROCEDURES, SERVICES, OR SUPPLIES (Explain Unusual Circumstances)		E DIAGNOSIS CODE	F $ CHARGES	G DAYS OR UNITS	H EPSDT Family Plan	I EMG	J COB	K RESERVED FOR LOCAL USE
From MM	DD	YY	To MM	DD	YY			CPT/HCPCS	MODIFIER							
1																
2																
3																
4																
5																
6																

25. FEDERAL TAX I.D. NUMBER   SSN ☐   EIN ☐

26. PATIENT'S ACCOUNT NO.

27. ACCEPT ASSIGNMENT?
(For govt. claims, see back)
☐ YES   ☐ NO

28. TOTAL CHARGE
$

29. AMOUNT PAID
$

30. BALANCE DUE
$

31. SIGNATURE OF PHYSICIAN OR SUPPLIER INCLUDING DEGREES OR CREDENTIALS
(I certify that the statements on the reverse apply to this bill and are made a part thereof.)

SIGNED _____ DATE _____

32. NAME AND ADDRESS OF FACILITY WHERE SERVICES WERE RENDERED (If other than home or office)

33. PHYSICIAN'S, SUPPLIER'S BILLING NAME, ADDRESS, ZIP CODE & PHONE #

PIN#   GRP#

PHYSICIAN OR SUPPLIER INFORMATION

221

PLEASE
DO NOT
STAPLE
IN THIS
AREA

| | PICA

HEALTH INSURANCE CLAIM FORM

PICA | | |

1. MEDICARE	MEDICAID	CHAMPUS	CHAMPVA	GROUP HEALTH PLAN	FECA BLK LUNG	OTHER	1a. INSURED'S I.D. NUMBER	(FOR PROGRAM IN ITEM 1)
☐ (Medicare #)	☐ (Medicaid #)	☐ (Sponsor's SSN)	☐ (VA File #)	☐ (SSN or ID)	☐ (SSN)	☐ (ID)		

2. PATIENT'S NAME (Last Name, First Name, Middle Initial)

3. PATIENT'S BIRTH DATE MM | DD | YY   SEX M ☐ F ☐

4. INSURED'S NAME (Last Name, First Name, Middle Initial)

5. PATIENT'S ADDRESS (No. Street)

6. PATIENT RELATIONSHIP TO INSURED
Self ☐ Spouse ☐ Child ☐ Other ☐

7. INSURED'S ADDRESS (No. Street)

CITY   STATE

8. PATIENT STATUS
Single ☐   Married ☐   Other ☐
Employed ☐   Full-Time Student ☐   Part-Time Student ☐

CITY   STATE

ZIP CODE   TELEPHONE (Include Area Code) ( )

ZIP CODE   TELEPHONE (INCLUDE AREA CODE) ( )

9. OTHER INSURED'S NAME (Last Name, First Name, Middle Initial)

10. IS PATIENT'S CONDITION RELATED TO:

11. INSURED'S POLICY GROUP OR FECA NUMBER

a. OTHER INSURED'S POLICY OR GROUP NUMBER

a. EMPLOYMENT? (CURRENT OR PREVIOUS)
☐ YES   ☐ NO

a. INSURED'S DATE OF BIRTH MM | DD | YY   SEX M ☐ F ☐

b. OTHER INSURED'S DATE OF BIRTH MM | DD | YY   SEX M ☐ F ☐

b. AUTO ACCIDENT?   PLACE (State)
☐ YES   ☐ NO

b. EMPLOYER'S NAME OR SCHOOL NAME

c. EMPLOYER'S NAME OR SCHOOL NAME

c. OTHER ACCIDENT?
☐ YES   ☐ NO

c. INSURANCE PLAN NAME OR PROGRAM NAME

d. INSURANCE PLAN NAME OR PROGRAM NAME

10d. RESERVED FOR LOCAL USE

d. IS THERE ANOTHER HEALTH BENEFIT PLAN?
☐ YES   ☐ NO   If yes, return to and complete item 9 a – d.

READ BACK OF FORM BEFORE COMPLETING & SIGNING THIS FORM.
12. PATIENT'S OR AUTHORIZED PERSON'S SIGNATURE I authorize the release of any medical or other information necessary to process this claim. I also request payment of government benefits either to myself or to the party who accepts assignment below.

SIGNED _____ DATE _____

13. INSURED'S OR AUTHORIZED PERSON'S SIGNATURE I authorize payment of medical benefits to the undersigned physician or supplier for services described below.

SIGNED _____

14. DATE OF CURRENT: ◀ ILLNESS (First symptom) OR INJURY (Accident) OR PREGNANCY (LMP)
MM | DD | YY

15. IF PATIENT HAS HAD SAME OR SIMILAR ILLNESS, GIVE FIRST DATE MM | DD | YY

16. DATES PATIENT UNABLE TO WORK IN CURRENT OCCUPATION
FROM MM | DD | YY   TO MM | DD | YY

17. NAME OF REFERRING PHYSICIAN OR OTHER SOURCE

17a. I.D. NUMBER OF REFERRING PHYSICIAN

18. HOSPITALIZATION DATES RELATED TO CURRENT SERVICES
FROM MM | DD | YY   TO MM | DD | YY

19. RESERVED FOR LOCAL USE

20. OUTSIDE LAB? $ CHARGES
☐ YES   ☐ NO

21. DIAGNOSIS OR NATURE OF ILLNESS OR INJURY. (RELATE ITEMS 1, 2, 3, OR 4 TO ITEM 24E BY LINE)
1. |___.___| 3. |___.___| ▼
2. |___.___| 4. |___.___|

22. MEDICAID RESUBMISSION CODE   ORIGINAL REF. NO.

23. PRIOR AUTHORIZATION NUMBER

24. A DATE(S) OF SERVICE						B Place of Service	C Type of Service	D PROCEDURES, SERVICES, OR SUPPLIES (Explain Unusual Circumstances)		E DIAGNOSIS CODE	F $ CHARGES	G DAYS OR UNITS	H EPSDT Family Plan	I EMG	J COB	K RESERVED FOR LOCAL USE
From MM	DD	YY	To MM	DD	YY			CPT/HCPCS	MODIFIER							
1																
2																
3																
4																
5																
6																

25. FEDERAL TAX I.D. NUMBER   SSN ☐ EIN ☐

26. PATIENT'S ACCOUNT NO.

27. ACCEPT ASSIGNMENT? (For govt. claims, see back)
☐ YES   ☐ NO

28. TOTAL CHARGE $

29. AMOUNT PAID $

30. BALANCE DUE $

31. SIGNATURE OF PHYSICIAN OR SUPPLIER INCLUDING DEGREES OR CREDENTIALS
(I certify that the statements on the reverse apply to this bill and are made a part thereof.)

SIGNED _____ DATE _____

32. NAME AND ADDRESS OF FACILITY WHERE SERVICES WERE RENDERED (If other than home or office)

33. PHYSICIAN'S, SUPPLIER'S BILLING NAME, ADDRESS, ZIP CODE & PHONE #

PIN#   GRP#

PLEASE PRINT OR TYPE

SAMPLE FORM 1500
SAMPLE FORM 1500 SAMPLE FORM 1500

(SAMPLE ONLY - NOT APPROVED FOR USE)

CARRIER

□□ PICA

HEALTH INSURANCE CLAIM FORM   PICA □□

1. MEDICARE MEDICAID CHAMPUS CHAMPVA GROUP HEALTH PLAN FECA BLK LUNG OTHER	1a. INSURED'S I.D. NUMBER (FOR PROGRAM IN ITEM 1)

□ (Medicare #) □ (Medicaid #) □ (Sponsor's SSN) □ (VA File #) □ (SSN or ID) □ (SSN) □ (ID)

2. PATIENT'S NAME (Last Name, First Name, Middle Initial)	3. PATIENT'S BIRTH DATE MM DD YY SEX M □ F □	4. INSURED'S NAME (Last Name, First Name, Middle Initial)

5. PATIENT'S ADDRESS (No. Street)	6. PATIENT RELATIONSHIP TO INSURED Self □ Spouse □ Child □ Other □	7. INSURED'S ADDRESS (No. Street)

CITY STATE	8. PATIENT STATUS Single □ Married □ Other □	CITY STATE

ZIP CODE TELEPHONE (Include Area Code) ( )	Employed □ Full-Time Student □ Part-Time Student □	ZIP CODE TELEPHONE (INCLUDE AREA CODE) ( )

9. OTHER INSURED'S NAME (Last Name, First Name, Middle Initial)	10. IS PATIENT'S CONDITION RELATED TO:	11. INSURED'S POLICY GROUP OR FECA NUMBER

a. OTHER INSURED'S POLICY OR GROUP NUMBER	a. EMPLOYMENT? (CURRENT OR PREVIOUS) □ YES □ NO	a. INSURED'S DATE OF BIRTH MM DD YY SEX M □ F □

b. OTHER INSURED'S DATE OF BIRTH MM DD YY SEX M □ F □	b. AUTO ACCIDENT? PLACE (State) □ YES □ NO	b. EMPLOYER'S NAME OR SCHOOL NAME

c. EMPLOYER'S NAME OR SCHOOL NAME	c. OTHER ACCIDENT? □ YES □ NO	c. INSURANCE PLAN NAME OR PROGRAM NAME

d. INSURANCE PLAN NAME OR PROGRAM NAME	10d. RESERVED FOR LOCAL USE	d. IS THERE ANOTHER HEALTH BENEFIT PLAN? □ YES □ NO If yes, return to and complete item 9 a – d.

READ BACK OF FORM BEFORE COMPLETING & SIGNING THIS FORM.
12. PATIENT'S OR AUTHORIZED PERSON'S SIGNATURE I authorize the release of any medical or other information necessary to process this claim. I also request payment of government benefits either to myself or to the party who accepts assignment below.

SIGNED _____   DATE _____

13. INSURED'S OR AUTHORIZED PERSON'S SIGNATURE I authorize payment of medical benefits to the undersigned physician or supplier for services described below.

SIGNED _____

PATIENT AND INSURED INFORMATION

14. DATE OF CURRENT: ILLNESS (First symptom) OR INJURY (Accident) OR PREGNANCY (LMP) MM DD YY	15. IF PATIENT HAS HAD SAME OR SIMILAR ILLNESS, GIVE FIRST DATE MM DD YY	16. DATES PATIENT UNABLE TO WORK IN CURRENT OCCUPATION MM DD YY FROM TO MM DD YY

17. NAME OF REFERRING PHYSICIAN OR OTHER SOURCE	17a. I.D. NUMBER OF REFERRING PHYSICIAN	18. HOSPITALIZATION DATES RELATED TO CURRENT SERVICES MM DD YY FROM TO MM DD YY

19. RESERVED FOR LOCAL USE		20. OUTSIDE LAB? □ YES □ NO $ CHARGES

21. DIAGNOSIS OR NATURE OF ILLNESS OR INJURY. (RELATE ITEMS 1, 2, 3, OR 4 TO ITEM 24E BY LINE)

1. L___ 3. L___

2. L___ 4. L___

22. MEDICAID RESUBMISSION CODE   ORIGINAL REF. NO.
23. PRIOR AUTHORIZATION NUMBER

24. A DATE(S) OF SERVICE From To MM DD YY MM DD YY	B Place of Service	C Type of Service	D PROCEDURES, SERVICES, OR SUPPLIES (Explain Unusual Circumstances) CPT/HCPCS MODIFIER	E DIAGNOSIS CODE	F $ CHARGES	G DAYS OR UNITS	H EPSDT Family Plan	I EMG	J COB	K RESERVED FOR LOCAL USE
1										
2										
3										
4										
5										
6										

25. FEDERAL TAX I.D. NUMBER SSN □ EIN □	26. PATIENT'S ACCOUNT NO.	27. ACCEPT ASSIGNMENT? (For govt. claims, see back) YES □ NO □	28. TOTAL CHARGE $	29. AMOUNT PAID $	30. BALANCE DUE $

31. SIGNATURE OF PHYSICIAN OR SUPPLIER INCLUDING DEGREES OR CREDENTIALS (I certify that the statements on the reverse apply to this bill and are made a part thereof.) SIGNED DATE	32. NAME AND ADDRESS OF FACILITY WHERE SERVICES WERE RENDERED (If other than home or office)	33. PHYSICIAN'S, SUPPLIER'S BILLING NAME, ADDRESS, ZIP CODE & PHONE # PIN# GRP#

PHYSICIAN OR SUPPLIER INFORMATION

(SAMPLE ONLY - NOT APPROVED FOR USE)

PLEASE PRINT OR TYPE

SAMPLE FORM 1500
SAMPLE FORM 1500 SAMPLE FORM 1500

223

(SAMPLE, ONLY - NOT APPROVED FOR USE)

CARRIER

☐☐☐ PICA

HEALTH INSURANCE CLAIM FORM

PICA ☐☐☐

| 1. MEDICARE ☐ (Medicare #) | MEDICAID ☐ (Medicaid #) | CHAMPUS ☐ (Sponsor's SSN) | CHAMPVA ☐ (VA File #) | GROUP HEALTH PLAN ☐ (SSN or ID) | FECA BLK LUNG ☐ (SSN) | OTHER ☐ (ID) | 1a. INSURED'S I.D. NUMBER | (FOR PROGRAM IN ITEM 1) |

2. PATIENT'S NAME (Last Name, First Name, Middle Initial)

3. PATIENT'S BIRTH DATE
MM | DD | YY   SEX   M ☐   F ☐

4. INSURED'S NAME (Last Name, First Name, Middle Initial)

5. PATIENT'S ADDRESS (No. Street)

6. PATIENT RELATIONSHIP TO INSURED
Self ☐   Spouse ☐   Child ☐   Other ☐

7. INSURED'S ADDRESS (No. Street)

CITY   STATE

8. PATIENT STATUS
Single ☐   Married ☐   Other ☐
Employed ☐   Full-Time Student ☐   Part-Time Student ☐

CITY   STATE

ZIP CODE   TELEPHONE (Include Area Code)
(   )

ZIP CODE   TELEPHONE (INCLUDE AREA CODE)
(   )

9. OTHER INSURED'S NAME (Last Name, First Name, Middle Initial)

10. IS PATIENT'S CONDITION RELATED TO:

11. INSURED'S POLICY GROUP OR FECA NUMBER

a. OTHER INSURED'S POLICY OR GROUP NUMBER

a. EMPLOYMENT? (CURRENT OR PREVIOUS)
☐ YES   ☐ NO

a. INSURED'S DATE OF BIRTH
MM | DD | YY   SEX   M ☐   F ☐

b. OTHER INSURED'S DATE OF BIRTH
MM | DD | YY   SEX   M ☐   F ☐

b. AUTO ACCIDENT?   PLACE (State)
☐ YES   ☐ NO

b. EMPLOYER'S NAME OR SCHOOL NAME

c. EMPLOYER'S NAME OR SCHOOL NAME

c. OTHER ACCIDENT?
☐ YES   ☐ NO

c. INSURANCE PLAN NAME OR PROGRAM NAME

d. INSURANCE PLAN NAME OR PROGRAM NAME

10d. RESERVED FOR LOCAL USE

d. IS THERE ANOTHER HEALTH BENEFIT PLAN?
☐ YES   ☐ NO   If yes, return to and complete item 9 a – d.

READ BACK OF FORM BEFORE COMPLETING & SIGNING THIS FORM.
12. PATIENT'S OR AUTHORIZED PERSON'S SIGNATURE I authorize the release of any medical or other information necessary to process this claim. I also request payment of government benefits either to myself or to the party who accepts assignment below.

SIGNED _____   DATE _____

13. INSURED'S OR AUTHORIZED PERSON'S SIGNATURE I authorize payment of medical benefits to the undersigned physician or supplier for services described below.

SIGNED _____

14. DATE OF CURRENT: ILLNESS (First symptom) OR INJURY (Accident) OR PREGNANCY (LMP)
MM | DD | YY

15. IF PATIENT HAS HAD SAME OR SIMILAR ILLNESS, GIVE FIRST DATE   MM | DD | YY

16. DATES PATIENT UNABLE TO WORK IN CURRENT OCCUPATION
FROM MM | DD | YY   TO MM | DD | YY

17. NAME OF REFERRING PHYSICIAN OR OTHER SOURCE

17a. I.D. NUMBER OF REFERRING PHYSICIAN

18. HOSPITALIZATION DATES RELATED TO CURRENT SERVICES
FROM MM | DD | YY   TO MM | DD | YY

19. RESERVED FOR LOCAL USE

20. OUTSIDE LAB? $ CHARGES
☐ YES   ☐ NO

21. DIAGNOSIS OR NATURE OF ILLNESS OR INJURY. (RELATE ITEMS 1, 2, 3, OR 4 TO ITEM 24E BY LINE)
1. ⌐__ . __
2. ⌐__ . __
3. ⌐__ . __
4. ⌐__ . __

22. MEDICAID RESUBMISSION
CODE   ORIGINAL REF. NO.

23. PRIOR AUTHORIZATION NUMBER

24. A DATE(S) OF SERVICE						B Place of Service	C Type of Service	D PROCEDURES, SERVICES, OR SUPPLIES (Explain Unusual Circumstances)		E DIAGNOSIS CODE	F $ CHARGES	G DAYS OR UNITS	H EPSDT Family Plan	I EMG	J COB	K RESERVED FOR LOCAL USE
From MM	DD	YY	To MM	DD	YY			CPT/HCPCS	MODIFIER							
1																
2																
3																
4																
5																
6																

25. FEDERAL TAX I.D. NUMBER   SSN ☐ EIN ☐

26. PATIENT'S ACCOUNT NO.

27. ACCEPT ASSIGNMENT? (For govt. claims, see back)
☐ YES   ☐ NO

28. TOTAL CHARGE
$

29. AMOUNT PAID
$

30. BALANCE DUE
$

31. SIGNATURE OF PHYSICIAN OR SUPPLIER INCLUDING DEGREES OR CREDENTIALS (I certify that the statements on the reverse apply to this bill and are made a part thereof.)

SIGNED _____   DATE _____

32. NAME AND ADDRESS OF FACILITY WHERE SERVICES WERE RENDERED (If other than home or office)

33. PHYSICIAN'S, SUPPLIER'S BILLING NAME, ADDRESS, ZIP CODE & PHONE #

PIN#   GRP#

(SAMPLE ONLY - NOT APPROVED FOR USE)

PLEASE PRINT OR TYPE

SAMPLE FORM 1500
SAMPLE FORM 1500 SAMPLE FORM 1500

PLEASE
DO NOT
STAPLE
IN THIS
AREA

| | PICA

CARRIER

HEALTH INSURANCE CLAIM FORM

PICA | |

| 1. MEDICARE ☐ (Medicare #) MEDICAID ☐ (Medicaid #) CHAMPUS ☐ (Sponsor's SSN) CHAMPVA ☐ (VA File #) GROUP HEALTH PLAN ☐ (SSN or ID) FECA BLK LUNG ☐ (SSN) OTHER ☐ (ID) | 1a. INSURED'S I.D. NUMBER (FOR PROGRAM IN ITEM 1) |

| 2. PATIENT'S NAME (Last Name, First Name, Middle Initial) | 3. PATIENT'S BIRTH DATE MM | DD | YY SEX M ☐ F ☐ | 4. INSURED'S NAME (Last Name, First Name, Middle Initial) |

| 5. PATIENT'S ADDRESS (No. Street) | 6. PATIENT RELATIONSHIP TO INSURED Self ☐ Spouse ☐ Child ☐ Other ☐ | 7. INSURED'S ADDRESS (No. Street) |

CITY | STATE | 8. PATIENT STATUS Single ☐ Married ☐ Other ☐ | CITY | STATE

ZIP CODE | TELEPHONE (Include Area Code) ( ) | Employed ☐ Full-Time Student ☐ Part-Time Student ☐ | ZIP CODE | TELEPHONE (INCLUDE AREA CODE) ( )

| 9. OTHER INSURED'S NAME (Last Name, First Name, Middle Initial) | 10. IS PATIENT'S CONDITION RELATED TO: | 11. INSURED'S POLICY GROUP OR FECA NUMBER |

| a. OTHER INSURED'S POLICY OR GROUP NUMBER | a. EMPLOYMENT? (CURRENT OR PREVIOUS) YES ☐ NO ☐ | a. INSURED'S DATE OF BIRTH MM | DD | YY SEX M ☐ F ☐ |

| b. OTHER INSURED'S DATE OF BIRTH MM | DD | YY SEX M ☐ F ☐ | b. AUTO ACCIDENT? PLACE (State) YES ☐ NO ☐ | b. EMPLOYER'S NAME OR SCHOOL NAME |

| c. EMPLOYER'S NAME OR SCHOOL NAME | c. OTHER ACCIDENT? YES ☐ NO ☐ | c. INSURANCE PLAN NAME OR PROGRAM NAME |

| d. INSURANCE PLAN NAME OR PROGRAM NAME | 10d. RESERVED FOR LOCAL USE | d. IS THERE ANOTHER HEALTH BENEFIT PLAN? YES ☐ NO ☐ If yes, return to and complete item 9 a – d. |

READ BACK OF FORM BEFORE COMPLETING & SIGNING THIS FORM.
12. PATIENT'S OR AUTHORIZED PERSON'S SIGNATURE I authorize the release of any medical or other information necessary to process this claim. I also request payment of government benefits either to myself or to the party who accepts assignment below.

SIGNED _____ DATE _____

13. INSURED'S OR AUTHORIZED PERSON'S SIGNATURE I authorize payment of medical benefits to the undersigned physician or supplier for services described below.

SIGNED _____

PATIENT AND INSURED INFORMATION

| 14. DATE OF CURRENT: ILLNESS (First symptom) OR INJURY (Accident) OR PREGNANCY (LMP) MM | DD | YY | 15. IF PATIENT HAS HAD SAME OR SIMILAR ILLNESS, GIVE FIRST DATE MM | DD | YY | 16. DATES PATIENT UNABLE TO WORK IN CURRENT OCCUPATION MM | DD | YY MM | DD | YY FROM TO |

| 17. NAME OF REFERRING PHYSICIAN OR OTHER SOURCE | 17a. I.D. NUMBER OF REFERRING PHYSICIAN | 18. HOSPITALIZATION DATES RELATED TO CURRENT SERVICES MM | DD | YY MM | DD | YY FROM TO |

| 19. RESERVED FOR LOCAL USE | 20. OUTSIDE LAB? YES ☐ NO ☐ $ CHARGES |

21. DIAGNOSIS OR NATURE OF ILLNESS OR INJURY. (RELATE ITEMS 1, 2, 3, OR 4 TO ITEM 24E BY LINE)

1. _____   3. _____

2. _____   4. _____

22. MEDICAID RESUBMISSION CODE | ORIGINAL REF. NO.

23. PRIOR AUTHORIZATION NUMBER

24. A DATE(S) OF SERVICE						B Place of Service	C Type of Service	D PROCEDURES, SERVICES, OR SUPPLIES (Explain Unusual Circumstances)		E DIAGNOSIS CODE	F $ CHARGES	G DAYS OR UNITS	H EPSDT Family Plan	I EMG	J COB	K RESERVED FOR LOCAL USE
From MM	DD	YY	To MM	DD	YY			CPT/HCPCS	MODIFIER							
1																
2																
3																
4																
5																
6																

| 25. FEDERAL TAX I.D. NUMBER SSN ☐ EIN ☐ | 26. PATIENT'S ACCOUNT NO. | 27. ACCEPT ASSIGNMENT? (For govt. claims, see back) YES ☐ NO ☐ | 28. TOTAL CHARGE $ | 29. AMOUNT PAID $ | 30. BALANCE DUE $ |

| 31. SIGNATURE OF PHYSICIAN OR SUPPLIER INCLUDING DEGREES OR CREDENTIALS (I certify that the statements on the reverse apply to this bill and are made a part thereof.) SIGNED _____ DATE _____ | 32. NAME AND ADDRESS OF FACILITY WHERE SERVICES WERE RENDERED (If other than home or office) | 33. PHYSICIAN'S, SUPPLIER'S BILLING NAME, ADDRESS, ZIP CODE & PHONE # PIN# GRP# |

PHYSICIAN OR SUPPLIER INFORMATION

PLEASE PRINT OR TYPE

SAMPLE FORM 1500
SAMPLE FORM 1500 SAMPLE FORM 1500

PLEASE
DO NOT
STAPLE
IN THIS
AREA

(SAMPLE ONLY - NOT APPROVED FOR USE)

CARRIER

☐☐☐ PICA

HEALTH INSURANCE CLAIM FORM   PICA ☐☐☐

1. MEDICARE MEDICAID CHAMPUS CHAMPVA GROUP HEALTH PLAN FECA BLK LUNG OTHER							1a. INSURED'S I.D. NUMBER (FOR PROGRAM IN ITEM 1)
☐ (Medicare #)	☐ (Medicaid #)	☐ (Sponsor's SSN)	☐ (VA File #)	☐ (SSN or ID)	☐ (SSN)	☐ (ID)	

2. PATIENT'S NAME (Last Name, First Name, Middle Initial)	3. PATIENT'S BIRTH DATE MM DD YY SEX M☐ F☐	4. INSURED'S NAME (Last Name, First Name, Middle Initial)

5. PATIENT'S ADDRESS (No. Street)	6. PATIENT RELATIONSHIP TO INSURED Self☐ Spouse☐ Child☐ Other☐	7. INSURED'S ADDRESS (No. Street)
CITY STATE	8. PATIENT STATUS Single☐ Married☐ Other☐	CITY STATE
ZIP CODE TELEPHONE (Include Area Code) ( )	Employed☐ Full-Time Student☐ Part-Time Student☐	ZIP CODE TELEPHONE (INCLUDE AREA CODE) ( )

9. OTHER INSURED'S NAME (Last Name, First Name, Middle Initial)	10. IS PATIENT'S CONDITION RELATED TO:	11. INSURED'S POLICY GROUP OR FECA NUMBER
a. OTHER INSURED'S POLICY OR GROUP NUMBER	a. EMPLOYMENT? (CURRENT OR PREVIOUS) ☐YES ☐NO	a. INSURED'S DATE OF BIRTH MM DD YY SEX M☐ F☐
b. OTHER INSURED'S DATE OF BIRTH MM DD YY SEX M☐ F☐	b. AUTO ACCIDENT? PLACE (State) ☐YES ☐NO	b. EMPLOYER'S NAME OR SCHOOL NAME
c. EMPLOYER'S NAME OR SCHOOL NAME	c. OTHER ACCIDENT? ☐YES ☐NO	c. INSURANCE PLAN NAME OR PROGRAM NAME
d. INSURANCE PLAN NAME OR PROGRAM NAME	10d. RESERVED FOR LOCAL USE	d. IS THERE ANOTHER HEALTH BENEFIT PLAN? ☐YES ☐NO If yes, return to and complete item 9 a – d.

READ BACK OF FORM BEFORE COMPLETING & SIGNING THIS FORM.
12. PATIENT'S OR AUTHORIZED PERSON'S SIGNATURE I authorize the release of any medical or other information necessary to process this claim. I also request payment of government benefits either to myself or to the party who accepts assignment below.

SIGNED _____   DATE _____

13. INSURED'S OR AUTHORIZED PERSON'S SIGNATURE I authorize payment of medical benefits to the undersigned physician or supplier for services described below.

SIGNED _____

PATIENT AND INSURED INFORMATION

14. DATE OF CURRENT: ILLNESS (First symptom) OR INJURY (Accident) OR PREGNANCY (LMP) MM DD YY	15. IF PATIENT HAS HAD SAME OR SIMILAR ILLNESS, GIVE FIRST DATE MM DD YY	16. DATES PATIENT UNABLE TO WORK IN CURRENT OCCUPATION MM DD YY MM DD YY FROM TO
17. NAME OF REFERRING PHYSICIAN OR OTHER SOURCE	17a. I.D. NUMBER OF REFERRING PHYSICIAN	18. HOSPITALIZATION DATES RELATED TO CURRENT SERVICES MM DD YY MM DD YY FROM TO
19. RESERVED FOR LOCAL USE		20. OUTSIDE LAB? $ CHARGES ☐YES ☐NO

21. DIAGNOSIS OR NATURE OF ILLNESS OR INJURY. (RELATE ITEMS 1, 2, 3, OR 4 TO ITEM 24E BY LINE)	22. MEDICAID RESUBMISSION CODE ORIGINAL REF. NO.
1.⌊___.___ 3.⌊___.___ 2.⌊___.___ 4.⌊___.___	23. PRIOR AUTHORIZATION NUMBER

24. A DATE(S) OF SERVICE From To MM DD YY MM DD YY	B Place of Service	C Type of Service	D PROCEDURES, SERVICES, OR SUPPLIES (Explain Unusual Circumstances) CPT/HCPCS MODIFIER	E DIAGNOSIS CODE	F $ CHARGES	G DAYS OR UNITS	H EPSDT Family Plan	I EMG	J COB	K RESERVED FOR LOCAL USE
1										
2										
3										
4										
5										
6										

25. FEDERAL TAX I.D. NUMBER SSN EIN ☐ ☐	26. PATIENT'S ACCOUNT NO.	27. ACCEPT ASSIGNMENT? (For govt. claims, see back) ☐YES ☐NO	28. TOTAL CHARGE $	29. AMOUNT PAID $	30. BALANCE DUE $
31. SIGNATURE OF PHYSICIAN OR SUPPLIER INCLUDING DEGREES OR CREDENTIALS (I certify that the statements on the reverse apply to this bill and are made a part thereof.) SIGNED DATE	32. NAME AND ADDRESS OF FACILITY WHERE SERVICES WERE RENDERED (If other than home or office)	33. PHYSICIAN'S, SUPPLIER'S BILLING NAME, ADDRESS, ZIP CODE & PHONE # PIN# GRP#			

PHYSICIAN OR SUPPLIER INFORMATION

(SAMPLE ONLY - NOT APPROVED FOR USE)   *PLEASE PRINT OR TYPE*   SAMPLE FORM 1500
SAMPLE FORM 1500 SAMPLE FORM 1500

(SAMPLE ONLY - NOT APPROVED FOR USE)

CARRIER

| | PICA | | **HEALTH INSURANCE CLAIM FORM** | PICA | |

1. MEDICARE ☐ (Medicare #)   MEDICAID ☐ (Medicaid #)   CHAMPUS ☐ (Sponsor's SSN)   CHAMPVA ☐ (VA File #)   GROUP HEALTH PLAN ☐ (SSN or ID)   FECA BLK LUNG ☐ (SSN)   OTHER ☐ (ID)

1a. INSURED'S I.D. NUMBER   (FOR PROGRAM IN ITEM 1)

2. PATIENT'S NAME (Last Name, First Name, Middle Initial)

3. PATIENT'S BIRTH DATE   MM | DD | YY   SEX   M ☐ F ☐

4. INSURED'S NAME (Last Name, First Name, Middle initial)

5. PATIENT'S ADDRESS (No. Street)

6. PATIENT RELATIONSHIP TO INSURED   Self ☐ Spouse ☐ Child ☐ Other ☐

7. INSURED'S ADDRESS (No. Street)

CITY   STATE

8. PATIENT STATUS   Single ☐ Married ☐ Other ☐

CITY   STATE

ZIP CODE   TELEPHONE (Include Area Code) ( )

Employed ☐   Full-Time Student ☐   Part-Time Student ☐

ZIP CODE   TELEPHONE (INCLUDE AREA CODE) ( )

9. OTHER INSURED'S NAME (Last Name, First Name, Middle Initial)

10. IS PATIENT'S CONDITION RELATED TO:

11. INSURED'S POLICY GROUP OR FECA NUMBER

a. OTHER INSURED'S POLICY OR GROUP NUMBER

a. EMPLOYMENT? (CURRENT OR PREVIOUS)   ☐ YES ☐ NO

a. INSURED'S DATE OF BIRTH   MM | DD | YY   SEX   M ☐ F ☐

b. OTHER INSURED'S DATE OF BIRTH   MM | DD | YY   SEX   M ☐ F ☐

b. AUTO ACCIDENT?   PLACE (State)   ☐ YES ☐ NO

b. EMPLOYER'S NAME OR SCHOOL NAME

c. EMPLOYER'S NAME OR SCHOOL NAME

c. OTHER ACCIDENT?   ☐ YES ☐ NO

c. INSURANCE PLAN NAME OR PROGRAM NAME

d. INSURANCE PLAN NAME OR PROGRAM NAME

10d. RESERVED FOR LOCAL USE

d. IS THERE ANOTHER HEALTH BENEFIT PLAN?   ☐ YES ☐ NO   If yes, return to and complete item 9 a – d.

PATIENT AND INSURED INFORMATION

READ BACK OF FORM BEFORE COMPLETING & SIGNING THIS FORM.

12. PATIENT'S OR AUTHORIZED PERSON'S SIGNATURE I authorize the release of any medical or other information necessary to process this claim. I also request payment of government benefits either to myself or to the party who accepts assignment below.

SIGNED _____ DATE _____

13. INSURED'S OR AUTHORIZED PERSON'S SIGNATURE I authorize payment of medical benefits to the undersigned physician or supplier for services described below.

SIGNED _____

14. DATE OF CURRENT: ILLNESS (First symptom) OR INJURY (Accident) OR PREGNANCY (LMP)   MM | DD | YY

15. IF PATIENT HAS HAD SAME OR SIMILAR ILLNESS, GIVE FIRST DATE   MM | DD | YY

16. DATES PATIENT UNABLE TO WORK IN CURRENT OCCUPATION   MM | DD | YY FROM   MM | DD | YY TO

17. NAME OF REFERRING PHYSICIAN OR OTHER SOURCE

17a. I.D. NUMBER OF REFERRING PHYSICIAN

18. HOSPITALIZATION DATES RELATED TO CURRENT SERVICES   MM | DD | YY FROM   MM | DD | YY TO

19. RESERVED FOR LOCAL USE

20. OUTSIDE LAB?   ☐ YES ☐ NO $ CHARGES

21. DIAGNOSIS OR NATURE OF ILLNESS OR INJURY. (RELATE ITEMS 1, 2, 3, OR 4 TO ITEM 24E BY LINE)

1. |___|.|___|
2. |___|.|___|
3. |___|.|___|
4. |___|.|___|

22. MEDICAID RESUBMISSION CODE   ORIGINAL REF. NO.

23. PRIOR AUTHORIZATION NUMBER

24. A				B	C	D		E	F	G	H	I	J	K
DATE(S) OF SERVICE				Place of Service	Type of Service	PROCEDURES, SERVICES, OR SUPPLIES (Explain Unusual Circumstances)		DIAGNOSIS CODE	$ CHARGES	DAYS OR UNITS	EPSDT Family Plan	EMG	COB	RESERVED FOR LOCAL USE
From MM	DD	YY	To MM DD YY			CPT/HCPCS	MODIFIER							
1														
2														
3														
4														
5														
6														

PHYSICIAN OR SUPPLIER INFORMATION

25. FEDERAL TAX I.D. NUMBER   SSN ☐ EIN ☐

26. PATIENT'S ACCOUNT NO.

27. ACCEPT ASSIGNMENT? (For govt. claims, see back)   YES ☐ NO ☐

28. TOTAL CHARGE $

29. AMOUNT PAID $

30. BALANCE DUE $

31. SIGNATURE OF PHYSICIAN OR SUPPLIER INCLUDING DEGREES OR CREDENTIALS (I certify that the statements on the reverse apply to this bill and are made a part thereof.)

SIGNED _____ DATE _____

32. NAME AND ADDRESS OF FACILITY WHERE SERVICES WERE RENDERED (If other than home or office)

33. PHYSICIAN'S, SUPPLIER'S BILLING NAME, ADDRESS, ZIP CODE & PHONE #

PIN#   GRP#

(SAMPLE ONLY - NOT APPROVED FOR USE)

PLEASE PRINT OR TYPE

SAMPLE FORM 1500
SAMPLE FORM 1500   SAMPLE FORM 1500

227

PLEASE
DO NOT
STAPLE
IN THIS
AREA

CARRIER

☐☐ PICA

HEALTH INSURANCE CLAIM FORM

PICA ☐☐☐

| 1. MEDICARE ☐ (Medicare #) MEDICAID ☐ (Medicaid #) CHAMPUS ☐ (Sponsor's SSN) CHAMPVA ☐ (VA File #) GROUP HEALTH PLAN ☐ (SSN or ID) FECA BLK LUNG ☐ (SSN) OTHER ☐ (ID) | 1a. INSURED'S I.D. NUMBER (FOR PROGRAM IN ITEM 1) |

| 2. PATIENT'S NAME (Last Name, First Name, Middle Initial) | 3. PATIENT'S BIRTH DATE MM ┆ DD ┆ YY SEX M ☐ F ☐ | 4. INSURED'S NAME (Last Name, First Name, Middle Initial) |

| 5. PATIENT'S ADDRESS (No. Street) | 6. PATIENT RELATIONSHIP TO INSURED Self ☐ Spouse ☐ Child ☐ Other ☐ | 7. INSURED'S ADDRESS (No. Street) |

| CITY | STATE | 8. PATIENT STATUS Single ☐ Married ☐ Other ☐ | CITY | STATE |

| ZIP CODE | TELEPHONE (Include Area Code) ( ) | Employed ☐ Full-Time Student ☐ Part-Time Student ☐ | ZIP CODE | TELEPHONE (INCLUDE AREA CODE) ( ) |

| 9. OTHER INSURED'S NAME (Last Name, First Name, Middle Initial) | 10. IS PATIENT'S CONDITION RELATED TO: | 11. INSURED'S POLICY GROUP OR FECA NUMBER |

| a. OTHER INSURED'S POLICY OR GROUP NUMBER | a. EMPLOYMENT? (CURRENT OR PREVIOUS) ☐ YES ☐ NO | a. INSURED'S DATE OF BIRTH MM ┆ DD ┆ YY SEX M ☐ F ☐ |

| b. OTHER INSURED'S DATE OF BIRTH MM ┆ DD ┆ YY SEX M ☐ F ☐ | b. AUTO ACCIDENT? PLACE (State) ☐ YES ☐ NO | b. EMPLOYER'S NAME OR SCHOOL NAME |

| c. EMPLOYER'S NAME OR SCHOOL NAME | c. OTHER ACCIDENT? ☐ YES ☐ NO | c. INSURANCE PLAN NAME OR PROGRAM NAME |

| d. INSURANCE PLAN NAME OR PROGRAM NAME | 10d. RESERVED FOR LOCAL USE | d. IS THERE ANOTHER HEALTH BENEFIT PLAN? ☐ YES ☐ NO If yes, return to and complete item 9 a – d. |

READ BACK OF FORM BEFORE COMPLETING & SIGNING THIS FORM.
12. PATIENT'S OR AUTHORIZED PERSON'S SIGNATURE I authorize the release of any medical or other information necessary to process this claim. I also request payment of government benefits either to myself or to the party who accepts assignment below.

SIGNED _____ DATE _____

13. INSURED'S OR AUTHORIZED PERSON'S SIGNATURE I authorize payment of medical benefits to the undersigned physician or supplier for services described below.

SIGNED _____

PATIENT AND INSURED INFORMATION

| 14. DATE OF CURRENT: ◀ ILLNESS (First symptom) OR INJURY (Accident) OR PREGNANCY (LMP) MM ┆ DD ┆ YY | 15. IF PATIENT HAS HAD SAME OR SIMILAR ILLNESS, GIVE FIRST DATE MM ┆ DD ┆ YY | 16. DATES PATIENT UNABLE TO WORK IN CURRENT OCCUPATION MM ┆ DD ┆ YY MM ┆ DD ┆ YY FROM TO |

| 17. NAME OF REFERRING PHYSICIAN OR OTHER SOURCE | 17a. I.D. NUMBER OF REFERRING PHYSICIAN | 18. HOSPITALIZATION DATES RELATED TO CURRENT SERVICES MM ┆ DD ┆ YY MM ┆ DD ┆ YY FROM TO |

| 19. RESERVED FOR LOCAL USE | 20. OUTSIDE LAB? ☐ YES ☐ NO $ CHARGES |

| 21. DIAGNOSIS OR NATURE OF ILLNESS OR INJURY. (RELATE ITEMS 1, 2, 3, OR 4 TO ITEM 24E BY LINE) 1. └─┆─┘ 3. └─┆─┘ 2. └─┆─┘ 4. └─┆─┘ | 22. MEDICAID RESUBMISSION CODE ORIGINAL REF. NO. 23. PRIOR AUTHORIZATION NUMBER |

24. A. DATE(S) OF SERVICE From To MM DD YY MM DD YY	B. Place of Service	C. Type of Service	D. PROCEDURES, SERVICES, OR SUPPLIES (Explain Unusual Circumstances) CPT/HCPCS MODIFIER	E. DIAGNOSIS CODE	F. $ CHARGES	G. DAYS OR UNITS	H. EPSDT Family Plan	I. EMG	J. COB	K. RESERVED FOR LOCAL USE
1										
2										
3										
4										
5										
6										

| 25. FEDERAL TAX I.D. NUMBER SSN ☐ EIN ☐ | 26. PATIENT'S ACCOUNT NO. | 27. ACCEPT ASSIGNMENT? (For govt. claims, see back) YES ☐ NO ☐ | 28. TOTAL CHARGE $ | 29. AMOUNT PAID $ | 30. BALANCE DUE $ |

| 31. SIGNATURE OF PHYSICIAN OR SUPPLIER INCLUDING DEGREES OR CREDENTIALS (I certify that the statements on the reverse apply to this bill and are made a part thereof.) SIGNED _____ DATE _____ | 32. NAME AND ADDRESS OF FACILITY WHERE SERVICES WERE RENDERED (If other than home or office) | 33. PHYSICIAN'S, SUPPLIER'S BILLING NAME, ADDRESS, ZIP CODE & PHONE # PIN# GRP# |

PHYSICIAN OR SUPPLIER INFORMATION

PLEASE PRINT OR TYPE

SAMPLE FORM 1500
SAMPLE FORM 1500 SAMPLE FORM 1500

PLEASE
DO NOT
STAPLE
IN THIS
AREA

CARRIER

| | PICA

HEALTH INSURANCE CLAIM FORM

PICA | |

1. MEDICARE MEDICAID CHAMPUS CHAMPVA GROUP HEALTH PLAN FECA BLK LUNG OTHER	1a. INSURED'S I.D. NUMBER (FOR PROGRAM IN ITEM 1)
☐ (Medicare #) ☐ (Medicaid #) ☐ (Sponsor's SSN) ☐ (VA File #) ☐ (SSN or ID) ☐ (SSN) ☐ (ID)	

2. PATIENT'S NAME (Last Name, First Name, Middle Initial)	3. PATIENT'S BIRTH DATE MM DD YY SEX M ☐ F ☐	4. INSURED'S NAME (Last Name, First Name, Middle Initial)

5. PATIENT'S ADDRESS (No. Street)	6. PATIENT RELATIONSHIP TO INSURED Self ☐ Spouse ☐ Child ☐ Other ☐	7. INSURED'S ADDRESS (No. Street)

CITY	STATE	8. PATIENT STATUS Single ☐ Married ☐ Other ☐	CITY	STATE

ZIP CODE	TELEPHONE (Include Area Code) ( )	Employed ☐ Full-Time Student ☐ Part-Time Student ☐	ZIP CODE	TELEPHONE (INCLUDE AREA CODE) ( )

9. OTHER INSURED'S NAME (Last Name, First Name, Middle Initial)	10. IS PATIENT'S CONDITION RELATED TO:	11. INSURED'S POLICY GROUP OR FECA NUMBER

a. OTHER INSURED'S POLICY OR GROUP NUMBER	a. EMPLOYMENT? (CURRENT OR PREVIOUS) ☐ YES ☐ NO	a. INSURED'S DATE OF BIRTH MM DD YY SEX M ☐ F ☐

b. OTHER INSURED'S DATE OF BIRTH MM DD YY SEX M ☐ F ☐	b. AUTO ACCIDENT? PLACE (State) ☐ YES ☐ NO	b. EMPLOYER'S NAME OR SCHOOL NAME

c. EMPLOYER'S NAME OR SCHOOL NAME	c. OTHER ACCIDENT? ☐ YES ☐ NO	c. INSURANCE PLAN NAME OR PROGRAM NAME

d. INSURANCE PLAN NAME OR PROGRAM NAME	10d. RESERVED FOR LOCAL USE	d. IS THERE ANOTHER HEALTH BENEFIT PLAN? ☐ YES ☐ NO If yes, return to and complete item 9 a – d.

READ BACK OF FORM BEFORE COMPLETING & SIGNING THIS FORM.
12. PATIENT'S OR AUTHORIZED PERSON'S SIGNATURE I authorize the release of any medical or other information necessary to process this claim. I also request payment of government benefits either to myself or to the party who accepts assignment below.

SIGNED _____   DATE _____

13. INSURED'S OR AUTHORIZED PERSON'S SIGNATURE I authorize payment of medical benefits to the undersigned physician or supplier for services described below.

SIGNED _____

PATIENT AND INSURED INFORMATION

14. DATE OF CURRENT: MM DD YY ◄ ILLNESS (First symptom) OR INJURY (Accident) OR PREGNANCY (LMP)	15. IF PATIENT HAS HAD SAME OR SIMILAR ILLNESS, GIVE FIRST DATE MM DD YY	16. DATES PATIENT UNABLE TO WORK IN CURRENT OCCUPATION MM DD YY MM DD YY FROM TO

17. NAME OF REFERRING PHYSICIAN OR OTHER SOURCE	17a. I.D. NUMBER OF REFERRING PHYSICIAN	18. HOSPITALIZATION DATES RELATED TO CURRENT SERVICES MM DD YY MM DD YY FROM TO

19. RESERVED FOR LOCAL USE		20. OUTSIDE LAB? ☐ YES ☐ NO $ CHARGES

21. DIAGNOSIS OR NATURE OF ILLNESS OR INJURY. (RELATE ITEMS 1, 2, 3, OR 4 TO ITEM 24E BY LINE) 1. ____ . ____ 3. ____ . ____ 2. ____ . ____ 4. ____ . ____	22. MEDICAID RESUBMISSION CODE ORIGINAL REF. NO. 23. PRIOR AUTHORIZATION NUMBER

24. A DATE(S) OF SERVICE From To MM DD YY MM DD YY	B Place of Service	C Type of Service	D PROCEDURES, SERVICES, OR SUPPLIES (Explain Unusual Circumstances) CPT/HCPCS	MODIFIER	E DIAGNOSIS CODE	F $ CHARGES	G DAYS OR UNITS	H EPSDT Family Plan	I EMG	J COB	K RESERVED FOR LOCAL USE
1											
2											
3											
4											
5											
6											

25. FEDERAL TAX I.D. NUMBER SSN ☐ EIN ☐	26. PATIENT'S ACCOUNT NO.	27. ACCEPT ASSIGNMENT? (For govt. claims, see back) ☐ YES ☐ NO	28. TOTAL CHARGE $	29. AMOUNT PAID $	30. BALANCE DUE $

31. SIGNATURE OF PHYSICIAN OR SUPPLIER INCLUDING DEGREES OR CREDENTIALS (I certify that the statements on the reverse apply to this bill and are made a part thereof.) SIGNED DATE	32. NAME AND ADDRESS OF FACILITY WHERE SERVICES WERE RENDERED (If other than home or office)	33. PHYSICIAN'S, SUPPLIER'S BILLING NAME, ADDRESS, ZIP CODE & PHONE # PIN# GRP#

PHYSICIAN OR SUPPLIER INFORMATION

PLEASE PRINT OR TYPE

SAMPLE FORM 1500
SAMPLE FORM 1500 SAMPLE FORM 1500

229

(SAMPLE ONLY - NOT APPROVED FOR USE)

CARRIER

☐ ☐ PICA

HEALTH INSURANCE CLAIM FORM

PICA ☐ ☐

1. MEDICARE MEDICAID CHAMPUS CHAMPVA GROUP HEALTH PLAN FECA BLK LUNG OTHER	1a. INSURED'S I.D. NUMBER (FOR PROGRAM IN ITEM 1)
☐ (Medicare #) ☐ (Medicaid #) ☐ (Sponsor's SSN) ☐ (VA File #) ☐ (SSN or ID) ☐ (SSN) ☐ (ID)	

2. PATIENT'S NAME (Last Name, First Name, Middle Initial)	3. PATIENT'S BIRTH DATE MM DD YY SEX M ☐ F ☐	4. INSURED'S NAME (Last Name, First Name, Middle Initial)

5. PATIENT'S ADDRESS (No. Street)	6. PATIENT RELATIONSHIP TO INSURED Self ☐ Spouse ☐ Child ☐ Other ☐	7. INSURED'S ADDRESS (No. Street)

CITY	STATE	8. PATIENT STATUS Single ☐ Married ☐ Other ☐	CITY	STATE

ZIP CODE	TELEPHONE (Include Area Code) ( )	Employed ☐ Full-Time Student ☐ Part-Time Student ☐	ZIP CODE	TELEPHONE (INCLUDE AREA CODE) ( )

9. OTHER INSURED'S NAME (Last Name, First Name, Middle Initial)	10. IS PATIENT'S CONDITION RELATED TO:	11. INSURED'S POLICY GROUP OR FECA NUMBER
a. OTHER INSURED'S POLICY OR GROUP NUMBER	a. EMPLOYMENT? (CURRENT OR PREVIOUS) ☐ YES ☐ NO	a. INSURED'S DATE OF BIRTH MM DD YY SEX M ☐ F ☐
b. OTHER INSURED'S DATE OF BIRTH MM DD YY SEX M ☐ F ☐	b. AUTO ACCIDENT? PLACE (State) ☐ YES ☐ NO	b. EMPLOYER'S NAME OR SCHOOL NAME
c. EMPLOYER'S NAME OR SCHOOL NAME	c. OTHER ACCIDENT? ☐ YES ☐ NO	c. INSURANCE PLAN NAME OR PROGRAM NAME
d. INSURANCE PLAN NAME OR PROGRAM NAME	10d. RESERVED FOR LOCAL USE	d. IS THERE ANOTHER HEALTH BENEFIT PLAN? ☐ YES ☐ NO If yes, return to and complete item 9 a – d.

READ BACK OF FORM BEFORE COMPLETING & SIGNING THIS FORM.
12. PATIENT'S OR AUTHORIZED PERSON'S SIGNATURE I authorize the release of any medical or other information necessary to process this claim. I also request payment of government benefits either to myself or to the party who accepts assignment below.

SIGNED _____ DATE _____

13. INSURED'S OR AUTHORIZED PERSON'S SIGNATURE I authorize payment of medical benefits to the undersigned physician or supplier for services described below.

SIGNED _____

PATIENT AND INSURED INFORMATION

14. DATE OF CURRENT: MM DD YY ◄ ILLNESS (First symptom) OR INJURY (Accident) OR PREGNANCY (LMP)	15. IF PATIENT HAS HAD SAME OR SIMILAR ILLNESS, GIVE FIRST DATE MM DD YY	16. DATES PATIENT UNABLE TO WORK IN CURRENT OCCUPATION MM DD YY MM DD YY FROM TO
17. NAME OF REFERRING PHYSICIAN OR OTHER SOURCE	17a. I.D. NUMBER OF REFERRING PHYSICIAN	18. HOSPITALIZATION DATES RELATED TO CURRENT SERVICES MM DD YY MM DD YY FROM TO
19. RESERVED FOR LOCAL USE		20. OUTSIDE LAB? ☐ YES ☐ NO $ CHARGES
21. DIAGNOSIS OR NATURE OF ILLNESS OR INJURY. (RELATE ITEMS 1, 2, 3, OR 4 TO ITEM 24E BY LINE) 1. ____ 3. ____ 2. ____ 4. ____		22. MEDICAID RESUBMISSION CODE ORIGINAL REF. NO. 23. PRIOR AUTHORIZATION NUMBER

24. A DATE(S) OF SERVICE		B Place of Service	C Type of Service	D PROCEDURES, SERVICES, OR SUPPLIES (Explain Unusual Circumstances)		E DIAGNOSIS CODE	F $ CHARGES	G DAYS OR UNITS	H EPSDT Family Plan	I EMG	J COB	K RESERVED FOR LOCAL USE
From MM DD YY	To MM DD YY			CPT/HCPCS	MODIFIER							
1												
2												
3												
4												
5												
6												

25. FEDERAL TAX I.D. NUMBER SSN ☐ EIN ☐	26. PATIENT'S ACCOUNT NO.	27. ACCEPT ASSIGNMENT? (For govt. claims, see back) ☐ YES ☐ NO	28. TOTAL CHARGE $	29. AMOUNT PAID $	30. BALANCE DUE $

31. SIGNATURE OF PHYSICIAN OR SUPPLIER INCLUDING DEGREES OR CREDENTIALS (I certify that the statements on the reverse apply to this bill and are made a part thereof.) SIGNED _____ DATE _____	32. NAME AND ADDRESS OF FACILITY WHERE SERVICES WERE RENDERED (if other than home or office)	33. PHYSICIAN'S, SUPPLIER'S BILLING NAME, ADDRESS, ZIP CODE & PHONE # PIN# GRP#

PHYSICIAN OR SUPPLIER INFORMATION

(SAMPLE ONLY - NOT APPROVED FOR USE)

PLEASE PRINT OR TYPE

SAMPLE FORM 1500
SAMPLE FORM 1500 SAMPLE FORM 1500

230

(SAMPLE ONLY - NOT APPROVED FOR USE)

CARRIER

☐☐ PICA

HEALTH INSURANCE CLAIM FORM

PICA ☐☐

1.	MEDICARE	MEDICAID	CHAMPUS	CHAMPVA	GROUP HEALTH PLAN	FECA BLK LUNG	OTHER	1a. INSURED'S I.D. NUMBER	(FOR PROGRAM IN ITEM 1)
	☐ (Medicare #)	☐ (Medicaid #)	☐ (Sponsor's SSN)	☐ (VA File #)	☐ (SSN or ID)	☐ (SSN)	☐ (ID)		

2. PATIENT'S NAME (Last Name, First Name, Middle Initial)

3. PATIENT'S BIRTH DATE
MM | DD | YY   SEX   M ☐   F ☐

4. INSURED'S NAME (Last Name, First Name, Middle Initial)

5. PATIENT'S ADDRESS (No. Street)

6. PATIENT RELATIONSHIP TO INSURED
Self ☐   Spouse ☐   Child ☐   Other ☐

7. INSURED'S ADDRESS (No. Street)

CITY   STATE

8. PATIENT STATUS
Single ☐   Married ☐   Other ☐
Employed ☐   Full-Time Student ☐   Part-Time Student ☐

CITY   STATE

ZIP CODE   TELEPHONE (Include Area Code)
(   )

ZIP CODE   TELEPHONE (INCLUDE AREA CODE)
(   )

9. OTHER INSURED'S NAME (Last Name, First Name, Middle Initial)

10. IS PATIENT'S CONDITION RELATED TO:

11. INSURED'S POLICY GROUP OR FECA NUMBER

a. OTHER INSURED'S POLICY OR GROUP NUMBER

a. EMPLOYMENT? (CURRENT OR PREVIOUS)
☐ YES   ☐ NO

a. INSURED'S DATE OF BIRTH
MM | DD | YY   SEX   M ☐   F ☐

b. OTHER INSURED'S DATE OF BIRTH
MM | DD | YY   SEX   M ☐   F ☐

b. AUTO ACCIDENT?   PLACE (State)
☐ YES   ☐ NO

b. EMPLOYER'S NAME OR SCHOOL NAME

c. EMPLOYER'S NAME OR SCHOOL NAME

c. OTHER ACCIDENT?
☐ YES   ☐ NO

c. INSURANCE PLAN NAME OR PROGRAM NAME

d. INSURANCE PLAN NAME OR PROGRAM NAME

10d. RESERVED FOR LOCAL USE

d. IS THERE ANOTHER HEALTH BENEFIT PLAN?
☐ YES   ☐ NO   If yes, return to and complete item 9 a – d.

READ BACK OF FORM BEFORE COMPLETING & SIGNING THIS FORM.
12. PATIENT'S OR AUTHORIZED PERSON'S SIGNATURE I authorize the release of any medical or other information necessary to process this claim. I also request payment of government benefits either to myself or to the party who accepts assignment below.

SIGNED _____   DATE _____

13. INSURED'S OR AUTHORIZED PERSON'S SIGNATURE I authorize payment of medical benefits to the undersigned physician or supplier for services described below.

SIGNED _____

PATIENT AND INSURED INFORMATION

14. DATE OF CURRENT: ▶ ILLNESS (First symptom) OR
MM | DD | YY   INJURY (Accident) OR
PREGNANCY (LMP)

15. IF PATIENT HAS HAD SAME OR SIMILAR ILLNESS,
GIVE FIRST DATE   MM | DD | YY

16. DATES PATIENT UNABLE TO WORK IN CURRENT OCCUPATION
MM | DD | YY   MM | DD | YY
FROM   TO

17. NAME OF REFERRING PHYSICIAN OR OTHER SOURCE

17a. I.D. NUMBER OF REFERRING PHYSICIAN

18. HOSPITALIZATION DATES RELATED TO CURRENT SERVICES
MM | DD | YY   MM | DD | YY
FROM   TO

19. RESERVED FOR LOCAL USE

20. OUTSIDE LAB? $ CHARGES
☐ YES   ☐ NO

21. DIAGNOSIS OR NATURE OF ILLNESS OR INJURY. (RELATE ITEMS 1, 2, 3, OR 4 TO ITEM 24E BY LINE)

1. ____.____
2. ____.____
3. ____.____
4. ____.____

22. MEDICAID RESUBMISSION
CODE   ORIGINAL REF. NO.

23. PRIOR AUTHORIZATION NUMBER

24. A DATE(S) OF SERVICE						B Place of Service	C Type of Service	D PROCEDURES, SERVICES, OR SUPPLIES (Explain Unusual Circumstances)		E DIAGNOSIS CODE	F $ CHARGES	G DAYS OR UNITS	H EPSDT Family Plan	I EMG	J COB	K RESERVED FOR LOCAL USE
From MM	DD	YY	To MM	DD	YY			CPT/HCPCS	MODIFIER							
1																
2																
3																
4																
5																
6																

25. FEDERAL TAX I.D. NUMBER   SSN ☐ EIN ☐

26. PATIENT'S ACCOUNT NO.

27. ACCEPT ASSIGNMENT? (For govt. claims, see back)
☐ YES   ☐ NO

28. TOTAL CHARGE $

29. AMOUNT PAID $

30. BALANCE DUE $

31. SIGNATURE OF PHYSICIAN OR SUPPLIER INCLUDING DEGREES OR CREDENTIALS
(I certify that the statements on the reverse apply to this bill and are made a part thereof.)

SIGNED _____   DATE _____

32. NAME AND ADDRESS OF FACILITY WHERE SERVICES WERE RENDERED (If other than home or office)

33. PHYSICIAN'S, SUPPLIER'S BILLING NAME, ADDRESS, ZIP CODE & PHONE #

PIN#   GRP#

PHYSICIAN OR SUPPLIER INFORMATION

(SAMPLE ONLY - NOT APPROVED FOR USE)

PLEASE PRINT OR TYPE

SAMPLE FORM 1500
SAMPLE FORM 1500 SAMPLE FORM 1500

231

PLEASE
DO NOT
STAPLE
IN THIS
AREA

[ ][ ] PICA

HEALTH INSURANCE CLAIM FORM

PICA [ ][ ]

1. MEDICARE MEDICAID CHAMPUS CHAMPVA GROUP HEALTH PLAN FECA BLK LUNG OTHER
[ ] (Medicare #) [ ] (Medicaid #) [ ] (Sponsor's SSN) [ ] (VA File #) [ ] (SSN or ID) [ ] (SSN) [ ] (ID)

1a. INSURED'S I.D. NUMBER   (FOR PROGRAM IN ITEM 1)

2. PATIENT'S NAME (Last Name, First Name, Middle Initial)

3. PATIENT'S BIRTH DATE MM | DD | YY   SEX M [ ] F [ ]

4. INSURED'S NAME (Last Name, First Name, Middle Initial)

5. PATIENT'S ADDRESS (No. Street)

6. PATIENT RELATIONSHIP TO INSURED
Self [ ] Spouse [ ] Child [ ] Other [ ]

7. INSURED'S ADDRESS (No. Street)

CITY   STATE

8. PATIENT STATUS
Single [ ] Married [ ] Other [ ]

Employed [ ] Full-Time Student [ ] Part-Time Student [ ]

CITY   STATE

ZIP CODE   TELEPHONE (Include Area Code)
(   )

ZIP CODE   TELEPHONE (INCLUDE AREA CODE)
(   )

9. OTHER INSURED'S NAME (Last Name, First Name, Middle Initial)

10. IS PATIENT'S CONDITION RELATED TO:

11. INSURED'S POLICY GROUP OR FECA NUMBER

a. OTHER INSURED'S POLICY OR GROUP NUMBER

a. EMPLOYMENT? (CURRENT OR PREVIOUS)
[ ] YES [ ] NO

a. INSURED'S DATE OF BIRTH MM | DD | YY   SEX M [ ] F [ ]

b. OTHER INSURED'S DATE OF BIRTH MM | DD | YY   SEX M [ ] F [ ]

b. AUTO ACCIDENT?   PLACE (State)
[ ] YES [ ] NO

b. EMPLOYER'S NAME OR SCHOOL NAME

c. EMPLOYER'S NAME OR SCHOOL NAME

c. OTHER ACCIDENT?
[ ] YES [ ] NO

c. INSURANCE PLAN NAME OR PROGRAM NAME

d. INSURANCE PLAN NAME OR PROGRAM NAME

10d. RESERVED FOR LOCAL USE

d. IS THERE ANOTHER HEALTH BENEFIT PLAN?
[ ] YES [ ] NO If yes, return to and complete item 9 a – d.

READ BACK OF FORM BEFORE COMPLETING & SIGNING THIS FORM.
12. PATIENT'S OR AUTHORIZED PERSON'S SIGNATURE I authorize the release of any medical or other information necessary to process this claim. I also request payment of government benefits either to myself or to the party who accepts assignment below.

SIGNED _____ DATE _____

13. INSURED'S OR AUTHORIZED PERSON'S SIGNATURE I authorize payment of medical benefits to the undersigned physician or supplier for services described below.

SIGNED _____

14. DATE OF CURRENT: ILLNESS (First symptom) OR MM | DD | YY INJURY (Accident) OR PREGNANCY (LMP)

15. IF PATIENT HAS HAD SAME OR SIMILAR ILLNESS, GIVE FIRST DATE MM | DD | YY

16. DATES PATIENT UNABLE TO WORK IN CURRENT OCCUPATION MM | DD | YY FROM   TO MM | DD | YY

17. NAME OF REFERRING PHYSICIAN OR OTHER SOURCE

17a. I.D. NUMBER OF REFERRING PHYSICIAN

18. HOSPITALIZATION DATES RELATED TO CURRENT SERVICES MM | DD | YY FROM   TO MM | DD | YY

19. RESERVED FOR LOCAL USE

20. OUTSIDE LAB? $ CHARGES
[ ] YES [ ] NO

21. DIAGNOSIS OR NATURE OF ILLNESS OR INJURY. (RELATE ITEMS 1, 2, 3, OR 4 TO ITEM 24E BY LINE)
1. |___.___
2. |___.___
3. |___.___
4. |___.___

22. MEDICAID RESUBMISSION CODE   ORIGINAL REF. NO.

23. PRIOR AUTHORIZATION NUMBER

24. A. DATE(S) OF SERVICE						B. Place of Service	C. Type of Service	D. PROCEDURES, SERVICES, OR SUPPLIES (Explain Unusual Circumstances)		E. DIAGNOSIS CODE	F. $ CHARGES	G. DAYS OR UNITS	H. EPSDT Family Plan	I. EMG	J. COB	K. RESERVED FOR LOCAL USE
From MM	DD	YY	To MM	DD	YY			CPT/HCPCS	MODIFIER							
1																
2																
3																
4																
5																
6																

25. FEDERAL TAX I.D. NUMBER SSN [ ] EIN [ ]

26. PATIENT'S ACCOUNT NO.

27. ACCEPT ASSIGNMENT? (For govt. claims, see back) YES [ ] NO [ ]

28. TOTAL CHARGE $

29. AMOUNT PAID $

30. BALANCE DUE $

31. SIGNATURE OF PHYSICIAN OR SUPPLIER INCLUDING DEGREES OR CREDENTIALS (I certify that the statements on the reverse apply to this bill and are made a part thereof.)

SIGNED _____ DATE _____

32. NAME AND ADDRESS OF FACILITY WHERE SERVICES WERE RENDERED (If other than home or office)

33. PHYSICIAN'S, SUPPLIER'S BILLING NAME, ADDRESS, ZIP CODE & PHONE #

PIN# _____   GRP# _____

PLEASE PRINT OR TYPE

SAMPLE FORM 1500
SAMPLE FORM 1500 SAMPLE FORM 1500

PLEASE
DO NOT
STAPLE
IN THIS
AREA

CARRIER

	PICA					

HEALTH INSURANCE CLAIM FORM

PICA | | |

1. MEDICARE	MEDICAID	CHAMPUS	CHAMPVA	GROUP HEALTH PLAN	FECA BLK LUNG	OTHER	1a. INSURED'S I.D. NUMBER	(FOR PROGRAM IN ITEM 1)
☐ (Medicare #)	☐ (Medicaid #)	☐ (Sponsor's SSN)	☐ (VA File #)	☐ (SSN or ID)	☐ (SSN)	☐ (ID)		

2. PATIENT'S NAME (Last Name, First Name, Middle Initial)

3. PATIENT'S BIRTH DATE MM   DD   YY   SEX   M ☐   F ☐

4. INSURED'S NAME (Last Name, First Name, Middle Initial)

5. PATIENT'S ADDRESS (No. Street)

6. PATIENT RELATIONSHIP TO INSURED   Self ☐   Spouse ☐   Child ☐   Other ☐

7. INSURED'S ADDRESS (No. Street)

CITY   STATE

8. PATIENT STATUS   Single ☐   Married ☐   Other ☐

CITY   STATE

ZIP CODE   TELEPHONE (Include Area Code) (   )

Employed ☐   Full-Time Student ☐   Part-Time Student ☐

ZIP CODE   TELEPHONE (INCLUDE AREA CODE) (   )

9. OTHER INSURED'S NAME (Last Name, First Name, Middle Initial)

10. IS PATIENT'S CONDITION RELATED TO:

11. INSURED'S POLICY GROUP OR FECA NUMBER

a. OTHER INSURED'S POLICY OR GROUP NUMBER

a. EMPLOYMENT? (CURRENT OR PREVIOUS)   ☐ YES   ☐ NO

a. INSURED'S DATE OF BIRTH   MM   DD   YY   SEX   M ☐   F ☐

b. OTHER INSURED'S DATE OF BIRTH   MM   DD   YY   SEX   M ☐   F ☐

b. AUTO ACCIDENT?   ☐ YES   ☐ NO   PLACE (State)

b. EMPLOYER'S NAME OR SCHOOL NAME

c. EMPLOYER'S NAME OR SCHOOL NAME

c. OTHER ACCIDENT?   ☐ YES   ☐ NO

c. INSURANCE PLAN NAME OR PROGRAM NAME

d. INSURANCE PLAN NAME OR PROGRAM NAME

10d. RESERVED FOR LOCAL USE

d. IS THERE ANOTHER HEALTH BENEFIT PLAN?   ☐ YES   ☐ NO   If yes, return to and complete item 9 a – d.

READ BACK OF FORM BEFORE COMPLETING & SIGNING THIS FORM.
12. PATIENT'S OR AUTHORIZED PERSON'S SIGNATURE I authorize the release of any medical or other information necessary to process this claim. I also request payment of government benefits either to myself or to the party who accepts assignment below.

SIGNED _____ DATE _____

13. INSURED'S OR AUTHORIZED PERSON'S SIGNATURE I authorize payment of medical benefits to the undersigned physician or supplier for services described below.

SIGNED _____

PATIENT AND INSURED INFORMATION

14. DATE OF CURRENT: MM   DD   YY   ILLNESS (First symptom) OR INJURY (Accident) OR PREGNANCY (LMP)

15. IF PATIENT HAS HAD SAME OR SIMILAR ILLNESS, GIVE FIRST DATE   MM   DD   YY

16. DATES PATIENT UNABLE TO WORK IN CURRENT OCCUPATION   MM   DD   YY   FROM   TO   MM   DD   YY

17. NAME OF REFERRING PHYSICIAN OR OTHER SOURCE

17a. I.D. NUMBER OF REFERRING PHYSICIAN

18. HOSPITALIZATION DATES RELATED TO CURRENT SERVICES   MM   DD   YY   FROM   TO   MM   DD   YY

19. RESERVED FOR LOCAL USE

20. OUTSIDE LAB?   ☐ YES   ☐ NO $ CHARGES

21. DIAGNOSIS OR NATURE OF ILLNESS OR INJURY. (RELATE ITEMS 1, 2, 3, OR 4 TO ITEM 24E BY LINE)

1. |___.___| 3. |___.___|

2. |___.___| 4. |___.___|

22. MEDICAID RESUBMISSION CODE   ORIGINAL REF. NO.

23. PRIOR AUTHORIZATION NUMBER

24. A DATE(S) OF SERVICE						B Place of Service	C Type of Service	D PROCEDURES, SERVICES, OR SUPPLIES (Explain Unusual Circumstances) CPT/HCPCS | MODIFIER	E DIAGNOSIS CODE	F $ CHARGES	G DAYS OR UNITS	H EPSDT Family Plan	I EMG	J COB	K RESERVED FOR LOCAL USE
From MM	DD	YY	To MM	DD	YY										
1															
2															
3															
4															
5															
6															

25. FEDERAL TAX I.D. NUMBER   SSN ☐   EIN ☐

26. PATIENT'S ACCOUNT NO.

27. ACCEPT ASSIGNMENT? (For govt. claims, see back)   ☐ YES   ☐ NO

28. TOTAL CHARGE $

29. AMOUNT PAID $

30. BALANCE DUE $

31. SIGNATURE OF PHYSICIAN OR SUPPLIER INCLUDING DEGREES OR CREDENTIALS (I certify that the statements on the reverse apply to this bill and are made a part thereof.)

SIGNED _____ DATE _____

32. NAME AND ADDRESS OF FACILITY WHERE SERVICES WERE RENDERED (If other than home or office)

33. PHYSICIAN'S, SUPPLIER'S BILLING NAME, ADDRESS, ZIP CODE & PHONE #

PIN#   GRP#

PHYSICIAN OR SUPPLIER INFORMATION

PLEASE PRINT OR TYPE

SAMPLE FORM 1500
SAMPLE FORM 1500 SAMPLE FORM 1500

(SAMPLE ONLY - NOT APPROVED FOR USE)

CARRIER

| | PICA |

HEALTH INSURANCE CLAIM FORM

PICA | | |

1. MEDICARE ☐ (Medicare #)   MEDICAID ☐ (Medicaid #)   CHAMPUS ☐ (Sponsor's SSN)   CHAMPVA ☐ (VA File #)   GROUP HEALTH PLAN ☐ (SSN or ID)   FECA BLK LUNG ☐ (SSN)   OTHER ☐ (ID)

1a. INSURED'S I.D. NUMBER   (FOR PROGRAM IN ITEM 1)

2. PATIENT'S NAME (Last Name, First Name, Middle Initial)

3. PATIENT'S BIRTH DATE   MM ☐ DD ☐ YY   SEX   M ☐   F ☐

4. INSURED'S NAME (Last Name, First Name, Middle Initial)

5. PATIENT'S ADDRESS (No. Street)

6. PATIENT RELATIONSHIP TO INSURED   Self ☐   Spouse ☐   Child ☐   Other ☐

7. INSURED'S ADDRESS (No. Street)

CITY   STATE

8. PATIENT STATUS   Single ☐   Married ☐   Other ☐
Employed ☐   Full-Time Student ☐   Part-Time Student ☐

CITY   STATE

ZIP CODE   TELEPHONE (Include Area Code)   ( )

ZIP CODE   TELEPHONE (INCLUDE AREA CODE)   ( )

9. OTHER INSURED'S NAME (Last Name, First Name, Middle Initial)

10. IS PATIENT'S CONDITION RELATED TO:

11. INSURED'S POLICY GROUP OR FECA NUMBER

a. OTHER INSURED'S POLICY OR GROUP NUMBER

a. EMPLOYMENT? (CURRENT OR PREVIOUS)   ☐ YES   ☐ NO

a. INSURED'S DATE OF BIRTH   MM ☐ DD ☐ YY   SEX   M ☐   F ☐

b. OTHER INSURED'S DATE OF BIRTH   MM ☐ DD ☐ YY   SEX   M ☐   F ☐

b. AUTO ACCIDENT?   PLACE (State)   ☐ YES   ☐ NO

b. EMPLOYER'S NAME OR SCHOOL NAME

c. EMPLOYER'S NAME OR SCHOOL NAME

c. OTHER ACCIDENT?   ☐ YES   ☐ NO

c. INSURANCE PLAN NAME OR PROGRAM NAME

d. INSURANCE PLAN NAME OR PROGRAM NAME

10d. RESERVED FOR LOCAL USE

d. IS THERE ANOTHER HEALTH BENEFIT PLAN?   ☐ YES   ☐ NO   If yes, return to and complete item 9 a – d.

READ BACK OF FORM BEFORE COMPLETING & SIGNING THIS FORM.
12. PATIENT'S OR AUTHORIZED PERSON'S SIGNATURE I authorize the release of any medical or other information necessary to process this claim. I also request payment of government benefits either to myself or to the party who accepts assignment below.

SIGNED _____   DATE _____

13. INSURED'S OR AUTHORIZED PERSON'S SIGNATURE I authorize payment of medical benefits to the undersigned physician or supplier for services described below.

SIGNED _____

PATIENT AND INSURED INFORMATION

14. DATE OF CURRENT: MM ☐ DD ☐ YY   ILLNESS (First symptom) OR INJURY (Accident) OR PREGNANCY (LMP)

15. IF PATIENT HAS HAD SAME OR SIMILAR ILLNESS, GIVE FIRST DATE   MM ☐ DD ☐ YY

16. DATES PATIENT UNABLE TO WORK IN CURRENT OCCUPATION   MM ☐ DD ☐ YY   FROM   TO   MM ☐ DD ☐ YY

17. NAME OF REFERRING PHYSICIAN OR OTHER SOURCE

17a. I.D. NUMBER OF REFERRING PHYSICIAN

18. HOSPITALIZATION DATES RELATED TO CURRENT SERVICES   MM ☐ DD ☐ YY   FROM   TO   MM ☐ DD ☐ YY

19. RESERVED FOR LOCAL USE

20. OUTSIDE LAB?   ☐ YES   ☐ NO $ CHARGES

21. DIAGNOSIS OR NATURE OF ILLNESS OR INJURY. (RELATE ITEMS 1, 2, 3, OR 4 TO ITEM 24E BY LINE)
1. └___ . __   3. └___ . __
2. └___ . __   4. └___ . __

22. MEDICAID RESUBMISSION CODE   ORIGINAL REF. NO.

23. PRIOR AUTHORIZATION NUMBER

24. A DATE(S) OF SERVICE						B Place of Service	C Type of Service	D PROCEDURES, SERVICES, OR SUPPLIES (Explain Unusual Circumstances)		E DIAGNOSIS CODE	F $ CHARGES	G DAYS OR UNITS	H EPSDT Family Plan	I EMG	J COB	K RESERVED FOR LOCAL USE
From MM	DD	YY	To MM	DD	YY			CPT/HCPCS	MODIFIER							
1																
2																
3																
4																
5																
6																

25. FEDERAL TAX I.D. NUMBER   SSN ☐   EIN ☐

26. PATIENT'S ACCOUNT NO.

27. ACCEPT ASSIGNMENT? (For govt. claims, see back)   ☐ YES   ☐ NO

28. TOTAL CHARGE $

29. AMOUNT PAID $

30. BALANCE DUE $

31. SIGNATURE OF PHYSICIAN OR SUPPLIER INCLUDING DEGREES OR CREDENTIALS (I certify that the statements on the reverse apply to this bill and are made a part thereof.)

SIGNED _____   DATE _____

32. NAME AND ADDRESS OF FACILITY WHERE SERVICES WERE RENDERED (If other than home or office)

33. PHYSICIAN'S, SUPPLIER'S BILLING NAME, ADDRESS, ZIP CODE & PHONE #

PIN#   GRP#

PHYSICIAN OR SUPPLIER INFORMATION

(SAMPLE ONLY - NOT APPROVED FOR USE)

PLEASE PRINT OR TYPE

SAMPLE FORM 1500
SAMPLE FORM 1500 SAMPLE FORM 1500

PLEASE
DO NOT
STAPLE
IN THIS
AREA

CARRIER

PICA

HEALTH INSURANCE CLAIM FORM

PICA

1.	MEDICARE	MEDICAID	CHAMPUS	CHAMPVA	GROUP HEALTH PLAN	FECA BLK LUNG	OTHER	1a. INSURED'S I.D. NUMBER (FOR PROGRAM IN ITEM 1)

(Medicare #) (Medicaid #) (Sponsor's SSN) (VA File #) (SSN or ID) (SSN) (ID)

2. PATIENT'S NAME (Last Name, First Name, Middle Initial)

3. PATIENT'S BIRTH DATE
MM DD YY   SEX   M   F

4. INSURED'S NAME (Last Name, First Name, Middle Initial)

5. PATIENT'S ADDRESS (No. Street)

6. PATIENT RELATIONSHIP TO INSURED
Self   Spouse   Child   Other

7. INSURED'S ADDRESS (No. Street)

CITY   STATE

8. PATIENT STATUS
Single   Married   Other

CITY   STATE

ZIP CODE   TELEPHONE (Include Area Code)
(   )

Employed   Full-Time Student   Part-Time Student

ZIP CODE   TELEPHONE (INCLUDE AREA CODE)
(   )

9. OTHER INSURED'S NAME (Last Name, First Name, Middle Initial)

10. IS PATIENT'S CONDITION RELATED TO:

11. INSURED'S POLICY GROUP OR FECA NUMBER

a. OTHER INSURED'S POLICY OR GROUP NUMBER

a. EMPLOYMENT? (CURRENT OR PREVIOUS)
YES   NO

a. INSURED'S DATE OF BIRTH
MM DD YY   SEX   M   F

b. OTHER INSURED'S DATE OF BIRTH
MM DD YY   SEX   M   F

b. AUTO ACCIDENT?   PLACE (State)
YES   NO

b. EMPLOYER'S NAME OR SCHOOL NAME

c. EMPLOYER'S NAME OR SCHOOL NAME

c. OTHER ACCIDENT?
YES   NO

c. INSURANCE PLAN NAME OR PROGRAM NAME

d. INSURANCE PLAN NAME OR PROGRAM NAME

10d. RESERVED FOR LOCAL USE

d. IS THERE ANOTHER HEALTH BENEFIT PLAN?
YES   NO   If yes, return to and complete item 9 a – d.

READ BACK OF FORM BEFORE COMPLETING & SIGNING THIS FORM.
12. PATIENT'S OR AUTHORIZED PERSON'S SIGNATURE I authorize the release of any medical or other information necessary to process this claim. I also request payment of government benefits either to myself or to the party who accepts assignment below.

SIGNED _____   DATE _____

13. INSURED'S OR AUTHORIZED PERSON'S SIGNATURE I authorize payment of medical benefits to the undersigned physician or supplier for services described below.

SIGNED _____

14. DATE OF CURRENT: ILLNESS (First symptom) OR INJURY (Accident) OR PREGNANCY (LMP)
MM DD YY

15. IF PATIENT HAS HAD SAME OR SIMILAR ILLNESS, GIVE FIRST DATE   MM DD YY

16. DATES PATIENT UNABLE TO WORK IN CURRENT OCCUPATION
MM DD YY   MM DD YY
FROM   TO

17. NAME OF REFERRING PHYSICIAN OR OTHER SOURCE

17a. I.D. NUMBER OF REFERRING PHYSICIAN

18. HOSPITALIZATION DATES RELATED TO CURRENT SERVICES
MM DD YY   MM DD YY
FROM   TO

19. RESERVED FOR LOCAL USE

20. OUTSIDE LAB? $ CHARGES
YES   NO

21. DIAGNOSIS OR NATURE OF ILLNESS OR INJURY. (RELATE ITEMS 1, 2, 3, OR 4 TO ITEM 24E BY LINE)

1. _____ . _____   3. _____ . _____

2. _____ . _____   4. _____ . _____

22. MEDICAID RESUBMISSION CODE   ORIGINAL REF. NO.

23. PRIOR AUTHORIZATION NUMBER

24. A DATE(S) OF SERVICE						B Place of Service	C Type of Service	D PROCEDURES, SERVICES, OR SUPPLIES (Explain Unusual Circumstances)		E DIAGNOSIS CODE	F $ CHARGES	G DAYS OR UNITS	H EPSDT Family Plan	I EMG	J COB	K RESERVED FOR LOCAL USE
From MM	DD	YY	To MM	DD	YY			CPT/HCPCS	MODIFIER							
1																
2																
3																
4																
5																
6																

25. FEDERAL TAX I.D. NUMBER   SSN   EIN

26. PATIENT'S ACCOUNT NO.

27. ACCEPT ASSIGNMENT? (For govt. claims, see back)
YES   NO

28. TOTAL CHARGE $

29. AMOUNT PAID $

30. BALANCE DUE $

31. SIGNATURE OF PHYSICIAN OR SUPPLIER INCLUDING DEGREES OR CREDENTIALS
(I certify that the statements on the reverse apply to this bill and are made a part thereof.)

SIGNED _____   DATE _____

32. NAME AND ADDRESS OF FACILITY WHERE SERVICES WERE RENDERED (If other than home or office)

33. PHYSICIAN'S, SUPPLIER'S BILLING NAME, ADDRESS, ZIP CODE & PHONE #

PIN#   GRP#

PLEASE PRINT OR TYPE

SAMPLE FORM 1500
SAMPLE FORM 1500 SAMPLE FORM 1500

235

(SAMPLE ONLY - NOT APPROVED FOR USE)

CARRIER

☐☐ PICA

HEALTH INSURANCE CLAIM FORM   PICA ☐☐☐

1.	MEDICARE	MEDICAID	CHAMPUS	CHAMPVA	GROUP HEALTH PLAN	FECA BLK LUNG	OTHER	1a. INSURED'S I.D. NUMBER	(FOR PROGRAM IN ITEM 1)
	☐ (Medicare #)	☐ (Medicaid #)	☐ (Sponsor's SSN)	☐ (VA File #)	☐ (SSN or ID)	☐ (SSN)	☐ (ID)		

2. PATIENT'S NAME (Last Name, First Name, Middle Initial)

3. PATIENT'S BIRTH DATE   MM   DD   YY   SEX   M ☐   F ☐

4. INSURED'S NAME (Last Name, First Name, Middle Initial)

5. PATIENT'S ADDRESS (No. Street)

6. PATIENT RELATIONSHIP TO INSURED   Self ☐   Spouse ☐   Child ☐   Other ☐

7. INSURED'S ADDRESS (No. Street)

CITY   STATE

8. PATIENT STATUS   Single ☐   Married ☐   Other ☐

CITY   STATE

ZIP CODE   TELEPHONE (Include Area Code) (   )

Employed ☐   Full-Time Student ☐   Part-Time Student ☐

ZIP CODE   TELEPHONE (INCLUDE AREA CODE) (   )

9. OTHER INSURED'S NAME (Last Name, First Name, Middle Initial)

10. IS PATIENT'S CONDITION RELATED TO:

11. INSURED'S POLICY GROUP OR FECA NUMBER

a. OTHER INSURED'S POLICY OR GROUP NUMBER

a. EMPLOYMENT? (CURRENT OR PREVIOUS)   ☐ YES   ☐ NO

a. INSURED'S DATE OF BIRTH   MM   DD   YY   SEX   M ☐   F ☐

b. OTHER INSURED'S DATE OF BIRTH   MM   DD   YY   SEX   M ☐   F ☐

b. AUTO ACCIDENT?   PLACE (State)   ☐ YES   ☐ NO

b. EMPLOYER'S NAME OR SCHOOL NAME

c. EMPLOYER'S NAME OR SCHOOL NAME

c. OTHER ACCIDENT?   ☐ YES   ☐ NO

c. INSURANCE PLAN NAME OR PROGRAM NAME

d. INSURANCE PLAN NAME OR PROGRAM NAME

10d. RESERVED FOR LOCAL USE

d. IS THERE ANOTHER HEALTH BENEFIT PLAN?   ☐ YES   ☐ NO   If yes, return to and complete item 9 a – d.

READ BACK OF FORM BEFORE COMPLETING & SIGNING THIS FORM.
12. PATIENT'S OR AUTHORIZED PERSON'S SIGNATURE I authorize the release of any medical or other information necessary to process this claim. I also request payment of government benefits either to myself or to the party who accepts assignment below.

SIGNED   DATE

13. INSURED'S OR AUTHORIZED PERSON'S SIGNATURE I authorize payment of medical benefits to the undersigned physician or supplier for services described below.

SIGNED

PATIENT AND INSURED INFORMATION

14. DATE OF CURRENT: MM   DD   YY   ◄ ILLNESS (First symptom) OR INJURY (Accident) OR PREGNANCY (LMP)

15. IF PATIENT HAS HAD SAME OR SIMILAR ILLNESS, GIVE FIRST DATE   MM   DD   YY

16. DATES PATIENT UNABLE TO WORK IN CURRENT OCCUPATION   MM   DD   YY   FROM   TO   MM   DD   YY

17. NAME OF REFERRING PHYSICIAN OR OTHER SOURCE

17a. I.D. NUMBER OF REFERRING PHYSICIAN

18. HOSPITALIZATION DATES RELATED TO CURRENT SERVICES   MM   DD   YY   FROM   TO   MM   DD   YY

19. RESERVED FOR LOCAL USE

20. OUTSIDE LAB?   ☐ YES   ☐ NO $ CHARGES

21. DIAGNOSIS OR NATURE OF ILLNESS OR INJURY. (RELATE ITEMS 1, 2, 3, OR 4 TO ITEM 24E BY LINE)

1. └___ . ___   3. └___ . ___

2. └___ . ___   4. └___ . ___

22. MEDICAID RESUBMISSION CODE   ORIGINAL REF. NO.

23. PRIOR AUTHORIZATION NUMBER

24. A DATE(S) OF SERVICE From MM DD YY To MM DD YY	B Place of Service	C Type of Service	D PROCEDURES, SERVICES, OR SUPPLIES (Explain Unusual Circumstances) CPT/HCPCS	MODIFIER	E DIAGNOSIS CODE	F $ CHARGES	G DAYS OR UNITS	H EPSDT Family Plan	I EMG	J COB	K RESERVED FOR LOCAL USE
1											
2											
3											
4											
5											
6											

25. FEDERAL TAX I.D. NUMBER   SSN ☐   EIN ☐

26. PATIENT'S ACCOUNT NO.

27. ACCEPT ASSIGNMENT? (For govt. claims, see back)   ☐ YES   ☐ NO

28. TOTAL CHARGE $

29. AMOUNT PAID $

30. BALANCE DUE $

31. SIGNATURE OF PHYSICIAN OR SUPPLIER INCLUDING DEGREES OR CREDENTIALS (I certify that the statements on the reverse apply to this bill and are made a part thereof.)

SIGNED   DATE

32. NAME AND ADDRESS OF FACILITY WHERE SERVICES WERE RENDERED (If other than home or office)

33. PHYSICIAN'S, SUPPLIER'S BILLING NAME, ADDRESS, ZIP CODE & PHONE #

PIN#   GRP#

PHYSICIAN OR SUPPLIER INFORMATION

PLEASE PRINT OR TYPE

SAMPLE FORM 1500
SAMPLE FORM 1500   SAMPLE FORM 1500

(SAMPLE ONLY - NOT APPROVED FOR USE)

CARRIER

| | PICA | | **HEALTH INSURANCE CLAIM FORM** | PICA | | |

| 1. | MEDICARE | MEDICAID | CHAMPUS | CHAMPVA | GROUP HEALTH PLAN | FECA BLK LUNG | OTHER | 1a. INSURED'S I.D. NUMBER | (FOR PROGRAM IN ITEM 1) |

☐ (Medicare #) ☐ (Medicaid #) ☐ (Sponsor's SSN) ☐ (VA File #) ☐ (SSN or ID) ☐ (SSN) ☐ (ID)

2. PATIENT'S NAME (Last Name, First Name, Middle Initial)

3. PATIENT'S BIRTH DATE MM DD YY SEX M ☐ F ☐

4. INSURED'S NAME (Last Name, First Name, Middle Initial)

5. PATIENT'S ADDRESS (No. Street)

6. PATIENT RELATIONSHIP TO INSURED Self ☐ Spouse ☐ Child ☐ Other ☐

7. INSURED'S ADDRESS (No. Street)

CITY   STATE

8. PATIENT STATUS Single ☐ Married ☐ Other ☐

CITY   STATE

ZIP CODE   TELEPHONE (Include Area Code) (   )

Employed ☐ Full-Time Student ☐ Part-Time Student ☐

ZIP CODE   TELEPHONE (INCLUDE AREA CODE) (   )

9. OTHER INSURED'S NAME (Last Name, First Name, Middle Initial)

10. IS PATIENT'S CONDITION RELATED TO:

11. INSURED'S POLICY GROUP OR FECA NUMBER

a. OTHER INSURED'S POLICY OR GROUP NUMBER

a. EMPLOYMENT? (CURRENT OR PREVIOUS) ☐ YES ☐ NO

a. INSURED'S DATE OF BIRTH MM DD YY SEX M ☐ F ☐

b. OTHER INSURED'S DATE OF BIRTH MM DD YY SEX M ☐ F ☐

b. AUTO ACCIDENT? PLACE (State) ☐ YES ☐ NO

b. EMPLOYER'S NAME OR SCHOOL NAME

c. EMPLOYER'S NAME OR SCHOOL NAME

c. OTHER ACCIDENT? ☐ YES ☐ NO

c. INSURANCE PLAN NAME OR PROGRAM NAME

d. INSURANCE PLAN NAME OR PROGRAM NAME

10d. RESERVED FOR LOCAL USE

d. IS THERE ANOTHER HEALTH BENEFIT PLAN? ☐ YES ☐ NO If yes, return to and complete item 9 a - d.

READ BACK OF FORM BEFORE COMPLETING & SIGNING THIS FORM.
12. PATIENT'S OR AUTHORIZED PERSON'S SIGNATURE I authorize the release of any medical or other information necessary to process this claim. I also request payment of government benefits either to myself or to the party who accepts assignment below.

SIGNED _____ DATE _____

13. INSURED'S OR AUTHORIZED PERSON'S SIGNATURE I authorize payment of medical benefits to the undersigned physician or supplier for services described below.

SIGNED _____

PATIENT AND INSURED INFORMATION

14. DATE OF CURRENT: MM DD YY ILLNESS (First symptom) OR INJURY (Accident) OR PREGNANCY (LMP)

15. IF PATIENT HAS HAD SAME OR SIMILAR ILLNESS, GIVE FIRST DATE MM DD YY

16. DATES PATIENT UNABLE TO WORK IN CURRENT OCCUPATION MM DD YY FROM TO MM DD YY

17. NAME OF REFERRING PHYSICIAN OR OTHER SOURCE

17a. I.D. NUMBER OF REFERRING PHYSICIAN

18. HOSPITALIZATION DATES RELATED TO CURRENT SERVICES MM DD YY FROM TO MM DD YY

19. RESERVED FOR LOCAL USE

20. OUTSIDE LAB? ☐ YES ☐ NO $ CHARGES

21. DIAGNOSIS OR NATURE OF ILLNESS OR INJURY. (RELATE ITEMS 1, 2, 3, OR 4 TO ITEM 24E BY LINE)

1. |___.___   3. |___.___

2. |___.___   4. |___.___

22. MEDICAID RESUBMISSION CODE   ORIGINAL REF. NO.

23. PRIOR AUTHORIZATION NUMBER

24. A DATE(S) OF SERVICE						B Place of Service	C Type of Service	D PROCEDURES, SERVICES, OR SUPPLIES (Explain Unusual Circumstances)		E DIAGNOSIS CODE	F $ CHARGES	G DAYS OR UNITS	H EPSDT Family Plan	I EMG	J COB	K RESERVED FOR LOCAL USE
From			To					CPT/HCPCS	MODIFIER							
MM	DD	YY	MM	DD	YY											
1																
2																
3																
4																
5																
6																

25. FEDERAL TAX I.D. NUMBER SSN ☐ EIN ☐

26. PATIENT'S ACCOUNT NO.

27. ACCEPT ASSIGNMENT? (For govt. claims, see back) ☐ YES ☐ NO

28. TOTAL CHARGE $

29. AMOUNT PAID $

30. BALANCE DUE $

31. SIGNATURE OF PHYSICIAN OR SUPPLIER INCLUDING DEGREES OR CREDENTIALS (I certify that the statements on the reverse apply to this bill and are made a part thereof.)

SIGNED _____ DATE _____

32. NAME AND ADDRESS OF FACILITY WHERE SERVICES WERE RENDERED (If other than home or office)

33. PHYSICIAN'S, SUPPLIER'S BILLING NAME, ADDRESS, ZIP CODE & PHONE #

PIN#   GRP#

PHYSICIAN OR SUPPLIER INFORMATION

(SAMPLE ONLY - NOT APPROVED FOR USE)

PLEASE PRINT OR TYPE

SAMPLE FORM 1500
SAMPLE FORM 1500 SAMPLE FORM 1500

(SAMPLE ONLY - NOT APPROVED FOR USE)

CARRIER

[ ] [ ] PICA

HEALTH INSURANCE CLAIM FORM

PICA [ ] [ ]

1. MEDICARE MEDICAID CHAMPUS CHAMPVA GROUP HEALTH PLAN FECA BLK LUNG OTHER	1a. INSURED'S I.D. NUMBER (FOR PROGRAM IN ITEM 1)

1. MEDICARE [ ] (Medicare #)   MEDICAID [ ] (Medicaid #)   CHAMPUS [ ] (Sponsor's SSN)   CHAMPVA [ ] (VA File #)   GROUP HEALTH PLAN [ ] (SSN or ID)   FECA BLK LUNG [ ] (SSN)   OTHER [ ] (ID)

1a. INSURED'S I.D. NUMBER (FOR PROGRAM IN ITEM 1)

2. PATIENT'S NAME (Last Name, First Name, Middle Initial)

3. PATIENT'S BIRTH DATE   MM [ ] DD [ ] YY   SEX   M [ ]   F [ ]

4. INSURED'S NAME (Last Name, First Name, Middle Initial)

5. PATIENT'S ADDRESS (No. Street)

6. PATIENT RELATIONSHIP TO INSURED   Self [ ] Spouse [ ] Child [ ] Other [ ]

7. INSURED'S ADDRESS (No. Street)

CITY   STATE

8. PATIENT STATUS   Single [ ] Married [ ] Other [ ]

CITY   STATE

ZIP CODE   TELEPHONE (Include Area Code) (   )

Employed [ ]   Full-Time Student [ ]   Part-Time Student [ ]

ZIP CODE   TELEPHONE (INCLUDE AREA CODE) (   )

9. OTHER INSURED'S NAME (Last Name, First Name, Middle Initial)

10. IS PATIENT'S CONDITION RELATED TO:

11. INSURED'S POLICY GROUP OR FECA NUMBER

a. OTHER INSURED'S POLICY OR GROUP NUMBER

a. EMPLOYMENT? (CURRENT OR PREVIOUS)   YES [ ]   NO [ ]

a. INSURED'S DATE OF BIRTH   MM [ ] DD [ ] YY   SEX   M [ ] F [ ]

b. OTHER INSURED'S DATE OF BIRTH   MM [ ] DD [ ] YY   SEX   M [ ] F [ ]

b. AUTO ACCIDENT?   YES [ ]   NO [ ]   PLACE (State) [ ]

b. EMPLOYER'S NAME OR SCHOOL NAME

c. EMPLOYER'S NAME OR SCHOOL NAME

c. OTHER ACCIDENT?   YES [ ]   NO [ ]

c. INSURANCE PLAN NAME OR PROGRAM NAME

d. INSURANCE PLAN NAME OR PROGRAM NAME

10d. RESERVED FOR LOCAL USE

d. IS THERE ANOTHER HEALTH BENEFIT PLAN?   YES [ ]   NO [ ]   If yes, return to and complete item 9 a – d.

READ BACK OF FORM BEFORE COMPLETING & SIGNING THIS FORM.

12. PATIENT'S OR AUTHORIZED PERSON'S SIGNATURE I authorize the release of any medical or other information necessary to process this claim. I also request payment of government benefits either to myself or to the party who accepts assignment below.

SIGNED _____   DATE _____

13. INSURED'S OR AUTHORIZED PERSON'S SIGNATURE I authorize payment of medical benefits to the undersigned physician or supplier for services described below.

SIGNED _____

PATIENT AND INSURED INFORMATION

14. DATE OF CURRENT: MM [ ] DD [ ] YY   ILLNESS (First symptom) OR INJURY (Accident) OR PREGNANCY (LMP)

15. IF PATIENT HAS HAD SAME OR SIMILAR ILLNESS, GIVE FIRST DATE   MM [ ] DD [ ] YY

16. DATES PATIENT UNABLE TO WORK IN CURRENT OCCUPATION   FROM MM [ ] DD [ ] YY   TO MM [ ] DD [ ] YY

17. NAME OF REFERRING PHYSICIAN OR OTHER SOURCE

17a. I.D. NUMBER OF REFERRING PHYSICIAN

18. HOSPITALIZATION DATES RELATED TO CURRENT SERVICES   FROM MM [ ] DD [ ] YY   TO MM [ ] DD [ ] YY

19. RESERVED FOR LOCAL USE

20. OUTSIDE LAB?   YES [ ]   NO [ ] $ CHARGES

21. DIAGNOSIS OR NATURE OF ILLNESS OR INJURY. (RELATE ITEMS 1, 2, 3, OR 4 TO ITEM 24E BY LINE)

1. |___.___| 3. |___.___|

2. |___.___| 4. |___.___|

22. MEDICAID RESUBMISSION CODE   ORIGINAL REF. NO.

23. PRIOR AUTHORIZATION NUMBER

24. A. DATE(S) OF SERVICE						B. Place of Service	C. Type of Service	D. PROCEDURES, SERVICES, OR SUPPLIES (Explain Unusual Circumstances) CPT/HCPCS MODIFIER	E. DIAGNOSIS CODE	F. $ CHARGES	G. DAYS OR UNITS	H. EPSDT Family Plan	I. EMG	J. COB	K. RESERVED FOR LOCAL USE
From MM	DD	YY	To MM	DD	YY										
1															
2															
3															
4															
5															
6															

25. FEDERAL TAX I.D. NUMBER   SSN [ ] EIN [ ]

26. PATIENT'S ACCOUNT NO.

27. ACCEPT ASSIGNMENT? (For govt. claims, see back)   YES [ ]   NO [ ]

28. TOTAL CHARGE $

29. AMOUNT PAID $

30. BALANCE DUE $

31. SIGNATURE OF PHYSICIAN OR SUPPLIER INCLUDING DEGREES OR CREDENTIALS (I certify that the statements on the reverse apply to this bill and are made a part thereof.)

SIGNED _____   DATE _____

32. NAME AND ADDRESS OF FACILITY WHERE SERVICES WERE RENDERED (If other than home or office)

33. PHYSICIAN'S, SUPPLIER'S BILLING NAME, ADDRESS, ZIP CODE & PHONE #

PIN# _____   GRP# _____

PHYSICIAN OR SUPPLIER INFORMATION

(SAMPLE ONLY - NOT APPROVED FOR USE)

PLEASE PRINT OR TYPE

SAMPLE FORM 1500
SAMPLE FORM 1500 SAMPLE FORM 1500

(SAMPLE ONLY - NOT APPROVED FOR USE)

CARRIER

☐☐ PICA

HEALTH INSURANCE CLAIM FORM PICA ☐☐

1.	MEDICARE	MEDICAID	CHAMPUS	CHAMPVA	GROUP HEALTH PLAN	FECA BLK LUNG	OTHER	1a. INSURED'S I.D. NUMBER	(FOR PROGRAM IN ITEM 1)
	☐ (Medicare #)	☐ (Medicaid #)	☐ (Sponsor's SSN)	☐ (VA File #)	☐ (SSN or ID)	☐ (SSN)	☐ (ID)		

2. PATIENT'S NAME (Last Name, First Name, Middle Initial)

3. PATIENT'S BIRTH DATE   MM ┆ DD ┆ YY   SEX   M ☐ F ☐

4. INSURED'S NAME (Last Name, First Name, Middle Initial)

5. PATIENT'S ADDRESS (No. Street)

6. PATIENT RELATIONSHIP TO INSURED   Self ☐ Spouse ☐ Child ☐ Other ☐

7. INSURED'S ADDRESS (No. Street)

CITY   STATE

8. PATIENT STATUS   Single ☐ Married ☐ Other ☐

CITY   STATE

ZIP CODE   TELEPHONE (Include Area Code) (   )

Employed ☐   Full-Time Student ☐   Part-Time Student ☐

ZIP CODE   TELEPHONE (INCLUDE AREA CODE) (   )

9. OTHER INSURED'S NAME (Last Name, First Name, Middle Initial)

10. IS PATIENT'S CONDITION RELATED TO:

11. INSURED'S POLICY GROUP OR FECA NUMBER

a. OTHER INSURED'S POLICY OR GROUP NUMBER

a. EMPLOYMENT? (CURRENT OR PREVIOUS)   ☐ YES ☐ NO

a. INSURED'S DATE OF BIRTH   MM ┆ DD ┆ YY   SEX   M ☐ F ☐

b. OTHER INSURED'S DATE OF BIRTH   MM ┆ DD ┆ YY   SEX   M ☐ F ☐

b. AUTO ACCIDENT?   PLACE (State)   ☐ YES ☐ NO

b. EMPLOYER'S NAME OR SCHOOL NAME

c. EMPLOYER'S NAME OR SCHOOL NAME

c. OTHER ACCIDENT?   ☐ YES ☐ NO

c. INSURANCE PLAN NAME OR PROGRAM NAME

d. INSURANCE PLAN NAME OR PROGRAM NAME

10d. RESERVED FOR LOCAL USE

d. IS THERE ANOTHER HEALTH BENEFIT PLAN?   ☐ YES ☐ NO   If yes, return to and complete item 9 a – d.

READ BACK OF FORM BEFORE COMPLETING & SIGNING THIS FORM.
12. PATIENT'S OR AUTHORIZED PERSON'S SIGNATURE I authorize the release of any medical or other information necessary to process this claim. I also request payment of government benefits either to myself or to the party who accepts assignment below.

SIGNED _____   DATE _____

13. INSURED'S OR AUTHORIZED PERSON'S SIGNATURE I authorize payment of medical benefits to the undersigned physician or supplier for services described below.

SIGNED _____

14. DATE OF CURRENT: MM ┆ DD ┆ YY ◀ ILLNESS (First symptom) OR INJURY (Accident) OR PREGNANCY (LMP)

15. IF PATIENT HAS HAD SAME OR SIMILAR ILLNESS, GIVE FIRST DATE MM ┆ DD ┆ YY

16. DATES PATIENT UNABLE TO WORK IN CURRENT OCCUPATION MM ┆ DD ┆ YY   FROM   TO   MM ┆ DD ┆ YY

17. NAME OF REFERRING PHYSICIAN OR OTHER SOURCE

17a. I.D. NUMBER OF REFERRING PHYSICIAN

18. HOSPITALIZATION DATES RELATED TO CURRENT SERVICES MM ┆ DD ┆ YY   FROM   TO   MM ┆ DD ┆ YY

19. RESERVED FOR LOCAL USE

20. OUTSIDE LAB?   ☐ YES ☐ NO $ CHARGES

21. DIAGNOSIS OR NATURE OF ILLNESS OR INJURY. (RELATE ITEMS 1, 2, 3, OR 4 TO ITEM 24E BY LINE)

1. └___ . ___   3. └___ . ___

2. └___ . ___   4. └___ . ___

22. MEDICAID RESUBMISSION CODE   ORIGINAL REF. NO.

23. PRIOR AUTHORIZATION NUMBER

24. A DATE(S) OF SERVICE						B Place of Service	C Type of Service	D PROCEDURES, SERVICES, OR SUPPLIES (Explain Unusual Circumstances)		E DIAGNOSIS CODE	F $ CHARGES	G DAYS OR UNITS	H EPSDT Family Plan	I EMG	J COB	K RESERVED FOR LOCAL USE
From MM	DD	YY	To MM	DD	YY			CPT/HCPCS	MODIFIER							
1																
2																
3																
4																
5																
6																

25. FEDERAL TAX I.D. NUMBER   SSN ☐ EIN ☐

26. PATIENT'S ACCOUNT NO.

27. ACCEPT ASSIGNMENT? (For govt. claims, see back)   ☐ YES ☐ NO

28. TOTAL CHARGE $

29. AMOUNT PAID $

30. BALANCE DUE $

31. SIGNATURE OF PHYSICIAN OR SUPPLIER INCLUDING DEGREES OR CREDENTIALS (I certify that the statements on the reverse apply to this bill and are made a part thereof.)

SIGNED _____   DATE _____

32. NAME AND ADDRESS OF FACILITY WHERE SERVICES WERE RENDERED (If other than home or office)

33. PHYSICIAN'S, SUPPLIER'S BILLING NAME, ADDRESS, ZIP CODE & PHONE #

PIN#   GRP#

PHYSICIAN OR SUPPLIER INFORMATION

PATIENT AND INSURED INFORMATION

CARRIER

☐☐ PICA

HEALTH INSURANCE CLAIM FORM

PICA ☐☐☐

| 1. MEDICARE ☐ (Medicare #) | MEDICAID ☐ (Medicaid #) | CHAMPUS ☐ (Sponsor's SSN) | CHAMPVA ☐ (VA File #) | GROUP HEALTH PLAN ☐ (SSN or ID) | FECA BLK LUNG ☐ (SSN) | OTHER ☐ (ID) | 1a. INSURED'S I.D. NUMBER (FOR PROGRAM IN ITEM 1) |

| 2. PATIENT'S NAME (Last Name, First Name, Middle Initial) | 3. PATIENT'S BIRTH DATE MM ┆ DD ┆ YY   SEX M ☐ F ☐ | 4. INSURED'S NAME (Last Name, First Name, Middle Initial) |

| 5. PATIENT'S ADDRESS (No. Street) | 6. PATIENT RELATIONSHIP TO INSURED Self ☐ Spouse ☐ Child ☐ Other ☐ | 7. INSURED'S ADDRESS (No. Street) |

| CITY | STATE | 8. PATIENT STATUS Single ☐ Married ☐ Other ☐ | CITY | STATE |

| ZIP CODE | TELEPHONE (Include Area Code) ( ) | Employed ☐ Full-Time Student ☐ Part-Time Student ☐ | ZIP CODE | TELEPHONE (INCLUDE AREA CODE) ( ) |

| 9. OTHER INSURED'S NAME (Last Name, First Name, Middle Initial) | 10. IS PATIENT'S CONDITION RELATED TO: | 11. INSURED'S POLICY GROUP OR FECA NUMBER |

| a. OTHER INSURED'S POLICY OR GROUP NUMBER | a. EMPLOYMENT? (CURRENT OR PREVIOUS) ☐ YES ☐ NO | a. INSURED'S DATE OF BIRTH MM ┆ DD ┆ YY   SEX M ☐ F ☐ |

| b. OTHER INSURED'S DATE OF BIRTH MM ┆ DD ┆ YY   SEX M ☐ F ☐ | b. AUTO ACCIDENT?   PLACE (State) ☐ YES ☐ NO | b. EMPLOYER'S NAME OR SCHOOL NAME |

| c. EMPLOYER'S NAME OR SCHOOL NAME | c. OTHER ACCIDENT? ☐ YES ☐ NO | c. INSURANCE PLAN NAME OR PROGRAM NAME |

| d. INSURANCE PLAN NAME OR PROGRAM NAME | 10d. RESERVED FOR LOCAL USE | d. IS THERE ANOTHER HEALTH BENEFIT PLAN? ☐ YES ☐ NO   If yes, return to and complete item 9 a – d. |

READ BACK OF FORM BEFORE COMPLETING & SIGNING THIS FORM.

12. PATIENT'S OR AUTHORIZED PERSON'S SIGNATURE I authorize the release of any medical or other information necessary to process this claim. I also request payment of government benefits either to myself or to the party who accepts assignment below.

SIGNED _____   DATE _____

13. INSURED'S OR AUTHORIZED PERSON'S SIGNATURE I authorize payment of medical benefits to the undersigned physician or supplier for services described below.

SIGNED _____

PATIENT AND INSURED INFORMATION

| 14. DATE OF CURRENT: MM ┆ DD ┆ YY ◀ ILLNESS (First symptom) OR INJURY (Accident) OR PREGNANCY (LMP) | 15. IF PATIENT HAS HAD SAME OR SIMILAR ILLNESS, GIVE FIRST DATE MM ┆ DD ┆ YY | 16. DATES PATIENT UNABLE TO WORK IN CURRENT OCCUPATION MM ┆ DD ┆ YY   MM ┆ DD ┆ YY FROM _____ TO _____ |

| 17. NAME OF REFERRING PHYSICIAN OR OTHER SOURCE | 17a. I.D. NUMBER OF REFERRING PHYSICIAN | 18. HOSPITALIZATION DATES RELATED TO CURRENT SERVICES MM ┆ DD ┆ YY   MM ┆ DD ┆ YY FROM _____ TO _____ |

| 19. RESERVED FOR LOCAL USE | 20. OUTSIDE LAB? $ CHARGES ☐ YES ☐ NO |

| 21. DIAGNOSIS OR NATURE OF ILLNESS OR INJURY. (RELATE ITEMS 1, 2, 3, OR 4 TO ITEM 24E BY LINE) 1. └__ . __┘   3. └__ . __┘ 2. └__ . __┘   4. └__ . __┘ | 22. MEDICAID RESUBMISSION CODE _____ ORIGINAL REF. NO. _____ 23. PRIOR AUTHORIZATION NUMBER |

24. A DATE(S) OF SERVICE						B Place of Service	C Type of Service	D PROCEDURES, SERVICES, OR SUPPLIES (Explain Unusual Circumstances)		E DIAGNOSIS CODE	F $ CHARGES	G DAYS OR UNITS	H EPSDT Family Plan	I EMG	J COB	K RESERVED FOR LOCAL USE
From			To					CPT/HCPCS	MODIFIER							
MM	DD	YY	MM	DD	YY											
1																
2																
3																
4																
5																
6																

| 25. FEDERAL TAX I.D. NUMBER   SSN ☐ EIN ☐ | 26. PATIENT'S ACCOUNT NO. | 27. ACCEPT ASSIGNMENT? (For govt. claims, see back) YES ☐ NO ☐ | 28. TOTAL CHARGE $ | 29. AMOUNT PAID $ | 30. BALANCE DUE $ |

| 31. SIGNATURE OF PHYSICIAN OR SUPPLIER INCLUDING DEGREES OR CREDENTIALS (I certify that the statements on the reverse apply to this bill and are made a part thereof.) SIGNED _____ DATE _____ | 32. NAME AND ADDRESS OF FACILITY WHERE SERVICES WERE RENDERED (If other than home or office) | 33. PHYSICIAN'S, SUPPLIER'S BILLING NAME, ADDRESS, ZIP CODE & PHONE # PIN# _____ GRP# _____ |

PHYSICIAN OR SUPPLIER INFORMATION

PLEASE PRINT OR TYPE

SAMPLE FORM 1500
SAMPLE FORM 1500 SAMPLE FORM 1500

(SAMPLE ONLY - NOT APPROVED FOR USE)

CARRIER

| | PICA

HEALTH INSURANCE CLAIM FORM

PICA | | |

1.	MEDICARE	MEDICAID	CHAMPUS	CHAMPVA	GROUP HEALTH PLAN	FECA BLK LUNG	OTHER	1a. INSURED'S I.D. NUMBER	(FOR PROGRAM IN ITEM 1)
	(Medicare #)	(Medicaid #)	(Sponsor's SSN)	(VA File #)	(SSN or ID)	(SSN)	(ID)		

2. PATIENT'S NAME (Last Name, First Name, Middle Initial)

3. PATIENT'S BIRTH DATE
MM | DD | YY   SEX
M | | F |

4. INSURED'S NAME (Last Name, First Name, Middle Initial)

5. PATIENT'S ADDRESS (No. Street)

6. PATIENT RELATIONSHIP TO INSURED
Self | | Spouse | | Child | | Other | |

7. INSURED'S ADDRESS (No. Street)

CITY   STATE

8. PATIENT STATUS
Single | | Married | | Other | |
Employed | | Full-Time Student | | Part-Time Student | |

CITY   STATE

ZIP CODE   TELEPHONE (Include Area Code)
( )

ZIP CODE   TELEPHONE (INCLUDE AREA CODE)
( )

9. OTHER INSURED'S NAME (Last Name, First Name, Middle Initial)

10. IS PATIENT'S CONDITION RELATED TO:

11. INSURED'S POLICY GROUP OR FECA NUMBER

a. OTHER INSURED'S POLICY OR GROUP NUMBER

a. EMPLOYMENT? (CURRENT OR PREVIOUS)
YES | | NO | |

a. INSURED'S DATE OF BIRTH
MM | DD | YY   SEX
M | | F |

b. OTHER INSURED'S DATE OF BIRTH
MM | DD | YY   SEX
M | | F |

b. AUTO ACCIDENT?   PLACE (State)
YES | | NO | |

b. EMPLOYER'S NAME OR SCHOOL NAME

c. EMPLOYER'S NAME OR SCHOOL NAME

c. OTHER ACCIDENT?
YES | | NO | |

c. INSURANCE PLAN NAME OR PROGRAM NAME

d. INSURANCE PLAN NAME OR PROGRAM NAME

10d. RESERVED FOR LOCAL USE

d. IS THERE ANOTHER HEALTH BENEFIT PLAN?
YES | | NO | | If yes, return to and complete item 9 a – d.

READ BACK OF FORM BEFORE COMPLETING & SIGNING THIS FORM.
12. PATIENT'S OR AUTHORIZED PERSON'S SIGNATURE I authorize the release of any medical or other information necessary to process this claim. I also request payment of government benefits either to myself or to the party who accepts assignment below.

SIGNED _____ DATE _____

13. INSURED'S OR AUTHORIZED PERSON'S SIGNATURE I authorize payment of medical benefits to the undersigned physician or supplier for services described below.

SIGNED _____

PATIENT AND INSURED INFORMATION

14. DATE OF CURRENT: ILLNESS (First symptom) OR
MM | DD | YY   INJURY (Accident) OR
PREGNANCY (LMP)

15. IF PATIENT HAS HAD SAME OR SIMILAR ILLNESS, GIVE FIRST DATE MM | DD | YY

16. DATES PATIENT UNABLE TO WORK IN CURRENT OCCUPATION
MM | DD | YY   MM | DD | YY
FROM   TO

17. NAME OF REFERRING PHYSICIAN OR OTHER SOURCE

17a. I.D. NUMBER OF REFERRING PHYSICIAN

18. HOSPITALIZATION DATES RELATED TO CURRENT SERVICES
MM | DD | YY   MM | DD | YY
FROM   TO

19. RESERVED FOR LOCAL USE

20. OUTSIDE LAB? $ CHARGES
YES | | NO | |

21. DIAGNOSIS OR NATURE OF ILLNESS OR INJURY. (RELATE ITEMS 1, 2, 3, OR 4 TO ITEM 24E BY LINE)

1. |____| . |____|
2. |____| . |____|
3. |____| . |____|
4. |____| . |____|

22. MEDICAID RESUBMISSION CODE   ORIGINAL REF. NO.

23. PRIOR AUTHORIZATION NUMBER

24. A DATE(S) OF SERVICE					B Place of Service	C Type of Service	D PROCEDURES, SERVICES, OR SUPPLIES (Explain Unusual Circumstances)		E DIAGNOSIS CODE	F $ CHARGES	G DAYS OR UNITS	H EPSDT Family Plan	I EMG	J COB	K RESERVED FOR LOCAL USE
From MM	DD	YY	To MM	DD	YY			CPT/HCPCS	MODIFIER							
1															
2															
3															
4															
5															
6															

25. FEDERAL TAX I.D. NUMBER   SSN | | EIN | |

26. PATIENT'S ACCOUNT NO.

27. ACCEPT ASSIGNMENT? (For govt. claims, see back)
YES | | NO | |

28. TOTAL CHARGE $

29. AMOUNT PAID $

30. BALANCE DUE $

31. SIGNATURE OF PHYSICIAN OR SUPPLIER INCLUDING DEGREES OR CREDENTIALS (I certify that the statements on the reverse apply to this bill and are made a part thereof.)

SIGNED _____ DATE _____

32. NAME AND ADDRESS OF FACILITY WHERE SERVICES WERE RENDERED (If other than home or office)

33. PHYSICIAN'S, SUPPLIER'S BILLING NAME, ADDRESS, ZIP CODE & PHONE #

PIN# _____ GRP# _____

PHYSICIAN OR SUPPLIER INFORMATION

(SAMPLE ONLY - NOT APPROVED FOR USE)

PLEASE PRINT OR TYPE

SAMPLE FORM 1500
SAMPLE FORM 1500 SAMPLE FORM 1500

(SAMPLE ONLY - NOT APPROVED FOR USE)

CARRIER

| | PICA | **HEALTH INSURANCE CLAIM FORM** | PICA | | |

1. MEDICARE ☐ (Medicare #) MEDICAID ☐ (Medicaid #) CHAMPUS ☐ (Sponsor's SSN) CHAMPVA ☐ (VA File #) GROUP HEALTH PLAN ☐ (SSN or ID) FECA BLK LUNG ☐ (SSN) OTHER ☐ (ID)

1a. INSURED'S I.D. NUMBER (FOR PROGRAM IN ITEM 1)

2. PATIENT'S NAME (Last Name, First Name, Middle Initial)

3. PATIENT'S BIRTH DATE MM ☐ DD ☐ YY SEX M ☐ F ☐

4. INSURED'S NAME (Last Name, First Name, Middle Initial)

5. PATIENT'S ADDRESS (No. Street)

6. PATIENT RELATIONSHIP TO INSURED Self ☐ Spouse ☐ Child ☐ Other ☐

7. INSURED'S ADDRESS (No. Street)

CITY STATE

8. PATIENT STATUS Single ☐ Married ☐ Other ☐

Employed ☐ Full-Time Student ☐ Part-Time Student ☐

CITY STATE

ZIP CODE TELEPHONE (Include Area Code) (   )

ZIP CODE TELEPHONE (INCLUDE AREA CODE) (   )

9. OTHER INSURED'S NAME (Last Name, First Name, Middle Initial)

10. IS PATIENT'S CONDITION RELATED TO:

11. INSURED'S POLICY GROUP OR FECA NUMBER

a. OTHER INSURED'S POLICY OR GROUP NUMBER

a. EMPLOYMENT? (CURRENT OR PREVIOUS) ☐ YES ☐ NO

a. INSURED'S DATE OF BIRTH MM ☐ DD ☐ YY SEX M ☐ F ☐

b. OTHER INSURED'S DATE OF BIRTH MM ☐ DD ☐ YY SEX M ☐ F ☐

b. AUTO ACCIDENT? PLACE (State) ☐ YES ☐ NO

b. EMPLOYER'S NAME OR SCHOOL NAME

c. EMPLOYER'S NAME OR SCHOOL NAME

c. OTHER ACCIDENT? ☐ YES ☐ NO

c. INSURANCE PLAN NAME OR PROGRAM NAME

d. INSURANCE PLAN NAME OR PROGRAM NAME

10d. RESERVED FOR LOCAL USE

d. IS THERE ANOTHER HEALTH BENEFIT PLAN? ☐ YES ☐ NO If yes, return to and complete item 9 a – d.

READ BACK OF FORM BEFORE COMPLETING & SIGNING THIS FORM.
12. PATIENT'S OR AUTHORIZED PERSON'S SIGNATURE I authorize the release of any medical or other information necessary to process this claim. I also request payment of government benefits either to myself or to the party who accepts assignment below.

SIGNED _____ DATE _____

13. INSURED'S OR AUTHORIZED PERSON'S SIGNATURE I authorize payment of medical benefits to the undersigned physician or supplier for services described below.

SIGNED _____

14. DATE OF CURRENT: MM ☐ DD ☐ YY ◄ ILLNESS (First symptom) OR INJURY (Accident) OR PREGNANCY (LMP)

15. IF PATIENT HAS HAD SAME OR SIMILAR ILLNESS, GIVE FIRST DATE MM ☐ DD ☐ YY

16. DATES PATIENT UNABLE TO WORK IN CURRENT OCCUPATION MM ☐ DD ☐ YY FROM TO MM ☐ DD ☐ YY

17. NAME OF REFERRING PHYSICIAN OR OTHER SOURCE

17a. I.D. NUMBER OF REFERRING PHYSICIAN

18. HOSPITALIZATION DATES RELATED TO CURRENT SERVICES MM ☐ DD ☐ YY FROM TO MM ☐ DD ☐ YY

19. RESERVED FOR LOCAL USE

20. OUTSIDE LAB? ☐ YES ☐ NO $ CHARGES

21. DIAGNOSIS OR NATURE OF ILLNESS OR INJURY. (RELATE ITEMS 1, 2, 3, OR 4 TO ITEM 24E BY LINE)
1. ____ . ____   3. ____ . ____
2. ____ . ____   4. ____ . ____

22. MEDICAID RESUBMISSION CODE ORIGINAL REF. NO.

23. PRIOR AUTHORIZATION NUMBER

24. A. DATE(S) OF SERVICE						B. Place of Service	C. Type of Service	D. PROCEDURES, SERVICES, OR SUPPLIES (Explain Unusual Circumstances)		E. DIAGNOSIS CODE	F. $ CHARGES	G. DAYS OR UNITS	H. EPSDT Family Plan	I. EMG	J. COB	K. RESERVED FOR LOCAL USE
From MM	DD	YY	To MM	DD	YY			CPT/HCPCS	MODIFIER							
1																
2																
3																
4																
5																
6																

25. FEDERAL TAX I.D. NUMBER SSN ☐ EIN ☐

26. PATIENT'S ACCOUNT NO.

27. ACCEPT ASSIGNMENT? (For govt. claims, see back) ☐ YES ☐ NO

28. TOTAL CHARGE $

29. AMOUNT PAID $

30. BALANCE DUE $

31. SIGNATURE OF PHYSICIAN OR SUPPLIER INCLUDING DEGREES OR CREDENTIALS (I certify that the statements on the reverse apply to this bill and are made a part thereof.)

SIGNED _____ DATE _____

32. NAME AND ADDRESS OF FACILITY WHERE SERVICES WERE RENDERED (If other than home or office)

33. PHYSICIAN'S, SUPPLIER'S BILLING NAME, ADDRESS, ZIP CODE & PHONE #

PIN# GRP#

PHYSICIAN OR SUPPLIER INFORMATION

PATIENT AND INSURED INFORMATION

(SAMPLE ONLY - NOT APPROVED FOR USE)

PLEASE PRINT OR TYPE

SAMPLE FORM 1500
SAMPLE FORM 1500 SAMPLE FORM 1500

CARRIER

| | PICA | | | | | | | | **HEALTH INSURANCE CLAIM FORM** | PICA | |

MEDICARE	MEDICAID	CHAMPUS	CHAMPVA	GROUP HEALTH PLAN	FECA BLK LUNG	OTHER	1a. INSURED'S I.D. NUMBER	(FOR PROGRAM IN ITEM 1)
(Medicare #)	(Medicaid #)	(Sponsor's SSN)	(VA File #)	(SSN or ID)	(SSN)	(ID)		

2. PATIENT'S NAME (Last Name, First Name, Middle Initial)

3. PATIENT'S BIRTH DATE MM | DD | YY   SEX   M [ ] F [ ]

4. INSURED'S NAME (Last Name, First Name, Middle Initial)

5. PATIENT'S ADDRESS (No. Street)

6. PATIENT RELATIONSHIP TO INSURED   Self [ ] Spouse [ ] Child [ ] Other [ ]

7. INSURED'S ADDRESS (No. Street)

CITY   STATE

8. PATIENT STATUS   Single [ ] Married [ ] Other [ ]

CITY   STATE

ZIP CODE   TELEPHONE (Include Area Code) ( )

Employed [ ] Full-Time Student [ ] Part-Time Student [ ]

ZIP CODE   TELEPHONE (INCLUDE AREA CODE) ( )

9. OTHER INSURED'S NAME (Last Name, First Name, Middle Initial)

10. IS PATIENT'S CONDITION RELATED TO:

11. INSURED'S POLICY GROUP OR FECA NUMBER

a. OTHER INSURED'S POLICY OR GROUP NUMBER

a. EMPLOYMENT? (CURRENT OR PREVIOUS) YES [ ] NO [ ]

a. INSURED'S DATE OF BIRTH MM | DD | YY   SEX   M [ ] F [ ]

b. OTHER INSURED'S DATE OF BIRTH MM | DD | YY   SEX   M [ ] F [ ]

b. AUTO ACCIDENT?   PLACE (State)   YES [ ] NO [ ]

b. EMPLOYER'S NAME OR SCHOOL NAME

c. EMPLOYER'S NAME OR SCHOOL NAME

c. OTHER ACCIDENT? YES [ ] NO [ ]

c. INSURANCE PLAN NAME OR PROGRAM NAME

d. INSURANCE PLAN NAME OR PROGRAM NAME

10d. RESERVED FOR LOCAL USE

d. IS THERE ANOTHER HEALTH BENEFIT PLAN? YES [ ] NO [ ] If yes, return to and complete item 9 a - d.

READ BACK OF FORM BEFORE COMPLETING & SIGNING THIS FORM.
12. PATIENT'S OR AUTHORIZED PERSON'S SIGNATURE I authorize the release of any medical or other information necessary to process this claim. I also request payment of government benefits either to myself or to the party who accepts assignment below.

SIGNED _____   DATE _____

13. INSURED'S OR AUTHORIZED PERSON'S SIGNATURE I authorize payment of medical benefits to the undersigned physician or supplier for services described below.

SIGNED _____

PATIENT AND INSURED INFORMATION

14. DATE OF CURRENT: MM | DD | YY   ILLNESS (First symptom) OR INJURY (Accident) OR PREGNANCY (LMP)

15. IF PATIENT HAS HAD SAME OR SIMILAR ILLNESS, GIVE FIRST DATE MM | DD | YY

16. DATES PATIENT UNABLE TO WORK IN CURRENT OCCUPATION MM | DD | YY FROM   TO MM | DD | YY

17. NAME OF REFERRING PHYSICIAN OR OTHER SOURCE

17a. I.D. NUMBER OF REFERRING PHYSICIAN

18. HOSPITALIZATION DATES RELATED TO CURRENT SERVICES MM | DD | YY FROM   TO MM | DD | YY

19. RESERVED FOR LOCAL USE

20. OUTSIDE LAB? YES [ ] NO [ ] $ CHARGES

21. DIAGNOSIS OR NATURE OF ILLNESS OR INJURY. (RELATE ITEMS 1, 2, 3, OR 4 TO ITEM 24E BY LINE)

1. |___.___| 3. |___.___|

2. |___.___| 4. |___.___|

22. MEDICAID RESUBMISSION CODE   ORIGINAL REF. NO.

23. PRIOR AUTHORIZATION NUMBER

24. A DATE(S) OF SERVICE			B Place of Service	C Type of Service	D PROCEDURES, SERVICES, OR SUPPLIES (Explain Unusual Circumstances) CPT/HCPCS | MODIFIER	E DIAGNOSIS CODE	F $ CHARGES	G DAYS OR UNITS	H EPSDT Family Plan	I EMG	J COB	K RESERVED FOR LOCAL USE
From MM DD YY	To MM DD YY											
1												
2												
3												
4												
5												
6												

PHYSICIAN OR SUPPLIER INFORMATION

25. FEDERAL TAX I.D. NUMBER SSN [ ] EIN [ ]

26. PATIENT'S ACCOUNT NO.

27. ACCEPT ASSIGNMENT? (For govt. claims, see back) YES [ ] NO [ ]

28. TOTAL CHARGE $

29. AMOUNT PAID $

30. BALANCE DUE $

31. SIGNATURE OF PHYSICIAN OR SUPPLIER INCLUDING DEGREES OR CREDENTIALS (I certify that the statements on the reverse apply to this bill and are made a part thereof.)

SIGNED _____   DATE _____

32. NAME AND ADDRESS OF FACILITY WHERE SERVICES WERE RENDERED (If other than home or office)

33. PHYSICIAN'S, SUPPLIER'S BILLING NAME, ADDRESS, ZIP CODE & PHONE #

PIN# _____   GRP# _____

PLEASE PRINT OR TYPE

SAMPLE FORM 1500
SAMPLE FORM 1500 SAMPLE FORM 1500

(SAMPLE ONLY - NOT APPROVED FOR USE)

CARRIER

HEALTH INSURANCE CLAIM FORM

PICA [ ] [ ] PICA [ ] [ ]

1. MEDICARE MEDICAID CHAMPUS CHAMPVA GROUP FECA OTHER	1a. INSURED'S I.D. NUMBER (FOR PROGRAM IN ITEM 1)
[ ] (Medicare #) [ ] (Medicaid #) [ ] (Sponsor's SSN) [ ] (VA File #) HEALTH PLAN BLK LUNG [ ] (SSN or ID) [ ] (SSN) [ ] (ID)	

2. PATIENT'S NAME (Last Name, First Name, Middle Initial)

3. PATIENT'S BIRTH DATE MM | DD | YY   SEX M [ ] F [ ]

4. INSURED'S NAME (Last Name, First Name, Middle Initial)

5. PATIENT'S ADDRESS (No. Street)

6. PATIENT RELATIONSHIP TO INSURED
Self [ ] Spouse [ ] Child [ ] Other [ ]

7. INSURED'S ADDRESS (No. Street)

CITY   STATE

8. PATIENT STATUS
Single [ ] Married [ ] Other [ ]
Employed [ ] Full-Time Student [ ] Part-Time Student [ ]

CITY   STATE

ZIP CODE   TELEPHONE (Include Area Code) ( )

ZIP CODE   TELEPHONE (INCLUDE AREA CODE) ( )

9. OTHER INSURED'S NAME (Last Name, First Name, Middle Initial)

10. IS PATIENT'S CONDITION RELATED TO:

11. INSURED'S POLICY GROUP OR FECA NUMBER

a. OTHER INSURED'S POLICY OR GROUP NUMBER

a. EMPLOYMENT? (CURRENT OR PREVIOUS) [ ] YES [ ] NO

a. INSURED'S DATE OF BIRTH MM | DD | YY   SEX M [ ] F [ ]

b. OTHER INSURED'S DATE OF BIRTH MM | DD | YY   SEX M [ ] F [ ]

b. AUTO ACCIDENT?   PLACE (State) [ ] YES [ ] NO

b. EMPLOYER'S NAME OR SCHOOL NAME

c. EMPLOYER'S NAME OR SCHOOL NAME

c. OTHER ACCIDENT? [ ] YES [ ] NO

c. INSURANCE PLAN NAME OR PROGRAM NAME

d. INSURANCE PLAN NAME OR PROGRAM NAME

10d. RESERVED FOR LOCAL USE

d. IS THERE ANOTHER HEALTH BENEFIT PLAN?
[ ] YES [ ] NO   If yes, return to and complete item 9 a – d.

READ BACK OF FORM BEFORE COMPLETING & SIGNING THIS FORM.
12. PATIENT'S OR AUTHORIZED PERSON'S SIGNATURE I authorize the release of any medical or other information necessary to process this claim. I also request payment of government benefits either to myself or to the party who accepts assignment below.

SIGNED _____   DATE _____

13. INSURED'S OR AUTHORIZED PERSON'S SIGNATURE I authorize payment of medical benefits to the undersigned physician or supplier for services described below.

SIGNED _____

14. DATE OF CURRENT: MM | DD | YY   ILLNESS (First symptom) OR INJURY (Accident) OR PREGNANCY (LMP)

15. IF PATIENT HAS HAD SAME OR SIMILAR ILLNESS, GIVE FIRST DATE MM | DD | YY

16. DATES PATIENT UNABLE TO WORK IN CURRENT OCCUPATION FROM MM | DD | YY   TO MM | DD | YY

17. NAME OF REFERRING PHYSICIAN OR OTHER SOURCE

17a. I.D. NUMBER OF REFERRING PHYSICIAN

18. HOSPITALIZATION DATES RELATED TO CURRENT SERVICES FROM MM | DD | YY   TO MM | DD | YY

19. RESERVED FOR LOCAL USE

20. OUTSIDE LAB? $ CHARGES
[ ] YES [ ] NO

21. DIAGNOSIS OR NATURE OF ILLNESS OR INJURY. (RELATE ITEMS 1, 2, 3, OR 4 TO ITEM 24E BY LINE)
1. |___|.|__| 3. |___|.|__|
2. |___|.|__| 4. |___|.|__|

22. MEDICAID RESUBMISSION CODE   ORIGINAL REF. NO.

23. PRIOR AUTHORIZATION NUMBER

24. A DATE(S) OF SERVICE						B Place of Service	C Type of Service	D PROCEDURES, SERVICES, OR SUPPLIES (Explain Unusual Circumstances)		E DIAGNOSIS CODE	F $ CHARGES	G DAYS OR UNITS	H EPSDT Family Plan	I EMG	J COB	K RESERVED FOR LOCAL USE
From MM	DD	YY	To MM	DD	YY			CPT/HCPCS	MODIFIER							
1																
2																
3																
4																
5																
6																

25. FEDERAL TAX I.D. NUMBER   SSN [ ] EIN [ ]

26. PATIENT'S ACCOUNT NO.

27. ACCEPT ASSIGNMENT? (For govt. claims, see back) [ ] YES [ ] NO

28. TOTAL CHARGE $

29. AMOUNT PAID $

30. BALANCE DUE $

31. SIGNATURE OF PHYSICIAN OR SUPPLIER INCLUDING DEGREES OR CREDENTIALS (I certify that the statements on the reverse apply to this bill and are made a part thereof.)

SIGNED _____   DATE _____

32. NAME AND ADDRESS OF FACILITY WHERE SERVICES WERE RENDERED (If other than home or office)

33. PHYSICIAN'S, SUPPLIER'S BILLING NAME, ADDRESS, ZIP CODE & PHONE #

PIN# _____   GRP# _____

(SAMPLE ONLY - NOT APPROVED FOR USE)

PLEASE PRINT OR TYPE

SAMPLE FORM 1500
SAMPLE FORM 1500 SAMPLE FORM 1500

PATIENT AND INSURED INFORMATION

PHYSICIAN OR SUPPLIER INFORMATION

(SAMPLE ONLY - NOT APPROVED FOR USE)

CARRIER

☐☐ PICA

HEALTH INSURANCE CLAIM FORM

PICA ☐☐☐

| 1. MEDICARE ☐ (Medicare #) | MEDICAID ☐ (Medicaid #) | CHAMPUS ☐ (Sponsor's SSN) | CHAMPVA ☐ (VA File #) | GROUP HEALTH PLAN ☐ (SSN or ID) | FECA BLK LUNG ☐ (SSN) | OTHER ☐ (ID) | 1a. INSURED'S I.D. NUMBER (FOR PROGRAM IN ITEM 1) |

| 2. PATIENT'S NAME (Last Name, First Name, Middle Initial) | 3. PATIENT'S BIRTH DATE MM ⏐ DD ⏐ YY   SEX M☐ F☐ | 4. INSURED'S NAME (Last Name, First Name, Middle Initial) |

| 5. PATIENT'S ADDRESS (No. Street) | 6. PATIENT RELATIONSHIP TO INSURED Self ☐ Spouse ☐ Child ☐ Other ☐ | 7. INSURED'S ADDRESS (No. Street) |

| CITY | STATE | 8. PATIENT STATUS Single ☐ Married ☐ Other ☐ | CITY | STATE |

| ZIP CODE | TELEPHONE (Include Area Code) ( ) | Employed ☐ Full-Time Student ☐ Part-Time Student ☐ | ZIP CODE | TELEPHONE (INCLUDE AREA CODE) ( ) |

| 9. OTHER INSURED'S NAME (Last Name, First Name, Middle Initial) | 10. IS PATIENT'S CONDITION RELATED TO: | 11. INSURED'S POLICY GROUP OR FECA NUMBER |

| a. OTHER INSURED'S POLICY OR GROUP NUMBER | a. EMPLOYMENT? (CURRENT OR PREVIOUS) ☐ YES ☐ NO | a. INSURED'S DATE OF BIRTH MM ⏐ DD ⏐ YY   SEX M☐ F☐ |

| b. OTHER INSURED'S DATE OF BIRTH MM ⏐ DD ⏐ YY   SEX M☐ F☐ | b. AUTO ACCIDENT? PLACE (State) ☐ YES ☐ NO | b. EMPLOYER'S NAME OR SCHOOL NAME |

| c. EMPLOYER'S NAME OR SCHOOL NAME | c. OTHER ACCIDENT? ☐ YES ☐ NO | c. INSURANCE PLAN NAME OR PROGRAM NAME |

| d. INSURANCE PLAN NAME OR PROGRAM NAME | 10d. RESERVED FOR LOCAL USE | d. IS THERE ANOTHER HEALTH BENEFIT PLAN? ☐ YES ☐ NO If yes, return to and complete item 9 a – d. |

READ BACK OF FORM BEFORE COMPLETING & SIGNING THIS FORM.

12. PATIENT'S OR AUTHORIZED PERSON'S SIGNATURE I authorize the release of any medical or other information necessary to process this claim. I also request payment of government benefits either to myself or to the party who accepts assignment below.

SIGNED _____ DATE _____

13. INSURED'S OR AUTHORIZED PERSON'S SIGNATURE I authorize payment of medical benefits to the undersigned physician or supplier for services described below.

SIGNED _____

PATIENT AND INSURED INFORMATION

| 14. DATE OF CURRENT: MM ⏐ DD ⏐ YY ◀ ILLNESS (First symptom) OR INJURY (Accident) OR PREGNANCY (LMP) | 15. IF PATIENT HAS HAD SAME OR SIMILAR ILLNESS, GIVE FIRST DATE MM ⏐ DD ⏐ YY | 16. DATES PATIENT UNABLE TO WORK IN CURRENT OCCUPATION MM ⏐ DD ⏐ YY   MM ⏐ DD ⏐ YY FROM   TO |

| 17. NAME OF REFERRING PHYSICIAN OR OTHER SOURCE | 17a. I.D. NUMBER OF REFERRING PHYSICIAN | 18. HOSPITALIZATION DATES RELATED TO CURRENT SERVICES MM ⏐ DD ⏐ YY   MM ⏐ DD ⏐ YY FROM   TO |

| 19. RESERVED FOR LOCAL USE | 20. OUTSIDE LAB? ☐ YES ☐ NO $ CHARGES |

| 21. DIAGNOSIS OR NATURE OF ILLNESS OR INJURY. (RELATE ITEMS 1, 2, 3, OR 4 TO ITEM 24E BY LINE) 1. L___ . ___   3. L___ . ___   2. L___ . ___   4. L___ . ___ | 22. MEDICAID RESUBMISSION CODE   ORIGINAL REF. NO. 23. PRIOR AUTHORIZATION NUMBER |

24. A DATE(S) OF SERVICE From To MM DD YY MM DD YY	B Place of Service	C Type of Service	D PROCEDURES, SERVICES, OR SUPPLIES (Explain Unusual Circumstances) CPT/HCPCS ⏐ MODIFIER	E DIAGNOSIS CODE	F $ CHARGES	G DAYS OR UNITS	H EPSDT Family Plan	I EMG	J COB	K RESERVED FOR LOCAL USE
1										
2										
3										
4										
5										
6										

| 25. FEDERAL TAX I.D. NUMBER SSN ☐ EIN ☐ | 26. PATIENT'S ACCOUNT NO. | 27. ACCEPT ASSIGNMENT? (For govt. claims, see back) ☐ YES ☐ NO | 28. TOTAL CHARGE $ | 29. AMOUNT PAID $ | 30. BALANCE DUE $ |

| 31. SIGNATURE OF PHYSICIAN OR SUPPLIER INCLUDING DEGREES OR CREDENTIALS (I certify that the statements on the reverse apply to this bill and are made a part thereof.) SIGNED _____ DATE _____ | 32. NAME AND ADDRESS OF FACILITY WHERE SERVICES WERE RENDERED (If other than home or office) | 33. PHYSICIAN'S, SUPPLIER'S BILLING NAME, ADDRESS, ZIP CODE & PHONE # PIN#   GRP# |

PHYSICIAN OR SUPPLIER INFORMATION

(SAMPLE ONLY - NOT APPROVED FOR USE)

PLEASE PRINT OR TYPE

SAMPLE FORM 1500
SAMPLE FORM 1500 SAMPLE FORM 1500

CARRIER

(SAMPLE ONLY - NOT APPROVED FOR USE)

☐☐ PICA

HEALTH INSURANCE CLAIM FORM   PICA ☐☐☐

1. MEDICARE	MEDICAID	CHAMPUS	CHAMPVA	GROUP HEALTH PLAN	FECA BLK LUNG	OTHER	1a. INSURED'S I.D. NUMBER (FOR PROGRAM IN ITEM 1)
☐ (Medicare #)	☐ (Medicaid #)	☐ (Sponsor's SSN)	☐ (VA File #)	☐ (SSN or ID)	☐ (SSN)	☐ (ID)	

2. PATIENT'S NAME (Last Name, First Name, Middle Initial)

3. PATIENT'S BIRTH DATE MM | DD | YY   SEX M ☐ F ☐

4. INSURED'S NAME (Last Name, First Name, Middle Initial)

5. PATIENT'S ADDRESS (No. Street)

6. PATIENT RELATIONSHIP TO INSURED Self ☐ Spouse ☐ Child ☐ Other ☐

7. INSURED'S ADDRESS (No. Street)

CITY   STATE

8. PATIENT STATUS Single ☐ Married ☐ Other ☐

Employed ☐ Full-Time Student ☐ Part-Time Student ☐

CITY   STATE

ZIP CODE   TELEPHONE (Include Area Code) ( )

ZIP CODE   TELEPHONE (INCLUDE AREA CODE) ( )

9. OTHER INSURED'S NAME (Last Name, First Name, Middle Initial)

10. IS PATIENT'S CONDITION RELATED TO:

11. INSURED'S POLICY GROUP OR FECA NUMBER

a. OTHER INSURED'S POLICY OR GROUP NUMBER

a. EMPLOYMENT? (CURRENT OR PREVIOUS) ☐ YES ☐ NO

a. INSURED'S DATE OF BIRTH MM | DD | YY   SEX M ☐ F ☐

b. OTHER INSURED'S DATE OF BIRTH MM | DD | YY   SEX M ☐ F ☐

b. AUTO ACCIDENT?   PLACE (State) ☐ YES ☐ NO

b. EMPLOYER'S NAME OR SCHOOL NAME

c. EMPLOYER'S NAME OR SCHOOL NAME

c. OTHER ACCIDENT? ☐ YES ☐ NU

c. INSURANCE PLAN NAME OR PROGRAM NAME

d. INSURANCE PLAN NAME OR PROGRAM NAME

10d. RESERVED FOR LOCAL USE

d. IS THERE ANOTHER HEALTH BENEFIT PLAN? ☐ YES ☐ NO If yes, return to and complete item 9 a – d.

READ BACK OF FORM BEFORE COMPLETING & SIGNING THIS FORM.
12. PATIENT'S OR AUTHORIZED PERSON'S SIGNATURE I authorize the release of any medical or other information necessary to process this claim. I also request payment of government benefits either to myself or to the party who accepts assignment below.

SIGNED _____   DATE _____

13. INSURED'S OR AUTHORIZED PERSON'S SIGNATURE I authorize payment of medical benefits to the undersigned physician or supplier for services described below.

SIGNED _____

PATIENT AND INSURED INFORMATION

14. DATE OF CURRENT: MM | DD | YY ILLNESS (First symptom) OR INJURY (Accident) OR PREGNANCY (LMP)

15. IF PATIENT HAS HAD SAME OR SIMILAR ILLNESS, GIVE FIRST DATE MM | DD | YY

16. DATES PATIENT UNABLE TO WORK IN CURRENT OCCUPATION MM | DD | YY FROM TO MM | DD | YY

17. NAME OF REFERRING PHYSICIAN OR OTHER SOURCE

17a. I.D. NUMBER OF REFERRING PHYSICIAN

18. HOSPITALIZATION DATES RELATED TO CURRENT SERVICES MM | DD | YY FROM TO MM | DD | YY

19. RESERVED FOR LOCAL USE

20. OUTSIDE LAB? ☐ YES ☐ NO $ CHARGES

21. DIAGNOSIS OR NATURE OF ILLNESS OR INJURY. (RELATE ITEMS 1, 2, 3, OR 4 TO ITEM 24E BY LINE)

1. ____ . ____   3. ____ . ____

2. ____ . ____   4. ____ . ____

22. MEDICAID RESUBMISSION CODE   ORIGINAL REF. NO.

23. PRIOR AUTHORIZATION NUMBER

24. A DATE(S) OF SERVICE						B Place of Service	C Type of Service	D PROCEDURES, SERVICES, OR SUPPLIES (Explain Unusual Circumstances) CPT/HCPCS	MODIFIER	E DIAGNOSIS CODE	F $ CHARGES	G DAYS OR UNITS	H EPSDT Family Plan	I EMG	J COB	K RESERVED FOR LOCAL USE
From MM	DD	YY	To MM	DD	YY											
1																
2																
3																
4																
5																
6																

PHYSICIAN OR SUPPLIER INFORMATION

25. FEDERAL TAX I.D. NUMBER   SSN ☐ EIN ☐

26. PATIENT'S ACCOUNT NO.

27. ACCEPT ASSIGNMENT? (For govt. claims, see back) ☐ YES ☐ NO

28. TOTAL CHARGE $

29. AMOUNT PAID $

30. BALANCE DUE $

31. SIGNATURE OF PHYSICIAN OR SUPPLIER INCLUDING DEGREES OR CREDENTIALS (I certify that the statements on the reverse apply to this bill and are made a part thereof.)

SIGNED _____ DATE _____

32. NAME AND ADDRESS OF FACILITY WHERE SERVICES WERE RENDERED (If other than home or office)

33. PHYSICIAN'S, SUPPLIER'S BILLING NAME, ADDRESS, ZIP CODE & PHONE #

PIN# _____   GRP# _____

PLEASE PRINT OR TYPE

SAMPLE FORM 1500
SAMPLE FORM 1500 SAMPLE FORM 1500

PLEASE
DO NOT
STAPLE
IN THIS
AREA

CARRIER

☐☐ PICA

HEALTH INSURANCE CLAIM FORM

PICA ☐☐

| 1. MEDICARE ☐ (Medicare #) | MEDICAID ☐ (Medicaid #) | CHAMPUS ☐ (Sponsor's SSN) | CHAMPVA ☐ (VA File #) | GROUP HEALTH PLAN ☐ (SSN or ID) | FECA BLK LUNG ☐ (SSN) | OTHER ☐ (ID) | 1a. INSURED'S I.D. NUMBER | (FOR PROGRAM IN ITEM 1) |

2. PATIENT'S NAME (Last Name, First Name, Middle Initial)

3. PATIENT'S BIRTH DATE MM ┊ DD ┊ YY   SEX   M ☐   F ☐

4. INSURED'S NAME (Last Name, First Name, Middle Initial)

5. PATIENT'S ADDRESS (No. Street)

6. PATIENT RELATIONSHIP TO INSURED   Self ☐   Spouse ☐   Child ☐   Other ☐

7. INSURED'S ADDRESS (No. Street)

CITY   STATE

8. PATIENT STATUS   Single ☐   Married ☐   Other ☐

CITY   STATE

ZIP CODE   TELEPHONE (Include Area Code) (   )

Employed ☐   Full-Time Student ☐   Part-Time Student ☐

ZIP CODE   TELEPHONE (INCLUDE AREA CODE) (   )

9. OTHER INSURED'S NAME (Last Name, First Name, Middle Initial)

10. IS PATIENT'S CONDITION RELATED TO:

11. INSURED'S POLICY GROUP OR FECA NUMBER

a. OTHER INSURED'S POLICY OR GROUP NUMBER

a. EMPLOYMENT? (CURRENT OR PREVIOUS)   YES ☐   NO ☐

a. INSURED'S DATE OF BIRTH MM ┊ DD ┊ YY   SEX   M ☐   F ☐

b. OTHER INSURED'S DATE OF BIRTH MM ┊ DD ┊ YY   SEX   M ☐   F ☐

b. AUTO ACCIDENT?   PLACE (State)   YES ☐   NO ☐

b. EMPLOYER'S NAME OR SCHOOL NAME

c. EMPLOYER'S NAME OR SCHOOL NAME

c. OTHER ACCIDENT?   YES ☐   NO ☐

c. INSURANCE PLAN NAME OR PROGRAM NAME

d. INSURANCE PLAN NAME OR PROGRAM NAME

10d. RESERVED FOR LOCAL USE

d. IS THERE ANOTHER HEALTH BENEFIT PLAN?   YES ☐   NO ☐   If yes, return to and complete item 9 a – d.

READ BACK OF FORM BEFORE COMPLETING & SIGNING THIS FORM.
12. PATIENT'S OR AUTHORIZED PERSON'S SIGNATURE I authorize the release of any medical or other information necessary to process this claim. I also request payment of government benefits either to myself or to the party who accepts assignment below.

SIGNED _____   DATE _____

13. INSURED'S OR AUTHORIZED PERSON'S SIGNATURE I authorize payment of medical benefits to the undersigned physician or supplier for services described below.

SIGNED _____

PATIENT AND INSURED INFORMATION

14. DATE OF CURRENT: ILLNESS (First symptom) OR INJURY (Accident) OR PREGNANCY (LMP) MM ┊ DD ┊ YY

15. IF PATIENT HAS HAD SAME OR SIMILAR ILLNESS, GIVE FIRST DATE MM ┊ DD ┊ YY

16. DATES PATIENT UNABLE TO WORK IN CURRENT OCCUPATION MM ┊ DD ┊ YY   FROM _____ TO _____

17. NAME OF REFERRING PHYSICIAN OR OTHER SOURCE

17a. I.D. NUMBER OF REFERRING PHYSICIAN

18. HOSPITALIZATION DATES RELATED TO CURRENT SERVICES MM ┊ DD ┊ YY   FROM _____ TO _____

19. RESERVED FOR LOCAL USE

20. OUTSIDE LAB?   YES ☐   NO ☐ $ CHARGES

21. DIAGNOSIS OR NATURE OF ILLNESS OR INJURY. (RELATE ITEMS 1, 2, 3, OR 4 TO ITEM 24E BY LINE)

1. └──.──   3. └──.──
2. └──.──   4. └──.──

22. MEDICAID RESUBMISSION CODE   ORIGINAL REF. NO.

23. PRIOR AUTHORIZATION NUMBER

24. A DATE(S) OF SERVICE						B Place of Service	C Type of Service	D PROCEDURES, SERVICES, OR SUPPLIES (Explain Unusual Circumstances) CPT/HCPCS ┊ MODIFIER	E DIAGNOSIS CODE	F $ CHARGES	G DAYS OR UNITS	H EPSDT Family Plan	I EMG	J COB	K RESERVED FOR LOCAL USE
From MM	DD	YY	To MM	DD	YY										
1															
2															
3															
4															
5															
6															

25. FEDERAL TAX I.D. NUMBER   SSN ☐   EIN ☐

26. PATIENT'S ACCOUNT NO.

27. ACCEPT ASSIGNMENT? (For govt. claims, see back)   YES ☐   NO ☐

28. TOTAL CHARGE $

29. AMOUNT PAID $

30. BALANCE DUE $

31. SIGNATURE OF PHYSICIAN OR SUPPLIER INCLUDING DEGREES OR CREDENTIALS (I certify that the statements on the reverse apply to this bill and are made a part thereof.)

SIGNED _____   DATE _____

32. NAME AND ADDRESS OF FACILITY WHERE SERVICES WERE RENDERED (If other than home or office)

33. PHYSICIAN'S, SUPPLIER'S BILLING NAME, ADDRESS, ZIP CODE & PHONE #

PIN# _____   GRP# _____

PHYSICIAN OR SUPPLIER INFORMATION

PLEASE PRINT OR TYPE

SAMPLE FORM 1500
SAMPLE FORM 1500 SAMPLE FORM 1500

PLEASE
DO NOT
STAPLE
IN THIS
AREA

(SAMPLE ONLY - NOT APPROVED FOR USE)

CARRIER

[ ][ ] PICA

HEALTH INSURANCE CLAIM FORM

PICA [ ][ ]

1. MEDICARE MEDICAID CHAMPUS CHAMPVA GROUP HEALTH PLAN FECA BLK LUNG OTHER	1a. INSURED'S I.D. NUMBER (FOR PROGRAM IN ITEM 1)

1. MEDICARE [ ] (Medicare #)   MEDICAID [ ] (Medicaid #)   CHAMPUS [ ] (Sponsor's SSN)   CHAMPVA [ ] (VA File #)   GROUP HEALTH PLAN [ ] (SSN or ID)   FECA BLK LUNG [ ] (SSN)   OTHER [ ] (ID)

1a. INSURED'S I.D. NUMBER   (FOR PROGRAM IN ITEM 1)

2. PATIENT'S NAME (Last Name, First Name, Middle Initial)

3. PATIENT'S BIRTH DATE   MM | DD | YY   SEX   M [ ]   F [ ]

4. INSURED'S NAME (Last Name, First Name, Middle Initial)

5. PATIENT'S ADDRESS (No. Street)

6. PATIENT RELATIONSHIP TO INSURED   Self [ ]   Spouse [ ]   Child [ ]   Other [ ]

7. INSURED'S ADDRESS (No. Street)

CITY   STATE

8. PATIENT STATUS   Single [ ]   Married [ ]   Other [ ]   Employed [ ]   Full-Time Student [ ]   Part-Time Student [ ]

CITY   STATE

ZIP CODE   TELEPHONE (Include Area Code) (   )

ZIP CODE   TELEPHONE (INCLUDE AREA CODE) (   )

9. OTHER INSURED'S NAME (Last Name, First Name, Middle Initial)

10. IS PATIENT'S CONDITION RELATED TO:

11. INSURED'S POLICY GROUP OR FECA NUMBER

a. OTHER INSURED'S POLICY OR GROUP NUMBER

a. EMPLOYMENT? (CURRENT OR PREVIOUS)   [ ] YES   [ ] NO

a. INSURED'S DATE OF BIRTH   MM | DD | YY   SEX   M [ ]   F [ ]

b. OTHER INSURED'S DATE OF BIRTH   MM | DD | YY   SEX   M [ ]   F [ ]

b. AUTO ACCIDENT?   PLACE (State)   [ ] YES   [ ] NO

b. EMPLOYER'S NAME OR SCHOOL NAME

c. EMPLOYER'S NAME OR SCHOOL NAME

c. OTHER ACCIDENT?   [ ] YES   [ ] NO

c. INSURANCE PLAN NAME OR PROGRAM NAME

d. INSURANCE PLAN NAME OR PROGRAM NAME

10d. RESERVED FOR LOCAL USE

d. IS THERE ANOTHER HEALTH BENEFIT PLAN?   [ ] YES   [ ] NO   If yes, return to and complete item 9 a – d.

READ BACK OF FORM BEFORE COMPLETING & SIGNING THIS FORM.
12. PATIENT'S OR AUTHORIZED PERSON'S SIGNATURE   I authorize the release of any medical or other information necessary to process this claim. I also request payment of government benefits either to myself or to the party who accepts assignment below.

SIGNED _____   DATE _____

13. INSURED'S OR AUTHORIZED PERSON'S SIGNATURE   I authorize payment of medical benefits to the undersigned physician or supplier for services described below.

SIGNED _____

14. DATE OF CURRENT: MM | DD | YY   ILLNESS (First symptom) OR   INJURY (Accident) OR   PREGNANCY (LMP)

15. IF PATIENT HAS HAD SAME OR SIMILAR ILLNESS, GIVE FIRST DATE   MM | DD | YY

16. DATES PATIENT UNABLE TO WORK IN CURRENT OCCUPATION   MM | DD | YY   FROM   TO   MM | DD | YY

17. NAME OF REFERRING PHYSICIAN OR OTHER SOURCE

17a. I.D. NUMBER OF REFERRING PHYSICIAN

18. HOSPITALIZATION DATES RELATED TO CURRENT SERVICES   MM | DD | YY   FROM   TO   MM | DD | YY

19. RESERVED FOR LOCAL USE

20. OUTSIDE LAB?   [ ] YES   [ ] NO $ CHARGES

21. DIAGNOSIS OR NATURE OF ILLNESS OR INJURY. (RELATE ITEMS 1, 2, 3, OR 4 TO ITEM 24E BY LINE)

1. |___.___   3. |___.___

2. |___.___   4. |___.___

22. MEDICAID RESUBMISSION CODE   ORIGINAL REF. NO.

23. PRIOR AUTHORIZATION NUMBER

24. A. DATE(S) OF SERVICE						B. Place of Service	C. Type of Service	D. PROCEDURES, SERVICES, OR SUPPLIES (Explain Unusual Circumstances) CPT/HCPCS MODIFIER	E. DIAGNOSIS CODE	F. $ CHARGES	G. DAYS OR UNITS	H. EPSDT Family Plan	I. EMG	J. COB	K. RESERVED FOR LOCAL USE
From MM	DD	YY	To MM	DD	YY										
1															
2															
3															
4															
5															
6															

25. FEDERAL TAX I.D. NUMBER   SSN [ ]   EIN [ ]

26. PATIENT'S ACCOUNT NO.

27. ACCEPT ASSIGNMENT? (For govt. claims, see back)   [ ] YES   [ ] NO

28. TOTAL CHARGE $

29. AMOUNT PAID $

30. BALANCE DUE $

31. SIGNATURE OF PHYSICIAN OR SUPPLIER INCLUDING DEGREES OR CREDENTIALS (I certify that the statements on the reverse apply to this bill and are made a part thereof.)

SIGNED _____   DATE _____

32. NAME AND ADDRESS OF FACILITY WHERE SERVICES WERE RENDERED (If other than home or office)

33. PHYSICIAN'S, SUPPLIER'S BILLING NAME, ADDRESS, ZIP CODE & PHONE #

PIN#   GRP#

PATIENT AND INSURED INFORMATION

PHYSICIAN OR SUPPLIER INFORMATION

(SAMPLE ONLY - NOT APPROVED FOR USE)

PLEASE PRINT OR TYPE

SAMPLE FORM 1500
SAMPLE FORM 1500 SAMPLE FORM 1500

(SAMPLE ONLY - NOT APPROVED FOR USE)

CARRIER

☐☐ PICA

HEALTH INSURANCE CLAIM FORM   PICA ☐☐

1. MEDICARE ☐ (Medicare #) MEDICAID ☐ (Medicaid #) CHAMPUS ☐ (Sponsor's SSN) CHAMPVA ☐ (VA File #) GROUP HEALTH PLAN ☐ (SSN or ID) FECA BLK LUNG ☐ (SSN) OTHER ☐ (ID)	1a. INSURED'S I.D. NUMBER (FOR PROGRAM IN ITEM 1)

2. PATIENT'S NAME (Last Name, First Name, Middle Initial)

3. PATIENT'S BIRTH DATE MM ┊ DD ┊ YY   SEX   M ☐   F ☐

4. INSURED'S NAME (Last Name, First Name, Middle Initial)

5. PATIENT'S ADDRESS (No. Street)

6. PATIENT RELATIONSHIP TO INSURED   Self ☐   Spouse ☐   Child ☐   Other ☐

7. INSURED'S ADDRESS (No. Street)

CITY   STATE

8. PATIENT STATUS   Single ☐   Married ☐   Other ☐
   Employed ☐   Full-Time Student ☐   Part-Time Student ☐

CITY   STATE

ZIP CODE   TELEPHONE (Include Area Code) ( )

ZIP CODE   TELEPHONE (INCLUDE AREA CODE) ( )

9. OTHER INSURED'S NAME (Last Name, First Name, Middle Initial)

10. IS PATIENT'S CONDITION RELATED TO:

11. INSURED'S POLICY GROUP OR FECA NUMBER

a. OTHER INSURED'S POLICY OR GROUP NUMBER

a. EMPLOYMENT? (CURRENT OR PREVIOUS)   ☐ YES   ☐ NO

a. INSURED'S DATE OF BIRTH MM ┊ DD ┊ YY   SEX   M ☐   F ☐

b. OTHER INSURED'S DATE OF BIRTH MM ┊ DD ┊ YY   SEX   M ☐   F ☐

b. AUTO ACCIDENT?   PLACE (State)   ☐ YES   ☐ NO

b. EMPLOYER'S NAME OR SCHOOL NAME

c. EMPLOYER'S NAME OR SCHOOL NAME

c. OTHER ACCIDENT?   ☐ YES   ☐ NO

c. INSURANCE PLAN NAME OR PROGRAM NAME

d. INSURANCE PLAN NAME OR PROGRAM NAME

10d. RESERVED FOR LOCAL USE

d. IS THERE ANOTHER HEALTH BENEFIT PLAN?   ☐ YES   ☐ NO   If yes, return to and complete item 9 a – d.

READ BACK OF FORM BEFORE COMPLETING & SIGNING THIS FORM.
12. PATIENT'S OR AUTHORIZED PERSON'S SIGNATURE I authorize the release of any medical or other information necessary to process this claim. I also request payment of government benefits either to myself or to the party who accepts assignment below.

SIGNED _____   DATE _____

13. INSURED'S OR AUTHORIZED PERSON'S SIGNATURE I authorize payment of medical benefits to the undersigned physician or supplier for services described below.

SIGNED _____

PATIENT AND INSURED INFORMATION

14. DATE OF CURRENT: ILLNESS (First symptom) OR INJURY (Accident) OR PREGNANCY (LMP) MM ┊ DD ┊ YY

15. IF PATIENT HAS HAD SAME OR SIMILAR ILLNESS, GIVE FIRST DATE   MM ┊ DD ┊ YY

16. DATES PATIENT UNABLE TO WORK IN CURRENT OCCUPATION FROM MM ┊ DD ┊ YY TO MM ┊ DD ┊ YY

17. NAME OF REFERRING PHYSICIAN OR OTHER SOURCE

17a. I.D. NUMBER OF REFERRING PHYSICIAN

18. HOSPITALIZATION DATES RELATED TO CURRENT SERVICES FROM MM ┊ DD ┊ YY TO MM ┊ DD ┊ YY

19. RESERVED FOR LOCAL USE

20. OUTSIDE LAB?   ☐ YES   ☐ NO $ CHARGES

21. DIAGNOSIS OR NATURE OF ILLNESS OR INJURY. (RELATE ITEMS 1, 2, 3, OR 4 TO ITEM 24E BY LINE)
1. └___ . ___   3. └___ . ___
2. └___ . ___   4. └___ . ___

22. MEDICAID RESUBMISSION CODE   ORIGINAL REF. NO.

23. PRIOR AUTHORIZATION NUMBER

24. A DATE(S) OF SERVICE						B Place of Service	C Type of Service	D PROCEDURES, SERVICES, OR SUPPLIES (Explain Unusual Circumstances)		E DIAGNOSIS CODE	F $ CHARGES	G DAYS OR UNITS	H EPSDT Family Plan	I EMG	J COB	K RESERVED FOR LOCAL USE
From MM	DD	YY	To MM	DD	YY			CPT/HCPCS	MODIFIER							
1																
2																
3																
4																
5																
6																

25. FEDERAL TAX I.D. NUMBER   SSN ☐ EIN ☐

26. PATIENT'S ACCOUNT NO.

27. ACCEPT ASSIGNMENT? (For govt. claims, see back)   ☐ YES   ☐ NO

28. TOTAL CHARGE $

29. AMOUNT PAID $

30. BALANCE DUE $

31. SIGNATURE OF PHYSICIAN OR SUPPLIER INCLUDING DEGREES OR CREDENTIALS (I certify that the statements on the reverse apply to this bill and are made a part thereof.)

SIGNED _____   DATE _____

32. NAME AND ADDRESS OF FACILITY WHERE SERVICES WERE RENDERED (If other than home or office)

33. PHYSICIAN'S, SUPPLIER'S BILLING NAME, ADDRESS, ZIP CODE & PHONE #

PIN#   GRP#

PHYSICIAN OR SUPPLIER INFORMATION

(SAMPLE ONLY - NOT APPROVED FOR USE)

PLEASE PRINT OR TYPE

SAMPLE FORM 1500
SAMPLE FORM 1500 SAMPLE FORM 1500

249

(SAMPLE ONLY - NOT APPROVED FOR USE)

CARRIER

☐☐ PICA

HEALTH INSURANCE CLAIM FORM

PICA ☐☐☐

1. MEDICARE	MEDICAID	CHAMPUS	CHAMPVA	GROUP HEALTH PLAN	FECA BLK LUNG	OTHER	1a. INSURED'S I.D. NUMBER (FOR PROGRAM IN ITEM 1)
☐ (Medicare #)	☐ (Medicaid #)	☐ (Sponsor's SSN)	☐ (VA File #)	☐ (SSN or ID)	☐ (SSN)	☐ (ID)	

2. PATIENT'S NAME (Last Name, First Name, Middle Initial)

3. PATIENT'S BIRTH DATE MM ☐ DD ☐ YY   SEX   M ☐   F ☐

4. INSURED'S NAME (Last Name, First Name, Middle Initial)

5. PATIENT'S ADDRESS (No. Street)

6. PATIENT RELATIONSHIP TO INSURED   Self ☐ Spouse ☐ Child ☐ Other ☐

7. INSURED'S ADDRESS (No. Street)

CITY   STATE

8. PATIENT STATUS   Single ☐   Married ☐   Other ☐

CITY   STATE

ZIP CODE   TELEPHONE (Include Area Code) (   )

Employed ☐   Full-Time Student ☐   Part-Time Student ☐

ZIP CODE   TELEPHONE (INCLUDE AREA CODE) (   )

9. OTHER INSURED'S NAME (Last Name, First Name, Middle Initial)

10. IS PATIENT'S CONDITION RELATED TO:

11. INSURED'S POLICY GROUP OR FECA NUMBER

a. OTHER INSURED'S POLICY OR GROUP NUMBER

a. EMPLOYMENT? (CURRENT OR PREVIOUS)   ☐ YES   ☐ NO

a. INSURED'S DATE OF BIRTH MM ☐ DD ☐ YY   SEX   M ☐   F ☐

b. OTHER INSURED'S DATE OF BIRTH MM ☐ DD ☐ YY   SEX   M ☐   F ☐

b. AUTO ACCIDENT?   PLACE (State)   ☐ YES   ☐ NO ☐

b. EMPLOYER'S NAME OR SCHOOL NAME

c. EMPLOYER'S NAME OR SCHOOL NAME

c. OTHER ACCIDENT?   ☐ YES   ☐ NO

c. INSURANCE PLAN NAME OR PROGRAM NAME

d. INSURANCE PLAN NAME OR PROGRAM NAME

10d. RESERVED FOR LOCAL USE

d. IS THERE ANOTHER HEALTH BENEFIT PLAN?   ☐ YES   ☐ NO   If yes, return to and complete item 9 a – d.

READ BACK OF FORM BEFORE COMPLETING & SIGNING THIS FORM.

12. PATIENT'S OR AUTHORIZED PERSON'S SIGNATURE I authorize the release of any medical or other information necessary to process this claim. I also request payment of government benefits either to myself or to the party who accepts assignment below.

SIGNED _____   DATE _____

13. INSURED'S OR AUTHORIZED PERSON'S SIGNATURE I authorize payment of medical benefits to the undersigned physician or supplier for services described below.

SIGNED _____

PATIENT AND INSURED INFORMATION

14. DATE OF CURRENT: ILLNESS (First symptom) OR INJURY (Accident) OR PREGNANCY (LMP) MM ☐ DD ☐ YY

15. IF PATIENT HAS HAD SAME OR SIMILAR ILLNESS, GIVE FIRST DATE   MM ☐ DD ☐ YY

16. DATES PATIENT UNABLE TO WORK IN CURRENT OCCUPATION   FROM MM ☐ DD ☐ YY   TO MM ☐ DD ☐ YY

17. NAME OF REFERRING PHYSICIAN OR OTHER SOURCE

17a. I.D. NUMBER OF REFERRING PHYSICIAN

18. HOSPITALIZATION DATES RELATED TO CURRENT SERVICES   FROM MM ☐ DD ☐ YY   TO MM ☐ DD ☐ YY

19. RESERVED FOR LOCAL USE

20. OUTSIDE LAB?   ☐ YES   ☐ NO $ CHARGES

21. DIAGNOSIS OR NATURE OF ILLNESS OR INJURY. (RELATE ITEMS 1, 2, 3, OR 4 TO ITEM 24E BY LINE)

1. ☐__ . __   3. ☐__ . __

2. ☐__ . __   4. ☐__ . __

22. MEDICAID RESUBMISSION CODE   ORIGINAL REF. NO.

23. PRIOR AUTHORIZATION NUMBER

24. A DATE(S) OF SERVICE						B Place of Service	C Type of Service	D PROCEDURES, SERVICES, OR SUPPLIES (Explain Unusual Circumstances)		E DIAGNOSIS CODE	F $ CHARGES	G DAYS OR UNITS	H EPSDT Family Plan	I EMG	J COB	K RESERVED FOR LOCAL USE
From MM	DD	YY	To MM	DD	YY			CPT/HCPCS	MODIFIER							
1																
2																
3																
4																
5																
6																

25. FEDERAL TAX I.D. NUMBER   SSN ☐ EIN ☐

26. PATIENT'S ACCOUNT NO.

27. ACCEPT ASSIGNMENT? (For govt. claims, see back)   ☐ YES   ☐ NO

28. TOTAL CHARGE $

29. AMOUNT PAID $

30. BALANCE DUE $

31. SIGNATURE OF PHYSICIAN OR SUPPLIER INCLUDING DEGREES OR CREDENTIALS (I certify that the statements on the reverse apply to this bill and are made a part thereof.)

SIGNED _____ DATE _____

32. NAME AND ADDRESS OF FACILITY WHERE SERVICES WERE RENDERED (If other than home or office)

33. PHYSICIAN'S, SUPPLIER'S BILLING NAME, ADDRESS, ZIP CODE & PHONE #

PIN# _____   GRP# _____

PHYSICIAN OR SUPPLIER INFORMATION

(SAMPLE ONLY - NOT APPROVED FOR USE)

PLEASE PRINT OR TYPE

SAMPLE FORM 1500
SAMPLE FORM 1500 SAMPLE FORM 1500

(SAMPLE ONLY - NOT APPROVED FOR USE)

CARRIER

☐☐ PICA

HEALTH INSURANCE CLAIM FORM   PICA ☐☐

1. MEDICARE ☐ (Medicare #)   MEDICAID ☐ (Medicaid #)   CHAMPUS ☐ (Sponsor's SSN)   CHAMPVA ☐ (VA File #)   GROUP HEALTH PLAN ☐ (SSN or ID)   FECA BLK LUNG ☐ (SSN)   OTHER ☐ (ID) | 1a. INSURED'S I.D. NUMBER   (FOR PROGRAM IN ITEM 1)

2. PATIENT'S NAME (Last Name, First Name, Middle Initial)

3. PATIENT'S BIRTH DATE MM | DD | YY   SEX   M ☐ F ☐

4. INSURED'S NAME (Last Name, First Name, Middle Initial)

5. PATIENT'S ADDRESS (No. Street)

6. PATIENT RELATIONSHIP TO INSURED   Self ☐   Spouse ☐   Child ☐   Other ☐

7. INSURED'S ADDRESS (No. Street)

CITY   STATE

8. PATIENT STATUS   Single ☐   Married ☐   Other ☐
Employed ☐   Full-Time Student ☐   Part-Time Student ☐

CITY   STATE

ZIP CODE   TELEPHONE (Include Area Code) ( )

ZIP CODE   TELEPHONE (INCLUDE AREA CODE) ( )

9. OTHER INSURED'S NAME (Last Name, First Name, Middle Initial)

10. IS PATIENT'S CONDITION RELATED TO:

11. INSURED'S POLICY GROUP OR FECA NUMBER

a. OTHER INSURED'S POLICY OR GROUP NUMBER

a. EMPLOYMENT? (CURRENT OR PREVIOUS)   YES ☐   NO ☐

a. INSURED'S DATE OF BIRTH MM | DD | YY   SEX   M ☐ · F ☐

b. OTHER INSURED'S DATE OF BIRTH MM | DD | YY   SEX   M ☐ F ☐

b. AUTO ACCIDENT?   PLACE (State)   YES ☐   NO ☐

b. EMPLOYER'S NAME OR SCHOOL NAME

c. EMPLOYER'S NAME OR SCHOOL NAME

c. OTHER ACCIDENT?   YES ☐   NO ☐

c. INSURANCE PLAN NAME OR PROGRAM NAME

d. INSURANCE PLAN NAME OR PROGRAM NAME

10d. RESERVED FOR LOCAL USE

d. IS THERE ANOTHER HEALTH BENEFIT PLAN?   YES ☐   NO ☐   If yes, return to and complete item 9 a – d.

READ BACK OF FORM BEFORE COMPLETING & SIGNING THIS FORM.
12. PATIENT'S OR AUTHORIZED PERSON'S SIGNATURE. I authorize the release of any medical or other information necessary to process this claim. I also request payment of government benefits either to myself or to the party who accepts assignment below.

SIGNED _____   DATE _____

13. INSURED'S OR AUTHORIZED PERSON'S SIGNATURE I authorize payment of medical benefits to the undersigned physician or supplier for services described below.

SIGNED _____

14. DATE OF CURRENT: MM | DD | YY   ILLNESS (First symptom) OR INJURY (Accident) OR PREGNANCY (LMP)

15. IF PATIENT HAS HAD SAME OR SIMILAR ILLNESS, GIVE FIRST DATE MM | DD | YY

16. DATES PATIENT UNABLE TO WORK IN CURRENT OCCUPATION MM | DD | YY   FROM   MM | DD | YY   TO

17. NAME OF REFERRING PHYSICIAN OR OTHER SOURCE

17a. I.D. NUMBER OF REFERRING PHYSICIAN

18. HOSPITALIZATION DATES RELATED TO CURRENT SERVICES MM | DD | YY   FROM   MM | DD | YY   TO

19. RESERVED FOR LOCAL USE

20. OUTSIDE LAB?   YES ☐   NO ☐ $ CHARGES

21. DIAGNOSIS OR NATURE OF ILLNESS OR INJURY. (RELATE ITEMS 1, 2, 3, OR 4 TO ITEM 24E BY LINE)
1. |___ . ___   3. |___ . ___
2. |___ . ___   4. |___ . ___

22. MEDICAID RESUBMISSION CODE   ORIGINAL REF. NO.

23. PRIOR AUTHORIZATION NUMBER

24. A DATE(S) OF SERVICE						B Place of Service	C Type of Service	D PROCEDURES, SERVICES, OR SUPPLIES (Explain Unusual Circumstances)		E DIAGNOSIS CODE	F $ CHARGES	G DAYS OR UNITS	H EPSDT Family Plan	I EMG	J COB	K RESERVED FOR LOCAL USE
From MM	DD	YY	To MM	DD	YY			CPT/HCPCS	MODIFIER							
1																
2																
3																
4																
5																
6																

25. FEDERAL TAX I.D. NUMBER   SSN ☐ EIN ☐

26. PATIENT'S ACCOUNT NO.

27. ACCEPT ASSIGNMENT? (For govt. claims, see back)   YES ☐   NO ☐

28. TOTAL CHARGE $

29. AMOUNT PAID $

30. BALANCE DUE $

31. SIGNATURE OF PHYSICIAN OR SUPPLIER INCLUDING DEGREES OR CREDENTIALS (I certify that the statements on the reverse apply to this bill and are made a part thereof.)

SIGNED _____   DATE _____

32. NAME AND ADDRESS OF FACILITY WHERE SERVICES WERE RENDERED (If other than home or office)

33. PHYSICIAN'S, SUPPLIER'S BILLING NAME, ADDRESS, ZIP CODE & PHONE #

PIN#   GRP#

(SAMPLE ONLY - NOT APPROVED FOR USE)   *PLEASE PRINT OR TYPE*

SAMPLE FORM 1500
SAMPLE FORM 1500 SAMPLE FORM 1500

(SAMPLE ONLY - NOT APPROVED FOR USE)

CARRIER

☐☐☐ PICA

HEALTH INSURANCE CLAIM FORM

PICA ☐☐☐

1.	MEDICARE	MEDICAID	CHAMPUS	CHAMPVA	GROUP HEALTH PLAN	FECA BLK LUNG	OTHER	1a. INSURED'S I.D. NUMBER	(FOR PROGRAM IN ITEM 1)
	☐ (Medicare #)	☐ (Medicaid #)	☐ (Sponsor's SSN)	☐ (VA File #)	☐ (SSN or ID)	☐ (SSN)	☐ (ID)		

2. PATIENT'S NAME (Last Name, First Name, Middle Initial)

3. PATIENT'S BIRTH DATE
MM | DD | YY   SEX   M ☐   F ☐

4. INSURED'S NAME (Last Name, First Name, Middle Initial)

5. PATIENT'S ADDRESS (No. Street)

6. PATIENT RELATIONSHIP TO INSURED
Self ☐   Spouse ☐   Child ☐   Other ☐

7. INSURED'S ADDRESS (No. Street)

CITY   STATE

8. PATIENT STATUS
Single ☐   Married ☐   Other ☐

CITY   STATE

ZIP CODE   TELEPHONE (Include Area Code)
(   )

Employed ☐   Full-Time Student ☐   Part-Time Student ☐

ZIP CODE   TELEPHONE (INCLUDE AREA CODE)
(   )

9. OTHER INSURED'S NAME (Last Name, First Name, Middle Initial)

10. IS PATIENT'S CONDITION RELATED TO:

11. INSURED'S POLICY GROUP OR FECA NUMBER

a. OTHER INSURED'S POLICY OR GROUP NUMBER

a. EMPLOYMENT? (CURRENT OR PREVIOUS)
☐ YES   ☐ NO

a. INSURED'S DATE OF BIRTH
MM | DD | YY   SEX   M ☐   F ☐

b. OTHER INSURED'S DATE OF BIRTH
MM | DD | YY   SEX   M ☐   F ☐

b. AUTO ACCIDENT?   PLACE (State)
☐ YES   ☐ NO

b. EMPLOYER'S NAME OR SCHOOL NAME

c. EMPLOYER'S NAME OR SCHOOL NAME

c. OTHER ACCIDENT?
☐ YES   ☐ NO

c. INSURANCE PLAN NAME OR PROGRAM NAME

d. INSURANCE PLAN NAME OR PROGRAM NAME

10d. RESERVED FOR LOCAL USE

d. IS THERE ANOTHER HEALTH BENEFIT PLAN?
☐ YES   ☐ NO   If yes, return to and complete item 9 a – d.

READ BACK OF FORM BEFORE COMPLETING & SIGNING THIS FORM.
12. PATIENT'S OR AUTHORIZED PERSON'S SIGNATURE I authorize the release of any medical or other information necessary to process this claim. I also request payment of government benefits either to myself or to the party who accepts assignment below.

SIGNED _____   DATE _____

13. INSURED'S OR AUTHORIZED PERSON'S SIGNATURE I authorize payment of medical benefits to the undersigned physician or supplier for services described below.

SIGNED _____

PATIENT AND INSURED INFORMATION

14. DATE OF CURRENT:
MM | DD | YY
ILLNESS (First symptom) OR
INJURY (Accident) OR
PREGNANCY (LMP)

15. IF PATIENT HAS HAD SAME OR SIMILAR ILLNESS, GIVE FIRST DATE   MM | DD | YY

16. DATES PATIENT UNABLE TO WORK IN CURRENT OCCUPATION
MM | DD | YY   MM | DD | YY
FROM   TO

17. NAME OF REFERRING PHYSICIAN OR OTHER SOURCE

17a. I.D. NUMBER OF REFERRING PHYSICIAN

18. HOSPITALIZATION DATES RELATED TO CURRENT SERVICES
MM | DD | YY   MM | DD | YY
FROM   TO

19. RESERVED FOR LOCAL USE

20. OUTSIDE LAB? $ CHARGES
☐ YES   ☐ NO

21. DIAGNOSIS OR NATURE OF ILLNESS OR INJURY. (RELATE ITEMS 1, 2, 3, OR 4 TO ITEM 24E BY LINE)

1. ⌊___.___   3. ⌊___.___

2. ⌊___.___   4. ⌊___.___

22. MEDICAID RESUBMISSION
CODE   ORIGINAL REF. NO.

23. PRIOR AUTHORIZATION NUMBER

24.	A DATE(S) OF SERVICE					B	C	D		E	F	G	H	I	J	K
	From			To			Place of Service	Type of Service	PROCEDURES, SERVICES, OR SUPPLIES (Explain Unusual Circumstances)		DIAGNOSIS CODE	$ CHARGES	DAYS OR UNITS	EPSDT Family Plan	EMG	COB	RESERVED FOR LOCAL USE
	MM	DD	YY	MM	DD	YY			CPT/HCPCS	MODIFIER							
1																	
2																	
3																	
4																	
5																	
6																	

25. FEDERAL TAX I.D. NUMBER   SSN ☐ EIN ☐

26. PATIENT'S ACCOUNT NO.

27. ACCEPT ASSIGNMENT?
(For govt. claims, see back)
☐ YES   ☐ NO

28. TOTAL CHARGE
$

29. AMOUNT PAID
$

30. BALANCE DUE
$

31. SIGNATURE OF PHYSICIAN OR SUPPLIER INCLUDING DEGREES OR CREDENTIALS
(I certify that the statements on the reverse apply to this bill and are made a part thereof.)

SIGNED _____   DATE _____

32. NAME AND ADDRESS OF FACILITY WHERE SERVICES WERE RENDERED (If other than home or office)

33. PHYSICIAN'S, SUPPLIER'S BILLING NAME, ADDRESS, ZIP CODE & PHONE #

PIN# _____   GRP# _____

PHYSICIAN OR SUPPLIER INFORMATION

PLEASE PRINT OR TYPE

SAMPLE FORM 1500
SAMPLE FORM 1500 SAMPLE FORM 1500

PLEASE
DO NOT
STAPLE
IN THIS
AREA

(SAMPLE ONLY - NOT APPROVED FOR USE)

CARRIER

| | PICA

HEALTH INSURANCE CLAIM FORM

PICA | |

1. MEDICARE   MEDICAID   CHAMPUS   CHAMPVA   GROUP HEALTH PLAN   FECA BLK LUNG   OTHER
(Medicare #)   (Medicaid #)   (Sponsor's SSN)   (VA File #)   (SSN or ID)   (SSN)   (ID)

1a. INSURED'S I.D. NUMBER   (FOR PROGRAM IN ITEM 1)

2. PATIENT'S NAME (Last Name, First Name, Middle Initial)

3. PATIENT'S BIRTH DATE
MM | DD | YY   SEX   M ☐   F ☐

4. INSURED'S NAME (Last Name, First Name, Middle Initial)

5. PATIENT'S ADDRESS (No. Street)

6. PATIENT RELATIONSHIP TO INSURED
Self ☐   Spouse ☐   Child ☐   Other ☐

7. INSURED'S ADDRESS (No. Street)

CITY   STATE

8. PATIENT STATUS
Single ☐   Married ☐   Other ☐
Employed ☐   Full-Time Student ☐   Part-Time Student ☐

CITY   STATE

ZIP CODE   TELEPHONE (Include Area Code)
(   )

ZIP CODE   TELEPHONE (INCLUDE AREA CODE)
(   )

9. OTHER INSURED'S NAME (Last Name, First Name, Middle Initial)

10. IS PATIENT'S CONDITION RELATED TO:

11. INSURED'S POLICY GROUP OR FECA NUMBER

a. OTHER INSURED'S POLICY OR GROUP NUMBER

a. EMPLOYMENT? (CURRENT OR PREVIOUS)
☐ YES   ☐ NO

a. INSURED'S DATE OF BIRTH
MM | DD | YY   SEX   M ☐   F ☐

b. OTHER INSURED'S DATE OF BIRTH
MM | DD | YY   SEX   M ☐   F ☐

b. AUTO ACCIDENT?   PLACE (State)
☐ YES   ☐ NO

b. EMPLOYER'S NAME OR SCHOOL NAME

c. EMPLOYER'S NAME OR SCHOOL NAME

c. OTHER ACCIDENT?
☐ YES   ☐ NO

c. INSURANCE PLAN NAME OR PROGRAM NAME

d. INSURANCE PLAN NAME OR PROGRAM NAME

10d. RESERVED FOR LOCAL USE

d. IS THERE ANOTHER HEALTH BENEFIT PLAN?
☐ YES   ☐ NO   If yes, return to and complete item 9 a – d.

READ BACK OF FORM BEFORE COMPLETING & SIGNING THIS FORM.
12. PATIENT'S OR AUTHORIZED PERSON'S SIGNATURE I authorize the release of any medical or other information necessary to process this claim. I also request payment of government benefits either to myself or to the party who accepts assignment below.

SIGNED _____   DATE _____

13. INSURED'S OR AUTHORIZED PERSON'S SIGNATURE I authorize payment of medical benefits to the undersigned physician or supplier for services described below.

SIGNED _____

PATIENT AND INSURED INFORMATION

14. DATE OF CURRENT: ILLNESS (First symptom) OR INJURY (Accident) OR PREGNANCY (LMP)
MM | DD | YY

15. IF PATIENT HAS HAD SAME OR SIMILAR ILLNESS, GIVE FIRST DATE   MM | DD | YY

16. DATES PATIENT UNABLE TO WORK IN CURRENT OCCUPATION
MM | DD | YY   MM | DD | YY
FROM   TO

17. NAME OF REFERRING PHYSICIAN OR OTHER SOURCE

17a. I.D. NUMBER OF REFERRING PHYSICIAN

18. HOSPITALIZATION DATES RELATED TO CURRENT SERVICES
MM | DD | YY   MM | DD | YY
FROM   TO

19. RESERVED FOR LOCAL USE

20. OUTSIDE LAB? $ CHARGES
☐ YES   ☐ NO

21. DIAGNOSIS OR NATURE OF ILLNESS OR INJURY. (RELATE ITEMS 1, 2, 3, OR 4 TO ITEM 24E BY LINE)
1. ____.____   3. ____.____
2. ____.____   4. ____.____

22. MEDICAID RESUBMISSION
CODE   ORIGINAL REF. NO.

23. PRIOR AUTHORIZATION NUMBER

24. A				B	C	D		E	F	G	H	I	J	K
DATE(S) OF SERVICE				Place of Service	Type of Service	PROCEDURES, SERVICES, OR SUPPLIES (Explain Unusual Circumstances)		DIAGNOSIS CODE	$ CHARGES	DAYS OR UNITS	EPSDT Family Plan	EMG	COB	RESERVED FOR LOCAL USE
From		To				CPT/HCPCS	MODIFIER							
MM DD YY	MM DD YY													
1														
2														
3														
4														
5														
6														

25. FEDERAL TAX I.D. NUMBER   SSN ☐ EIN ☐

26. PATIENT'S ACCOUNT NO.

27. ACCEPT ASSIGNMENT? (For govt. claims, see back)
☐ YES   ☐ NO

28. TOTAL CHARGE $

29. AMOUNT PAID $

30. BALANCE DUE $

31. SIGNATURE OF PHYSICIAN OR SUPPLIER INCLUDING DEGREES OR CREDENTIALS (I certify that the statements on the reverse apply to this bill and are made a part thereof.)

SIGNED _____   DATE _____

32. NAME AND ADDRESS OF FACILITY WHERE SERVICES WERE RENDERED (If other than home or office)

33. PHYSICIAN'S, SUPPLIER'S BILLING NAME, ADDRESS, ZIP CODE & PHONE #

PIN# _____   GRP# _____

PHYSICIAN OR SUPPLIER INFORMATION

(SAMPLE ONLY - NOT APPROVED FOR USE)

PLEASE PRINT OR TYPE

SAMPLE FORM 1500
SAMPLE FORM 1500   SAMPLE FORM 1500

253

(SAMPLE ONLY - NOT APPROVED FOR USE)

CARRIER

□□□ PICA

HEALTH INSURANCE CLAIM FORM

PICA □□□

1. MEDICARE □ (Medicare #)	MEDICAID □ (Medicaid #)	CHAMPUS □ (Sponsor's SSN)	CHAMPVA □ (VA File #)	GROUP HEALTH PLAN □ (SSN or ID)	FECA BLK LUNG □ (SSN)	OTHER □ (ID)

1a. INSURED'S I.D. NUMBER (FOR PROGRAM IN ITEM 1)

2. PATIENT'S NAME (Last Name, First Name, Middle Initial)

3. PATIENT'S BIRTH DATE MM ¦ DD ¦ YY   SEX M □ F □

4. INSURED'S NAME (Last Name, First Name, Middle Initial)

5. PATIENT'S ADDRESS (No. Street)

6. PATIENT RELATIONSHIP TO INSURED Self □ Spouse □ Child □ Other □

7. INSURED'S ADDRESS (No. Street)

CITY   STATE

8. PATIENT STATUS Single □ Married □ Other □
Employed □ Full-Time Student □ Part-Time Student □

CITY   STATE

ZIP CODE   TELEPHONE (Include Area Code) (   )

ZIP CODE   TELEPHONE (INCLUDE AREA CODE) (   )

9. OTHER INSURED'S NAME (Last Name, First Name, Middle Initial)

10. IS PATIENT'S CONDITION RELATED TO:

11. INSURED'S POLICY GROUP OR FECA NUMBER

a. OTHER INSURED'S POLICY OR GROUP NUMBER

a. EMPLOYMENT? (CURRENT OR PREVIOUS) □ YES □ NO

a. INSURED'S DATE OF BIRTH MM ¦ DD ¦ YY SEX M □ F □

b. OTHER INSURED'S DATE OF BIRTH MM ¦ DD ¦ YY SEX M □ F □

b. AUTO ACCIDENT? PLACE (State) □ YES □ NO

b. EMPLOYER'S NAME OR SCHOOL NAME

c. EMPLOYER'S NAME OR SCHOOL NAME

c. OTHER ACCIDENT? □ YES □ NO

c. INSURANCE PLAN NAME OR PROGRAM NAME

d. INSURANCE PLAN NAME OR PROGRAM NAME

10d. RESERVED FOR LOCAL USE

d. IS THERE ANOTHER HEALTH BENEFIT PLAN? □ YES □ NO If yes, return to and complete item 9 a – d.

READ BACK OF FORM BEFORE COMPLETING & SIGNING THIS FORM.
12. PATIENT'S OR AUTHORIZED PERSON'S SIGNATURE I authorize the release of any medical or other information necessary to process this claim. I also request payment of government benefits either to myself or to the party who accepts assignment below.

SIGNED _____ DATE _____

13. INSURED'S OR AUTHORIZED PERSON'S SIGNATURE I authorize payment of medical benefits to the undersigned physician or supplier for services described below.

SIGNED _____

14. DATE OF CURRENT: ILLNESS (First symptom) OR INJURY (Accident) OR PREGNANCY (LMP) MM ¦ DD ¦ YY

15. IF PATIENT HAS HAD SAME OR SIMILAR ILLNESS, GIVE FIRST DATE MM ¦ DD ¦ YY

16. DATES PATIENT UNABLE TO WORK IN CURRENT OCCUPATION MM ¦ DD ¦ YY FROM ___ TO ___ MM ¦ DD ¦ YY

17. NAME OF REFERRING PHYSICIAN OR OTHER SOURCE

17a. I.D. NUMBER OF REFERRING PHYSICIAN

18. HOSPITALIZATION DATES RELATED TO CURRENT SERVICES MM ¦ DD ¦ YY FROM ___ TO ___ MM ¦ DD ¦ YY

19. RESERVED FOR LOCAL USE

20. OUTSIDE LAB? □ YES □ NO $ CHARGES

21. DIAGNOSIS OR NATURE OF ILLNESS OR INJURY. (RELATE ITEMS 1, 2, 3, OR 4 TO ITEM 24E BY LINE)
1. └___ . ___
2. └___ . ___
3. └___ . ___
4. └___ . ___

22. MEDICAID RESUBMISSION CODE   ORIGINAL REF. NO.

23. PRIOR AUTHORIZATION NUMBER

24. A. DATE(S) OF SERVICE						B. Place of Service	C. Type of Service	D. PROCEDURES, SERVICES, OR SUPPLIES (Explain Unusual Circumstances)		E. DIAGNOSIS CODE	F. $ CHARGES	G. DAYS OR UNITS	H. EPSDT Family Plan	I. EMG	J. COB	K. RESERVED FOR LOCAL USE
From MM	DD	YY	To MM	DD	YY			CPT/HCPCS	MODIFIER							
1																
2																
3																
4																
5																
6																

25. FEDERAL TAX I.D. NUMBER SSN □ EIN □

26. PATIENT'S ACCOUNT NO.

27. ACCEPT ASSIGNMENT? (For govt. claims, see back) □ YES □ NO

28. TOTAL CHARGE $

29. AMOUNT PAID $

30. BALANCE DUE $

31. SIGNATURE OF PHYSICIAN OR SUPPLIER INCLUDING DEGREES OR CREDENTIALS (I certify that the statements on the reverse apply to this bill and are made a part thereof.)

SIGNED _____ DATE _____

32. NAME AND ADDRESS OF FACILITY WHERE SERVICES WERE RENDERED (if other than home or office)

33. PHYSICIAN'S, SUPPLIER'S BILLING NAME, ADDRESS, ZIP CODE & PHONE #

PIN# _____ GRP# _____

PATIENT AND INSURED INFORMATION

PHYSICIAN OR SUPPLIER INFORMATION

(SAMPLE ONLY - NOT APPROVED FOR USE)

PLEASE PRINT OR TYPE

SAMPLE FORM 1500
SAMPLE FORM 1500 SAMPLE FORM 1500

(SAMPLE ONLY - NOT APPROVED FOR USE)

CARRIER

| | PICA

HEALTH INSURANCE CLAIM FORM

PICA | |

1. MEDICARE MEDICAID CHAMPUS CHAMPVA GROUP HEALTH PLAN FECA BLK LUNG OTHER	1a. INSURED'S I.D. NUMBER (FOR PROGRAM IN ITEM 1)

☐ (Medicare #) ☐ (Medicaid #) ☐ (Sponsor's SSN) ☐ (VA File #) ☐ (SSN or ID) ☐ (SSN) ☐ (ID)

2. PATIENT'S NAME (Last Name, First Name, Middle Initial)	3. PATIENT'S BIRTH DATE MM DD YY SEX M ☐ F ☐	4. INSURED'S NAME (Last Name, First Name, Middle Initial)

5. PATIENT'S ADDRESS (No. Street)	6. PATIENT RELATIONSHIP TO INSURED Self ☐ Spouse ☐ Child ☐ Other ☐	7. INSURED'S ADDRESS (No. Street)

CITY	STATE	8. PATIENT STATUS Single ☐ Married ☐ Other ☐	CITY	STATE

ZIP CODE	TELEPHONE (Include Area Code) ( )	Employed ☐ Full-Time Student ☐ Part-Time Student ☐	ZIP CODE	TELEPHONE (INCLUDE AREA CODE) ( )

PATIENT AND INSURED INFORMATION

9. OTHER INSURED'S NAME (Last Name, First Name, Middle Initial)	10. IS PATIENT'S CONDITION RELATED TO:	11. INSURED'S POLICY GROUP OR FECA NUMBER

a. OTHER INSURED'S POLICY OR GROUP NUMBER	a. EMPLOYMENT? (CURRENT OR PREVIOUS) ☐ YES ☐ NO	a. INSURED'S DATE OF BIRTH MM DD YY SEX M ☐ F ☐

b. OTHER INSURED'S DATE OF BIRTH MM DD YY SEX M ☐ F ☐	b. AUTO ACCIDENT? PLACE (State) ☐ YES ☐ NO	b. EMPLOYER'S NAME OR SCHOOL NAME

c. EMPLOYER'S NAME OR SCHOOL NAME	c. OTHER ACCIDENT? ☐ YES ☐ NO	c. INSURANCE PLAN NAME OR PROGRAM NAME

d. INSURANCE PLAN NAME OR PROGRAM NAME	10d. RESERVED FOR LOCAL USE	d. IS THERE ANOTHER HEALTH BENEFIT PLAN? ☐ YES ☐ NO If yes, return to and complete item 9 a – d.

READ BACK OF FORM BEFORE COMPLETING & SIGNING THIS FORM.

12. PATIENT'S OR AUTHORIZED PERSON'S SIGNATURE I authorize the release of any medical or other information necessary to process this claim. I also request payment of government benefits either to myself or to the party who accepts assignment below.

SIGNED _____ DATE _____

13. INSURED'S OR AUTHORIZED PERSON'S SIGNATURE I authorize payment of medical benefits to the undersigned physician or supplier for services described below.

SIGNED _____

14. DATE OF CURRENT: ILLNESS (First symptom) OR INJURY (Accident) OR PREGNANCY (LMP) MM DD YY	15. IF PATIENT HAS HAD SAME OR SIMILAR ILLNESS, GIVE FIRST DATE MM DD YY	16. DATES PATIENT UNABLE TO WORK IN CURRENT OCCUPATION MM DD YY MM DD YY FROM TO

17. NAME OF REFERRING PHYSICIAN OR OTHER SOURCE	17a. I.D. NUMBER OF REFERRING PHYSICIAN	18. HOSPITALIZATION DATES RELATED TO CURRENT SERVICES MM DD YY MM DD YY FROM TO

19. RESERVED FOR LOCAL USE		20. OUTSIDE LAB? ☐ YES ☐ NO $ CHARGES

21. DIAGNOSIS OR NATURE OF ILLNESS OR INJURY. (RELATE ITEMS 1, 2, 3, OR 4 TO ITEM 24E BY LINE) 1. _____ 2. _____ 3. _____ 4. _____	22. MEDICAID RESUBMISSION CODE ORIGINAL REF. NO. 23. PRIOR AUTHORIZATION NUMBER

24. A DATE(S) OF SERVICE From To MM DD YY MM DD YY	B Place of Service	C Type of Service	D PROCEDURES, SERVICES, OR SUPPLIES (Explain Unusual Circumstances) CPT/HCPCS MODIFIER	E DIAGNOSIS CODE	F $ CHARGES	G DAYS OR UNITS	H EPSDT Family Plan	I EMG	J COB	K RESERVED FOR LOCAL USE
1										
2										
3										
4										
5										
6										

PHYSICIAN OR SUPPLIER INFORMATION

25. FEDERAL TAX I.D. NUMBER SSN ☐ EIN ☐	26. PATIENT'S ACCOUNT NO.	27. ACCEPT ASSIGNMENT? (For govt. claims, see back) ☐ YES ☐ NO	28. TOTAL CHARGE $	29. AMOUNT PAID $	30. BALANCE DUE $

31. SIGNATURE OF PHYSICIAN OR SUPPLIER INCLUDING DEGREES OR CREDENTIALS (I certify that the statements on the reverse apply to this bill and are made a part thereof.) SIGNED _____ DATE _____	32. NAME AND ADDRESS OF FACILITY WHERE SERVICES WERE RENDERED (If other than home or office)	33. PHYSICIAN'S, SUPPLIER'S BILLING NAME, ADDRESS, ZIP CODE & PHONE # PIN# _____ GRP# _____

(SAMPLE ONLY - NOT APPROVED FOR USE)

PLEASE PRINT OR TYPE

SAMPLE FORM 1500
SAMPLE FORM 1500 SAMPLE FORM 1500

(SAMPLE ONLY - NOT APPROVED FOR USE)

CARRIER

| | PICA

HEALTH INSURANCE CLAIM FORM

PICA | | |

| 1. MEDICARE ☐ (Medicare #) | MEDICAID ☐ (Medicaid #) | CHAMPUS ☐ (Sponsor's SSN) | CHAMPVA ☐ (VA File #) | GROUP HEALTH PLAN ☐ (SSN or ID) | FECA BLK LUNG ☐ (SSN) | OTHER ☐ (ID) | 1a. INSURED'S I.D. NUMBER (FOR PROGRAM IN ITEM 1) |

| 2. PATIENT'S NAME (Last Name, First Name, Middle Initial) | 3. PATIENT'S BIRTH DATE MM | DD | YY SEX M ☐ F ☐ | 4. INSURED'S NAME (Last Name, First Name, Middle Initial) |

| 5. PATIENT'S ADDRESS (No. Street) | 6. PATIENT RELATIONSHIP TO INSURED Self ☐ Spouse ☐ Child ☐ Other ☐ | 7. INSURED'S ADDRESS (No. Street) |

| CITY | STATE | 8. PATIENT STATUS Single ☐ Married ☐ Other ☐ | CITY | STATE |

| ZIP CODE | TELEPHONE (Include Area Code) ( ) | Employed ☐ Full-Time Student ☐ Part-Time Student ☐ | ZIP CODE | TELEPHONE (INCLUDE AREA CODE) ( ) |

| 9. OTHER INSURED'S NAME (Last Name, First Name, Middle Initial) | 10. IS PATIENT'S CONDITION RELATED TO: | 11. INSURED'S POLICY GROUP OR FECA NUMBER |

| a. OTHER INSURED'S POLICY OR GROUP NUMBER | a. EMPLOYMENT? (CURRENT OR PREVIOUS) ☐ YES ☐ NO | a. INSURED'S DATE OF BIRTH MM | DD | YY SEX M ☐ F ☐ |

| b. OTHER INSURED'S DATE OF BIRTH MM | DD | YY SEX M ☐ F ☐ | b. AUTO ACCIDENT? PLACE (State) ☐ YES ☐ NO | b. EMPLOYER'S NAME OR SCHOOL NAME |

| c. EMPLOYER'S NAME OR SCHOOL NAME | c. OTHER ACCIDENT? ☐ YES ☐ NO | c. INSURANCE PLAN NAME OR PROGRAM NAME |

| d. INSURANCE PLAN NAME OR PROGRAM NAME | 10d. RESERVED FOR LOCAL USE | d. IS THERE ANOTHER HEALTH BENEFIT PLAN? ☐ YES ☐ NO If yes, return to and complete item 9 a – d. |

READ BACK OF FORM BEFORE COMPLETING & SIGNING THIS FORM.

12. PATIENT'S OR AUTHORIZED PERSON'S SIGNATURE I authorize the release of any medical or other information necessary to process this claim. I also request payment of government benefits either to myself or to the party who accepts assignment below.

SIGNED _____ DATE _____

13. INSURED'S OR AUTHORIZED PERSON'S SIGNATURE I authorize payment of medical benefits to the undersigned physician or supplier for services described below.

SIGNED _____

| 14. DATE OF CURRENT: MM | DD | YY ☐ ILLNESS (First symptom) OR INJURY (Accident) OR PREGNANCY (LMP) | 15. IF PATIENT HAS HAD SAME OR SIMILAR ILLNESS, GIVE FIRST DATE MM | DD | YY | 16. DATES PATIENT UNABLE TO WORK IN CURRENT OCCUPATION MM | DD | YY FROM TO MM | DD | YY |

| 17. NAME OF REFERRING PHYSICIAN OR OTHER SOURCE | 17a. I.D. NUMBER OF REFERRING PHYSICIAN | 18. HOSPITALIZATION DATES RELATED TO CURRENT SERVICES MM | DD | YY FROM TO MM | DD | YY |

| 19. RESERVED FOR LOCAL USE | 20. OUTSIDE LAB? $ CHARGES ☐ YES ☐ NO |

| 21. DIAGNOSIS OR NATURE OF ILLNESS OR INJURY. (RELATE ITEMS 1, 2, 3, OR 4 TO ITEM 24E BY LINE) 1. ___.___ 2. ___.___ 3. ___.___ 4. ___.___ | 22. MEDICAID RESUBMISSION CODE ORIGINAL REF. NO. |
| | 23. PRIOR AUTHORIZATION NUMBER |

24. A DATE(S) OF SERVICE						B Place of Service	C Type of Service	D PROCEDURES, SERVICES, OR SUPPLIES (Explain Unusual Circumstances)		E DIAGNOSIS CODE	F $ CHARGES	G DAYS OR UNITS	H EPSDT Family Plan	I EMG	J COB	K RESERVED FOR LOCAL USE
From MM	DD	YY	To MM	DD	YY			CPT/HCPCS	MODIFIER							
1																
2																
3																
4																
5																
6																

| 25. FEDERAL TAX I.D. NUMBER SSN ☐ EIN ☐ | 26. PATIENT'S ACCOUNT NO. | 27. ACCEPT ASSIGNMENT? (For govt. claims, see back) YES ☐ NO ☐ | 28. TOTAL CHARGE $ | 29. AMOUNT PAID $ | 30. BALANCE DUE $ |

| 31. SIGNATURE OF PHYSICIAN OR SUPPLIER INCLUDING DEGREES OR CREDENTIALS (I certify that the statements on the reverse apply to this bill and are made a part thereof.) SIGNED _____ DATE _____ | 32. NAME AND ADDRESS OF FACILITY WHERE SERVICES WERE RENDERED (If other than home or office) | 33. PHYSICIAN'S, SUPPLIER'S BILLING NAME, ADDRESS, ZIP CODE & PHONE # PIN# GRP# |

PATIENT AND INSURED INFORMATION

PHYSICIAN OR SUPPLIER INFORMATION

(SAMPLE ONLY - NOT APPROVED FOR USE)

PLEASE PRINT OR TYPE

SAMPLE FORM 1500
SAMPLE FORM 1500 SAMPLE FORM 1500

InstaClaim Trial Version CD-ROM

SYSTEM REQUIREMENTS

- PC compatible, 486 or higher processor
- 8 MB RAM (memory)
- 256 color VGA monitor
- Windows® 95/NT or newer operating system
- 5 MB free disk space
- Mouse

CD-ROM SETUP INSTRUCTIONS

Installing to a Local Drive

1. Insert the installation CD into your computer.
2. The installation program should automatically begin to install. If for any reason it does not, use the instructions below. Otherwise, go on to step 3.
   a. Click the **Start** button.
   b. Select **Control Panel** (for Windows 9x, select **Settings** then **Control Panel**).
   c. Select **Add/Remove Programs.**
   d. Click the **Install** button. When the Install Program box appears, click the **Next** button.
   e. X:\setup.EXE (where "X" is the name or the letter assigned to your drive) will appear in the command line. Press **Return** or click the **Finish** button and installation begins.
3. Click the **I Agree to the License** button to accept the license agreement and begin the installation.
4. When the Welcome message appears, press **Enter** or click the **Next** button to continue.
5. You will be asked where you would like to install InstaClaim. The default folder is C:\Program Files\InstaCode Products\InstaClaim. If you would something different than this, click the **Browse** button to find or create the desired folder.

6. Follow the prompts until the "Installation Completed!" window appears. Press **Enter** or click the **Finish** button to complete the installation.

7. Remove the CD from the drive. You may be prompted to re-boot your computer.

8. You are ready to begin using InstaClaim. An icon is located on your desktop. A User Guide has also been installed. To view or print the user guide you need to have Adobe Acrobat Reader installed on your computer. Go into **Start**/All Programs/InstaClaim and select the User Guide to view or print.

Uninstalling the InstaClaim Software

To remove the InstaClaim software program from your computer, you can uninstall it by selecting **InstaClaim** from the Programs menu and then selecting **Uninstall.**

USING THE INSTACLAIM TRIAL VERSION CD-ROM

The InstaClaim Trial Version CD-ROM, included with this textbook, is designed to help you practice completing CMS-1500 claims using commercial medical practice management software. Up to three sample claims can be prepared using this software. The CD-ROM User Guide can be accessed after you load the software on your computer. It can be viewed on your computer screen or printed.

Using the InstaClaim Software

1. Double click on the InstaClaim icon that appears on your computer's desktop.

2. Click Continue.

   NOTE: This trial version of the software allows you to complete CMS-1500 claims for three patients.

3. Click Continue.

4. To enter a patient's CMS-1500 claim, click New.

   NOTE: Check with your instructor to determine the case studies to be used when completing CMS-1500 claims using the InstaClaim software (in addition to completing the InstaClaim Tutorial).

General Hints

- Press the Caps Lock key on your keyboard to activate it.
- Press the Num Lock key on your keyboard to activate it, before using the numeric keypad to enter long strings of numbers.
- Proofread each entry before moving to the next block of the CMS-1500 claim.
- Follow Optical Scanning Guidelines when completing each CMS-1500 claim.
- Enter reference numbers (not ICD code numbers) in Block 21.
- Enter the provider's full name and credentials in Block 31.

Optical Scanning Guidelines

- Do not enter the alpha character O for a zero (0) in a number.
- Do not enter the dollar sign ($) for charges, payments, or balances due.

- Enter a space instead of a:
  - ☐ decimal point in charges, payments, or balances
  - ☐ decimal point in an ICD diagnosis code number
  - ☐ dash in front of a procedure code number or a telephone number
- Do not keyboard parentheses when entering the area code of the telephone number (they are printed automatically on the form).
- Leave one blank space between the patient's/policyholder's last name, first name, and middle initial.
- Do not use any punctuation in a patient's/policyholder's name, except for a hyphen in a compound name.
- Do not use a patient's or policyholder's title or other designations such as Sr., Jr., II, or III on a claim unless they appear on the patient's insurance ID card.

EXAMPLE: The name on the ID card reads: Wm. F. Goodpatient, IV

This name is entered on the CMS-1500 claim as:

GOODPATIENT IV WILLIAM F

Special CMS-1500 Claims Completion Instructions

- Enter the active duty sponsor's rank or grade after the name for TRICARE (formerly CHAMPUS) claims.
- Enter two zeros (00) in the cents column when a fee or monetary total is expressed in whole dollars.

EXAMPLE: Six dollars is entered as 6 00

Six thousand dollars is entered as 6 000 00

- Enter dates as eight digits with spaces (MM DD YYYY) for the month, day, and year, except for Blocks 24A, 24B and 31 where dates are entered as eight digits without spaces (MMDDYYYY). Two-digit code numbers for the months are:

January	01
February	02
March	03
April	04
May	05
June	06
July	07
August	08
September	09
October	10
November	11
December	12

EXAMPLE: Enter 03 04 1897 for March 4, 1897

- Enter the hyphen in all Employer Identification Numbers (EIN).
- Enter social security numbers as a continuous number, without the hyphens or spaces.
- In Block 31, enter the provider's full name and credentials.
- Review the claim to be sure all blocks that require an X to be placed within the block are so marked.

INSTACLAIM TUTORIAL

This tutorial will introduce you to the completion of a CMS-1500 claim using the InstaClaim software. Complete this tutorial after having installed the InstaClaim software program on your computer.

1. Double click on the InstaClaim icon located on your computer's desktop (or click Start, InstaClaim, and the InstaClaim icon to start the program).

2. The title page of the InstaClaim software will briefly display.

3. Click Continue when the InstaClaim Trial Version screen displays.

4. Click Settings & Tools to enter the setup information for the medical practice as displayed on the Settings1 and Settings2 screens. (The default entries on the Tools1 and Tools2 screens are used, which means you don't need to change that setup information.)

5. Click Save and Close to return to the InstaClaim main page.

6. Click New (located to the right of Patient) to begin entering a CMS-1500 claim.

    NOTE: When the InstaClaim – CMS–1500 screen displays, notice that you will enter claims data on each of five screens:

    ☐ Patient Info

    ☐ Insured's Info

    ☐ Claim Info

    ☐ Diagnosis/Charges

    ☐ Provider Info

    Access each screens by clicking on the section heading (e.g., Insured's Info).

7. Click on the Patient Info screen, and enter the data as displayed on the screen.

InstaClaim - CMS-1500

Patient: KITTEN KITTY : 123456   Entry Date: 06 02 2005 : 7

Patient Info | Insured's Info | Claim Info | Diagnosis/Charges | Provider Info

(Right-Click on an item for QuickHelp)

Patient Name (2) KITTEN KITTY   (Last, First, Middle Initial)
Patient Signature (12) ☑ Signature on File   Date 06/02/2005
Account # (26) 123456   ☑ Accept Assignment? (27) (Check if Yes)
Birth Date (3) 05/09/1971   (Month/Day/Year)
Sex (3) ○ Male ● Female   ○ Not Specified
Status (8) ● Single ○ Married   ○ Other
○ Employed ○ Full Time Student ○ Part Time Student ○ Other
Address (5) 101 MAIN STREET
City/State ANYWHERE   US
Zip Code/Phone 12345   (101) 555-1234

Next

New | Print | Delete | (Note: Data is saved as it is entered.) | Close

8. Click on the Insured's Info section, and enter the data as displayed on the screen.

InstaClaim - CMS-1500

Patient: KITTEN KITTY : 123456   Entry Date: 06 02 2005 : 7

Patient Info | **Insured's Info** | Claim Info | Diagnosis/Charges | Provider Info

(Right-Click on an item for QuickHelp)

Insurance Type (1) OTHER (ID)
ID # (1a) 123456789
Patient Relationship to Insured (6) ● Self ○ Spouse ○ Child ○ Other
Insured's Name (4) (Last, First, Middle Initial) KITTEN KITTY
☑ Signature on File (13) Same
Insured's Address (7) 101 MAIN STREET
City/State ANYWHERE   US
Zip Code/Phone 12345   (101) 555-1234
Policy Grp or FECA # (11)
Birth Date/Sex (11a) 05/09/1971 ○ Male ● Female ○ N/S*   * N/S - Not Specified
Employer or School (11b)
Insurance Plan/Prg (11c)   ? Address Group # (33)

☐ Another Benefit Plan (11d)
Other Insured (9a-d)
(Last, First, Middle Initial) Same
Policy Number
Birthdate / /
Sex ○ Male ○ Female ● N/S*
Employer/School Name
Plan Name
PIN # (33) 11-1234562
Next

New | Print | Delete | (Note: Data is saved as it is entered.) | Close

9. Click on the Claim Info section, and enter the data as displayed on the screen.

InstaClaim - CMS-1500

Patient: KITTEN KITTY : 123456   Entry Date: 06 02 2005 : 7

Patient Info | Insured's Info | **Claim Info** | Diagnosis/Charges | Provider Info

(Right-Click on an item for QuickHelp)

Date of Injury, Illness or LMP (14) 06/01/2005
Patient Contidition Related To: ☐ Employment (10a) (Current or Previous)
☐ Auto Accident (10b) - State
☐ Other Accident (10c)
Reserved for Local Use (10d)
First Date of Same or Similar Illness (15) / /
Dates Patient Unable to Work (16) / / to / /
Dates Patient was Hospitalized (18) / / to / /
Medicaid Resubmission Code (22)   Original Ref. No.
Prior Authorization # (23)

Next

New | Print | Delete | (Note: Data is saved as it is entered.) | Close

10. Click on the Diagnosis/Charges section, and enter the data as displayed on the screen.

11. Click on the Provider Info section, and enter the data as displayed on the screen.

12. Click Close, which returns you to the InstaClaim main menu.
13. Click Reports (to generate a report about the claim you entered).
14. Select KITTEN KITTY from the For Patient drop down menu.
15. Click Claim Entry Report and Patient Name (next to Reports).
16. Select Preview from the Print To: drop down menu.
17. Click PRINT (and notice that the report displays on your computer screen).

18. Click on the X located in the upper right corner of the report to close that screen.
19. Click Close.
20. Click Exit.